First World War
and Army of Occupation
War Diary
France, Belgium and Germany

11 DIVISION
34 Infantry Brigade
Headquarters
1 July 1916 - 31 December 1917

WO95/1818

The Naval & Military Press Ltd
www.nmarchive.com
Published in association with The National Archives

Published by

The Naval & Military Press Ltd

Unit 10 Ridgewood Industrial Park,

Uckfield, East Sussex,

TN22 5QE England

Tel: +44 (0) 1825 749494

www.naval-military-press.com

www.nmarchive.com

This diary has been reprinted in facsimile from the original. Any imperfections are inevitably reproduced and the quality may fall short of modern type and cartographic standards.

© Crown Copyright
Images reproduced by permission of The National Archives, London, England, 2015.

Contents

Document type	Place/Title	Date From	Date To
Heading	11th Division 34th Infy Bde Bde Headquarters Jly 1916-Dec 1917		
War Diary	Ferdan Suez Canal.	01/07/1916	09/07/1916
War Diary	Marseilles	09/07/1916	19/07/1916
War Diary	Bretencourt	20/07/1916	31/07/1916
Miscellaneous	Appendix I With M A P.	02/08/1916	02/08/1916
Map	Ficheux Edition 2.		
Miscellaneous	Appendix LL.		
Miscellaneous	On His Majesty's Service.		
War Diary	Bretencourt France	01/08/1916	31/08/1916
Operation(al) Order(s)	34th Brigade Order No. 4.	15/08/1916	15/08/1916
Operation(al) Order(s)	34th Brigade Order No. 7.	19/08/1916	19/08/1916
Operation(al) Order(s)	34th Brigade Order No. 8.	30/08/1916	30/08/1916
Miscellaneous	3rd. Train.		
Miscellaneous	1st. Train.	31/08/1916	31/08/1916
Miscellaneous	Appendix II.		
Miscellaneous	1st Line Transport.	01/09/1916	01/09/1916
Operation(al) Order(s)	34th Infantry Brigade Order No. 5.	16/08/1916	16/08/1916
Miscellaneous	Move Table.		
Heading	Headquarters 34th Inf. Bde (11th Div.) August 1916		
Miscellaneous	On His Majesty's Service.		
Heading	War Diary of 34th B.H.Q Sept 1916		
War Diary	Houvin Houvignuel	01/09/1916	14/09/1916
War Diary	Bouzincourt	15/09/1916	30/09/1916
Operation(al) Order(s)	34th Infantry Brigade Order No. 9.	06/09/1916	06/09/1916
Operation(al) Order(s)	34th Infantry Brigade Order No. 10.	13/09/1916	13/09/1916
Operation(al) Order(s)	34th Infantry Brigade Order No. 4.	21/09/1916	21/09/1916
Operation(al) Order(s)	34th Infantry Brigade Order No. 13.	25/09/1916	25/09/1916
Miscellaneous	Artillery Programme.		
Miscellaneous	Communications.		
Miscellaneous	Report On Operations From September 22nd. to September 29th.	22/09/1916	22/09/1916
Miscellaneous	Appendix 2. Mouquet Farm.		
Map			
Miscellaneous	Appendix II. September 1916.	00/09/1916	00/09/1916
Heading	Headquarters, 34th Inf. Bde. (11th Div.) July 1916		
Heading	War Diary (Original) Headquarters 34th Infantry Brigade 1st. October 1916 To 31st. October 1916		
War Diary		01/10/1916	31/10/1916
Miscellaneous	Appendix. II. Strength of Unit from 1st to 7th October.	07/10/1916	07/10/1916
Miscellaneous	Amendment To 34th Infantry Brigade Order No. 16.	27/10/1916	27/10/1916
Operation(al) Order(s)	34th Infantry Brigade Order No. 16.	24/10/1916	24/10/1916
Miscellaneous	Time Table.		
Heading	34th Infantry Brigade War Diary From 1st November 1916 To 30th November 1916		
War Diary	Fransu	01/11/1916	14/11/1916
War Diary	Berteaucourt	15/11/1916	15/11/1916
War Diary	Contay	16/11/1916	17/11/1916
War Diary	Puchvillers	18/11/1916	19/11/1916
War Diary	Lealvillers	20/11/1916	21/11/1916

War Diary	St Pierre Divion.	22/11/1916	30/11/1916
Operation(al) Order(s)	34th Infantry Brigade Order No. 17. Appendix I	12/11/1916	12/11/1916
Miscellaneous	March Table.		
Operation(al) Order(s)	34th Infantry Brigade Order No. 18.	14/11/1916	14/11/1916
Miscellaneous	March Table.		
Operation(al) Order(s)	34th Infantry Brigade Order No. 19.	15/11/1916	15/11/1916
Miscellaneous	March Table.		
Operation(al) Order(s)	34th Infantry Brigade Order No. 20.	21/11/1916	21/11/1916
Operation(al) Order(s)	34th Infantry Brigade Order No. 21.	29/11/1916	29/11/1916
Miscellaneous	March Table.		
Miscellaneous	Appendix II. Strength of units from 1st. to 7th. Nov. 1916.	01/11/1916	01/11/1916
Map	Bois D'Holland		
Heading	War Diary 34th Infantry Brigade. Dec 1916		
War Diary	St Pierre Divion	01/12/1916	09/12/1916
War Diary	Forceville	10/12/1916	17/12/1916
War Diary	Q18A82	18/12/1916	25/12/1916
War Diary	Forceville	26/12/1916	31/12/1916
Operation(al) Order(s)	34th. Infantry Brigade Order No. 22		
Operation(al) Order(s)	34th Infantry Brigade Order No. 23.	22/12/1916	22/12/1916
Operation(al) Order(s)	34th Infantry Brigade Order No. 24.	23/12/1916	23/12/1916
Miscellaneous	Move Table.		
Operation(al) Order(s)	34th Infantry Brigade Order No 25.	30/12/1916	30/12/1916
Miscellaneous	Move Table.		
Miscellaneous	Appendix II Strength of units from 1st. to 7th. Dec. 1916.	01/12/1916	01/12/1916
Heading	Headquarters 34th Inf. Bde. (11th Div.) January 1917		
War Diary	Forceville	01/01/1917	02/01/1917
War Diary	Q 18 A 8 2.	03/01/1917	11/01/1917
War Diary	Forceville	12/01/1917	18/01/1917
War Diary	Beauquesne	19/01/1917	21/01/1917
War Diary	Fienvillers	21/01/1917	21/01/1917
War Diary	Fransu	22/01/1917	31/01/1917
Miscellaneous	Appendix II. Strength Of Units From 1st. 7th. Jan.	01/01/1917	01/01/1917
Miscellaneous	Report On Operation For Week Ending January 12th. In The Sector N. Of The Ancre.	12/01/1917	12/01/1917
Operation(al) Order(s)	34th Infantry Brigade Order No. 31.	15/01/1917	15/01/1917
Miscellaneous	Move Table		
Miscellaneous	Amendments To 34th Infantry Brigade Order No. 31.		
Miscellaneous	Move Table.		
Miscellaneous		19/01/1917	19/01/1917
Miscellaneous			
Miscellaneous	Move Table		
Operation(al) Order(s)	34th Infantry Brigade Order No 25.	30/12/1916	30/12/1916
Miscellaneous	Move Table.		
Operation(al) Order(s)	34th Infantry Brigade Order No. 29.	08/01/1917	08/01/1917
Miscellaneous	Amendment To 34th Infantry Brigade Order No. 29.		
Miscellaneous	34th Infantry Brigade Order No. 30.	09/01/1917	09/01/1917
Miscellaneous	Move Table.		
Heading	Headquarters, 34th Inf. Bde. (11th Div.) February 1917		
War Diary	Fransu	01/02/1917	23/02/1917
War Diary	Fieffes	24/02/1917	24/02/1917
War Diary	Beauquesne.	25/02/1917	28/02/1917
Miscellaneous	34th Infantry Brigade Preliminary Entraining Order.	21/02/1917	21/02/1917
Operation(al) Order(s)	34th Infantry Brigade Order No. 32.	22/02/1917	22/02/1917

Miscellaneous	March Table to Accompany 34th Infantry Brigade Order No. 32.		
Miscellaneous	(2nd) March Table to Accompany 34th Infantry Brigade Order No. 32.		
Operation(al) Order(s)	34th Infantry Brigade Order No. 33.	24/02/1917	24/02/1917
Miscellaneous	Appendix. II. February, 1917.	00/02/1917	00/02/1917
Miscellaneous	Cover for Documents. Nature of Enclosures.		
Heading	Headquarters, 34th Inf. Bde (11th Div) March 1917. Vol. 9.		
Heading	War Diary. March 1917. 34th. Infantry Brigade H.Q.		
War Diary	Beauquesne.	01/03/1917	31/03/1917
Operation(al) Order(s)	34th Infantry Brigade Order No. 34.	23/03/1917	23/03/1917
Miscellaneous	Appendix II. March 1917. Strength of Units from 1st. to 7th.	00/03/1917	00/03/1917
Miscellaneous	Cover for Documents. Nature of Enclosures.		
Heading	Headquarters, 34th Inf. Bde. (11th Div.) April 1917 Vol. 10.		
War Diary	Beauquesne.	01/04/1917	11/04/1917
War Diary	Acheux	12/04/1917	18/04/1917
War Diary	Bouzincourt	19/04/1917	19/04/1917
War Diary	Thilloy.	20/04/1917	24/04/1917
War Diary	Fremicourt	25/04/1917	30/04/1917
Miscellaneous	Appendix 1 for April 1917. Headquarters, 34th Infantry Brigade.		
Operation(al) Order(s)	34th Infantry Brigade Order No. 36.	18/04/1917	18/04/1917
Miscellaneous	March Table (Issued in conjunction with B.O. 36.)		
Operation(al) Order(s)	34th Infantry Brigade Order No. 37.	19/04/1917	19/04/1917
Miscellaneous	March Table (Issued in conjunction with B.O. 37. herewith)		
Operation(al) Order(s)	34th Infantry Brigade Order No. 38.	22/04/1917	22/04/1917
Operation(al) Order(s)	34th Infantry Brigade Order No. 39.	28/04/1917	28/04/1917
Miscellaneous	Relief Table (Issued in conjunction with B.O. No. 39.)		
Miscellaneous	Appendix II for April 1917. Headquarters, 34th Infantry Brigade.		
Miscellaneous	Appendix II.		
Miscellaneous	Appendix III for April 1917. Headquarters, 34th Infantry Brigade.		
Map	Fifth Army Area. (B)		
Miscellaneous	Cover for Documents. Nature of Enclosures.		
Heading	Headquarters, 34th Inf. Bde. (11th Div.) May 1917. Vol. II		
War Diary	Morchies	01/05/1917	31/05/1917
Miscellaneous	Appendix I for May 1917 Headquarters, 34th Infantry Brigade.		
Operation(al) Order(s)	34th Infantry Brigade Order No. 40.	01/05/1917	01/05/1917
Operation(al) Order(s)	34th Infantry Brigade Order No. 41.	04/05/1917	04/05/1917
Operation(al) Order(s)	34th Infantry Brigade Order No. 42.	12/05/1917	12/05/1917
Miscellaneous	Relief Table issued in conjunction with Brigade Order No. 42.		
Operation(al) Order(s)	34th Infantry Brigade Order No. 43.	13/05/1917	13/05/1917
Miscellaneous	March Table issued in conjunction with Brigade Order No. 43.		
Miscellaneous	Amended March Table for 2nd day's March detailed in Brigade Order No. 43.	15/05/1917	15/05/1917
Miscellaneous	To O.C.	18/05/1917	18/05/1917
Miscellaneous	Appendix		

Operation(al) Order(s)	34th Infantry Brigade Order No. 44.	20/05/1917	20/05/1917
Operation(al) Order(s)	34th. Infantry Brigade Order No. 45.	24/05/1917	24/05/1917
Miscellaneous	March Table issued in conjunction with Brigade Order No. 45.		
Miscellaneous	Appendix II for May 1917. Headquarters, 34th Infantry Brigade.		
Miscellaneous	Appendix II.		
Miscellaneous	Appendix III for May 1917. Headquarters, 34th Infantry Brigade.		
Miscellaneous	Nil		
Miscellaneous	Cover for Documents. Nature of Enclosures.		
Heading	War Diary for June 1917. Headquarters, 34th Infantry Brigade.		
War Diary	Mont Kokereele. R 16 D 65 Ref Map Sheet 27 1/40000.	01/06/1917	05/06/1917
War Diary	La Clytte.	07/06/1917	09/06/1917
War Diary	Chinese Wall N 23 B 5.2	10/06/1917	30/06/1917
Miscellaneous	Appendix I for June 1917 Headquarters, 34th Infantry Brigade.		
Operation(al) Order(s)	34th Infantry Brigade Order No. 46.	06/06/1917	06/06/1917
Miscellaneous	March Table issued in conjunction with 34th Brigade Order No. 46.		
Operation(al) Order(s)	34th Infantry Brigade Order No. 47.	08/06/1917	08/06/1917
Operation(al) Order(s)	34th Infantry Brigade Order No. 48.	09/06/1917	09/06/1917
Operation(al) Order(s)	34th Infantry Brigade Order No. 49.	10/06/1917	10/06/1917
Operation(al) Order(s)	34th Infantry Brigade Order No. 50.	16/06/1917	16/06/1917
Operation(al) Order(s)	34th Infantry Brigade Order No. 51.	19/06/1917	19/06/1917
Miscellaneous	Relief Table issued in conjunction with Brigade Order No. 51.		
Miscellaneous	March Table for 20th. in continuation of Brigade Order No. 51.		
Miscellaneous	March Table for 21st. in continuation of Brigade Order No. 51.		
Miscellaneous	March Table for 22nd. inst. continuation of Brigade Order No. 51.		
Miscellaneous	March Table for 23rd inst. continuation of Brigade Order No. 51		
Miscellaneous	March Table for 24th. inst. in continuation of Brigade Order No. 51.		
Miscellaneous	Appendix II for June 1917. Headquarters, 34th. Infantry Brigade.		
Miscellaneous	Appendix II June 1917.	00/06/1917	00/06/1917
Miscellaneous	Appendix III for June 1917. Headquarters, 34th Infantry Brigade.		
Miscellaneous	34th Infantry Brigade. Narrative of operation-7th-15th June.	18/06/1917	18/06/1917
Miscellaneous	Provisional Defence Scheme.	12/06/1917	12/06/1917
Heading	War Diary. 34th Infantry Brigade. H.Q.		
War Diary	Eperlecques	01/07/1917	24/07/1917
War Diary	Rubrouck	24/07/1917	25/07/1917
War Diary	Wormhoudt	25/07/1917	28/07/1917
War Diary	St. Jans-Ter-Biezen	29/07/1917	30/07/1917
War Diary	A.17.d.	31/07/1917	31/07/1917
Operation(al) Order(s)	34th Infantry Brigade Order No. 52.	19/07/1917	19/07/1917
Miscellaneous	March Table for 24th. July, 1917, Issued in conjunction with O.O. 52.		

Miscellaneous	March Table for 25th. July 1917, issued in continuation of Brigade Order 52.	22/07/1917	22/07/1917
Miscellaneous	March Table for 29th. July, 1917, issued in continuation of Bde. Order 52.	24/07/1917	24/07/1917
Miscellaneous	March Table for 30th. July, 1917, issued in continuation of Bde. Order 52.	28/07/1917	28/07/1917
Miscellaneous	Appendix II.		
Heading	War Diary of 34th Infantry Brigade From 1st To 31st August 1917		
War Diary	A.17.d (Sheet 28) Windmill Camp	01/08/1917	08/08/1917
War Diary	B.21.C Siege Camp	08/08/1917	09/08/1917
War Diary	B.21.C (Sheet 28) Siege Camp	10/08/1917	15/08/1917
War Diary	Foch Farm	15/08/1917	17/08/1917
War Diary	Foch Farm Siege Camp B.21.C.	18/08/1917	20/08/1917
War Diary	Siege Camp (B.21.C)	21/08/1917	30/08/1917
War Diary	Dirty Bucket Camp (A.30. Central)	31/08/1917	31/08/1917
Miscellaneous	Appendix I		
Operation(al) Order(s)	34th. Infantry Brigade Order No. 53.	06/08/1917	06/08/1917
Miscellaneous	March Table issued in conjunction with 34th Infantry Brigade Order No. 53 of 6/8/17.	06/08/1917	06/08/1917
Operation(al) Order(s)	34th Infantry Brigade Order No. 54.	10/08/1917	10/08/1917
Miscellaneous	Headquarters 34th Infantry Brigade	13/08/1917	13/08/1917
Miscellaneous	Headquarters 34th Infantry Brigade	11/08/1917	11/08/1917
Miscellaneous	Reference 34th Infantry Brigade Order No. 54 dated August 10th., Para 14.	13/08/1917	13/08/1917
Miscellaneous	Administrative Instructions (in connection with 11th. Divn. Order No. 95.)	11/08/1917	11/08/1917
Map	Map 'A'		
Operation(al) Order(s)	34th Infantry Brigade Order No. 55.	11/08/1917	11/08/1917
Miscellaneous	Movement Table issued with 34th Brigade Order No. 55.	11/08/1917	11/08/1917
Miscellaneous	A Form. Messages And Signals.		
Operation(al) Order(s)	34th Infantry Brigade Order No. 56.	28/08/1917	28/08/1917
Miscellaneous	Movement Table issued with 34th Brigade Order No. 56.		
Miscellaneous	Appendix 2		
Miscellaneous	Appendix II.		
Miscellaneous	Appendix 3.		
Miscellaneous	Special Order Of The Day.	20/08/1917	20/08/1917
Miscellaneous	Fifth Army. G.A. 790/9. 19th. Aug. 1917.	19/08/1917	19/08/1917
Miscellaneous	General Sir H. de la P. Gough, K.C.V.O., K.C.B., Commanding Fifth Army.	17/08/1917	17/08/1917
Miscellaneous	Report on the operations of the 34th Infantry Brigade on August 16th., /17th.	20/08/1917	20/08/1917
Map	Poelcappelle		
Miscellaneous	Cover for Documents. Nature of Enclosures.		
Heading	War Diary Headquarters 34th Infantry Brigade From 1st To 30th September		
War Diary	Dirty Bucket Camp (A.30. Central)	01/09/1917	04/09/1917
War Diary	L.13.Central (Sheet 27)	04/09/1917	10/09/1917
War Diary	L.13.Central D.7.C.5.1 (Sheet 27)	11/09/1917	20/09/1917
War Diary	D.7.C.5.1 (Sheet 27)	21/09/1917	30/09/1917
Miscellaneous	Reference this Office No. 11. 67 of today's date. March Table is as under.	03/09/1917	03/09/1917
Operation(al) Order(s)	34th Infantry Brigade Order No. 57.	10/09/1917	10/09/1917
Miscellaneous	March Table issued with 34th Brigade Order No. 57.		

Operation(al) Order(s)	34th. Infantry Brigade Order No. 58.	29/09/1917	29/09/1917
Miscellaneous	Movement Table to Accompany 34th Brigade Order No. 58.		
Heading	War Diary of 34th Infantry Brigade Headquarters From 1st October 1917 To 1st October 1917		
War Diary	D.7.C.5.1 (Sheet 27)	01/10/1917	01/10/1917
War Diary	Dirty Bucket Camp	01/10/1917	02/10/1917
War Diary	Cane Post	02/10/1917	03/10/1917
War Diary	Maison Bulgare	03/10/1917	08/10/1917
War Diary	Siege Camp	08/10/1917	08/10/1917
War Diary	Eperlecques	09/10/1917	10/10/1917
War Diary	Houlle	10/10/1917	18/10/1917
War Diary	Ecquedecques	18/10/1917	19/10/1917
War Diary	Vaudricourt	19/10/1917	20/10/1917
War Diary	Noeux-Lez-Mines	20/10/1917	21/10/1917
War Diary	Cite St. Pierre	22/10/1917	31/10/1917
Operation(al) Order(s)	34th Infantry Brigade Order No. 59.	29/09/1917	29/09/1917
Miscellaneous	Appendix 2. Machine Gun Arrangements.		
Miscellaneous	Appendix 3. To 34th Brigade Instructions issued under this Office No. M. 246, dated 30th. September, 1917.	30/09/1917	30/09/1917
Miscellaneous	Appendix 4. Tanks.		
Miscellaneous	Appendix 5. Contact Aeroplanes.		
Miscellaneous	Appendix 6. To 34th Brigade Instructions issued under this office No. M. 246 dated 30th. September, 1917.	30/09/1917	30/09/1917
Miscellaneous	Appendix 7. To 34th Brigade Instructions issued under this office No. M. 246 dated 30th. September, 1917.	30/09/1917	30/09/1917
Operation(al) Order(s)	34th Infantry Brigade Order No. 59.a.	01/10/1917	01/10/1917
Miscellaneous	Reference 34th Brigade Order No. 59.a.	02/10/1917	02/10/1917
Map	Edition. I.		
Miscellaneous	Administrative Instructions. For Move October 1st.-2nd. 1917.	01/10/1917	01/10/1917
Miscellaneous	Schedule. Bulow Farm.		
Operation(al) Order(s)	34th Infantry Brigade Order No. 60.	01/10/1917	01/10/1917
Miscellaneous			
Operation(al) Order(s)	34th Infantry Brigade Order No. 61.	05/10/1917	05/10/1917
Miscellaneous	34th Infantry Brigade. Defence Scheme.	06/10/1917	06/10/1917
Operation(al) Order(s)	34th Infantry Brigade Order No. 62.	06/10/1917	06/10/1917
Miscellaneous	Table to be road in conjunction with 34th Brigade Order No. 62.		
Miscellaneous	34th Infantry Brigade. Report On Recent Operations.	12/10/1917	12/10/1917
Miscellaneous	Special Order Of The Day.	14/10/1917	14/10/1917
Miscellaneous	11th. Division No. G.S. 1157	15/10/1917	15/10/1917
Operation(al) Order(s)	34th Infantry Brigade Order No. 63.	16/10/1917	16/10/1917
Miscellaneous			
Operation(al) Order(s)	34th Infantry Brigade Order No. 64.	17/10/1917	17/10/1917
Miscellaneous	Table to Accompany Brigade Order No 64		
Operation(al) Order(s)	34th Infantry Brigade Order No. 65.	19/10/1917	19/10/1917
Miscellaneous	Movement Table issued in conjunction with B.O. 65.		
Miscellaneous	34th Infantry Brigade. Defence Scheme. (Provisional)	28/10/1917	28/10/1917
Miscellaneous	Warning Order.	12/10/1917	12/10/1917
Miscellaneous	Schedule No. 1. (Issued in continuation of 34th Brigade Defence Scheme) Artillery.		
Miscellaneous	Schedule No. 2. (Issued in continuation of 34th Brigade Defence Scheme) Machine Guns and Trench Mortars.		
Miscellaneous	Schedule 3. S.A.A. and Bomb Stores.		

Miscellaneous	Schedule No.4. (Issued in continuation of 34th Brigade Defence Scheme.) Communications.		
Miscellaneous	Schedule 5. Evacuation Of Wounded.		
Operation(al) Order(s)	34th Infantry Brigade Order No. 66.	28/10/1917	28/10/1917
Miscellaneous	Administrative Instruction To Accompany 34th. Infantry Brigade Order No. 66.	28/10/1917	28/10/1917
Map	Poelcappelle		
Heading	War Diary of Headquarters 34th Infantry Brigade From 1st Nov To 30th Nov.		
War Diary	Gte St Pierre M.11.a.b.1 (Sheet 36c)	01/11/1917	07/11/1917
War Diary	Vaudricourt	08/11/1917	15/11/1917
War Diary	Elvaston Castle G.34.d.9.3 (Sheet 36c)	15/11/1917	30/11/1917
Operation(al) Order(s)	34th Infantry Brigade Order No. 67.	05/11/1917	05/11/1917
Miscellaneous	March Table.		
Operation(al) Order(s)	34th Infantry Brigade Order No. 68.	13/11/1917	13/11/1917
Miscellaneous	Relief Table issued in conjunction with 34th Brigade Order No. 68.		
Operation(al) Order(s)	34th Infantry Brigade Order No. 69.	17/11/1917	17/11/1917
Operation(al) Order(s)	34th Infantry Brigade Order No. 70.	21/11/1917	21/11/1917
Operation(al) Order(s)	34th Infantry Brigade Order No. 71.	21/11/1917	21/11/1917
Operation(al) Order(s)	34th Infantry Brigade Order No. 72.	25/11/1917	25/11/1917
Miscellaneous	34th Infantry Brigade Order No. 73.	25/11/1917	25/11/1917
Miscellaneous	34th Infantry Brigade Order No. 74.	29/11/1917	29/11/1917
Miscellaneous	Instructions In Event Of An Enemy Retirement. 34th Infantry Brigade No. M. 576.	19/11/1917	19/11/1917
Diagram etc	Formation for a Leash ? Company in a ?		
Operation(al) Order(s)	34th Infantry Brigade No. M. 636		
Operation(al) Order(s)	34th Infantry Brigade No. M. 711.	01/12/1917	01/12/1917
Miscellaneous	Defence Scheme for Brigade in Divisional Reserve	11/11/1917	11/11/1917
Miscellaneous	Amendment No. D.S./1. to 34th Infantry Brigade	04/11/1917	04/11/1917
Heading	War Diary of Headquarters 34th Infantry Brigade From 1st Dec 17 To 31st Dec 17		
War Diary	Elvaston Castle G 34.d.9.3 (Sheet 36 C)	01/12/1917	22/12/1917
War Diary	Noeux-Les-Mines	22/12/1917	23/12/1917
War Diary	Burbure	23/12/1917	31/12/1917
Miscellaneous	Report on the Blowing Up of German Bomb Store at No 4 Brickstack on Night of 2/12/17.	02/12/1917	02/12/1917
Operation(al) Order(s)	34th Infantry Brigade Order No. 75.	06/12/1917	06/12/1917
Miscellaneous	Centre Brigade Defence Scheme. (11th. Division Sector)	07/12/1917	07/12/1917
Miscellaneous	Appendix 1. to Centre Brigade Defence Scheme. Communications.		
Diagram etc			
Miscellaneous	Appendix II To Centre Brigade Defence Scheme.		
Operation(al) Order(s)	34th Infantry Brigade Order No. 76.	11/12/1917	11/12/1917
Operation(al) Order(s)	34th Infantry Brigade Order No. 77.	15/12/1917	15/12/1917
Operation(al) Order(s)	34th Infantry Brigade Order No. 78	19/12/1917	19/12/1917
Miscellaneous	Administrative Instruction No. 78. To Accompany 34th, Infantry Brigade Order No. 78.	19/12/1917	19/12/1917
Miscellaneous	Table "A" To Accompany 11th. Division Order No. 143.		

11TH DIVISION
34TH INFY BDE

BDE HEADQUARTERS
JLY 1916-DEC 1917

Army Form C. 2118.

WAR DIARY
or
34th INTELLIGENCE SUMMARY. Inf. Brigade.

(Erase heading not required.)

Place	Date	Hour	Summary of Events and Information	Remarks and references to Appendices
FERDAN SUEZ CANAL.	1st JULY 2nd	—	2nd Dismounted Brigade took over from 34th Brigade. Brigade Head Quarters. 5 Dorset Regt. Manchester Regt and 34 Machine Gun Company entrained at EL FERDAN at 11:30 a.m. and Embarked on arrival at ALEXANDRIA at H.M.T. TRANSYLVANIA and H.M.T. TORONTO.	
	3rd	—	8 N. Fusiliers and 9 Lanc Fusiliers and all details of Supply and Sanitary Section Entrained at EL FERDAN — arrived at ALEXANDRIA at 5 a.m. and Embarked on H.M.T. LLANDOVERIE CASTLE.	
	4th	6 pm	H.M.T. TRANSYLVANIA & TORONTO Sailed from ALEXANDRIA	
		6 pm	H.M.T. LLANDOVERIE CASTLE Sailed	"
	4th to 9th		At Sea	
	9th	7 a.m.	H.M.T. TRANSYLVANIA & TORONTO arrived at MARSEILLES. Manchester Regt and 5 Dorset Regt and 34 M. Gun Coy went into camp —	

WAR DIARY
or
INTELLIGENCE SUMMARY.

Army Form C. 2118.

Place	Date	Hour	Summary of Events and Information	Remarks and references to Appendices
MARSEILLES	9		B de H Qrs entrained for ST POL.	
	10		8 N. Fusiliers & 9 Lanc Fusiliers arrived at Marseilles and entrained for St Pol.	
			11 Man Regt, 5 Dorset Regt and 34 M.G. Coy entrained for St Pol.	
	11		B de Head Quarters arrived at St Pol.	
	12	-		
	13		B de arrived and went into Billets near IZEL-LE-HAMEAU	
			B de Head Quarters moved to IZEL-LE-HAMEAU.	
	14	-		
	15	-		
	17	-	B de moved to GRAND ROULLECOURT.	
			Officers went from Battalions to reconnoitre line held by 16 S Brigade prior to taking over the	
	18	-	Brigade moved to BEAUMETZ -	
	19	-	11 MANCHESTER Regt took over trenches 180 to 192 inclusive from 6th LIVERPOOL Regt.	
			34 M Gun Coy relieved 16 S M.G. Coy in F section. Whole relief completed without incident	

Army Form C. 2118.

WAR DIARY
or
INTELLIGENCE SUMMARY.
(Erase heading not required.)

Place	Date	Hour	Summary of Events and Information	Remarks and references to Appendices
BRETENCOURT	20th	8am	5th DORSET Regt took over trenches 167 & 179 inclusive from 7th KINGS LIVERPOOL Regt.	
		12 noon	R.N. Fusiliers moved into Billets in BRETENCOURT and became Brigade Reserve.	
		3 p.m	34 Brigade Head Quarters moved to BRETENCOURT and took over from 166 Bde 55th Division. R. Fusiliers moved into billets at SIMENCOURT and became Divisional Reserve.	
		5 p.m.	Relief of 166 Bde by 34 B rigade reported complete.	
	21st		Very quiet day. Right section of 60 F.A.B. relieved right section of 277 F.A.B. 86 Coy R.E. arrived and went into Billets at LE FERMONT.	
	22nd		Relief of 277 F.A.B. by 60 F.A.B. completed.	
	20 23		Enemy very quiet all day. 60 & 7 F A B reported on relieving sap heads and front line	
	23	9 a.m.	Gas Gongs and Klaxon Horns were heard on our left. the Gas alert was immediately ordered but events proved it was a false alarm.	

Army Form C. 2118.

WAR DIARY
or
INTELLIGENCE SUMMARY.
(Erase heading not required.)

Instructions regarding War Diaries and Intelligence Summaries are contained in F. S. Regs., Part II. and the Staff Manual respectively. Title pages will be prepared in manuscript.

Place	Date	Hour	Summary of Events and Information	Remarks and references to Appendices
	24.		Slight activity by our Artillery otherwise a very quiet day. Patrols were out all along the Bde front but no enemy were met and the patrols were not fired on.	
	25.		Enemy shells Right Sub-sector with field guns and Howitzers (4.5) causing no casualties. Our artillery replied on their sap heads and front line. Patrols were out all night but met no opposition. One bombing party threw eight bombs into enemy's sap head opposite Right Sub Sector. Our working parties were unmolested.	
	26.		Same as for 25th	
	27.		Lt Col C. C. HANNAY rejoined 5 Dorset Regt and took over command from Lt Col POLLOCK, 52nd Regt. Beyond slight artillery activity on both sides a very quiet day. Usual patrolling and wiring at night without interruption.	

1577 Wt.W10791/1773 500,000 1/15 D. D. & L. A.D.S.S./Forms/C. 2118.

Army Form C. 2118.

WAR DIARY
or
INTELLIGENCE SUMMARY.
(Erase heading not required.)

Instructions regarding War Diaries and Intelligence Summaries are contained in F. S. Regs., Part II. and the Staff Manual respectively. Title pages will be prepared in manuscript.

Place	Date	Hour	Summary of Events and Information	Remarks and references to Appendices
	28		9 have few in Divisional Reserve marched to ARRAS and took over a Sub sector of I Sector on the left of 3.3.3.- Brigade. They were attached to 33rd Brigade. Feetubert very quiet.	
	29.		Exceptionally quiet day on Feetubert front. 5 Northumberland Fusiliers relieved 11 Manchester Regt in left Sub Sector trenches 180 to 192 inclusive by day without event.	
		5.35'	Relief reports complete. 11 Manchester Regt relieved one Coy 5 N. Fus. in village line and were disposed as follows. 1 Platoon in BRASSERIE, " " PETIT MOULIN. " " WAILLY KEEP " " PETIT CHATEAU. The remaining 3 Coys went into billets in BRETENCOURT and became Bde Reserve.	

1577 Wt.W10791/1773 500,000 1/15 D.D.&L. A.D.S.S./Forms/C. 2118.

Army Form C. 2118.

WAR DIARY
or
INTELLIGENCE SUMMARY.
(Erase heading not required.)

Instructions regarding War Diaries and Intelligence Summaries are contained in F. S. Regs., Part II. and the Staff Manual respectively. Title pages will be prepared in manuscript.

Place	Date	Hour	Summary of Events and Information	Remarks and references to Appendices
	30. 31.		Very quiet days. Practically no shelling by ourselves or the enemy. Patrolling and wiring carried out without interference. <u>Weather</u> Mist every morning from about 4.30 am to 7 am. During the day bright sunshine and hot. Nights warm. Wind almost entirely N to N.E. No rain. <u>Health</u> Good vide Appendix II.	

A.H. Clerke Capt.
B.M. 34 BDe

Appendix I.
with MAP.

Reference attached map.

"F" SECTOR. Trenches 167 to 192 (both inclusive).

        Consists of Firing Line.
                Support Line.
                Reserve Line.
                Village Line.

Average distance from front line to Support Line is 150 yards.

Average distance from Support Line to Reserve Line is 400 yards.

A sunken road runs the whole length of the line and on an average 150 yards in rear of Reserve Line.

The Village Line on the BRETENCOURT - WAILLY Road is some 400 yards behind this sunken road.

The Sector is divided into :-

        Right Sub-Sector 167 to 179 (both inclusive).
        Left Sub-Sector 180 to 192 (both inclusive).

Each Sub-Sector is held by one Battalion.

The Village Line is held by one Company from Battalion in Reserve at BRETENCOURT and 8 machine guns.

The fourth Battalion being Divisional Reserve.

THE GROUND. About 150 yards in front of the firing line is the crest of a ridge running N.E. and S.W.. From the crest the ground slopes down to the BRETENCOURT - WAILLY Road whence it rises again N.W.

The Germans held this ridge and have their front line running along the reverse slope, but maintain observation and offensive action by means of many saps pushed over the crest of the hill

The average distance of the enemys line from our line is 150 yards, but most of the sap heads are only about 50 yards distant.

OBSERVATION. Owing to the above most of the enemy's line is hidden from our front line and can only be seen from the top of the ridge N. of the BRETENCOURT - WAILLY Road, whereas the whole of our system of trenches can be seen from several points in the enemy's front.

G.H.G. Elton Capt.

Bde Major. ~~Brigadier~~ ~~General~~,
~~Commanding~~ 34th. Infantry Brigade.

2 : 8 : 16.

APPENDIX LL.

Unit.   Strength.   Casualties.

From 1st. July to 7th. July.

			Officers.				Other Ranks.		
	Officers.	O.R.	K.	W.	M.		K.	W.	M.
8/North.Fusr.	35.	994.	-	-	-	-	-	-	-
9/Lancs.Fusr.	35.	899.	-	-	-	-	-	-	-
5/Dorset Regt.	32.	872½	-	-	-	-	-	-	-
11/Manchester Regt.	35.	993.	-	-	-	-	-	-	-
34th.M.Gun Coy.	10.	129.	-	-	-	-	-	-	-

From 7th. July to 14th. July.

8/North.Fusr.	35.	994.	-	-	-	-	-	-	-
9/Lans.Fusr.	35.	899.	-	-	-	-	-	-	-
5/Dorset Regt.	32.	872.	-	-	-	-	-	-	-
11/Manch.Regt.	35.	993.	-	-	-	-	-	-	-
34th.M.G.Coy.	10.	129½	-	-	-	-	-	-	-

From 14th. July to 21st. July.

8/North.Fusr.	34.	985.	-	-	-	-	-	-	-
9/Lans.Fusr.	34.	891.	-	-	-	-	-	-	-
5/Dorset Regt.	31.	857	-	-	-	-	-	-	-
11/Manch.Regt.	34.	896.	-ø	2.	-	-	-ø	2.	-
34th.M.G.Coy.	10.	126.	-	-	-	-	-	-	-

From 21st. July to 31st. July.

8/North.Fusr.	34½	984.	-	-	-	-	2-	1.	-
9/Lancs.Fusr.	35.	886.	-	-	-	-	-	-	-
5/Dorset Regt.	30.	841.	-	✱1.	-	-	-	2.	-
11/Manch.Regt.	31.	967.	-	-	-	-	-	-	-
34/M.G.Coy.	10.	161.	-	-	-	-	-	-	-

Reinforcements 1 Officer for North.Fusr and 1 Officers for 5th.Dorsets

ø Captain E. Mc.A. REIDY.
ø Lieut. H.H.O' PEARY.   ✱ 2/Lieut N.J.O. WICKHAM.

Captain E. Mc A REIDY since died of wounds.

F.F. Elton Capt.
B.M. 34th Brigade.

On His Majesty's Service.

Historical Section,
Military Branch,
C.J.A.
Audit House,
Victoria Embankment,
London E.C.4.

WAR DIARY 34 INF. BRIGADE
or
INTELLIGENCE SUMMARY. AUGUST Vol 2

Army Form C. 2118.
(Erase heading not required.)

Hour, Date, Place	Summary of Events and Information	Remarks and references to Appendices
BRETENCOURT. FRANCE. AUGUST 1st.	F Sector. Holding trenches — 5th North Regt. & N. Fusiliers Bde Reserve — 11 Manchester Regt. & gave two batt. attached to 33 @ Bde.	
1.	Very quiet day. Brigade Commander visited the Brigade area and went round trenches of the Left Sub-Sector.	
8.25/m	False gas alarm.	
10.15/m	Rocket lost — Rockets found to be useless owing to exposure for many weeks.	
2.	Exceptionally quiet day. During the night enemy reported to be working hard on his South Keeps and front line.	
3.	Officers of 6th K.E.O. Cavalry and 19th Cavalry visited the area to reconnoitre approaches and main communication trenches.	
4.	Very quiet — Nothing of note to record.	

Army Form C. 2118.

WAR DIARY
or
INTELLIGENCE SUMMARY.
(Erase heading not required.)

Instructions regarding War Diaries and Intelligence Summaries are contained in F.S. Regs., Part II. and the Staff Manual respectively. Title pages will be prepared in manuscript.

Hour, Date, Place	Summary of Events and Information	Remarks and references to Appendices
4th	An exceptionally quiet day. Work progressed satisfactorily in repairing support LINE. Six dug outs starts mon rampit of support line of Right Sub Sector. Two Vickers Machine Gun Emplacements completed in WOOD STREET to fill gap in Village line between BRETENCOURT AND SUGAR FACTORY. Officers patrols were out all along the front line. No enemy was met with.	Village line very strong now.
5th 6th 7th	Quiet days nothing of importance to record. Enemy fired some aerial torpedoes daily * causing a few casualties. Nights were very quiet except apparently busy wiring and digging. Our patrols were out every night in our sector. No enemy patrols.	* a little larger than rifle grenade.
8th	11 Manchester Regt relieved 5th Dorset Regt in Right Sub Sector Trenches 167 to 179 both inclusive. Relief was carried out by day and was completed by 11.45 a.m.	

(73989) W4141—463. 400,000. 9/14. H.&J.Ltd. Forms/C. 2118/10.

Army Form C. 2118.

WAR DIARY
or
INTELLIGENCE SUMMARY.
(Erase heading not required.)

Instructions regarding War Diaries and Intelligence Summaries are contained in F. S. Regs., Part II. and the Staff Manual respectively. Title pages will be prepared in manuscript.

Hour, Date, Place	Summary of Events and Information	Remarks and references to Appendices
9th	Light trench mortars fired to terral tins at Enemys front line behind C+D Saps. Morin trench mortars fired on N.E corner of BLAIRVILLE WOOD. Enemy retaliated with aerial torpedoes. Brig General Corkran 139 Bde on our Right visited Gen Hill by arrangement and discussed the dividing line between the Brigades and defence of that area. Bde issued orders for E.W Fusiliers to carry out a raid on Enemys Sap heads C+D.	Ammt. casualty causing 2 cas. privates. * Range found to be at least 300 x quality superior to our Rifle grenade
10.	Hottest day since 15th July. Night was abnormally quiet. Our patrols were out from 1 am to 3 am but saw no signs of the enemy. Very heavy thunderstorm fell at 2 am and did not clear until 8.30 am.	

WAR DIARY
or
INTELLIGENCE SUMMARY.
(Erase heading not required.)

Army Form C. 2118.

Hour, Date, Place	Summary of Events and Information	Remarks and references to Appendices
11th	Medium Trench Mortar Batty tried at Saps C & D with view of cutting the wire but this was a failure. It was its first time this Batty had been in action. Operation ordered for P.M. this evening should have taken place this night. It was the wire round C & D gaps was not cut the operation was postponed.	
12th 13th	Very quiet. Nothing of interest to record.	
14th	Captn Hon E.S. Hewitt Staff Captn. was appointed to command 1st Battn DORSET Regt and left the Brigade.	
15th	Orders received from Division for relief of 3rd Brigade by 37th Bde to be complete by 6 a.m. on 22nd inst.	Appendix I.

Army Form C. 2118.

WAR DIARY
or
INTELLIGENCE SUMMARY.
(Erase heading not required.)

Instructions regarding War Diaries and Intelligence Summaries are contained in F.S. Regs., Part II and the Staff Manual respectively. Title pages will be prepared in manuscript.

Hour, Date, Place	Summary of Events and Information	Remarks and references to Appendices
16	Very quiet day – Our patrols were out all night and saw no enemy patrols or working parties.	
17th	Very quiet day until 7pm when the 60th A.B. bombarded a sector of the enemy's trenches vide attached orders – Enemy made no retaliation	Appendix I.
18th	Heavy thunder showers made the trenches very bad – wet and muddy –	
19th	More rain – Another quiet day with nothing of importance to record – Capt. E.A.B. Orr. Royal Berkshire Regt. arrived & took over duties of Staff Captain. More heavy rain – Brigade Orders issued for relief of 34th Brigade by 37th Bde. also Move Table Appendix II At 8.55 p.m. Two parties of one Sgt. one Corporal & 7	Appendix II
8.55 p.m		

WAR DIARY
OR
INTELLIGENCE SUMMARY.
(Erase heading not required.)

Army Form C. 2118.

Hour, Date, Place	Summary of Events and Information	Remarks and references to Appendices
20th	men each of the 8th N/Hy Fusiliers under Lieuts. Armstrong & Ash raided enemy Sap. C.R.29.d.95.55. Lieut Armstrong succeeded by three Bayonet men, worked along the Sap. Sentries were posted over two dug outs. Lieut Armstrong & Lt. Thompson succeeded further but meting opposition the enemy throwing bombs one of which dropped without exploding, were immediately thrown back wounding a German who was taken prisoner but died on reaching our fire trench. We had no casualties. The operation lasted twenty minutes. The information obtained proved of great value. It was found that no relief opposite this sector had taken place for some time.	(78th Landwehr Regt.) Vide Appendix I.
21st	The 60.F.A.B. bombarded the enemy's trenches in attacked Orders- The enemy made no retaliation. Remainder of day quiet. The 37th Brigade relieved 34th Brigade in F. Sector. Relief was carried out by day and was complete by 3.40 p.m. - 34th Brigade HQ. moved to Sombrin	
3.40 p.m.	5 Dorset Regt marched to Sombrin thence into Billets	

WAR DIARY
or
INTELLIGENCE SUMMARY.
(Erase heading not required.)

Army Form C. 2118.

Hour, Date, Place	Summary of Events and Information	Remarks and references to Appendices
22nd	8th North'n Fusiliers, Lancashire Fusiliers & 11th Manchester Regt. billeted in GRAND RULLECOURT. 34th M.G. Coy. billeted in LIENCOURT.	
23rd	Major Campbell, Gordon Highlanders, lectured on "Bayonet Fighting" to the 8th N.F., 11th Man. Regt. 34th M.G. Coy, Brigade H.Q. & L.T.M. Battery, at GRAND RULLECOURT at 9 Lancs, two 4.5" Howrs at P.3. Training area.	
24th	Training all day – nothing of note to record.	
25th	Training all day – G.O.C. 11th Division visited 34 Bde Area.	
26th	Training all day – Heavy rain – B.G.O.C. 34"Bde. inspected Brigade transport – Demonstration of the Flammenwerfer at GOUY-EN-ARTOIS.	
27th	Church Parades. Remainder of day – rest.	
28th	Orders to move to new Area – HOUVAIN, HOUVENEUL, GOUEY-EN-TOURNOIS, MAZIERES – received. Training all day	

Army Form C. 2118.

WAR DIARY
or
INTELLIGENCE SUMMARY.
(Erase heading not required.)

Place	Date	Hour	Summary of Events and Information	Remarks and references to Appendices
	29th		Training all day. Very heavy rain.	
	30th		Brigade moved to new Area - B.H.Q. at HOUVIN - HOUVENEUL - Rained all day	
	31st		Training all day. Fine weather. Orders issued for transfer of Division to Reserve Army - Vide Orders - Appendix I.	Appendix I.

R.H. Ratcliffe Lieut
34th Inf. Brigade H.Q.

SECRET.   Copy No. 2

34th BRIGADE ORDER No. 4.

Reference Trench Map FICHEUX.- 1/10,000.

1. A bombardment of enemy's lines in Area R.30.a. - M.19.d. - M.25.b. by 60th F. A. B. will take place on 18 : 8 : 16.

2. TIME.   7 p.m. to ~~7 p.m.~~ 7.20 p.m.

3. OBJECT.   Destruction of suspected Trench Mortar emplacements and communications in that area.

4. Light Trench Mortar Batteries will co-operate.

   (a) Four guns firing on Saps B. C. D. and the wire in front of these.

   (b) Two guns will fire on enemy trenches on each flank of the bombardment.

   (c) Ammunition to be used :- 1,000 Rounds.

5. 34th Machine Gun Company will co-operate and will fire indirect fire on enemy main approaches behind above area, and on the WAILLY - FICHEUX Road where it passes through FICHEUX.

6. Owing to proximity of our front line to enemy trenches opposite above area, trenches 178 to 183 will be cleared from 6.55 p.m. till after the bombardment.

7. In view of probable retaliation, there will be as little movement as possible during the bombardment. All men not on duty to be under cover from 6.55 p.m. to 7.30 p.m.

8. Brigade Intelligence Officer will arrange to collect reports as to enemy's action.

9. Reports to B. H. Q.

Issued at. 5 p.m.

Copy No. 1. Office.
"   "   2. War Diary.
"   "   3. 8th North. Fus.
"   "   4. 5th Dorset Rgt.
"   "   5. 11th Manchester Rgt.
"   "   6. 34th Machine Gun Coy.
"   "   7. Light Trench Mortar Batty.
"   "   8. Medium Trench Mortar Batty.
"   "   9. 86th Field Company R.E.
"   " 10. "C" Coy. 6th E. Yorks.
"   " 11. 60th. F. A. B.
"   " 12. 32nd Brigade.
"   " 13. 139th Brigade.
"   " 14. 11th Division.

15 : 8 : 16.

Captain,
Brigade Major, 34th. Inf. Brigade.

Appendix F

SECRET.   Copy No. 2

34th BRIGADE ORDER No. 7.

Reference   Trench Map FICHEUX 1/10,000.

1. A bombardment of enemy's lines in Areas :-

   R.29.d. 80.85.
   R.29.d. 90.87.
   R.30.a. 15.10.
   R.30.a. 25.25.

   by 60th. F. A. B. will take place tomorrow.

2. TIME.   10 a.m. to 10.42 a.m.

3. OBJECT.   Destruction of Sapheads and Communication trenches.

4. Medium Trench Mortar Battery will co-operate and fire on Saps A.B.C.D.   Steady rate of fire from 10. a.m. to 10.18 . Rounds 40.

5. Light Trench Mortars will co-operate and fire on Sapheads A.B.C.D. Fire at steady rate from 10. a.m. to 10.18 a.m.   Rounds 1,000.

6. Front Line Trenches in front of this area will be cleared by 9.50 a.m. until after the bombardment.

7. In view of probable retaliation all working parties and those not on duty will be under cover by 9.50 a.m. until after the bombardment.

8. Brigade Intelligence Officer will arrange to collect reports.

Issued at

Copy No. 1. Office,
  "   " 2. War Diary.
  "   " 3. 8th North. Fus.
  "   " 4. 5th Dorset Rgt.
  "   " 5. 11th Manchester Rgt.
  "   " 6. 86th Field Coy. R.E.
  "   " 7. 34th M. G. Coy.
  "   " 8. M. T. M. B.
  "   " 9. L. T. M. B.
  "   " 10. "C" Coy. 6th E. Yorks.
  "   " 11. 32nd Inf. Brigade.
  "   " 12. 33th Inf. Brigade.
  "   " 13. 60th. F. A. B.
  "   " 14. 11th. Division.

                                                    Captain,
19 : 8 : 16.   Brigade Major, 34th Infantry Brigade.

SECRET.   Copy No. 4

34th BRIGADE ORDER No. 8.

Reference Maps LENS 11. 1/100,000.   August 30th. 1916.

1. The 11th Division (less Artillery) will be transferred to 2nd Corps, Reserve Army, on 3rd September and will be concentrated in Area "O" Reserve Army.

2. 34th Infantry Brigade will move as per attached tables to ACHEUX thence to Billets in PUCHEVILLERS.

3. Transport moving by road will be Brigaded and march under Lieut KING, 5th Dorset Regiment.

4. Supply Railhead for the 11th Division will change from TINQUES to BOUQUEMAISON on 3rd September.
   Supply Railhead for 4th September will be in Reserve Army Area.

5. Brigade Headquarters will move to PUCHEVILLERS on 3rd September.

6. Completion of all moves to be reported to B.H.Q.

Issued at 6 p.m.

Copy No. 1. Office.
" " 2. "
" " 3. Brigade Signals.
" " 4. War Diary.
" " 5. 8th North. Fus.
" " 6. 9th Lancs. Fus.
" " 7. 5th Dorset Rgt.
" " 8. 11th Manchesters.
" " 9. 34th Machine G. Coy.
" " 10. 34th Light Trench Mortars.
" " 11. Lieut. KING.
" " 12. 11th Division.

                                                                 Captain,

                               Brigade Major, 34th Infantry Brigade.

3rd. TRAIN.   PREVENT Depart 8.38 A.M.
ACHEUX Arrive 1.35 P.M.

Unit.	Officers.	O.R.	Animals.	G.S. Wagons.	Cookers.	Limbered G.S.	Carts.	Trench Mortars.
BRIGADE HEADQUARTERS.	1.	24.	8.	-	-	1.	-	-
34th M.G. Coy.	9.	141.	44.	1.	-	9.	2.	-
Signal Section.	1.	26.	8.	-	-	3.	-	-
Cookers.	-	16.	32.	-	16.	-	-	-
32 Pack Mules. (2 Per Coy.)	-	32.	32.	-	-	-	-	-
4 Limbered G.S. Wagons for S.A.A. (1 Per Battn.)	3.	4.	8.	-	-	4.	-	-
34th Light Trench Mortars.	6.	66.	-	-	-	-	-	8.
	20.	309.	132.	1.	16.	17.	2.	8.

Unit.	Date.	Time.	From.	To	ROUTE.	Remarks.
				1st. TRAIN.	FREVENT Depart:- 4.38 A.M. ACHEUX Arrive:- 8.20 A.M.	
8th North. Fus.	2nd/3rd.	12 Midnight.	Billets.	ACHEUX.	March route via HOUVIGNEUL to FREVENT - Thence by Rail.	
5th Dorset Rgt.	-do-	-do-	-do-	-do-	March route via HOUVIN - HOUVIG -NEUL. HOUVIGNEUL to FREVENT. Thence by Rail.	
34th M.G. Coy.	-do-	12-20 A.M.	-do-	-do-	To follow 8th North. Fus.	Officers and O.R. not with Transport or 3rd Train will go by 1st Train.
				2nd. TRAIN.	FREVENT Depart:- 5.38 A.M. ACHEUX Arrive:- 9.25 A.M.	
9th Lancs. Fus.	3rd.	12.30 A.M.	-do-	-do-	March route to FREVENT via MAGNICOURT - HOUVIN - HOUVIGNEUL.	
11th Manchesters.	3rd.	-do-	-do-	-do-	March route to FREVENT via MAGNICOURT - HOUVIN - HOUVIGNEUL.	

All troops to be at the Station one hour before Entraining Time in cases of Trains Nos. 1 and 2, and three hours before Entraining Time in the case of No. 3 Train.

APPENDIX 11.

STRENGTH OF UNITS FOR WEEK 1st. to 7th. Aug.

	Off.	Other ranks.	Officers K.	W.	M.	Other ranks K.	W.	M.
8/North.Fus.	35.	973.	-	-	-	1.	2.	-
9th.Lancs.Fus.	35.	889.	-	-	-	-	-	-
5th.Dorset Regt.	31.	832.	-	-	-	1.	1.	-
11th.Manch.Regt.	31.	964.	-	-	-	-	-	-
34th.M.G.Coy.	11.	165.	-	-	-	-	-	-

STRENGTH OF UNITS FOR WEEK 8th. to 14th. Aug.

8th.North.Fus.	34.	971.	-	-	-	2.	8.	-
9th.Lancs.Fus.	With 33rd. Brigade.		-	-	-	-	-	-
5th.Dorset Regt.	31.	842.	ø 1.	-	-	2.	6.	-
11th.Manch.Regt.	29.	937.	-	-	-	1.	5.	-
34th.M.G.Coy.	11.	166.	-	-	-	-	-	-

ø Capt. H.E. KITCHER.

STRENGTH OF UNITS FOR WEEK 15th. to 21st. Aug.

8th. North. Fus.	34.	961.	-	-	-	2.	2.	-
9th.Lancs.Fus.	With 33rd. Brigade.		-	-	-	-	-	-
5th.Dorset Regt.	31.	833.	-	-	-	-	-	-
11th. Manch.Regt.	32.	937.	-	X 2.	-	1.	2.	-
34th.M.G.Coy.	12.	171.	-	ø1	-	-	-	-

X (Lt. C.M.S. CUNNINGHAM
(2/Lt. E.C. GRAY.
ø 2Lt. R.C.R. ALLERTON.

STRENGTH OF UNITS FOR WEEK 22nd. to 28th. Aug.

8th. North.Fus.	33.	979.	-	-	-	2.	-	-
9th. Lancs. Fus.	36.	879	-	-	-	-	-	-
5th. Dorset Regt.	40.	868.	-	-	-	-	-	-
11th. Manch.Regt.	31.	945.	-	-	-	-	-	-
34th.M.G.Coy.	11.	176.	-	-	-	-	-	-

<u>Reinforcements arrived during month.</u>   1 Officer and 20.O.R. North.Fusr.

9th. Lancs. Fus. 1 Officer.   5th. Dorset Regt. 15 Officers.

11th. Manchester Regt. 3 Officers. 30 O.R.   34th. M.G.Coy. 1 Officer.

Reference Map LENS 11. 1/100,000.

1st LINE TRANSPORT.

Unit.	Date.	Time.	From.	To.	Route.
BRIGADE HEADQUARTERS.	2nd.	9.30 A.M.	Billets.	PUCHEVILLERS.	ETREE WAMIN = BEAUDRICOURT = IVERGNY = LUCHEUX = HOLLOY = THIEVRES = VAUCHELLES = RAIECHEVAL.
8th North. Fus.	2nd.	9.30 A.M.	-do-	-do-	-ditto-
34th M. G. Coy.	2nd.	9.30 A.M.	-do-	-do-	To follow 8th North. Fus.
5th Dorset Rgt.	2nd.	9.15.A.M.	-do-	-do-	HOUVIN.
9th Lancs. Fus.	2nd.	9. 0 A.M.	-do-	-do-	MAGNICOURT.
11th Manchesters.	2nd.	8.50 A.M.	-do-	-do-	MAGNICOURT.

All 1st Line Transport and baggage wagons marching to PUCHEVILLERS will form up on MAGNICOURT = HOUVIN Road with head of the column just short of turning to ETREE WAMIN and proceed thence under Lieut. KING, 5th Dorset Regiment.

MOTOR TRANSPORT FOR SEPTEMBER 2nd.

1. Units will send guides to Brigade Headquarters at 12 Noon tomorrow to fetch the two Motor Lorries which have been allotted to their unit.
These Lorries will be loaded and will return to Brigade Headquarters by 2 P.M., where they will form up previous to departure.
Billeting officers will proceed with the Lorry, the Senior Billeting Officer Lieut. BARFOOT, 8th North. Fus, reporting to Brigade Headquarters for instructions at 2 P.M.

2. Two other Lorries have been allotted to the Brigade for transporting Lewis Guns and Officers Kits (if desired) to PREVENT Station. Guides to meet these Lorries will report at Brigade Headquarters at 4 P.M.
The Lorries will make two journeys if necessary.

Captain,

Brigade Major, 34th Infantry. Brigade.

1 : 9 : 16.

App IV

Copy No. 3

34th INFANTRY BRIGADE ORDER No. 5.

Map reference 1/40,000 Sheet 51 C.
1/10,000 Trench Map FICHEUX.   16 : 8 : 16.

1. 34th Infantry Brigade will be relieved in F Sector by 37th Infantry Brigade by 6 a.m. on 22nd.

2. On relief Units will move in accordance with attached table.

3. 86th Field Company R.E. and detachment East Yorks Pioneer Battalion will be relieved at a later date.

4. Light Trench Mortar detachments will be attached to 34th Machine Gun Company from 21st.

5. Vickers and Lewis Gun personnel, snipers, bombers, observers and telephonists of incoming Units will take over 24 hours before the commencement of Infantry reliefs.

6. All trench maps, air photos, defence schemes and log books will be handed over to relieving troops. Trench Stores will be handed over and receipts for same sent to B.H.Q.

7. One Officer and one N.C.O. per company in the front line will be left with the relieving Battalion for 24 hours after completion of the relief.

8. Brigade Headquarters will move to SOMBRIN on 21st after the relief is complete.

9. All reports to present B.H.Q.

Issued at 6.30 pm

Copy No. 1. Office.   Copy No. 8. 34th Machine Gun Coy.
"   " 2. Office.   "   " 9. 86th Field Company R.E.
"   " 3. War Diary.   "   " 10. Light Trench Mortar Batty.
"   " 4. 8th North. Fus.   "   " 11. 32nd Infantry Brigade.
"   " 5. 9th Lancs. Fus.   "   " 12. 139th Infantry Brigade.
"   " 6. 5th Dorset Rgt.   "   " 13. 60th. F. A. B.
"   " 7. 11th Manchester Rgt.   "   " 14. 11th Division.
"   " 15. 34th Field Ambulance

E.B.G. Elton   Captain,

16 : 8 : 16.   Brigade Major, 34th Infantry Brigade.

MOVE TABLE.

Unit.	Date of relief.	Destination on date of relief	Final Destination and date.	Remarks.
9th. Lancs. Fus.	18/19.	FOSSEUX	GRAND ROULLECOURT 21st.	Clear FOSSEUX by 9.30 a.m.
5th Dorset Rgt.	21st.	SOMBRIN	SOMBRIN 21st.	Will march via BASSEUX - LE BAC DU SUD - GOUY. With 10 minutes interval between platoons until they reach GOUY, thence by companies.
11th Manchester Rgt.	21st.	BEAUMETZ	GRAND ROULLECOURT 22nd.	To be clear of BEAUMETZ by 9.30 a.m. on 22nd. and march with 10 minutes interval between companies until 2 Miles clear of BEAUMETZ.
8th. North. Fus.	21st.	MONCHIET	GRAND ROULLECOURT 22nd.	To be clear of MONCHIET by 9 a.m.
34th M. G. Coy.	21st.	MONCHIET	SOMBRIN 22nd.	Will march half hour in rear of 8th North. Fus.
34th Field Amb.	21st.	SOMBRIN	SOMBRIN 21st.	To be clear of BARLY by 9.30 a.m. 21st.
Light Trench Mor. B.	21st.	MONCHIET	SOMBRIN 22nd.	March with Machine Gun Company.
Brigade Headquarters	21st.	SOMBRIN	SOMBRIN 21st.	

Headquarters,
34th Inf: Bde.
(11th Div)
August 1916

On His Majesty's Service.

Historical Section (Military Branch)
Audit House
Victoria Embankment
E.C.4

WAR DIARY

of

34th Bn

Sept 1916

vol 3

Army Form C. 2118.

34th Inf. Brigade
11th Division.

WAR DIARY
INTELLIGENCE SUMMARY
(Erase heading not required.)

September 1916

Place	Date	Hour	Summary of Events and Information	Remarks and references to Appendices
HOUVIN=	1		Training all day -	
HOUVIGNUEL	2	3.P.M.	34th Bde Headquarters moved to PUCHEVILLERS	
	2/3		34th Bde, including 4 Battns, 34th F.Amb, 86 Field Coy. R.E. 34th M.G. Coy & 34th L.T.M.B. arrived & billeted in PUCHEVILLERS.	
	4		Training all day -	
	5		Training all day -	
	6		Training all day - Orders issued for relief of 25th Division by 11th Division to be completed by 8th Sept. Vide Orders - Appendix	Appendix I
	7		Training all day - Demonstration to Brigade of Light Trench Mortars	
	8		34th Brigade H.Q. marched to BOUZINCOURT relieved 75th Inf. Bde.	
		2.15 P.M.	Relief completed at 2.15 P.M. = 34th Brigade on Divisional Reserve	
	9		Battalions training & cleaning up billets	
	10		34th Brigade supplied working parties to 32nd + 33rd Brigades - by day & night	
	11		34th Brigade supplied working parties to 32nd + 33rd Brigades - by day & night	
	12		34th Brigade supplied working parties to 32nd + 33rd Brigades - by day & night	
	13		Training -	
	14		32nd Brigade attacked & captured line R.31.d.98 - WONDER WORK. Vide Orders	App. I

Army Form C. 2118.

WAR DIARY
INTELLIGENCE SUMMARY.
(Erase heading not required.)

August 1916

Place	Date	Hour	Summary of Events and Information	Remarks and references to Appendices
Bouzincourt	15		Brigade ready to move at 2 hours notice - Orders received for relief of 8th Canadian Brigade.	
	16		5th Dorsets & 7th Lancs Fus. left BOUZINCOURT at 7.30 p.m. to relieve 2 Battalions 8th Canadian Brigade took over trenches in line R.28.d.51. 28.c.95.93.22.21.d.21.c R.27.a.91.b. R.33.b.59. through MOUQUET FARM to R.39.c.18. R.33.a.77.54. On the right the 8th Canadian Brigade reported having taken MOUQUET FARM & dug a line round it. At daybreak we found the situation was not as stated by them but the line runs through the FARM. - Relief completed without any casualties at 6.30 am	
	17	6.30 am	Brigade moved 16 X 15 Central took over from 8th Canadian Brigade	
	17	3.20 p.m.	8 No.1 R.Fusiliers and 11th Manchester Reg(t)s in Brigade reserve. Fine weather. The Brigade front runs from R.33 a 77 to R.28.C.21 and includes front of MOUQUET FARM - a length of about 800 yards held by one Battalion. Battalion Headquarters is just near the POZIERES Cemetery and there is only one communication trench up to the QUARRY about 400 yards in rear of the front line first beyond the QUARRY is a support line with communicating trenches from one end to the front line. When taken over all the trenches were very shallow and	
	18			

Army Form C. 2118.

WAR DIARY
INTELLIGENCE SUMMARY.
(Erase heading not required.)

Place	Date	Hour	Summary of Events and Information	Remarks and references to Appendices
	17		consisted of places of nothing but shell holes. The 9th Canadian Brigade was on our right and the 33rd Bde. on our left and there were gaps of about 100 to 200 yards between each. The FARM itself consists of three ruins one of which is behind our lines and two in front. A tunnel connects all three ruins and Germans are known to have used this to gain access to the rear of our front line and on Wednesday the 19th four Germans were shot in doing so. A deep dug out was known to be under the ruin about 40 yards in front of our line.	
	18		Wet day – 5 Dorsets & 9th Lancs Fus. holding trenches – both battalions relieved by 11th Manch. a Battalion of the 9th Canadian Brigade – The 5 Dorset Regt. took 4 Prisoners – 3 of which were stretcher bearers and the other all belonging to the 212 I.R. – The Lancs Fus. took one prisoner belonging to the 213 I.R.	
	19		Wet day which delayed Operations – The 5th Dorset Regt were relieved by the 11th Manchester Regt during night 19/20th. Relief completed by 10.25pm. 5 Dorsets went into billets in ALBERT. 11th Manr. Regt took one prisoner.	
	20	7 A.M.	(belong to 169 I.R. – 34th B.H.Q. moved to x 3 (OUVILLERS) Canadian Brigade at 7 A.M. being relieved by 9th Fair weather – Normal conditions – 11th Man Regt took one prisoner belonging to 126 I.R.	

Army Form C. 2118.

WAR DIARY
INTELLIGENCE SUMMARY.
(Erase heading not required.)

Place	Date	Hour	Summary of Events and Information	Remarks and references to Appendices
	21		Fine day - 11th Man. Regt. holding line with 9th Lancs. Fus. in reserve at 7.30 a.m. 8 prisoners, including a Sgt. Major belonging to I.R. 93 were brought in by 11th Man. Regt. - Orders issued - Vide App. I.	App. I
			For relief by 32nd Inf. Brigade. Capt. Hutchinson - 6th Lincolnshire Regt. arrived attached to 34th Inf. Bde. H.Q. as Assistant Staff Captain - For instructional purposes. Heavy shelling from 4.30 p.m. until midnight by enemy. He obtained direct hits on 6 - 18 pdr. Canadian Guns.	
	22		One prisoner belonging to the 212 I.R. was taken in the early morning. Fine weather. Heavy shelling by the enemy all day, about 6.50 p.m. the intensity of the Artillery duel increased which lasted practically all night - 11th Manchester Regt. was relieved by 6th York Lancs. Regt. (32nd Bde) relief being completed by 4.10 a.m. & the Brigade was disposed as follows - 8th Northumberland Fus. in ENGLEBELMER - 9th Lancashire Fusiliers in MAILLEY-MAILLET - 5th Dorset Regt. in ENGLEBELMER 11th Manchester Regt, 34 Machine Gun Coy. 34th Light Trench Mortar Battery in shelters south of CRUCIFIX CORNER. Bde. H.Q., in ENGLEBELMER, arriving at 1.10 p.m.	

Army Form C. 2118.

WAR DIARY
INTELLIGENCE SUMMARY.
(Erase heading not required.)

Place	Date	Hour	Summary of Events and Information	Remarks and references to Appendices
ENGLEBELMER	24		Lt. Col. B.A. Wright commanding 11th Man. Regt. was evacuated sick - left for Field Ambulance. Major Oliver took over command.	
	25		34th Brigade Headquarters moved to OVILLERS & took over dug outs - 8th North. Fus. & 9th Lancs Fus. took over trenches R.28.C.21, 33.6.59.55.34.a.28. 11th Manchesters & 5th Dorsets in reserve. Vide Orders - App. I. Orders issued for attack on enemy positions. Vide Orders - App. I.	App I T/77
	26/29	12.35 p.m.	Operations commenced - see attached report. Vide app. I. Also report on MOUQUET FARM operations - App. II. During night (29th) 8th North. Fusiliers, 9th Lancs Fus. & 5th Dorset Regt. went into dug outs in OVILLERS next morning whole Brigade less 11th Manchester Regt. moved to billets in ACHEUX & VARENNES.	
	30	4.50	Brigade H.Q. moved to VARENNES arriving at 4.50 p.m.	

R.W. Ratcliffe 2nd Lieut.
34th Inf. Brigade H.Q.

S E C R E T. Copy No. ....

34th INFANTRY BRIGADE ORDER No. 9.

Reference Map 1/40,000 Sheet 57. D.   6 - 9 - 16

1. The 11th Division (less Artillery) will commence to relieve the 25th Division (less Artillery) on 6th Inst. The relief will be completed on 8th. September.

2. 34th Infantry Brigade will march to BOUZINCOURT on 8th. Sept. Vide March Table, and be in Divisional Reserve.

3. STARTING POINT:- Cross Roads in N. 22. C.

4. MARCH TABLE :-

UNIT.	TIME OF CLEARING STARTING POINT.	ROUTE.
BRIGADE H. Q.	8.30 A.M.	)
8th North. Fus.	8.45 A.M.	)
9th Lancs. Fus.	9. 0 A.M.	) RAINCHEVAL.
5th Dorset Rgt.	9.15 A.M.	) ARQUEVES. LEALVILLERS.
11th Manch Rgt.	9.30 A.M.	) VARENNES. SENLIS.
34th M. G. Coy.	9.40 A.M.	)
34th L. T. M. B.	9.50 A.M.	)

5. 1st Line Transport will march with Battalions.

Issued at 1/pm

Copy No. 1. Office.
 - 2. -
 - 3. War Diary.
 - 4. Signals.
 - 5.)
 - 6.) Four
 - 7.) Battns.
 - 8.)
 - 9. 34th M. G. Coy.
 - 10. 34th L. T. M. B.
 - 11. 11th Division.
 - 12. A.P.M. 11th Division.

Captain,
Brigade Major, 34th. INF. Brigade.

SECRET. App. I Copy No......

34th INFANTRY BRIGADE ORDER No. 10.

Reference Map 1/5,000. Trench Map THIEPVAL. September 13th.
1/20,000. 57.d.S.E. Edition 2 d.

INTENTION. 1. The 11th Division will capture the line R.31.d.98 - WONDER WORK - b.23 - b.03.- A.91.- c.78, (the portion b.03 - A.91 - c.78 being organised as a defensive flank and a block formed on the right about R.32.c.08) on the afternoon of the 14th. September.

DISPOSITIONS. 2. "A". The 32nd Inf. Bde. is detailed for this task.
"B". The 33rd Inf. Bde. will bring machine gun fire to bear on approaches likely to be utilized by the enemy for reinforcing his troops South of THIEPVAL, especial attention being paid to communication trench R.32.a.26 - 28 - R.32.a.09, trench along the hedge running Northwards from R.32.a.77. to about R.26.c.74.
Trenches R.32.c.39 - 31.b.91 and 31.b.82. to b.23 should be fired on up to ZERO plus 7 minutes.
"C". 34th Inf. Bde. will be in Divisional Reserve and disposed as under :-
34th Inf. Bde will remain at BOUZINCOURT ready to move at an hours notice from ZERO hour until further notice.

DRESS. 3. Marching order - Filled water bottles - Iron rations.

LIAISON. 4. 9th Lancs. Fus will detail a Captain as Liaison Officer between 11th Division and 3rd Canadian Division.

ZERO HOUR. 5. ZERO will be at 6.30 P.M.

MEDICAL ARRANGEMENTS. 6. Medical arrangements will be as under :-

Main Dressing Stations (1) VARENNES - (for serious cases)
(2) EAST CLAIRFAYE - (for light cases)
Divisional Collecting Stations for walking cases -
(BOUZINCOURT.
Advanced Dressing Stations (1) BLACK HORSE BRIDGE.
(2) AVELUY CHATEAU.

WATCHES. 7. An Officer from each Battalion will report at B.H.Q. at 6 P.M. to correct watches.

REPORTS. 8. Reports to B.H.Q.

Issued to Signals at 2.30 p.m.

Copy No. 1. Office.
" " 2. Staff Captain.
" " 3. Bde. Sig. Off.
" " 4.)
" " 5.) Four
" " 6.) Batt^{ns}.
" " 7.)
" " 8. 34th M.G. Coy.
" " 9. 34th L. T. M. B.
" " 10. 11th Division.
" " 11. War Diary.

Captain,
Brigade Major, 34th Infantry Brigade.

34th INFANTRY BRIGADE ORDER No. 48.

Reference Map 1/5,000 - FERME DU MOUQUET.
1/20,000 - FRANCE-57.d.S.E.   September 21st.

1. The 32nd Inf. Bde. will relieve 34th and 33rd Inf. Brigades in the line on Night 22nd/23rd.

2. On relief 34th Inf. Bde. will be disposed as follows :-

   8th North. Fus. in ENGLEBELMER.
   9th Lancs. Fus. in MAILLEY - MAILLET.
   5th Dorset Rgt. in ENGLEBELMER.
   11th Manch Rgt. in shelters South of CRUCIFIX CORNER.
   34th M. G. Coy.   -ditto-
   34th L. T. M. B.   -ditto-

3. 6th York and Lancs Regt. will relieve 11th Manchester Rgt. Guides to be at OVILLERS CHURCH for advance party at 10 A.M. and for Battalion at 7.30 P.M.

4. (a) 9th West Yorks Regt. will relieve 9th Lancs. Fus.
   (b) 9th Lancs. Fus. will be clear of OVILLERS and halted off the Road by 3.30 P.M., where they will wait until 9th West Yorks Regt. have passed.
   (c) 9th Lancs. Fus. will provide guides for advanced party at OVILLERS CHURCH at 2 P.M.

5. 8th North. Fus. will complete the erection of shelters South of CRUCIFIX CORNER before marching off.

6. 32nd M. G. Coy. will relieve 34th M. G. Coy.

7. 32nd L. T. M. B. will relieve 34th L. T. M. B. Guide to H. Q. 34th L. T. M. B. to be at B. H. Q. at 2 P.M.

8. Details of reliefs to be made by C. Os. concerned.

9. Completion of reliefs to be reported by CODE Word "RABBITS".

10. 11th Manchester Regt., 34th M. G. Coy. and 34th L. T. M. B. will be at disposal of G.O.C. 32nd Brigade for tactical and working purposes.

11. Advance parties of 8th North. Fus. and 9th Lancs. Fus. will report to town Majors ENGLEBELMER and MAILLEY - MAILLET respectively.

12. 1st Line Transport will remain in its present position.

13. B. H. Q. will move to ENGLEBELMER on completion of relief.

Issued to Signals at 12 Midnight

Copy No. 1. Office.
"   "   2. Staff Captain.
"   "   3 Signals.
"   "   4. War Diary.
"   "   5. 8th North. Fus.
"   "   6. 9th Lancs. Fus.
"   "   7. 5th Dorset Rgt.
"   "   8. 11th Manchester Rgt.
"   "   9. 34th M. G. Coy.
"   " 10. 34th L. T. M. B.
"   " 11. 32nd Brigade.
"   " 12. 33rd Brigade.
"   " 13. 9th Canadian Inf. Bde.
"   " 14. 11th Division.

                                        Captain,
                            Brigade Major, 34th Infantry Brigade.

21. REPORTS.

To Brigade Headquarters at X.8.b.16.24.

Issued at................

Copy No. 1 & 2 Office.
"   "   3 Diary.
"   "   4 to 9 8th North. Fus.
"   "   10 to 14. 9th Lancs. Fus.
"   "   15 to 19. 5th Dorset Rgt.
"   "   20 to 24. 11th Manchester Rgt.
"   "   25 to 28. 34th M. G. Coy.
"   "   29 & 30. 34th L. T. M. B.
"   "   31. 11th Division.
"   "   32 to 35. C. R. A.
"   "   36. 33rd Inf. Brigade.
"   "   37. 32nd Inf. Brigade.
"   "   38. 2nd. Canadian Inf. Bde.
"   "   39. 86th Field Co. R.E.
"   "   40. Bde. Sigs. Officer.
"   "   41. Bde. Intell. Offcr.
"   "   42 & 43. Liaison Officers.

(signed) Captain,
Brigade Major, 34th Infantry Brigade.

SECRET.   Copy No. 3

34th INFANTRY BRIGADE ORDER No. 13.

Reference Maps :- GRANDCOURT.   )   September 25th.
                  ST. PIERRE DIVION.)
                  COURCELETTE.   ) Scale.
                  FERME DU MOUQUET.) 1/5,000.
                  THIEPVAL.   )
                  OVILLERS.   )

1. 2nd Corps will capture HESSIAN TRENCH, STUFF REDOUBT along the high ground to SCHWABEN REDOUBT, on a date to be detailed later.

INFORMATION.

2. INFORMATION OF OUR OWN FORCES.
   (a) The attack will form part of Offensive operations on a large scale.
   (b) 2nd Canadian Corps will attack at the same hour as 2nd Corps with 1st Canadian Division on our Right.
   (c) 1st Canadian Division will capture from M.19.d.35 to R.22.a.40 inclusive.
   (d) 11th Division will capture from R.21.d.99 inclusive along HESSIAN TRENCH - STUFF REDOUBT - R.20.d.10 inclusive.
   (e) 18th Division will capture from R.20.d.10 exclusive, along the HESSIAN TRENCH - SCHWABEN REDOUBT - R.19.d.00 inclusive.

DIVIDING LINES.

3. (a) Between 1st Canadian and 11th Divisions :-
   Road R.28.c.21 - 39 - a.64 to R.22.a.10 inclusive to the 1st Canadian Division.
   (b) Between 11th and 18th Divisions :-
   From well 32.c.78 - along hedge - through R.32.a.77 - 25.c.73 - XXX - R.26.a.80 - R.20.d.10 inclusive to the 11th Division.

OBJECTIVES.

4. (a) The attack will be delivered with the 33rd and 34th Infantry Brigades in the Front Line and the 32nd Infantry Brigade in Reserve.
   (b) RIGHT ATTACK :- 34th Infantry Brigade.
       1st Objective :- R.28.a.31 inclusive to R.27.c.54 inclusive.

       2nd Objective :- R.21.d.78 inclusive - ZOLLERN REDOUBT - along ZOLLERN TRENCH - R.26.b.86 inclusive.

       3rd Objective :- R.21.d.99 inclusive - along HESSIAN TRENCH - STUFF REDOUBT - R.20.d.91 Exclusive.
   (c) G.O.C. 33rd Infantry Brigade will give particular attention to the following points :-
       (i) Clearance of MIDWAY LINE.
       (ii) Formation of strong point to guard left flank of 11th. Division and connect with Right of 18th Division about R.26.c.93.

DISPOSITIONS.

ASSAULTING TROOPS.

5. RIGHT ATTACK :- 8th Northumberland Fusiliers.
   FORMING UP PLACES :- Firing Line and Support Line in Area R.28.c.21 - 33.b.59 - 55 - 34.a.28.

1st Objective - R.28.a.31 inclusive to R.27.b.51 inclusive.

2nd Objective - R.21.d.78 inclusive - ZOLLERN REDOUBT - to - R.21.b.01
(inclusive.

3rd Objective - R.21.d.99 inclusive - all HESSIAN TRENCH to R.21.c.97.

(b) O.C. 8th North. Fus. will detail small party to proceed along the Boundary Road and keep touch with the 1st Canadian Division.

(c) LEFT ATTACK. 9th Lancashire Fusiliers.
FORMING UP PLACES. Firing Line and Support Line in Area R.33.b.59 to 33.a.54 to QUARRY R.33.b.13 to R.33.b.55.

1st Objective - R.27.b.51 exclusive - along trench to R.27.c.54 inclusive.

2nd Objective - R.21.d.01 exclusive - along ZOLLERN TRENCH to R.26.b.86
(inclusive.

3rd Objective - R.21.a.97 exclusive - STUFF REDOUBT - R.20.d.91 exclusive.

(d) 1. O.C. 9th Lancs. Fus will detail a party to block the Northern exits from MOUQUET FARM provided that the place is not in our hands on day of attack.
2. Clear up points R.27.c.54 and 38.

SUPPORTS.

(e) 5th Dorset Regiment will assemble in Reserve Trench and Ration Trench and push forward to Front Trenches as soon as these become vacated, and follow closely behind the assualting Battalions in Artillery Formation.

RESERVE.

(f) 11th Manchester Regiment will remain in OVILLERS until ordered forward.

FORMATION OF ASSUALTING BATTALIONS.

6. Three Companies in Column of Platoons.
One Company in Support.
20 Yards between waves.
Men extended to 5 paces.

ACTION TO BE TAKEN BY ASSUALTING INFANTRY.

7. (a) Troops detailed for the various Objectives will follow one another closely under cover of the Artillery barrages.
On the 1st Objective being gained there will be a pause of 10 minutes in the advance when all men not actually occupying the 1st Objective will lie down.
At ZERO plus 24 minutes the troops will advance in successive waves to attack the 2nd Objective.
On the 2nd Objective being gained there will be a pause of 60 minutes in the advance when all men not actually occupying the 2nd Objective will lie down.
At ZERO plus 98 minutes the troops will advance in successive waves to attack the 3rd Objective.
As the troops detailed for the capture of the various objectives advance and vacate our forward trenches, Brigade Reserves will advance so as to be ready to press forward to support the assualting troops.
The enemy's positions must be assualted by wave after wave until all opposition is broken down.
Especial clearing up parties will be detailed to deal with any enemy left in the 1st and 2nd Objectives.

(b) The instructions contained in 11th Divl. Standing Battle Orders will be adhered to in all respects.
Especial attention is drawn to paras. 15 and 16.
Times will be detailed later.

(3)

(c) The strictest discipline must be maintained in the Formung Up Positions.
The importance of no unusual movement being observed by the enemy is to be impressed on all ranks.
The success of the operation depends on this.

ARTILLERY.

8. The following Artillery will cover the attack and destroy enemy's defences both prior to and during the attack.

(a) Part of the 2nd Corps Heavy Artillery.
(b) 11th Divisional Artillery.
(c) Part of the 25th Divisional Artillery.
(d) 48th Divisional Artillery.

At ZERO a heavy bombardment will be placed on the 1st Objective and ZOLLERN REDOUBT.
At ZERO plus A minutes fire will be transferred from the 1st. Objective and gradually from ZOLLERN REDOUBT on to the 2nd Objective.
At ZERO plus A plus B minutes fire will be transferred from the 2nd Objective on to the 3rd Objective.
At ZERO plus A plus B plus C minutes fire will be lifted from the 3rd Objective on to hostile lines of approach.
Times will be detailed later.

After the initial barrages one battery will be placed at direct disposal of each Infantry Brigadier.

ZERO HOUR.

9. ZERO hour will be notified later.

STOKES GUNS.

10. One section will be held in readiness to move to STUFF REDOUBT when ordered.

M. G. COMPANY.

11. Will act on a plan drawn up by the two Corps in order to ensure full co-operation and liaison between M. G. Companies of the Corps.
Details will follow.

TANKS.

12. Two tanks are allotted to the 11th Division. They will operate on the Right Flank in conjunction with the 34th Infantry Brigade, and will follow the assaulting troops.

CONSOLIDATION.

13. (a) Each Objective gained will be consolidated at once.
(b) Posts will be established forward of the 3rd Objective.
(c) Strong Points will be organised as under :-
   1. R.21.d.99.
   2. Northern Side of ZOLLERN REDOUBT.
   3. Northern Side of STUFF REDOUBT.
   4. R.20.d.12.
(d) Midway Line and the Western Face of ZOLLERN REDOUBT from about R.27.d.91 - 59 - b.51 - 03 - 21.d.01 - c.55 to be repaired to form communication trenches from our present front line to the captured positions.
(e) 86th Field Company R.E. will hold three sections ready to move when ordered to assist in construction of strong points :-
   One Section to R.21.d.99.
   One Section to Northern Side of ZOLLERN REDOUBT.
   One Section to Northern Side of STUFF REDOUBT.

13. (f) On 1st Objective being passed by assualting Battalions, 5th Dorset Rgt. will occupy, clear and consolidate it——paying especial attention to both flanks.
(g) On the two assualting Battalions leaving 2nd Objective 5th Dorset Rgt. will detach two platoons from each Company to occupy and carry on with the consolidation of it.
(h) On the Final Objective being taken it will be held from R.21.d.99 to R.21.c.97 by two Companies of the 8th North. Fus. and eight Lewis Guns. The other two Companies will return to the 2nd Objective relieving 6 platoons of the 5th Dorset Rgt. who will return to 1st Objective.
The 9th Lancs. Fus. will hold from R.21.c.97 to R.20.d.91 until the barrage lifts from the North Side of STUFF REDOUBT, when it will be assualted. While this barrage is taking place the trench from R.21.c.55 to 18 and from R.55.c.87 should be cleared by bombers. It is known that there are deep dug-outs along the former. Eight Lewis Guns will be taken to the final Objective.

14. LOCATION OF POSITION.

The Infantry will light flares and wave YELLOW flags on their arrival at each Objective to show their position to Aeroplanes. Should parties be without flares men should wave their Trench Helmets whenever an Aeroplane passes over them during the hours of daylight.
Communications - See Appendix 1.

15. MEASURES FOR KEEPING DIRECTION.

Officers and N.C.Os. detailed to take part in the assualt must study the ground beforehand and impress landmarks on their memory. Compass bearings will be taken beforehand.
The Left Battalion of the 34th Infantry Brigade will direct and will march with its Right on Trench R.27.d.91 - 59 - B.51 - 08 -21.d.01 - c.55. It must be remembered that the 34th Brigade will have a Road on its Right and that the 33rd Inf. Bde. will have a distinct valley on its left.

16. LIAISON.

5th Dorset Rgt. will detail an Officer to be attached to 33rd. Inf. Bde.
11th Manchester Rgt. will detail an Officer to be attached to 2nd Canadian Infantry Brigade.

17. MEDICAL ARRANGEMENTS.

Advanced Dressing Stations have been formed at :-
(1) X.8.b.7.4.
(2) AVELUY CHATEAU.
(3) Divisional Collecting Station for walking cases - AVELUY CHATEAU.
(4) Battalions will arrange their own aid posts as most convenient.

18. ADMINISTRATIVE.

For Administrative arrangements less Medical see Appendix 2 attached.

19. WATCHES.

Watches will be sychronised at 6 A.M., 8 A.M., 10 A.M.

20. PRISONERS OF WAR.

Any prisoners taken will be marched down to CRUCIFIX CORNER under escort, which will be kept as small as possible, and be handed over to the A.P.M. or Representative.

ARTILLERY PROGRAMME.

1. At ZERO a heavy bombardment will be placed on HIGH TRENCH, lifting at ZERO plus 4, when it will be assualted and passed over.
The specially detailed party from 9th Lancs. Fus. will assualt the Farm at the same time, being assisted in doing so by two flanks.

2. From ZERO plus 4 the barrage will creep towards 1st Objective, lifting from 27.c.5.4 to 27.b.5.1 at
 ZERO plus 8.
 From 27.b.51 to 82 at ZERO plus 12.
 From 27.b.82 to 28.a.36 at ZERO plus 14.

3. (a) Troops will follow as close as possible behind the barrage, assualting immediately it lifts from the part of the Objective to their immediate Front.
(b) The greatest care must be taken to prevent men running through our own barrage when they see troops on their flanks assualting.
(c) There will be a pause of ten minutes in the 1st Objective.

4. At ZERO plus 24 the assualting troops will leave the 1st Objective for the 2nd Objective following close on the Barrage which will lift from the 2nd Objective at ZERO plus 38, when troops will assualt.

5. It will be noticed that the EASTERN Flank of the 2nd Objective is much in advance of the Centre.
The 8th North. Fus. left will therefore have to mark time at point R.27.b.09 while the Right swings forward close under the barrage, as it does the same, finally assualting as the barrage lifts from the Right Flank of the 2nd Objective.
There will be a pause of 60 minutes in the 2nd Objective, which should be utilised to the fullest extent for consolidation.

6. At ZERO plus one hour and 38 minutes the advance on the final Objective will commence.
At ZERO plus one hour and 44 minutes the barrage lifts to a line 200 Yards North of Final Objective EXCLUSIVE of STUFF REDOUBT.
At ZERO plus two hours and 15 minutes the barrage from Northern Face of STUFF REDOUBT will lift and be assualted by 9th Lancs. Fus.

34th STOKES MORTAR PROGRAMME.

1. The 34th L. T. M. B. will take part in the attack on HIGH TRENCH and MOUQUET FARM.

2. Eight guns will be in position by daylight 26th instant, to fire on these two Objectives - up to ZERO plus 4.

COMMUNICATIONS.

1. **TELEPHONE.**

   Brigade Headquarters will be connected direct to Battalion Headquarters in line through Test Stations at CEMETERY, POZIERES X.4.a.49 and Brigade Observation Station at R.33.d.6.9.
   Attacking Battalions will carry forward 6 lines each from their Battalion Headquarters.
   Brigades on Left and Right will be in direct communication with Brigade Headquarters.

2. **VISUAL.**

   Brigade Forward Visual Station will be at Brigade Observation Station R.33.d.6.9. Visual messages received there, from Forward will be sent back to Brigade Headquarters from there.

   In the event of wires being cut between Brigade Headquarters and CEMETERY Test Stations, visual communication between these places will be established.

3. **RUNNERS.**

   Runner Relay Stations will be at Brigade Observation Station R.33.d.6.9, CEMETERY Test Station and at original Battalion Headquarters.

4. **PIGEONS.**

   Attacking Battalions will carry Pigeons with them.

5. **WIRELESS.**

   Brigade Headquarters will be in direct communication with Corps Wireless Station.

REPORT ON OPERATIONS

FROM September 22nd. to September 29th.

1. On the night 22nd/23rd the 32nd Infantry Brigade relieved the 34th Infantry Brigade in the Trenches opposite MOUQUET FARM.
The 34th Infantry Brigade went into Billets in ENGLEBELMER and MAILLEY - MAILLET.
This was a preparatory step to allow the 34th Infantry Brigade to prepare for the Offensive which was to take place on the 26th, and the 32nd Infantry Brigade to improve the existing trenches and dig others for the assembling of the assaulting troops.
On the night of the 25th/26th the 34th Infantry Brigade relieved the 32nd Infantry Brigade in the same trenches.
In each case the relief was carried out with few casualties

SEPTEMBER 26th

2. On September 26th Offensive operations were carried out by the British and French from THIEPVAL Southwards.
The 11th Division attacked in conjunction with the Canadian Corps on their Right and the 18th Division on their Left.
The 11th Divisional Front was allotted to the 34th Infantry Brigade on the Right and the 33rd Infantry Brigade on Left with the 32nd Infantry Brigade in Divisional Reserve.
The Front allotted to the 34th Infantry Brigade was from R.28.c.21 to R.33.a.54.
The Objectives being :-
(1) The line R.28.a.36 through the Southern End of ZOLLERN REDOUBT along the trench to R.27.c.54 inclusive.
    A Front of 1100 Yards.
(2) R.21.d.78 inclusive - ZOLLERN REDOUBT to R.26.b.86.
    A Front of 1200 Yards.
(3) R.21.d.99 inclusive - along HESSIAN TRENCH - STUFF REDOUBT to R.20.d.91 exclusive.
    A Front of 1700 Yards.
It will be noticed that the ground to be captured included:-
(a) MOUQUET FARM.
(b) HIGH TRENCH.
(c) Portions of SCHWABEN TRENCH, MIDWAY LINE, HESSIAN TRENCH.
(d) Whole of ZOLLERN REDOUBT.
(e) Whole of STUFF REDOUBT.
An average Front of 1200 Yards to a depth of 1500 Yards.

3. Furthermore owing to the 1st.and 2nd Objectives being at an angle to the assaulting line it necessitated in the 1st case of the barrage lifting at different periods along the line.
In the 2nd Case the Right of the line had to Left Wheel with the barrage, the inner flank marking time.
These were two very difficult movements.

4. This task was allotted to 8th Northumberland Fusiliers and 9th Lancashire Fusiliers with 5th Dorset Regiment in Support and 11th Manchester Regiment in Brigade Reserve.

TIME.
DAYBREAK. Assaulting Troops were in position. The concentration was apparently a surprise to the enemy as there was little shelling of our trenches before ZERO Hour.

12.35 P.M. ZERO.
At this hour an intense bombardment by the Artillery on HIGH TRENCH and the 34th Light Trench Mortar Battery on MOUQUET FARM and HIGH TRENCH opened.

(2)

ZERO + 1.	A bombing party of 9th Lancashire Fusiliers rushed and held the entrances to the FARM, while the assaulting troops left the trenches for 1st Objective, 5th Dorset Regiment following 500 Yards in rear in Artillery Formation.
ZERO + 2.	The barrage moved slowly forward towards 1st Objective.
	Although the concentration of the assaulting troops was apparently unknown to the enemy he must have been expecting some form of assualt, perhaps only against MOUQUET FARM, as his barrage was on our Front Trenches before the assualting troops were out of them, causing many casualties. The 5th Dorset Regiment following in Support also lost heavily.
12.50 P.M.	1st Objective was reported to have been gained with apparently slight casualties.
1.18 P.M.	2nd Objective was reported to have been gained with apparently slight casualties.
2.30 P.M.	One section 34th Machine Gun Company was ordered forward to Northern end of ZOLLERN REDOUBT. One section 86th Field Company R.E. to move to Northern end of ZOLLERN REDOUBT to construct a strong point.
3. 0 P.M.	Artillery Observing Officer reported "Our Infantry now in STUFF REDOUBT. About 100 prisoners were taken. Enemy are now shelling STUFF REDOUBT heavily".
3. 0 P.M.	11th Manchester Regiment in Brigade Reserve ordered to occupy our original Front Line Trenches. It being thought unwise to push them further forward for fear of overcrowding the new trenches which were being consolidated and certain to be heavily shelled.
3.30 P.M.	No reports having been received from the assualting Battns. Battalion Commanders were ordered to push forward to gain touch with their Battalions and report. Staff Officer from Brigade was sent forward to report on the situation.
6.25 P.M.	Report that the Final Objective had been taken was corroborated by 2 wounded men from 9th Lancashire Fusiliers stating they had come from the REDOUBT.
6.40 P.M.	A wounded Officer of 9th Lancashire Fusiliers stated he had come straight back from STUFF REDOUBT and that his men were consolidating there.
6.45 P.M.	MOUQUET FARM finally cleared of Germans, one Officer and 35 men being taken prisoner (See Appendix 2.) About this time messages were received from Flank Brigades and Observation Posts, stating it to be doubtful whether our troops were in the Final Objective.
8.P.M.	5th Dorset Regiment ordered to send 2 Companies through ZOLLERN REDOUBT to 2nd Objective. 11th Manchester Regiment to send 2 Companies to 1st Objective and 2 Companies to HIGH TRENCH.
10.P.M.	It was reported that two parties of the enemy with Machine Guns were in Southern end of ZOLLERN REDOUBT and were causing many casualties and completely stopping all communication with the forward troops. These Germans must have been passed over by the 8th Northumberland Fusiliers and not dealt with by the clearing up parties.
10.15.P.M.	5th Dorset Regiment ordered to clear up situation at ZOLLERN

(3)

REDOUBT and gain touch with the Brigade on our Right.

11. P.M. Officers patrols were sent forward from each Battalion to endeavour to locate the exact positions of their units.

SEPTEMBER 27th.
3.30 A.M. Orders issued that by daybreak the situation was to be cleared up as follows :-

(a) 8th Northumberland Fusiliers to gain touch with 2nd Canadian Brigade at R.21.d.99.
(b) 9th Lancashire Fusiliers to gain touch with 33rd Inf. Brigade at R.28.a.36.
(c) 5th Dorset Regiment to send one company to reinforce 8th Northumberland Fusiliers.
One company to reinforce 9th Lancashire Fusiliers in Final Objective.
Two companies to remain in ZOLLERN TRENCH ready to support Front Line if necessary.
(d) 11th Manchester Regiment to detail one company to clear up ZOLLERN REDOUBT.
One platoon to move up Road in R.28.c. and get touch with 2nd Canadian Brigade at R.28.a.36.

6.30 A.M. ZOLLERN REDOUBT reported clear of enemy.

8.25 A.M. Aeroplane report received that neither Germans nor our men could be seen in STUFF REDOUBT.

8.30 A.M. 11th Manchester Regiment ordered to push forward and occupy STUFF REDOUBT and HESSIAN TRENCH.
They were finally held up by Machine Gun Fire from HESSIAN TRENCH, East of the REDOUBT.

Situation was now found to be as per attached map - shown in Red.
From subsequent reports the positions gained on the night of September 26th are marked in Blue on attached map.
Apparently the 8th Northumberland Fusiliers and 9th Lancashire Fusiliers reached the 1st Objective with comparatively slight casualties. On advancing from this line they came under a heavy barrage and Machine Gun Fire from ZOLLERN REDOUBT and HESSIAN TRENCH and STUFF REDOUBT.
The platoon of 8th Northumberland Fusiliers on the Right detailed to keep touch with the Canadians, was wiped out with the exception of four men, who established a bombing post with the Canadians about R.28.a.32.
Several of the 8th Northumberland Fusiliers joined with the Canadians in the attack and two letters have since been received from Canadian Officers commending their services.

Every Officer who went forward with this battalion was either killed or wounded with the exception of Lieut. MACDONALD who, with one man reached a point about 200 Yards East of R.27.b.46. He at once collected all the men in that vicinity and dug in with 54 men of his Battalion and 5 men and a Lewis Gun of the 5th Dorset Regiment.
The Company attacking ZOLLERN REDOUBT lost very heavily, and parties told off as "Clearing up parties" had become casualties, with the result that although many Germans were found dead in the dug-outs, some had not been dealt with and these held up the operations until Daybreak on the 27th.

On the Left the 9th Lancs. Fusiliers suffered equally severely, every Officer but one being killed or wounded.
In this case there was no Redoubt to encounter and some of the 9th Lancashire Fusiliers undoubtedly reached the Final Objective.

(4)

TIME.	
	An examination of the ground in the 1st Objective and up MIDWAY LINE showed what fighting they had done. Many Germans lay killed with the bayonet.
SEPTEMBER 27th. 1 P.M.	Division issued orders that two Battalions of 32nd Inf. Brigade, supported by 11th Manchester Regiment were to attack HESSIAN TRENCH and STUFF REDOUBT at 3 P.M.
3 P.M.	The West Yorks. Regt. attacking R.26.c.45 to R.20.d.91 reached ZOLLERN TRENCH with scarcely a casualty but, not being quite up to time, the barrage was ahead of them and lifted from STUFF REDOUBT as they reached ZOL-LERN TRENCH, and so made it impossible for them to ad-vance further. The Artillery however saw this and put another barrage on this line and after some eight minutes the Infantry on their own initiative went forward : the guns stopped and the Infantry took the position and got a footing into STUFF REDOUBT. Large quantities of Bombs were now needed and were supplied by parties of 11th Manches-ter Regiment and 5th Dorset Regiment.
9 P.M.	11th Manchester Regiment was ordered to bomb along trench R.21.d.10 - 32 - 78 and endeavour to gain touch with the Canadians on the Right. This was done as far as point 78.
10 P.M.	The Command of the Area North of MOUQUET FARM passed to G.O.C. 32nd Infantry Brigade.
SEPTEMBER 28th.	Severe fighting went on throughout the day at STUFF RE-DOUBT. At nightfall the 34th Infantry Brigade less 11th Manch-ester Regiment was withdrawn to OVILLERS and held in Divisional Reserve. 11th Manchester Regiment remained in the line attached to 32nd Infantry Brigade.

CASUALTIES.

	KILLED. O.	KILLED. O.R.	WOUNDED. O.	WOUNDED. O.R.	MISSING. O.	MISSING. O.R.
8th North. Fus.	5.	60.	12.	271.	-	45.
9th Lancs. Fus.	3.	26.	7.	188.	2.	84.
5th Dorset Rgt.	5.	58.	5.	255.	3.	56.
11th Manch' Rgt.	3.	61.	2.	221.	-	16.
34th M. G. Coy.	-	1.	-	18.	-	-
34th L. T. M. B.	-	1.	-	19.	-	2.
R. A. M. C.	2.	-	2.	-	-	-
	18.	207.	28.	972.	5.	203.

TOTALS.

	OFFICERS.	O.R.
KILLED.	18.	207.
WOUNDED.	28.	972.
MISSING.	5.	203.
	51.	1382.

APPENDIX 2.

MOUQUET FARM.

MOUQUET FARM was known to be held by about 50 Germans with at least one machine gun. In order to prevent this party interfering with the advance of the assaulting troops, special bombing party was detailed from 9th Lancashire Fusiliers to rush all the entrances to the FARM half a minute before the remainder of the troops were to leave the trenches.

This party was completely successful in its mission and was relieved by a similar party from 11th Manchester Regt. under Lieut. COOPER who was killed shortly afterwards.

To assist this operation of clearing the FARM, the two TANKS allotted to the Brigade were to pass the FARM on their way to ZOLLERN REDOUBT.

1.30 P.M. They both drove into a deep hole and remained stuck there for the next three days.

Had these TANKS been able to push on to ZOLLERN REDOUBT they would have been invaluable.

4.30 P.M. At this time the occupants of the FARM were causing many casualties, so, Lieut. DANCER, 5th Dorset Regiment, the Officer of the TANK No. 542 and its crew and Lieut. KOHNSTAMM and six men of 11th Manchester Regiment and a Sergeant and six men of the 6th East Yorkshire Pioneers lined the top of a mound on the building, and placed 2 Machine Guns from the TANKS to cover the Western and Northern entrances to the FARM, while two bombing parties of the 11th Manchester Regiment threw bombs down the entrances to the FARM with no visible result.

5.30 P.M. Lieut. LOW of 11th Manchester Regiment threw smoke bombs down the entrances and shortly afterwards the occupants came out.
One Officer and 55 other ranks in all.
On examination 3 machine guns, 2 FLAMMENWERFERS and two gas cylinders were found in the FARM.

The actual taking of the FARM cannot be claimed by any one unit as

    6th East Yorkshire Pioneers,
    11th Manchester Regiment,
    5th Dorset Regiment,
    No. 542 TANK.

were all represented. The clearing of the FARM was undoubtedly effected by the smoke bombs thrown by Lieut. LOWE.

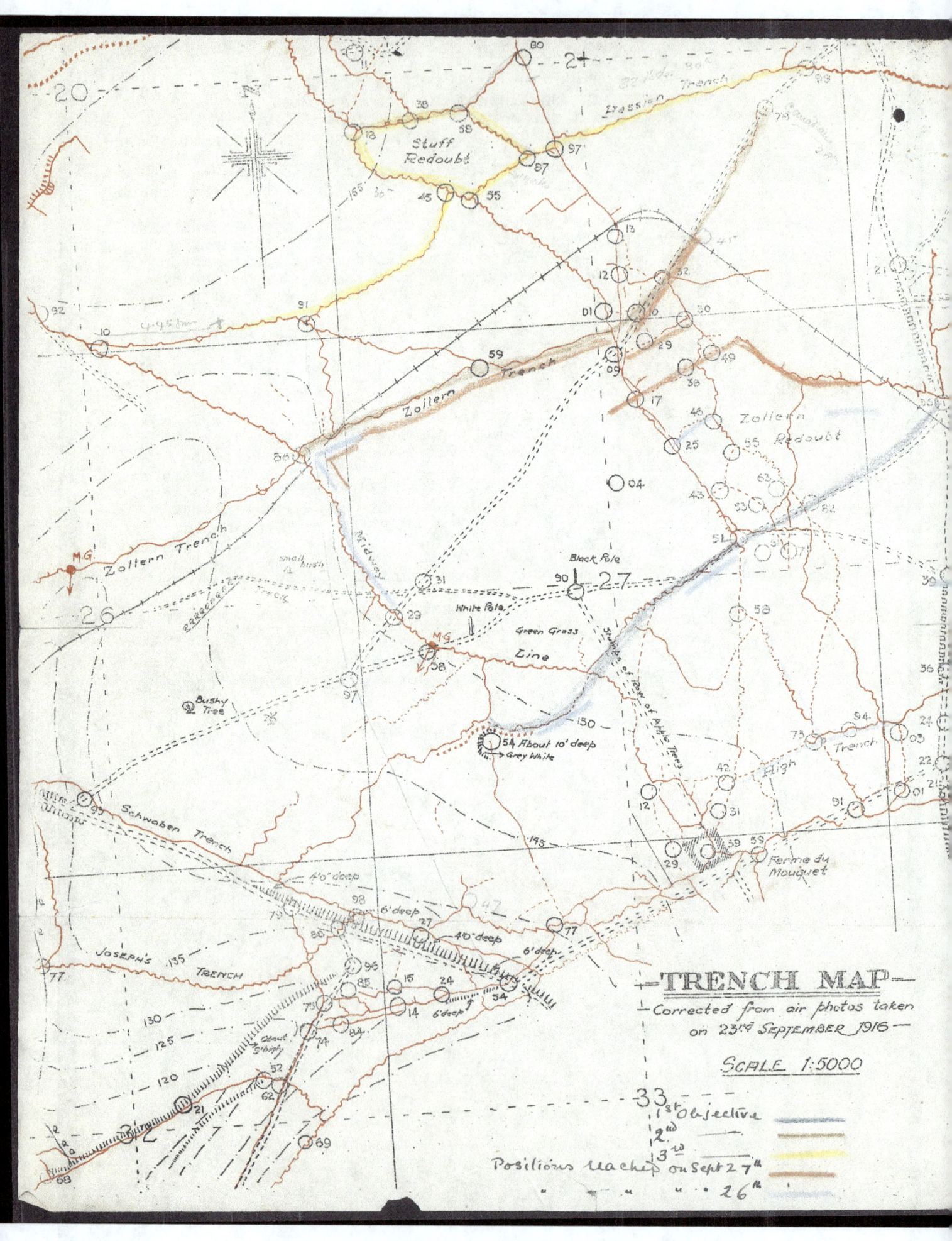

APPENDIX 11. September 1916.

Unit	Officers	O. Ranks	Officers K. W. M.	O. Ranks K. W. M.
Strength of units from 1st. to 7th. Sept.				
8/North.Fus.	32.	958.	- - -	- - -
9/Lancs.Fus.	36.	882.	- - -	- - -
5/Dorsets.	43.	867.	- - -	- - -
11/Manchesters.	35.	998.	- - -	- 1. -
34th.M.G.Coy.	12.	221.	- - -	- - -
Strength of units from 8th. to 14th. Sept.				
8/North.Fusr.	32.	950.	- - -	- 1 -
9/Lancs.Fusr	36.	953.	1. - -	1. 3. -
5/Dorset Regt.	42.	880.	- - -	- - -
11/Manchesters.	35.	989	- - -	1. 1. -
34th. M.G. Coy.	11.	167.	- - -	- - 1.
Strength of Units from 15th. to 21st. Sept.				
8/North.Fusrs.	32.	950.	- - -	- 3 -
9/Lancs. Fusrs	35.	942.	1. 1. -	15.48.3.
5/Dorset Regt.	44.	906.	- 6 -	12.23.-
11th.Manchesters.	33.	1013.	1. - -	3.17.1.
34th.M.G. Coy.	11.	218.	- 1 -	1. 2. 6.
Strength of Units from 22nd. to 28th. Sept.				
8/North.Fus.	34.	961.	5. 13. -	60.271. 45.
9/Lancs.Fus	31.	880.	3. 7. 2.	26.188. 84.
5/Dorsets.	39.	859.	5. 5. 3.	58.255. 56.
11th.Manchesters.	32.	963.	3. 3. -	61.221. 16.
34th.M.G. Coy.	8.	203.	1. 1. -	1. 18. -
Strength of units from 29th. to 30th. Sept.				
8th.North.Fusr.	18.	511.	- - -	- - -
9th. Lancs.Fus.	19.	475.	- 3 -	- - -
5th.Dorsets.	31.	454.	- - -	- - -
11th.Manchesters.	23.	668.	- - -	- - -

REINFORCEMENTS.	from 1st to 9th.	from 10th to 16th.	From 17th. to 23rd.	From 24th. to 30th.
8th.North.Fusiliers.	Nil.	7.O.R.	3.O. 22.O.R.	2 Off. 2.O.R.
9th.Lancs.Fusr.	82.O.R.	1 Off.7.O.R.	17.O.R.	NIL.
5th.Dorsets.	19.O.R.	3Off.37.O.R	1 Off.12.O.R.	5 Off.
11th.Manchesters.	NIL.	37.O.R.	1 Off.24.O.R.	
34th.M.G.Coy.	9. O.R.	4 O.R.	NIL.	1 Off. 5 O.R.

Headquarters,
34th Inf. Bde.
(11th Div)

July 1916

May 1916.

Dec 1917

Vol 4

Confidential

WAR DIARY.
(ORIGINAL)

HEADQUATERS
34th INFANTRY BRIGADE
1st. OCTOBER 1916
TO
31st. OCTOBER 1916

Army Form C. 2118.

WAR DIARY
34th Inf. Brigade H.Q.
INTELLIGENCE SUMMARY. 11 Division.

(Erase heading not required.)

Instructions regarding War Diaries and Intelligence Summaries are contained in F. S. Regs., Part II. and the Staff Manual respectively. Title pages will be prepared in manuscript.

Place	Date	Hour	Summary of Events and Information	Remarks and references to Appendices
RIBEAUCOURT	1		34th Inf. Brigade moved to billets in "A" area + B.H.Q. were at RIBEAUCOURT.	
	2		Very wet day - Brigade cleaning up generally.	
	3		Wet day - Brigade marched to billets in "B" area was disposed as follows - B.H.Q. & 11th Manchester Regt. at FRANSU - 8th North Fusiliers ST. OUEN. 9th Lancashire Fus. and 5th Dorsets at FRANQUEVILLE - 34th M.Gun Coy & 34th L.T.M. Battery at SURCAMPS.	
	4		Very wet day - Brigade resting	
	5		Very wet day - 8th North. Fus. moved to billets in DOMQUER	
	6		Training all day.	
	7		Wet day - 5th Dorset Regt. moved to billets in DOMQUER.	
	8		Wet day - Holiday + Church Parades.	
	9		Training all day	
	10		Training all day	
	11		Fair - The Commander-in-Chief (Sir Douglas Haig) inspected the Brigade.	
	12		Training all day	

Army Form C. 2118.

WAR DIARY
INTELLIGENCE SUMMARY.
(Erase heading not required.)

34th Inf Brigade H.Q. 11th Division

Title pages 1/6

Place	Date	Hour	Summary of Events and Information	Remarks and references to Appendices
	13		Training all day	
	14		do.	
	15		Week day - Holiday - Church Parades.	
	16		Training all day -	
	17		do. Major V.T.R. Ford 6th K.O. Lancaster Regt. arrived & took over command of the 8th No K.O.R. Fusiliers	
	18		Training all day - Major F.P. Worsley - 9th West Yorkshire Regt. arrived & took over command of 9th Lancashire Fus.	
	19		Wet day "	
	20		Fine day - Training - Lieut. Col. Sir. T.D. Jackson, Bart. M.V.O., A.D.C. King's Own Royal Lancaster Regt. arrived & took over command of 11th Manchester Regt.	
	21		Fine day - Training all day	
	22		Fair - Holiday & Church Parades	
	23		Training all day - Orders received from 11th Division for the Brigade to move to "P" area to morrow - 10.30 Move was postponed for 24 hours -	

Army Form C. 2118.

WAR DIARY
or
INTELLIGENCE SUMMARY. 34th Inf. Brigade. H.Q.
11th Division

(Erase heading not required.)

Instructions regarding War Diaries and Intelligence Summaries are contained in F. S. Regs., Part II. and the Staff Manual respectively. Title pages will be prepared in manuscript.

Place	Date	Hour	Summary of Events and Information	Remarks and references to Appendices
	24		Wet day. Training. Move again postponed for 48 hours	
	25		Wet day. Training. Move postponed until 29th inst.	
	26		Fine day. G.O.C. 34th Brigade presented the Military Medals awarded to the N.C.O.s + men of the Brigade, for the recent action on 26/28th Sept, at a Brigade Parade held near FRANSU.	
	27		Wet day. Training. Cleaning up, including Hot Baths at DOMART	
	28		Wet day. Training all day	
	29		Fair weather. Holiday + Church Parades. Move postponed until 4th prox.	
	30		Wet day. Training all day.	
	31		Fine day. Training all day. Major V.B. Thurston, Dorset Regt. took over command of 9th Lancashire Fusiliers vice Major F.P. Worsley who continued to hand over command of 9th West Yorkshire Regt.	

H.J. Ratcliffe 2nd Lieut.
34th Inf. Brigade H.Q.

APPENDIX. II.

Strength of Unit from 1st to 7th October.

UNIT.	OFFICERS.	OTHER RANKS.	OFFICERS. K.	W.	M.	OTHER RANK. K.	W.	M.
8th Northumberland Fusiliers.	18.	512.	-	-	-	-	-	-
9th Lancs.Fus.,	19.	499.	1.	-	-	-	-	-
5th Dorset Regt.,	30.	593.	-	-	-	-	-	2.
11th Manchesters.	23.	668.	3.	2.	-	6.	228.	17.
34th M.G.Coy.,	7.	206.	-	-	-	-	2.	-

Strength of Unit from 8th to 14th October.

UNIT.	OFFICERS.	OTHER RANKS.	K.	W.	M.	K.	W.	M.
8th Northd. Fus.	25.	525.	-	-	-	-	-	-
9th Lancs., Fus.	24.	674.	-	-	-	-	-	-
5th Dorset Rgt.,	34.	786.	-	-	-	-	-	-
11th Manchesters.	23.	676.	-	-	-	-	-	-
34th M.G.Coy.,	9.	207.	-	-	-	-	-	-

Strength of Unit from 15th to 21st October.

UNIT.	OFFICERS.	OTHER RANKS.	K.	W.	M.	K.	W.	M.
8th Northd. Fus.,	29.	902.	-	-	-	-	1.	-
9th Lancs. Fus.,	25.	865.	-	-	-	-	1.	-
5th Dorset Rgt.,	35.	1074.	-	-	-	-	-	-
11th Manchesters.	21.	945.	-	-	-	-	-	-
34th M.G.Coy.,	6.	208.	-	-	-	-	-	-

Strength of Unit from 22nd to 31st October.

UNIT.	OFFICERS.	OTHER RANKS.	K.	W.	M.	K.	W.	M.
8th Northd. Fus.	30.	934.	-	-	-	-	-	-
9th Lancs. Fus.	26.	902.	-	-	-	-	4	-
5th Dorset Rgt.,	35.	1111.	-	-	-	-	-	-
11th Manchesters.	21.	993.	-	1.	-	-	5.	-
34th M.G.Coy.,	9.	202.	-	-	-	-	-	-

REINFORCEMENTS.

UNIT.	1st/7th Oct. O.	O.R.	8th/14th Oct. O.	O.R.	15/21st Oct. O.	O.R.	22nd/31st Oct O.	O.R.
8th Northd. Fus.	-	3.	12.	147.	1.	251.	-	-
9th Lancs. Fus.	5.	183.	3.	212.	1.	43.	-	19.
5th Dorset Rgt.,	4.	306.	2.	268.	-	41.	3.	19.
11th Manchesters.	-	15.	4.	268.	1.	50.	8.	23.
34th M.G.Coy.,	2.	4.	-	-	-	-	-	-

SECRET.

No. M.354
Date Oct 27
HEADQUARTERS 34th INFANTRY BRIGADE

AMENDMENT TO 34th INFANTRY BRIGADE ORDER No. 16.

Reference MOVE TABLE.

The 11th Manchester Regiment will move to HALLOY and **not** to LA VICOGNE as previously stated.

27 : 10 : 16.

[signature]

Captain,
Brigade Major, 34th. Infantry Brigade.

SECRET.   Copy No. 3

34th INFANTRY BRIGADE ORDER No. 16.

Reference Map LENS 11 - 1/100,000.   October 24th.

1. 11th Division (less detached Units) will move tomorrow from "B" Area to "R" Area.

2. 34th Infantry Brigade will march as per attached table.

3. 1st Line Transport will march with Units.

4. Brigade Headquarters will close at FRANSU at 7.30 A.M. and re-open at PERNOIS at 1 P.M.

Issued at 1. p.m.

Copy No. 1. Office.
"   " 2. Staff Captain.
"   " 3. War Diary.
"   " 4. Brigade Signals.
"   " 5.)
"   " 6.   Four
"   " 7. (Battns.
"   " 8.)
"   " 9. 34th L. T. M. B.
"   " 10. Supply Column.
"   " 11. 34th Field Ambulance.
"   " 12. 11th Division.

                                        Captain,
                        Brigade Major, 34th Infantry Brigade.

TIME TABLE.

UNIT.	FROM.	TO.	ROUTE.	REMARKS.
Bde. Hd. Qrs.	FRANSU.	PERNOIS.	FRANQUEVILLE - DOMART - ST. LEGER - BERTEAUCOURT - HALLOY - HAVERNAS - N. of NAOURS.	To march at head of 9th Lancs. Fus.
9th Lancs. Fus.	FRANQUEVILLE.	LA VICOGNE.	-do-	Tail to clear Church at 8.35 A.M.
11th Manch' Rgt.	FRANSU.	-do-	-do-	Head to pass FRANQUEVILLE Church at 8.36 A.M.
8th North. Fus.	DOMQUEUR.	HAVERNAS.	-do-	Head of column to be at junction of DOMQUEUR - FRANQUEVILLE Road and FRANSU - FRANQUEVILLE Road at 8.40 A.M. and follow in rear of 11th Manchester Rgt.
5th Dorset Rgt.	-to-	PERNOIS.	-do-	To follow 8th North Fus.
34th L.T.M.B.	SURCAMPS.	HALLOY.	-do-	Not to reach ST. LEGER before 11 A.M.
34th Field A.M'.	REDERIE FARM.	PERNOIS.	-do-	Not to reach ST. LEGER before 11 A.M.

The following transport will report to units at 6 P.M. tonight:- 1 Motor Lorry and 2 G.S. Wagons to each Battalion.

1 G.S. Wagon to 34th Field Ambulance.

1 G.S. Wagon to 34th L.T.M.B.

Confidential

34th Infantry Brigade

WAR DIARY

From 1st November 1916
To 30th November 1916

Vol 5

WAR DIARY

INTELLIGENCE SUMMARY. 34th Inf. Brigade. 11th Division

Month: September 1916

Army Form C. 2118.

Place	Date	Hour	Summary of Events and Information	Remarks and references to Appendices
FRANSU	1		Wet day - training all day.	
	2		Fine - Training all day.	
	3		Fine. Demonstration to Brigade of L.T. Mortars at work	
	4		Wet day - Training all day.	
	5		Fair - Holiday. Church parades & Football Match	
	6		Fair rather heavy rain - G.O.C. 34th Brigade presented the Medal ribbons to the Officers & N.C.O.'s men of the Brigade in the recent operations of 26/28th Septr. at a Brigade parade held	
near FRANSU	7		Very wet - training all day.	
	8		Fair - Training all day	
	9		Fine day - training all day -	
	10		Wet - given up to improvement of billets.	
	11			
	12		Sunday - Church parades & holiday -	
	13		Orders issued for the Brigade to move tomorrow to ST OUEN & ST LEGER	APP. I
	14		Bde Group marches in accordance with above orders -	

Army Form C. 2118.

WAR DIARY
or
INTELLIGENCE SUMMARY.
(Erase heading not required.)

Place	Date	Hour	Summary of Events and Information	Remarks and references to Appendices
BERTEAUCOURT	15.		The Brigade marched to BERTEAUCOURT – HALLOY and PERNOIS. Orders were received for a further march tomorrow.	AM. I
CONTAY	16.		The Brigade marched to CONTAY – VADENCOURT and HARPONVILLE.	"
	17.		The Brigade marched to PUCHVILLERS and RAINCHEVAL. Throughout the above moves the weather was high and frosty.	
PUCHVILLERS	18.		The whole Bde group was concentrated at PUCHVILLERS. Snow fell during the night 17/18th and rain during the day 18. Sunday – Bde remained at PUCHVILLERS.	
	19.	5 pm	Orders received to move tomorrow to HEDAUVILLE LEALVILLERS and ACHEUX, and for arrangements to be made for the Bde to take over the front being held by 19 Div.	
	20.		The Bde Group marched BHQ to HEDA LEALVILLERS. 5 N Fusiliers & L Fusiliers LTMB to LEALVILLERS. 5 DORSET Regt and 11 MANCHESTER Regt to ACHEUX. G.O.C. and Staff visited HQrs 56 Inf Bde at ST PIERRE DIVION and arranged relief of 56 Inf Bde to take place on 21st inst.	
LEALVILLERS				

Place	Date	Hour	Summary of Events and Information	Remarks and references to Appendices
	21		9. SHERWOOD FORESTERS. 33 Inf Bde were attached to 34 Inf Bde and under their orders took over the line held by 5-6 Inf Bde from R14 c 9.3 to the River ANCRE. Bde HQrs were established at ST PIERRE DIVION. 8 N. Fusiliers marched to BOUZINCOURT 9. L. Fusiliers " " " SENLIS 5 DORSET Regt " " " " " MANCHESTER Regt " " dugouts in ST PIERRE DIVION	Ref MAP BEAUMONT S-7 DSE 1/10,000. APPENDIX I.
		10 pm	The relief of 5-6 Inf Bde was complete without casualties	
ST PIERRE DIVION.	22		Arrangements were made to relieve the 5-8 Inf Bde in the line on the Right of the line taken over last night - The line extending from STUMP ROAD. R21A 67 along STUFF Trench to R 20 B 55 across the valley to R14 e 93 - with a strong point thrown forward to R14 D94. 8 N. Fusiliers took over this line and completed the relief by 11.30 pm without incident.	

WAR DIARY
or
INTELLIGENCE SUMMARY.
(Erase heading not required.)

Army Form C. 2118.

Place	Date	Hour	Summary of Events and Information	Remarks and references to Appendices
	22		11 MANCHESTER Regt relieved the 9 SHERWOOD FORESTERS who rejoined the 33rd Inf Bde. 9 LANC FUSILIERS moved to dug outs in THIEPVAL 5 DORSET Regt " " " ST PIERRE DIVION L.T.M.B. to MESNIL. 34 M.G. Coy to the line and THIEPVAL.	
	23. 24. 25. 26. 27. 28. 29.	}	During these days there was nothing of importance to report. Heavy rain fell on 24th and 25th which made the trenches very difficult to work in - The wind in many places being very deep. The Battns in the front line relieved their companies every 24 hours. The relieved coys being taken back to drying rooms and given hot food.	
	30.		The 9 K. Ins relieved the 5 N. Fusiliers in the right sector. The 5 Dorset Regt relieved 11 Manchester Regt in the left sector. Both reliefs were completed without casualties.	

A.K.G. Ellis C/M
Bt Major 34 Inf Bde

APPENDIX I & II an attached.
A.D.S.S./Forms/C. 2118.

APPENDIX I

SECRET.   Copy No. 3

34th INFANTRY BRIGADE ORDER No. 17.

Reference map LENS 11 - 1/100,000.

1. 11th Division less detached units will move tomorrow from YVRENCH Area to CANAPLES Area.

2. 34th Brigade Group (less Machine Gun Company) will move in accordance with attached March Table.

3. Brigade Headquarters will close at FRANSU at 12 Noon and re-open at ST. OUEN at the same hour.

Issued at 6 pm.

Copy No. 1. Office.
"   " 2. Staff Captain.
"   " 3. War Diary.
"   " 4. 8th North. Fus.
"   " 5. 9th Lancs. Fus.
"   " 6. 5th Dorset Rgt.
"   " 7. 11th Manchester Rgt.
"   " 8. 34th L. T. M. B.
"   " 9. 34th Field Ambulance.
"   " 10. No.4 Coy. Divsl. Train.
"   " 11. 11th Division.

G.D.G. Elton, Captain,

12 : 11 : 16.   Brigade Major, 34th Infantry Brigade.

MARCH TABLE.

DATE.	UNIT.	DESTINATION.	ROUTE.	REMARKS.
NOVEMBER 10th.	8th. North. Fus.	ST. OUEN.		Not to move before 11.45 A.M.
-do-	9th. Lancs. Fus.	FRANQUEVILLE. HOUDENCOURT.	FRANSU. -do-	Not to move before 11.15 A.M.
-do-	5th. Dorset Rgt.	ST. LEGER.	ST. OUEN.	Clear PLOUY by 11.15 A.M.
-do-	11th Manchester Rgt.	LANCHES. BA RLETTE.	FRANQUEVILLE.	Clear FRANSU by 11.15 A.M.
-do-	34th L.T.M.B.	SURCAMPS.	DOMQUEUR.	Not to move before 11 A.M.
-do-	34th Field Ambulance.	LA HAIE FARM.	DOMQUEUR.	Not to move before 11.30 A.M.
-do-	No.4 Coy.Div.Train.	SURCAMPS.		

SECRET.   Copy No. 3

34th INFANTRY BRIGADE ORDER No. 18.

Reference map LENS 11 - 1/100,000.   14 : 11 : 16.

1. 34th Infantry Brigade Group (less Machine Gun Company) will move tomorrow in accordance with attached march table.

2. Brigade Headquarters will close at St. OUEN at Noon and re-open at the same hour at BERTEAUCOURT.

Issued at 6-30 pm

Copy No. 1. Office.
" " 2. Staff Captain.
" " 3. War Diary.
" " 4. 8th North. Fus.
" " 5. 9th Lancs. Fus.
" " 6. 5th Dorset Rgt.
" " 7. 11th Manchester Rgt.
" " 8. 34th L. T. M. B.
" " 9. 34th Field Ambulance.
" " 10. No.4 Coy. Divsl. Train.
" " 11. 11th Division.

                          G. de G. Elliot, Captain,
         Brigade Major, 34th. Infantry Brigade.

MARCH TABLE.

UNIT.	DESTINATION.	ROUTE.	DATE.	REMARKS.
8th. North. Fus.	HALLOY.	BERTEAUCOURT.	NOV. 15th.	Tail of column to clear ST. OUEN at 10.30 A.M.
9th. Lancs. Fus.	PERNOIS.	DOMART - ST - LEGER.	-do-	To clear FRANQUEVILLE by 10 A.M.
5th. Dorset Rgt.	PERNOIS.	-do-	-do-	To clear Railway Crossing at 11.15 A.M.
11th. Manchester Rgt.	BERTEAUCOURT.	-do-	-do-	NOT to move before 10 A.M.
34th L.T.M.B.	-do-	ST. OUEN.	-do-	Not to reach ST. OUEN before 11 A.M.
34th Field Ambulance	-do-	-do-	-do-	Not to reach ST. OUEN before 11.30
No. 4. Coy. Divsl. Train.	-do-	-do-	-do-	

SECRET.   Copy No ...3....

34th INFANTRY BRIGADE ORDER No.19.

Reference maps LENS - 1/100,000.   NOV. 15th 1916.
                FRANCE - 1/40,000 - Sheet 57.D.

1. 34th Infantry Brigade group (less Machine Gun Company) will move on 16th and 17th in accordance with attached march tables.

2. Brigade Headquarters will close at BERTEAUCOURT and CONTAY on 16th and 17th respectively at 9 A.M. and re-open at CONTAY on 16th at 3 P.M. and AVELUY on 17th at 1 P.M.

Issued at 4.30 p.m.

Copy No. 1. Office.
"   "   2. Staff Captain.
"   "   3. War Diary.
"   "   4. Brigade Signals.
"   "   5. 8th. North. Fus.
"   "   6. 9th. Lancs. Fus.
"   "   7. 5th. Dorset Rgt.
"   "   8. 11th Manchester Rgt.
"   "   9. 34th L.T.M.B.
"   " 10. 34th Field Ambulance.
"   " 11. No.4.Coy.Divsl.Train.

                              G.D.G. Elton, Captain,
                       Brigade Major, 34th Infantry Brigade.

MARCH TABLE.

DATE.	UNIT.	DESTINATION.	ROUTE.	REMARKS.
NOV. 16th	Brigade H.Q.	CONTAY.	HAVERNAS.- WARGNIES.- NAOURS.- TALMAS.- HERISSART.	
-do-	8th. North. Fus	VADENCOURT.	-do-	To clear HALLOY by 9.45 A.M.
-do-	9th. Lancs. Fus	CONTAY.	-do-	To clear HALLOY at 10 A.M.
-do-	5th. Dorset Rgt	HARPONVILLE.	-do-	To clear PERNOIS at 10 A.M.
-do-	11th Manchester Rgt.	CONTAY.	-do-	To follow 9th. Lancs. Fus.
-do-	34th L.T.M.B.	CONTAY.	-do-	Not to start before 10.30 A.M.
-do-	34th Field Ambulance.	VADENCOURT.	-do-	To follow 34th Field Amb.
-do-	No.4.Coy.Divsl.Train.	HARPONVILLE.	-do-	To follow 11th Manchesters.

NOTE. Distance of 200 yards between companies and at least 400 yards between Battalions to be maintained on the march.

MARCH TABLE.

DATE.	UNIT.	DESTINATION.	ROUTE.	REMARKS.
Nov. 17th.	Brigade H.Q.	AVELUY.	SENLIS - BOUZINCOURT.	Clear VADENCOURT by 9.45 A.M.
-do-	8th. North. Fus.	-do-	-do-	Clear VADENCOURT by 10 A.M.
-do-	9th. Lancs. Fus.	-do-	-do-	Not to leave HARPONVILLE before 10.15 A.M.
-do-	5th. Dorset Rgt.	-do-	-do-	Head to pass CONTAY CHURCH at 10 A.M.
-do-	11th Manches.r Rgt.	-do-	-do-	Follow 5th. Dorset Rgt.
-do-	34th L.T.M.B.	-do-	-do-	Follow 11th Manchester Rgt.
-do-	34th Field Ambulance.	-do-	-do-	Follow 8th. North. Fus.
-do-	No.4.Coy.Divsl.Train.	-do-	-do-	

NOTE. Distance of 200 yards between companies and 400 yards between Battalions to be maintained on the march.

SECRET.   Copy No. 3

34th Infantry Brigade Order No. 20.

Reference Map 1/100,000 LENS.   Nov.21st 1916
"   "   1/10,000 BEAUMONT.

1. 34th Infantry Brigade will move to-morrow in accordance with attached March table.

2. Brigade Headquarters will close at LEALVILLERS at 12.30 p.m. to-morrow and reopen at ST.PIERRE DIVION at 4 p.m.

3. On night 22nd/23rd the 34th Infantry Brigade will relieve the 58th Infantry Brigade from about Point R.21.a6.8 to R.14 Central.

Issued at 10.-30 p.m.

Copy No. 1 Office.
"   "   2 Staff Captain.
"   "   3 War Diary.
"   "   4 Brigade Signals.
"   "   5 8th North. Fus,
"   "   6 9th Lanc. Fus.
"   "   7 5th Dorset Rgt.
"   "   8 11th Manchesters.
"   "   9 M.G.Coy.
"   " 10 L.T.M.B.
"   " 11 86th R.E.
"   " 12 No.4 Coy Train.
"   " 13 34th Field Ambl.
"   " 14 11th Division.

                                G.G. Elton. Captain.
                         Brigade Major 34th Infantry Bde.

SECRET.   COPY No 3

34th INFANTRY BRIGADE ORDER No.21.

Reference maps - BEAUMONT 57.d.S.E.- 1/10,000   Nov. 29th 1916.
                 GRANDCOURT   - 1/5,000.
                 BOIS D' HOLLAND.   - 1/5,000.

1. The following reliefs will take place on the night November 30th/December 1st.

2. 9th Lancashire Fusiliers will relieve 8th Northumberland Fusiliers in the Right Sector from STUMP ROAD inclusive to R.14.c.93 inclusive.

3. 5th Dorset Regiment will relieve 11th Manchester Regiment in Left Sector from R.14.c.93 exclusive to the River exclusive.

4. On completion of relief the 8th Northumberland Fusiliers and the 11th Manchester Regiment will occupy the dugouts vacated by their opposite numbers.

5. All detailed arrangements to be made between Commanding Officers concerned.

6. The outgoing unit will leave

          1 N.C.O. per company.
          1 man per Lewis gun in the line.
          1 Signaller per Signal Station.
    for 24 hours with the relieving unit.

7. Completion of reliefs will be reported by the Code word "HOORAY".

8. ACKNOWLEDGE.

Issued at 11 a.m.

Copy No. 1. Office.
  "   "   2. Staff Captain.
  "   "   3. War Diary.
  "   "   4. Brigade Signals.
  "   "   5. 8th North. Fus.
  "   "   6. 9th Lancs. Fus.
  "   "   7. 5th Dorset Rgt.
  "   "   8. 11th Manchester Rgt.
  "   "   9. 34th M. G. Coy.
  "   " 10. 34th L. T. M. B.
  "   " 11. 86th Field Co. R.E.
  "   " 12. 34th Field Ambulance.
  "   " 13. 32nd Brigade.
  "   " 14. 184th Brigade.
  "   " 15. 11th Division.

                                         G.A.G. Elton. Captain,
                                    Brigade Major, 34th Inf. Brigade.

MARCH TABLE.

DATE.	UNIT.	TO.	ROUTE.	REMARKS.
21st NOV.	8th. North. Fus.	BOUZINCOURT.	VARENNES and HEDAUVILLE.	Clear LEALVILLERS at 11.30 A.M.
-do-	9th. Lancs. Fus.	SENLIS.	VARENNES.	Not to move before 12 Noon.
-do-	5th. Dorset Rgt.	SENLIS.	HEDAUVILLE.	Clear ACHEUX by 12 Noon.
-do-	11th Manchesters.	ST. PIERRE DIVION.	ENGLEBELMER & MESNIL.	Clear ACHEUX at 11 A.M.
-do-	34th M. G. Coy. 2 Sections. 2 Sections.	THIEPVAL. SENLIS.	-do- HEDAUVILLE.	Clear FORCEVILLE by 11 A.M.)-ditto-(
-do-	86th Field Co. R.E.	BOUZINCOURT.	HEDAUVILLE.	Not to move till Manchester Rgt. has cleared FORCEVILLE.
-do-	34th L. T. M. Bn.	-do-	-do-	Clear ACHEUX 11.20 A.M.

Intervals to be maintaned as ordered.

APPENDIX II.

Strength of units from 1st. to 7th. Nov. 1916.

	Officers.	Other ranks.	Casualties Officers. K. W. M.	Other ranks. K. W. M.
8th. North. Fusr.	29.	914.	- 3/4 -	- - -
9th. Lancs. Fus.	25.	896.	- - -	- - -
5th. Dorsets.	34.	1120.	- - 3/4	- 3/4 -
11th. Manch. R.	28.	986.	- - 3/4	- - -
34th. M.G. Coy.	9.	202.	- - -	- - -

Strength from 8th. to 14th. November 1916.

8th. North. Fusr.	29.	907.	- - -	- - -
9th. Lancs. Fusr.	28.	888.	- - -	- - -
5th. Dorset Regt.	40.	1111.	- - -	- - -
11th. Manch. Regt.	30.	989.	- - -	- - -
34th. M.G. Coy.	detached from Brigade.			

Strength from 15th. to 21st. Nov. 1916.

8th. North. Fusr.	29.	908.	- - -	- - -
9th. Lancs. Fus.	28.	880.	- - -	- - -
5th. Dorset Regt.	41.	1115.	- - -	- - -
11th. Manch. Regt.	30.	981.	- - -	- - -
34th. M.G. Coy.	detached from Brigade.			

Strength from 22nd. to 30th. November 1916.

8th. North. Fus.	30.	906.	- 1. -	3. 32. -
9th. Lancs. Fus.	28.	887.	- - -	- 7. -
5th. Dorsets.	43.	1107.	- 3. -	7. 20. 2.
11th. Manch. Regt.	30.	975.	2. - -	16. 60. 1.
34th. M.G. Coy.	10.	195.	- - -	1. 4. -

Reinforcements.

	From 1st. to 7th. Novr.	From 8th. to 14th. Novr.	From 15th. to 21st. Novr.	From 22nd. to 30th. Novr.
8th. North. Fusr.	Nil.	Nil.	1 Off: 5.O.R.	Nil.
9th. Lancs. Fus.	5 Off: 2.O.R.	Nil.	8.O. Ranks.	1 Officer.
5th. Dorset R.	7 Off. 19.O.R.	2 Offrs. & 13 O. Ranks.	2 Off: 5.O.R.	Nil.
11th. Manch. R.	3 Off:	6.O. Ranks.	Nil.	Nil.
34th. M.G. Coy.	Nil.	Nil.	Nil.	2 Officers.

Vol 6

11 Dv

WAR DIARY

34th Infantry Brigade.
8th North'n Fusiliers.
9th Lancs. Fusiliers.
6th Dorset Regt.
11th Manchester Regt.
34th M.G.Coy.

Dec 1916

DECEMBER 1916 WAR DIARY 34th Inf Brigade
INTELLIGENCE SUMMARY.
Army Form C. 2118.

Place	Date	Hour	Summary of Events and Information	Remarks and references to Appendices
ST PIERRE DIVION	1 2 3 4 5 6 7		Nothing of importance took place during these days - The weather was fine and misty and work on the trenches progressed - A new trench was dug from R20B75 to R20B37 and a C.T. from R20D6.5 to R20B75. The 1st 3 Inf Bde 61st Divn took over the right of our line. They relieved the 9 Lancashire Fusiliers from STUMP ROAD to LUCKY WAY exclusive to them. The relief was completed without incident by 8pm -	
	8		The 33rd Inf Bde commenced to relief of 34 Bde today - The 11 Manchester Regt and 8 Northumberland Fusiliers marched to FORCEVILLE and ARQUEVES respectively -	
	9		7 Royal Fusiliers and 5 Dorset Regt were relieved in the front line by 6 Border Regt and 7 S. Staffords. The relief being complete by 8 pm - The Battns marched to billets at LEALVILLERS and FORCEVILLE respectively - Bn HQ moved to FORCEVILLE.	

Army Form C. 2118.

WAR DIARY
or
INTELLIGENCE SUMMARY.
(Erase heading not required.)

Instructions regarding War Diaries and Intelligence Summaries are contained in F. S. Regs., Part II. and the Staff Manual respectively. Title pages will be prepared in manuscript.

Place	Date	Hour	Summary of Events and Information	Remarks and references to Appendices
FORCEVILLE.	10			
	11		Bathing parades & road repairing	
	12		Much rain fell at intervals during three days.	
	13.		Orders received for the relief of 32nd Bde in sector N. of the RIVER ANCRE on nights 16/17th & 17/18th from RIVER ANCRE on the right to RYA 6.9.	
	14		Wet	
	15		Bathing parades & road repairing	
	16.		8th N. Fusiliers & 9th L. Fusiliers relieved 8th WEST RIDINGS & 9th WEST YORKS respectively in Right sub-sector. 34th M.G. Coy relieved 32nd M.G Coy. Reliefs completed by 2am without incident. BRIG. GEN. J. HILL. D.S.O. A.D.C. left for ENGLAND on leave. Lt Col E.C. HANNAY 5th DORSET REGT. took our temporary command of the Bde.	
	17.		11th MANCHESTER REGT & 5th DORSET Regt relieved 6th YORK + LANCS & 6th YORKSHIRE REGT. respectively in left sub-sector. 34th L.T.M.B relieved 32nd L.T.M.B. 34th Bde H.Q. relieved 32nd Bde H.Q. at Q18a 8.2. Relief completed by 12.15 pm without incident	

Army Form C. 2118.

WAR DIARY
or
INTELLIGENCE SUMMARY.
(Erase heading not required.)

Place	Date	Hour	Summary of Events and Information	Remarks and references to Appendices
Q.19.A.&.2		18	Shine & Stroat	
		19	Work carried out in SUVLA TRENCH & advanced posts by night & on	
		20	BEAUCOURT TRENCH & RAILWAY ALLEY by day	
		21	wet.	
		22	Owing to the rain digging was very difficult. The trenches in	
		23	many places falling in.	
		24.	32nd Infy Bde commenced relief of 34th Bde. The 11th MANCHESTER Regt & 9th LANCS Fusiliers moved to FORCEVILLE & LEALVILLERS respectively. The Batts were relieved by 5th YORKSHIRE Regt & 9th WEST YORKS Regt respectively. The 34th M.G. Coy was relieved by 32nd M.G. Coy reliefs were completed without casualties by 8.15 P.M.	
		25.	8th N. Fusiliers & 5th DORSET Regt were relieved by 6th YORK & LANCS Regt & 6th YORKSHIRE Regt (from reserve). Reliefs were completed by 8.30 P.M withdrawn. The Batts moved to ARQUEVES & FORCEVILLE respectively. 34th LTMB relieved by 32nd LTMB. 34th Bde. H.Q. was established at FORCEVILLE.	
FORCEVILLE		26.	Bathing parades & road repairing.	

Army Form C. 2118.

WAR DIARY
or
INTELLIGENCE SUMMARY.
(Erase heading not required.)

Place	Date	Hour	Summary of Events and Information	Remarks and references to Appendices
FORCEVILLE	27		BATHING parades & road repairing	
	28		"	
	29		"	
	30		"	
	31		Orders issued for relief of 32nd Bde.	

J.F. Wardidge Lt
34th Inf. Bde

SECRET.

Copy No... 2

34th. Infantry Brigade Order No.22

Reference Map 1/5,000 Bois D' Holland.
                     Pendant Copse.
                     Beaumont Hamel.
          1/40,000. Sheet 57.D.

1. 34th.Brigade will relieve 32nd.Brigade in the Sector N. of the ANCRE on nights 16th./17th., 17th./18th. December.

2. The area to be atken over extends from the River ANCRE inclusive on the Right to a line running from R.7.A.6.9. through R.12.Central.

3. This area is divided in two Sub-Sectors.

    Right Sub-Sector.

            From River ANCRE inclusive to a line from R.&.B.5.8. to R.7.C.9.8. -- 88. through junction of Railway Alley and Engine Trench.

    Left Sub)Sector.

            Remainder of the area.

4. On 16th./17th.December (a). 8th.North. Fusiliers and 9th.Lancs.Fusiliers will relieve 8th.West Ridings and 9th.West Yorks repectively in the Right Sub-Sector. 34th.M.G.Coy. will relieve 32nd.M.G.Coy.
   On 17th./18th.December
   (b)11th.Manchester Regiment will relieve 6th.York & Lancs Regt. in Left Sub-Sector.
   5th.Dorset Regt will relieve 6th.Yorkshire Regt. in Reserve.
   34th.L.T.M.B. will relieve 32nd. L.T.M.B.

5. All detailed arrangements to be made by C.O's concerned.

6. Copies of receipts for all trench stores taken over will be sent to B.H.Q. by 19th.December.

7. Outgoing Units will leave one man per Adv.Post. One man per Lewis and Vickers Gun. One Officer per Company in the Line for 24 hours after relief.

8. Work in hand will be very carefully taken over and carried on with.

9. A rough sketch shewing dispositions and location of Lewis Guns by Battalion Commanders and Vickers Guns by O.C., M.G.Coy, will be sent to Bde.Hd.Qrs. by 9.a.m. 19th.December.

2.

10. If possible busses will be supplied to convey units to LANCASHIRE DUMP.
Units marching will move via HEDAUVILLE - BOUZINCOURT -- AVELUY.

11. Bde.Hd.Qrs will be established at Q.18.a.8.2. on Completion of relief

12. Completion of reliefs will be reported by code word "GUM BOOTS."

13. ACKNOWLEDGE.

Issued at 4.p.m.

Copy No.		
1.	Office.	
2.	War diary.	
3.	Staff Capt.	
4.	Bde.Signals.	
5.	8th.North.Fus.	
6.	9th.Lancs.Fus.	
7.	5th.Dorsets.	
8.	11th.Manch.Regt.	
9.	34th.M.G.Coy.	
10.	34th.L.T.M.B.	
11.	183rd.Brigade.	
12.	11th.Division.	
13.	33rd.Brigade.	
14.	32nd.Brigade.	
15.	Bde.Supply Office.	
16.	No.4.Coy.Train.	

Captain.,
Brigade Major, 34th.Inf.Brigade.

SECRET.   COPY NO. 2

34th INFANTRY BRIGADE ORDER No. 23.

DEC. 22nd 1916.

1. 32nd Infantry Brigade will relieve 34th Infantry Brigade on Dec. 24th and 25th.

2. On the 24th :-
   (a) 8th West Riding Regt. will relieve 8th North. Fus.
   (b) 9th West Yorks. Regt. will relieve 9th Lancs. Fus.
   (c) 32nd Machine Gun Coy. will relieve 34th M. G. Coy.

3. On the 25th :-
   (a) 6th York & Lancs Rgt. will relieve 11th Manchesters.
   (b) 6th Yorkshire Regimt. will relieve 5th Dorset Rgt.
   (c) 32nd L. T. M. Batty. will relieve 34th L. T. M. B.

4. All arrangements to be made by Commanding Officers concerned.

5. All trench stores, maps and aeroplane photos are to be handed over and receipts forwarded to B.H.Q. by noon 26th.

6. On relief units will march to billets which they last vacated.

7. Completion of reliefs will be reported by code word HAPPY XMAS.

8. Brigade Headquarters will move to FORCEVILLE on 25th.

Issued at 7.30 p.m.

Copy No. 1. Office.
"   "   2. War Diary.
"   "   3. Staff Capt.
"   "   4. Bde. Signals.
"   "   5. 8th North. Fus.
"   "   6. 9th Lancs. Fus.
"   "   7. 5th Dorset Rgt.
"   "   8. 11th Manchesters.
"   "   9. 34th M. G. Coy.
"   " 10. 34th L. T. M. B.
"   " 11. 22nd Inf. Brigade.
"   " 12. 11th Division.
"   " 13. 33rd Brigade.
"   " 14. 32nd Brigade.
"   " 15. Bde. Supply Officer.
"   " 16. No. 4 Coy. Div. Train.

G.D.G. Ellis
Captain,
Brigade Major, 34th Infantry Brigade.

SECRET.   COPY NO. 2

34th INFANTRY BRIGADE ORDER No. 24.

Reference map - FRANCE - 1/10,000 - Sheet 57.d.   DEC. 23rd.

1. Brigade Order No. 23 is cancelled.

2. Relief of 34th Infantry Brigade by 32nd Infantry Brigade will be carried out in accordance with attached move table.

3. Tunnelling platoons will move with Battalions.

4. All details of relief to be arranged by Commanding Officers concerned.

5. Receipts for all trench stores to be forwarded to B.H.Q. by noon on 26th.

6. Completion of relief will be reported by code words HAPPY XMAS.

7. Staff Captain will be at B.H.Q. FORCEVILLE at 2 P.M. 25th. instant.

8. Movements will be by platoons at 200 yards interval.

9. ACKNOWLEDGE.

ISSUED AT 7.30 pm

COPY NO. 1. Office.
"   "   2. War Diary.
"   "   3. Staff Capt.
"   "   4. Bde. Sigs.
"   "   5. 8th North. Fus.
"   "   6. 9th Lancs. Fus.
"   "   7. 5th Dorset Rgt.
"   "   8. 11th Manchesters.
"   "   9. 34th M. G. Coy.
"   " 10. 34th L. T. M. B.
"   " 11. 22nd Inf. Brigade.
"   " 12. 11th Division.
"   2 13. C.R.A.
"   " 14. C.R.E.
"   " 15. 33rd Brigade.
"   " 16. 32nd Brigade.
"   " 17. Bde. Supply Officer.
"   " 18. No. 4. Coy. Divsl. Train.

G. D. G. Elton, Captain,
Brigade Major, 34th Infantry Brigade.

"   " 19. Town Major FORCEVILLE
"   " 20.   "   "   ARQUEVES
"   " 21.   "   "   LEALVILLERS
"   " 22. 86th Field Co. RE

MOVE TABLE.

DATE.	UNIT.	RELIEVED BY.	DESTINATION OF 34th BDE. UNIT.	REMARKS.
24th.	11th Manchesters.	6th Yorkshire Regt.	FORCEVILLE.	By bus leaving LANCASHIRE DUMP at 3 P.M. Busses to return to LANCASHIRE DUMP.
24th.	9th Lancs. Fus.	9th West Yorks Rgt.	LEALVILLERS.	By bus from LANCASHIRE DUMP.
24th.	34th M. G. Coy.	32nd M. G. Coy.	-do-	By busses at 3 P.M. and 11 P.M.
25th.	8th North. Fus.	6th York & Lancs Rgt.	ARQUEVES.	By bus from LANCASHIRE DUMP at 3.30 P.M. Busses to return to LANCASHIRE DUMP.
25th.	5th Dorset Rgt.	6th Yorkshire Regt. (FROM RESERVE)	FORCEVILLE.	By bus from LANCASHIRE DUMP.
25th.	34th L. T. M. B.	32nd L. T. M. B.	-do-	By march route.

On 24th Busses will remain at FORCEVILLE. Drivers being accomodated in Rest Camp.

SECRET.   COPY No. 2

34th INFANTRY BRIGADE ORDER No 25.

Reference maps - BEAUMONT - 1/10,000.
              LENS 11 - 1/100,000.   DEC. 30th 1916.

1. 34th Infantry Brigade will relieve 32nd Infantry Brigade in the Sector North of the ANCRE on January 1st and 2nd.

2. Relief to be carried out in accordance with attached table.

3. All detailed arrangements to be made by Commanding Officers concerned.

4. All work in hand is to be carefully taken over, to ensure continuity.

5. Duplicates of receipts given for trench stores are to be sent to Staff Captain by noon on 3rd inst.

6. Tunnelling platoons will move with their Battalions and commence work the day after their arrival.

7. Completion of relief will be reported by Code word "IMBROS".

8. ACKNOWLEDGE.

ISSUED AT 7 pm

COPY No. 1. Office.
"   "   2. War Diary.
"   "   3. Staff Capt.
"   "   4. Bde. Signals.
"   "   5. 8th North. Fus.
"   "   6. 9th Lancs. Fus.
"   "   7. 5th Dorset Rgt.
"   "   8. 11th Manchesters.
"   "   9. 34th M. G. Coy.
"   "   10. 34th L. T. M. B.
"   "   11. 22nd Brigade.
"   "   12. 11th Division.
"   "   13. C.R.A.
"   "   14. C.R.E.
"   "   15. 33rd Brigade.
"   "   16. 32nd Brigade.
"   "   17. Bde. Supply Officer.
"   "   18. No.4.Coy.Divsl.Train.
"   "   19. TOWN MAJOR - FORCEVILLE.
"   "   20.   "   "   - ARQUEVES.
"   "   21.   "   "   - LEALVILLERS.
"   "   22. 86th Field Coy. R.E.

                                                  Captain,
                                      Brigade Major, 34th. Infy. Brigade.

MOVE TABLE.

DATE.	UNIT.	FROM.	TO.	IN RELIEF OF.	REMARKS.
JAN. 1st.	5th Dorset Rgt. QD	FORCEVILLE.	OLD GERMAN FRONT LINE.	6th Yorkshire Regt. AV	Route March.
-do-	8th North. Fus. JV	ARQUEVES.	FRONT LINE RIGHT SECTOR.	8th West Riding Regt. AZ	By bus to LANCASHIRE DUMP.
-do-	34th M. G. Coy.	LEALVILLERS.	LINE.	32nd M. G. Coy.	By route march.
-do-	Half Bde. Sigs. Section.	FORCEVILLE.	B.H.Q.	32nd Bde. Sigs.	By route march.
JAN. 2nd.	5th Dorset Rgt.	OLD GERMAN FRONT LINE.	FRONT LINE LEFT SECTOR.	6th York & Lancs. Regt.	
-do-	11th Manchesters. ØH	FORCEVILLE.	OLD GERMAN FRONT LINE.	5th Dorset Rgt.	By route march.
-do-	9th Lancs. Fus. JZ	LEALVILLERS.	SUPPORT DUG-OUTS.	9th West Yorks. Regt. AR	By bus to LANCASHIRE DUMP.
-do-	34th L. T. M. B.	FORCEVILLE.	LINE.	32nd L. T. M. B.	By route march.
-do-	Half Bde. Sigs. Section.	FORCEVILLE.	B.H.Q.	32nd Bde. Sigs.	By route march.

Appendix 11

Strength of units from 1st. to 7th. Dec.1916.

Unit.	Officers.	Other Ranks.	Casualties. Officers.		Casualties. other ranks.		
			K.	W.	K.	W.	M.
8th. North. Fusiliers.	29.	844.	—	1.	3.	10.	—
9th. Lancs. Fusiliers.	29.	879.	—	—	10.	11.	—
5th. Dorset Regiment.	40.	1085.	—	—	3.	10.	—
11th. Manchester Regt.	27.	870.	—	—	1.	14.	1.
34th. M.G. Company.	11.	163.	—	—	—	3.	—

Strength from 8th. to 14th. December, 1916.

8th. North. Fusr.	28.	829.	—	—	—	—	—
9th. Lancs. Fusiliers.	29.	859½	1.	—	—	2.	—
5th. Dorset Regiment.	40.	1064.	—	—	1.	3.	—
11th. Manch. Regiment.	24.	848.	—	—	—	2.	—
34th. M.G. Company.	11.	174.	—	—	—	—	—

Strength from 15th. to 21st. December, 1916.

8th. North. Fusr.	28.	802.	—	—	3.	11.	—
9th. Lancs. Fusr.	28.	847.	—	—	—	5.	—
5th. Dorset Regt.	40.	1041.	—	—	—	—	—
11th. Manch. Regt.	24.	838.	1.	1.	—	11.	—
34th. M.G. Company.	11.	180.	—	—	—	—	—

Strength of from 22nd. to 31st. December, 1916.

8th. North. Fusiliers.	29.	760.	—	—	3.	7.	—
9th. Lancs. Fusiliers.	28.	840.	—	—	1.	3.	—
5th. Dorset Regiment.	42.	1008.	—	—	3.	3.	—
11th. Manch Regiment.	26.	802.	—	—	—	4.	—
34th. M.G. Company.	11.	177.	—	—	—	—	—

Reinforcements.

Unit.	From 1st. to 7th.	8th. to 14th.	15th. to 21st.	22nd. to 31st
8th. North. Fus.	—	—	—	109.
9th. Lancs. Fus.	—	—	—	—
5th. Dorset Regt.	—	—	—	—
1th. Manch. Regt.	—	—	—	195.
4th. M.G. Coy.	—	—	—	—

Vol I

Headquarters,
34th Inf. Bde.
(11th Div.)
January '91

34th Inf Bde

Army Form C. 2118.

WAR DIARY
or
INTELLIGENCE SUMMARY.

H.Q. 34th Infantry Brigade

(Erase heading not required.)

January 1917

Place	Date	Hour	Summary of Events and Information	Remarks and references to Appendices
FORCEVILLE		1.	Fine. 5th Dorset Regt & 8th N. Fus. relieved 6th Yorkshire Regt & 8th West Riding Regt in sector north of the ANCRE. 34th M.G. Coy relieved 32nd M.G. Coy. Relief completed without incident	JR
		2.	11th Man. Regt & 9th L. Fus relieved 6th York & Lanc & 9th West Yorks Regt respectively. 34th L.T.M.B. relieved 32nd L.T.M.B. 34th Bde HQ relieved 32nd Bde HQ. Reliefs were completed without incident by 8.15 pm.	
		3.	Wet. Work pushed forward in REDOUBT ALLEY, BEAUCORT & SUVLA TRENCHES & RAILWAY ALLEY.	
		4.		
		5.	Fine & clear. 9 L.Fus relieved 8 N.Fus in front line without incident.	
		6.	Fine. 11 Man Regt relieved 5 Dorset Regt " " "	
Q 18 A 8.2			Just Barrage on O.G.1+2.	
		7.	Fine } Work on trenches pushed forward	
		8.	Wet }	
		9.	Fine } Little of note happened these days	
		10.	Fine. Enemy artillery very active all day. 5th Dorset Regt relieved 11 Man Regt without incident. 8th N.Fus relieved by 6th W.Riding Regt. 9th L. Fus by 9th Arques having been relieved by 8th W. Riding Regt. Leavillers " " 9th W. Yorks Regt.	

WAR DIARY
or INTELLIGENCE SUMMARY

Army Form C. 2118.

34th Inf Bde.

January 1917

Place	Date	Hour	Summary of Events and Information	Remarks and references to Appendices
Q18 A & 2		11	W.O. for Operations see attached report, vide App: I. 5 Dorset Regt & 11th Man: Regt relieved by 6th York & Lancs Regt & 6th Yorkshire Regt & moved by bus to FORCEVILLE. 34 M.G. Coy relieved by 32 M.G. Coy. Reliefs completed by 12.10 am. Bde HQ moved to HORCEVILLE.	App. I.
FORCEVILLE		12, 13, 14, 15	Cleaning, Bathing & Road mending fatigues.	
		16	11th Man Regt proceeded to sector north of the ANCRE and occupied the reserve line. B.W. Cmde. returned from leave and took over command.	
		17	Brigade preparing to move and cleaning up area	
		18	5 Dorsets marched to RAINNEVILLE. 34 M.G Cy to BEAUQUESNE.	
		19	11th Manchesters were relieved without casualties and proceeded by bus to RAINNEVILLE. 11 Bn to BEAUQUESNE.	
BEAUQUESNE		20	N: Fus to BEAUQUESNE. 9 Lancs Fus to CANDAS	

Army Form C. 2118.

WAR DIARY
or
INTELLIGENCE SUMMARY.
(Erase heading not required.)

Place	Date	Hour	Summary of Events and Information	Remarks and references to Appendices
	21		8th W. Yorks: to BERNEUIL :. 9th Lancs Fus: BERNAVILLE : 5th Dorsets LEPLUOY 11th KNAN and Bde HQ to FIENVILLERS.	
FIENVILLERS				
FRANSU	22		Moved into rest area completed	
	23 to 27		Cleaning up and refitting — reorganizing section and platoons. Preliminary section and platoon drills and route marches. Weather very cold and sharp frost.	
	28 to 31st		Health of troops good. Platoon training — proceed to hold for drying owing to frost continuing.	

2/2/17.

J.M.T. Capt
o/c 11th Bde lng: 34th Bde.

APPENDIX 11.

STRENGTH OF UNITS FROM 1st.-7th. Jan.

	Off.	O.R.	\multicolumn{3}{c}{Casualties}				
			Officers			Other Ranks		
			K.	W.	M.	K.	W.	M.
8th. North. Fusirs.	30.	953.	-	-	-	7.	10.	
9th. Lancs. Fusr.	28.	815.	-	-	-	-	4	-
5th. Dorset Regt.	41.	981.	-	-	-	3.	1.	2.
11th. Manch. Regt.	26.	970.	-	-	-	-	-	-
34th. M.G.Company.	11.	193.	-	-	-	-	-	-

STRENGTH OF UNITS FROM 7st. to 14th. Jan.

	Off.	O.R.	K.	W.	M.	K.	W.	M.
8th. North. Fusr.	29.	908.	1	9	-	-	3	-
9th. Lancs. Fusr.	28.	1006.	-	-	-	5.	6.	2.
5th. Dorset. Regt.	39.	930.	1	3	2.	19.	46.	91.
11th. Manch. Regt.	31.	958.	1	-	-	11.	22	4.
34th. M.G.Company.	11.	176.	-	-	-	14.	2.	4.

STRENGTH OG UNITS FROM 15th. to 21st. Jan.

	Off.	O.R.	K.	W.	M.	K.	W.	M.
8th. North. Fusr.	29.	895.	-	-	-	-	-	-
9th. Lancs. Fusr.	31.	950.	-	-	-	-	-	-
5th. Dorset Regt.	37.	777.	-	-	-	-	-	2
11th. Manch. Regt.	34.	937.	-	-	-	-	-	-
34th. M.G.Company.	11.	173.	-	-	-	-	-	-

STRENGTH OF UNITS FROM 22nd. to 31st. Jan.

	Off.	O.R.	K.	W.	M.	K.	W.	M.
8th. North. Fusr.	29.	987.	-	-	-	-	-	-
9th. Lancs. Fusr.	33.	929.	-	-	-	-	-	-
5th. Dorset Regt.	42.	810.	-	-	-	-	-	-
11th. Manch. Regt.	32.	935.	-	-	-	-	-	-
34th. M.G.Company.	11.	171.	-	-	-	-	-	-

Reinforcements.

	From 1st. to 7th.		From 7th. to 14th.		From 14th. to 21st.		From 22nd. to 31st.	
	O.	O.R.	O.	O.R.	O.	O.R.	O.	O.R.
8th. North.Fus.	1	-	1	-	1.	80.	5.	-
9th. Lancs.Fus.	1.	-	3.	198.	1	-	3.	-
5th. Dorsets	-	-	1.	-	4	-	6.	80.
11th. Manchesters	5	-	5.	-	-	14.	2	10
34th. M.G.Coy.	-	-	-	-	-	-	-	-

REPORT ON OPERATION FOR WEEK ENDING JANUARY 12th.
IN THE SECTOR N. OF THE ANCRE.

Date.
6th to 10th.   Active patrolling was carried out along the whole front - particularly in R.1.D. and C.

Jan.11th.
1. The 34th Brigade attacked the spur in R.1.C. and D. in conjunction with the attack on MUNICH Trench in Q.6. by the 7th Division.
2. The 5th Dorset Regiment carried out the attack with 2 companies and 1½ companies 11th Manchester Regiment in Reserve.
3. ZERO - 6.40 A.M.
4. The Artillery Barrage was excellent and the attacking waves following closely under it gained their objective with very few casualties.
Fourteen prisoners belonging to the 135th Regt. 33rd Division were taken in the dug-outs at the "NEST" R.1.D.14.
Under normal conditions the spur in R.1.C. and D. is under direct observation from BEAUCOURT, but owing to a thick fog 50 yards was the maximum range of sight up till 10.A.M. from 10. A.M. to 10.30.A.M. there was a snow blizzard which made it impossible to see more then 20 yards. From 10.30.A.M. to 12.30.P.M. - 150 yards was the average range of sight.
At 12.30.P.M. the fog started to lift and had entirely gone by 1.30.P.M.
Owing to the means of communication (except by runner) having failed, reports took a considerable time to get back and it was not known until about 8.30.A.M. that the platoon detailed to clear up and hold the "CHALK PIT" had been attacked, from the bank above, with bombs, and driven out.
However the Officer in Command of this platoon (Lieut WANSTALL) although slightly wounded, collected more men from the Supporting Company and again attacked the "CHALK PIT", but was again wounded and failed to regain the pit. He estimated the strength of the enemy to be ¥ 50 men and a Machine Gun
It would appear that the enemy who regained the "CHALK PIT" from a dug-out under a broken in hut about R.1.D.1.2½. It is further thought that this dugAout is connected with those at the "NEST" R.1.D.14. which were reported to be very deep and hot air was rising from the entrance, which tends to show they held a large number of men.
A platoon was detailed to clear up the "NEST" in R.1.D.14, and in doing this the Officer and platoon Sergeant were wounded.
Four entrances were found and fourteen prisoners were taken out of one of them. Two of the others had been blown in by our shell fire, and while the mopping up party was trying to open up these, they were shot by the enemy who were found to be lining the top of the bank about R.1.D.24.

(2)

About 9.30.A.M Captain RITSON - Commanding "A" Company attacking the "NEST" returned to SUVLA TRENCH and brought up "C" Company under Captain CLAYTON to attack the enemy in the "CHALK PIT" and on the bank R.1.D2/4. and reported his action to his Commanding Officer who ordered 2 platoons of 11th Manchester Regiment forward to SUVLA Trench. While this attack was being organised the enemy reported to be 200 strong appeared from behind the bank at R.1.D.36. D Company who were on the right and had established posts at R.1.D.64-45-35 were fired on from the front and rear - Lieut SHEPHEARD in Command of the Company was killed and 90 men are missing. Before Lieut, SHEPHEARD was killed he ordered "A" Company, on his Left to retire Captain XXXXXX RITSON "A" Company's Commander was at this time with Captain CLAYTON.

Captain CLAYTON'S Company, who were preparing to attack, covered this retirement and then withdrew to SUVLA Trench and the original line of Posts.

NOTES.
1. The "CHALK PIT" was occupied in the first instance without opposition,
2. The dug-outs under the "NEST" were known to exist as Germans had constantly been seen to enter them just at Daybreak, but no one had been seen to use the entrance under the small broken hut - so this was not known of and not dealt with,

3. The fog prevented observation of any kind and so the Supporting Companies, who had orders to reinforce at once, if necessary were ignorant of the situation.

4. Captain RITSON had two runners killed while trying to take messages to Captain CLAYTON, before he went back himself.
He also had two direct hits on his Lewis Guns.

12 : 1 : 17.

Lieut COLONEL.
Commanding 34th. Infantry Bde.

S E C R E T.   Copy... 3 ...

34th INFANTRY BRIGADE ORDER No. 31.

Reference Map LENS. 11th

January 15th 1917.

1. The 11th Division (less Artillery) will be relieved in the line by the 63rd R.N. Division (less Artillery) on 18th, 19th, and 20th January and will move to the MARIEUX AREA.

2. The 34th Brigade will move in accordance with attached Move Table.

3. Permanent working parties attached to the Field Companys and Divisional R.E, will rejoin their units on 1th inst.

4. (a) One Company 11th Manchester Regiment working on YELLOW LINE will be relieved by a party from 189th Brigade on January 19th.

   (b) One Officer 11th Manchester Regiment will remain with the relieving unit until 20th inst to hand over work.

5. Distances of 200 yards between Companys and of 500 yards between larger units will be maintained on the march.

6. Brigade Headquarters will close at FORCEVILLE at 11.A.M. and reopen at BEAUQUESNE at the same hour.

7. ACKNOWLEDGE.

Issued at... ....

Copy No. 1. Office.
"   "   2. Staff Captain.
"   "   3. War Diary.
"   "   4. Brigade Signals.
"   "   5. 8th North Fus.
"   "   6. 9th Lancs. Fus.
"   "   7. 5th Dorset Rg.
"   "   8. 11th Manchesters.
"   "   9. 34th Machine Gun Coy.
"   " 10. 34th L.T. M.B.
"   " 11. No.4.Coy.Divsl.Train.
"   " 12. 11th Division.

H.J. Ratcliffe Lt. for Captain.
Brigade Major 34th Infantry Bde.

Move Table

Date	Unit	From	To	Route	Remarks
Jan 18th	5th Dorsets	FORCEVILLE	RAINCHEVAL	ACHEUX LEALVILLERS ARQUEVES	To pass FORCEVILLE VARENNES corner at 12-10 p.m.
"	11th Div Band	-do-	-do-	-do-	-do-
"	34th Bde S.M.B.	-do-	BEAUQUESNE	-do-	-do- 12 noon
"	34th M.G. Co.	LEALVILLERS	TERRA MESNIL	-do-	To pass Church 12-40 p.m.
Jan 19th	Bde Headqrs	FORCEVILLE	BEAUQUESNE	-do-	Not to move before 4 p.m.
"	11th Manchesters	LINE	FORCEVILLE		
Jan 20th	8th North Lanc.	ARQUEVES	BEAUQUESNE. RAINCHEVAL		To clear ARQUEVES by 12 noon
"	9th Lanc. Fus.	LEALVILLERS.	CANDAS	do	To clear LEALVILLERS by 12 noon
"	11th Manchesters	FORCEVILLE	RAINCHEVAL		Not to reach ARQUEVES before 12 noon
"	Mobile Vet Sect.	-do-	-do-	ACHEUX LEALVILLERS ARQUEVES.	—
"	S.A.A. Sect. D.A.C.	do	do	do	—
"	34th Field Ambulance	CLAIRFAYE	TERRA MESNIL	do	—

PROVISIONAL.

SECRET.   Copy No..........

AMENDMENTS TO
34th INFANTRY BRIGADE ORDER No.31.

The following amendments are published.

Para 2.   An amended Move Table is attached and is
          to be substituted.

Para 6.   Brigade Headquarters will close at
          FORCEVILLE at 11 a.m. on 19th inst.

ACKNOWLEDGE.

Issued to............

Copy No. 1. Office.
"   "   2. Staff Captain.
"   "   3. War Diary.
"   "   4. Brigade Signals.
"   "   5. 8th North.Fus.
"   "   6. 9th Lanc.Fus.
"   "   7. 5th Dorset Rgt.
"   "   8. 11th Manchester Rgt.
"   "   9. 34th Machine Gun Coy.
"   " 10. 34th L.T.M.B.
"   " 11. No.4. Coy. D.vel.Train.
"   " 12. 11th Division.
"   " 13. 11th Divisional Emm.
"   " 14. S.A.A.Sect.D.A.C.
"   " 15. 34th Field Ambulance.
"   " 16. Mob.Vet.Sect.

                                       ....
                                          Captain.
                              a/c Brigade Major 34th Infantry Bde.

Move Table.

Date	Unit	From	To	Route	Remarks
Jan 18th	Bde Hdqrs.	FORCEVILLE	BEAUQUESNE	ACHEUX LEALVILLERS ARQUEVES	To pass FORCEVILLE VARENNES corner at 11-45 a.m.
	11th Manchester Rgt	-do-	-do-	-do-	-do- 12 noon
	5th Dorset Rgt	-do-	RAINCHEVAL	-do-	-do- 12-20 p.m.
	3rd L.T.M.B.	-do-	BEAUQUESNE	-do-	-do- 12.40 "
	3rd M.G. Coy	LEALVILLERS	TERRA MESNIL	-do-	To pass Church 12-40 p.m.
Jan 20th	8th Manch. Fus.	ARQUEVES	BEAUQUESNE	RAINCHEVAL	To clear ARQUEVES 11-30 a.m.
"	9th Lanc. Fus.	LEALVILLERS	RAINCHEVAL	-do-	To clear ARQUEVES by 11-45 a.m.

To.

In continuation of Brigade Order No.31.

1. The additional move table is attached.

2. All columns will move closed up but an interval of 100 yards will be maintained between Battalions, Field Companies, Ambulances, etc.

3. Railhead will be on 20th. January at BELLE EGLISE.
   "   " " " 21st.   "   " CANAPLES.
   "   " " ") 22nd.   "   " CONTEVILLE.

4. Attention id directed to M.114 of 17th. December 1916.

5. Brigade Headquarters will close at BEAUQUESNES at 11.a.m 21st and will open at FIENVILLERS at 12 noon same day.

6. ACKNOWLEDGE.

                                                 Captain,

19 : 1 : 17.   a/ Brigade Major, 34th, Inf, Brigade.

UNIT.	FROM.	TO.	ROUTE.	REMARKS.
21st. 8th North. Fus.	BEAUQUESNE.	BERNEUIL.	BEAUVAL – CANDAS.	To be clear of BEAUQUESNE by 9.30 A.M.
" 9th. Lanc. Fus.	*CANDAS.	RIBEAUCOURT.	FIENVILLERS.	Not to enter FIENVILLERS before 9.30 a.m. To be clear of CANDAS by 10.30
" 5th. Dorset Regt. {11th. Divl. Band}	"	PLUOY.	— do —	✻ To be clear of CANDAS by 9.30 a.m.
" 11th. Manchesters	RAINCHEVAL.	FIENVILLERS.	BEAVAL – CANDAS.	To be clear of BEAUQUESNE by 9.30 a.m.
" No.4 Coy. Divl. Train.	"	"	"	To follow Mob Vety. Sect.
" 34th. M.G. Coy.	"	TERRA MESNIL	"	To follow 8th North. Fus.
" 34th. L.T.M.B.	"	BEAUQUESNE	"	To clear BEAUQUESNE – 8.30 a.m.
" Bde. Hd. Qrs.	"	"	"	
" S.A.A. Sect. D.A.C.	RAINCHEVAL.	BERNEUIL.	"	To follow 11th Manchesters
" Mob. Vety. Sect.	"	"	"	
" 34th Field Amb.	PUCHEVILLERS.	VACQUERIE.	"	Not to reach BEAUQUESNE before 9 a.m.

Move Table (Contd.)

Date.	Unit.	From.	To.	Route.	Remarks.
Jan. 22nd.	8th North. Fus.	BERNEUIL.	DOMQUEUR.	BERNEVILLE.	Not to reach BERNEVILLE before 10 a.m.
"	11th Manchesters.	FIENVILLERS.	FRANS U.	"	To be clear of FIENVILLERS by 9.30 a.m in order as detailed
"	34th M.G. Coy	"	MESNIL-DOMQUEUR.	"	
"	34th L.T.M.B.	"	"	"	
"	Bde. Hd. Qrs.	Bernil.	FRANSU.	"	
"	No 4. Amp. Sub. Train.	"	"		
"	11th Div. Band	PLUOY.	YRENCH.	Amy.	
"	S.A.A. Sect. ℥ D.A.C.	BERNEUIL.	BEAUVOIR.	BERNEVILLE.	Not to reach BERNEVILLE before 10.30 a.m
"	Mob. Vety. Sect.		CRAMONT FARM		"

SECRET.   COPY No...2...
----

                3 4th INFANTRY BRIGADE ORDER No 25.

Reference maps - BEAUMONT - 1/10,000.
                 LENS 11 - 1/100,000.   DEC. 30th 1916.

1. 3 4th Infantry Brigade will relieve 32nd Infantry Brigade
    in the Sector North of the ANCRE on January 1st and 2nd.

2. Relief to be carried out in accordance with attached table.

3. All detailed arrangements to be made by Commanding Officers
    concerned.

4. All work in hand is to be carefully taken over, to ensure
    continuity.

5. Duplicates of receipts given for trench stores are to be
    sent to Staff Captain by noon on 3rd inst.

6. Tunnelling platoons will move with their Battalions and
    commence work the day after their arrival.

7. Completion of relief will be reported by Code word "IMBROS".

8. ACKNOWLEDGE.

ISSUED AT

COPY No. 1. Office.
  "   "   2. War Diary.
  "   "   3. Staff Capt.
  "   "   4. Bde. Signals.
  "   "   5. 8th North. Fus.
  "   "   6. 9th Lancs. Fus.
  "   "   7. 5th Dorset Rgt.
  "   "   8. 11th Manchesters.
  "   "   9. 34th M. G. Coy.
  "   " 10. 32th L. T. M. B.
  "   " 11. 22nd Brigade.
  "   " 12. 11th Division.
  "   " 13. C.R.A.
  "   " 14. C.R.E.
  "   " 15. 33rd Brigade.
  "   " 16. 32nd Brigade.
  "   " 17. Bde. Supply Officer.
  "   " 18. No.4.Coy.Divsl.Train.
  "   " 19. TOWN MAJOR - FORCEVILLE.
  "   " 20.   "   "   - ARQUEVES.
  "   " 21.   "   "   - LEALVILLERS.
  "   " 22. 86th Field Coy. R.E.

                                         G. D. G. Elton Captain,
                                         Brigade Major, 34th. Infy. Brigade.

MOVE TABLE.

DATE.	UNIT.	FROM.	TO.	IN RELIEF OF.	REMARKS.
JAN. 1st.	5th Dorset Rgt.	FORCEVILLE.	OLD GERMAN FRONT LINE.	6th Yorkshire Regt.	Route March.
-do-	8th North. Fus.	ARQUEVES.	FRONT LINE RIGHT SECTOR.	8th West Riding Regt.	By bus to LANCASHIRE DUMP.
-do-	34th M. G. Coy.	LEALVILLERS.	LINE.	32nd M. G. Coy.	By route march.
-do-	Half Bde. Sigs. Section.	FORCEVILLE.	B.H.Q.	32nd Bde. Sigs.	By route march.
JAN. 2nd.	5th Dorset Rgt.	OLD GERMAN FRONT LINE.	FRONT LINE LEFT SECTOR.	6th York & Lancs. Regt.	By route march.
-do-	11th Manchesters.	FORCEVILLE.	OLD GERMAN FRONT LINE.	5th Dorset Rgt.	By route march.
-do-	9th Lancs. Fus.	LEALVILLERS.	SUPPORT DUG-OUTS.	9th West Yorks. Regt.	By bus to LANCASHIRE DUMP.
-do-	34th L. T. M. B.	FORCEVILLE.	LINE.	32nd L. T. M. B.	By route march.
-do-	Half Bde. Sigs. Section.	FORCEVILLE.	B.H.Q.	32nd Bde. Sigs.	By route march.

S E C R E T.

COPY No. 3

34th INFANTRY BRIGADE ORDER No.29.

Reference maps -1/5,000 - BOIS D' HOLLAND.
PENDANT COPSE.
BEAUMONT HAMEL.
REDAN.

JAN. 8th. 1917.

GENERAL.	1.	The 7th Division on our Left will capture MUNICH TRENCH.
INTENTION.	2.	The 34th Infantry Brigade will attack in conjunction with above and take up a line - BOIS D' HOLLAND - Existing posts in the Right Sub-Sector - thence a line R.1.D.4.5 - 3.5 - 1.5 - C.8.3½ - C.6.2.
INFORMATION ABOUT OUR TROOPS.	3.	Prior to and during the attack the Brigade in the Right Sector will demonstrate against O.G.1 and O.G.2 by Machine Gun Fire and rifle fire and vigorous patrolling - GRANDCOURT receiving special attention.
INFORMATION ABOUT THE ENEMY.	4.	(a) The 1st Bavarian Reserve Division is holding the line opposite to us in R.1 and 2. (b) The 18th Division holds PUISIEUX TRENCH. (c) An order issued in December by the German Command - stated that in view of their unfavourable position and the bad state of their trenches it might prove impossible to hold their present line, therefore in case of attack they would withdraw to a prepared line behind. (d) The enemy has no regular system of defences on the front to be attacked by this Brigade.
OBJECTIVES.	5.	(a) The spur in R.1.C and D - including the "NEST" at R.1.D.14, "CHALK PIT" at R.1.D.22 and trench from "NEST" to R.1.D.35. (b) Blocks will be established in the trench at R.1.D.46. R.1.C.86.
BOUNDARIES.	6.	RIGHT :- PUISIEUX ROAD (Inclusive). LEFT :- ARTILLERY LANE -do-
ASSAULTING TROOPS.	7.	The 5th Dorset Regiment will carry out the attack as follows :- (a) One platoon to move below Western bank R.1.D.20 to 35 OBJECTIVE "CHALK PIT" and its dug-outs and to establish posts at :- R.1.D.45. R.1.D.35. (b) Three waves on a one-platoon front OBJECTIVE Trench and "NEST" R.1.D.35 to R.1.C.94.

(2)

(c) Special parties will be detailed to push forward with the attack and establish posts at
R.1.D.6.4.
R.1.C.8.3.
R.1.C.6.2.

(d) Assualting troops will advance close under the barrage - scouts and Lewis Guns being sent forward of the objective while the position is being consolidated.

(e) The present line of posts will be occupied immediately the assualting troops have passed them and be ready to support the attack vigorously if necessary.

FORMING UP PLACES.   8.

(a) The garrison of the posts will be withdrawn by 5 A.M. on the day of the attack.

(b) The assualting troops will form up in and behind SUVLA TRENCH.

(c) Trench boards will be kept in readiness to throw across SUVLA TRENCH as bridges.

(d) Troops to be in position one hour before ZERO.

(e) It is to be impressed on all ranks that strict silence must be maintained throughout the forming up.

MACHINE GUN COMPANY.   9. Will co-operate with fire on ARTILLERY ALLEY in R.1.B and 2.A. - PUISIEUX TRENCH - SWAN TRENCH and PUISIEUX ROAD from junction with ARTILLERY ALLEY Northwards.

ARTILLERY.   10.

(a) The Heavy Artillery will bombard the "NEST" and "CHALK PIT" and dug-outs at R.1.D.58 on January 9th and 10th.

(b) The programme for the attack will be issued separately.

MEDICAL ARRANGE-MENTS.   11.

(a) The Battalion Dressing Station will be in a dug-out near junction of BEAUCOURT TRENCH and RAILWAY ALLEY.

(b) 33rd Field Ambulance Dressing Station at (Brigade Dump.
-ditto- at RAVINE - Q.12.D.

PRISONERS.   12. Will be passed back to the Brigade Dump, where they will be collected and taken to Divisional Cage at ENGLEBELMER.

WATCHES.   13. Will be synchronised every hour for four hours before ZERO.

ZERO.   14. To be communicated later.

(3)

BATTALION HEADQUARTERS.
---

15. Will be at R.7.A.1.3.

BRIGADE HEADQUARTERS.
---

16. Will remain in present position.

17. ACKNOWLEDGE.

Issued at 7.30 p.m.

Copy No. 1. Office.
" " 2. Staff Captain.
" " 3. War Diary.
" " 4. Bde. Signals.
" " 5. 8th North. Fus.
" " 6. 9th Lancs. Fus.
" " 7. 5th Dorset Rgt.
" " 8. 11th Manchester Rgt.
" " 9. 34th M. G. Coy.
" " 10. 34th L. T. M. B.
" " 11. 86th Field Coy. R.E.
" " 12. 11th Division.

Copy No. 13. C.R.A. 11th Division.
" " 14. 32nd Brigade.
" " 15. 33rd Brigade.
" " 16. 20th Brigade.
" " 17. 33rd Field Amb.
" " 18. 35th Field Amb.
" " 19. 60th F. A. B.
" " 20. 58th F. A. B.
" " 21. 59th F. A. B.
" " 22. Bde. Int. Officer.
" " 23.
24.

G. d G. Elton, Captain,
Brigade Major, 34th Infty. Brigade.

SECRET.   Copy No........

AMENDMENT TO 34th INFANTRY BRIGADE ORDER No.29.

Reference   Blocks will not be made.
Para 5 (b).

Reference   5th Dorset Regiment will attack as follows :-
Para 7
----------   (a) RIGHT ATTACK. - R.1.D.20 to PUISIEUX ROAD.

                    One platoon detailed to clear up "CHALK PIT"
                    and its dug-outs.

                    Three platoons to advance in three waves and
                    consolidate strong posts at
                                R.1.D.64.
                                R.1.D.45.
                                R.1.D.35.

                (b) LEFT ATTACK. - R.1.D.20 to R.1.C.90.
                    ----
                    1. Three platoon waves to advance and con-
                       solidate a line R.1.D.35 to R.1.C.95

                    2. One platoon will clear up and hold the
                       "NEST" at R.1.D.14.

                    3. One company will occupy original line
                       of posts.

                    4. One Company will occupy SUVLA TRENCH.

                       These companies will immediately re-in-
                       force the advancing companies should the
                       occasion demand it.

                    5. The 11th Manchester Regiment will move
                       1½ Companies to the CAVE by 6 A.M. on 11th.
                       These will be at the disposal of Officer
                       Commanding 5th Dorset Regiment.

           18. A subsidiary S.O.S. will be used by the attacking
                troops.
                This will consist of 3 White Very Lights fired in
                quick succession - One to the Right - One to the
                Centre and one to the Left - (Prince of Wales
                                                     Feathers.)

           19. O.C. 5th Dorset Regiment will see that the necessary
                gaps are made in the wire in front of SUVLA TRENCH
                on the night 10/11th.

           20. ACKNOWLEDGE.

           21. DIRECTION OF ATTACK - Due North.

                                         G.A.G.Elton,   Captain,
                                    Brigade Major, 34th Infantry Brigade.

SECRET.   COPY No. 2

34th INFANTRY BRIGADE ORDER No. 30.

Reference maps - BEAUMONT - 1/10,000.   JAN. 9th 1917.
                 LENS 11 - 1/100,000.

1. The 32nd Infantry Brigade will relieve the 34th Infantry Brigade in the Sector North of the RIVER ANCRE on the nights 10/11th and 11/12th.

2. The relief will be carried out in accordance with attached Move Table. (P.T.O)

3. Detailed arrangements will be made between Commanding Officers concerned.

4. The 5th Dorset Regiment will be responsible that all new posts captured by them in the morning are handed over.

5. Receipts for all trench stores and photos will be obtained in duplicate and a copy forwarded to Brigade Headquarters by 5 P.M. on 12th.

6. Completion of reliefs will be reported by the Code Word "HURRAH".

7. Staff Captain will be at Brigade Headquarters FORCEVILLE at 4 P.M. on 11th.

8. ACKNOWLEDGE..

ISSUED AT

COPY No. 1. Office.
 "   "   2. War Diary.
 "   "   3. Staff Captain.
 "   "   4. Bde. Signals.
 "   "   5. Bde. Int. Officer.
 "   "   6. 8th North. Fus.
 "   "   7. 9th Lancs. Fus.
 "   "   8. 5th Dorset Rgt.
 "   "   9. 11th Manchester Rgt.
 "   " 10. 34th M. G. Coy.
 "   " 11. 34th L. T. M. B.
 "   " 12. 20th Brigade.
 "   " 13. 11th Division.
 "   " 14. C.R.A. 11th Divn.
 "   " 15. C.R.E.   -do-
 "   " 16. 33rd Brigade.
 "   " 17. 32nd Brigade.
 "   " 18. Bde. Supply Officer.
 "   " 19. No.4.Coy.Divsl.Train.
 "   " 20. TOWN MAJOR - FORCEVILLE.
 "   " 21.   -do-   - ARQUEVES.
 "   " 22.   -do-   - LEALVILLERS.
 "   " 23. 86th Field Coy. R.E.

                                            G.B.G. Elton
                                                        Captain,
                                    Brigade Major, 34th Infty. Brigade.

MOVE TABLE.

DATE.	UNIT.	FROM.	TO.	TO BE RELIEVED BY	REMARKS.
10th.	8th North. Fus	Right Support.	ARQUEVES.	8th W. Riding Rgt.	By bus from LANCASHIRE DUMP.
10th.	9th Lancs. Fus.	Right Front Line.	LEALVILLERS.	9th W. Yorks. Rgt.	-do-
10th.	34th L.T.M.B.	Line.	FORCEVILLE.	32nd L T M B.	
11th.	11th Manchesters.	Reserve.	FORCEVILLE.		By Route March.
11th.	5th Dorset Rgt.	Left Front Line.	FORCEVILLE.		By bus from LANCASHIRE DUMP.
11th.	34th M.G. Coy.	Line.	LEA LVILLERS.	32nd M.G. Coy.	-do-

Vol. 8.

Headquarters,
34th Inf. Bde.
(11th Div.)
February 1917

WAR DIARY 34th Inf. Brigade
or INTELLIGENCE SUMMARY

Army Form C. 2118.

February 1917

Place	Date	Hour	Summary of Events and Information	Remarks and references to Appendices
FRANCE	1st and 2nd		Training continued.	
	3rd		Army Commander visited area and inspected 8th N.F. Tans.	
	5-9		Company training. Road fort continues.	
	10th		Brig. Genl. J. HILL, proceeded to ENGLAND. Brig. Gen. S.H. PEDLEY CB assumed command of the Brigade. Gen. Ritchie Div. Cmdt. inspected the special platoon 8th N.F. This platoon was adjudged the best platoon in the Division. 11th Div: now pass into the XIII Corps (Gen. Congreve)	
	11th		Sunday	
	12th		Gen. Ritchie proceeds on leave and Brig. Gen. Erskine's assumes command of the Division. Col. C. HANNAY returns from leave and takes on command of 5th DORSETS.	
	13th			
	14th 15th		11th Division to be in' G.H.Q. reserve when 31st Div move forward. Company Training	

Army Form C. 2118.

WAR DIARY
or
INTELLIGENCE SUMMARY.
(Erase heading not required.)

*Instructions regarding War Diaries and Intelligence Summaries are contained in F. S. Regs., Part II. and the Staff Manual respectively. Title pages will be prepared in manuscript.

Place	Date	Hour	Summary of Events and Information	Remarks and references to Appendices
FRANSU	16 17		Coy Training in the mornings. Rifle meeting in the afternoon. Bombing Competition - Lewis Gun Test - Bayonet fighting competition. The results were as per attached	Appendix V.
	18.		Sunday and holiday. Brigade transport show in the afternoon -	
	19. to 22		Battalion training. The 11 Division became the G.H.Q. reserve and orders were as below -	Appendix I.
	23.		The Brigade marched to FIEFFES - MONTRELET and BONNEVILLE area. Lancs Fusiliers marched to GEZAINCOURT. 34 M.G. coy marched to BEAUQUESNE.	
FIEFFES.	24.		The Brigade marched less 11 Manchester Regt - M.G. Coy and L.T.M.B. marched to BEAUQUESNE area - M.G. Coy marched to FOREEVILLE and was attached to 62nd DIVISION.	
BEAUQUESNE	25.		11 Manchester Regt and L.T.M.B. marched to TERRA NESRN and BEAUQUESNE respectively.	

Army Form C. 2118.

WAR DIARY
or
INTELLIGENCE SUMMARY.

(Erase heading not required.)

Place	Date	Hour	Summary of Events and Information	Remarks and references to Appendices
BEAUQUESNE	26.		9. Lancashire Fusiliers were split up into various working parties in DOULENS area.	
	27.		8 N. Fusiliers marched to FORCEVILLE and were attacked for work in that area. 62nd Division training in organisation	
	28.		9 Manchester Regt. and 5 Dorset Regt trained in new formations for the attack by the Coys and Battn. The weather throughout the month has been co-dry and foggy. In the first three weeks much useful training was carried out in the mornings and sports in the afternoons. During the last week the Brigade was moved in a whole horse and individual Battns were moved four times rendering all training almost impossible. G.A.S. Thom C.M Bde Maj. B Bde 1/2/17	

SECRET.   Copy No. 2

34th INFANTRY BRIGADE PRELIMINARY ENTRAINING ORDER.

1. The 11th Division is in G.H.Q. Reserve.

2. The 34th Infantry Brigade is to be ready to entrain at CANDAS at 24 hours notice.

3. ZERO hour will be the hour at which the first train leaves.

4. The Staff Captain will be at the Station 6 hours before ZERO, to organise the entraining parties, to arrange their billets, to control traffic at entraining Station, to find out watering arrangements etc. He will travel in the last train.

5. 11th Manchester Regiment will detail 1 Company for detraining duties.

6. (a) All trains consist of 1 Officers carriage, 17 flat trucks, 30 covered trucks.

   (b) Each flat truck will take an average of 4 axles.

   (c) Each covered truck will take 6 H. D. Horses.
                                    or 8 L. D.   "
                                    or 40 Men.

   (d) No personnel or stores will be allowed in the brake vans at each end of the train or on the roofs of the trucks.
       No covered trucks should be used for baggage.

7. Units transport will arrive at the Station 3 hours before the departure of the train and the personnel one an half hours.

8. A complete marching out state showing the numbers of Men, horses, G.S. limbered, G.S. and two wheeled wagons and bicycles will be sent down with the transport of every unit, so that accomodation in the train can be checked by the R.T.O. at the beginning of the entrainment, limbered G.S. wagons being counted as 2 - 2 wheeled on the state.

9. Supply and baggage wagons will accompany _their own units in every case._

10. The entrainment of all units must be completed half an hour before the time of departure of train, when it will be moved from the loading siding.

11. Breast ropes for horse trucks must be provided by the Units themselves; ropes for lashing vehicles on the flat trucks will be provided by the Railway. Units will take steps now to complete required number of breast ropes.

12. Piquets must be provided at all stops for each end of the train to prevent troops leaving.

13. ACKNOWLEDGE.

                                                   Captain,
21 : 2 : 17.   Brigade Major, 34th Infy. Bde.

Copy No 1. Office.   Copy No. 7. 5th Dorset Rgt.
 "   " 2. War Diary.   "   "   8. 11th Manchesters.
 "   " 3. Staff Capt.   "   "   9. 34th M. G. Coy.
 "   " 4. Bde. Sigs. Off.   "   " 10. 34th L. T. M. B,
 "   " 5. 8th North. Fus.   "   " 11. 11th Division.
 "   " 6. 9th Lancs. Fus.   "   " 12.
            Copy No. 13.
             "   " 14.
             "   " 15.

SECRET.

Copy No. 2

34th INFANTRY BRIGADE ORDER No. 32.

Reference map - LENS 11.   February 22nd.

1. The 11th Division (less Artillery and 33rd Infantry Brigade) will move from CANAPLES Area into Vth Corps Area on 23rd and 24th February.

2. The 34th Infantry Brigade will move in accordance with attached March Tables.

3. The Machine Gun Companies are placed at the disposal of G.O.C. 62nd Division from 10 a.m. 25th February for the purpose of relieving the Machine Gun Companies of 7th Division now covering the front of 62nd Division. They will join 62nd Division on 24th February.

4. Brigade Headquarters will close at FRANSU at 12 noon and re-open at FIEFFES at the same hour.

5. ACKNOWLEDGE.

ISSUED AT 7. p.m.

Captain,
Brigade Major, 34th. Infantry Brigade.

Copy No. 1. Office.
      2. War Diary.
      3. Staff Captain.
      4. Bde. Sigs.
      5. 8th North. Fus.
      6. 9th Lancs. Fus.
      7. 5th Dorset Rgt.
      8. 11th Manchesters.
      9. 34th M. G. Coy.
    10. 34th L. T. M. B.
    11. 11th Division.
    12. No. 4 Coy. Divsl. Train.

MARCH TABLE to accompany 34th Infantry Brigade Order No. 32.

DATE.	UNIT.	FROM.	TO.	ROUTE.	REMARKS.
23rd Feb.	Brigade Headquarters.	FRANSU.	FIEFFES.	FRANQUEVILLE - BERNEUIL.	Clear FRANSU - 9.15 a.m.
-do-	Bde. Signal Section.	-do-	-do-	-do-	-do-
-do-	11th Manchesters.	-do-	BONNEVILLE.	-do-	Clear FRANSU - 9.30 a.m.
-do-	5th Lancs. Fus.	RIBEAUCOURT.	-do-	-do-	
-do-	8th North. Fus.	DOMQUEUR.	MONTRELET.	-do-	Clear DOMQUEUR - 9.30 a.m.
-do-	5th Dorset Rgt.	-do-	FIEFFES.	-do-	To follow 8th North. Fus.
-do-	34th L. T. M. B.	MESNIL DOMQUEUR.	MONTRELET.	BERNAVILLE.	
-do-	34th M. G. Coy.	-do-	BEAUQUESNE.	-do-	

Transport of Brigade Headquarters, 11th Manchesters, 8th North. Fus. and 5th Dorsets will move via DOMART.

(2nd) MARCH TABLE to accompany 34th Infantry Brigade Order No. 32.

DATE.	UNIT.	FROM.	TO.	ROUTE	REMARKS.
24th Feb.	Bde. Brigade Headquarters.	FIEFFES.	BEAUQUESNE.	VALHEUREUX - Cross Roads N. of FERME du - ROSEL - BEAUQUESNE.	To clear BONNEVILLE by 9.5 a.m.
-do-	Bde. Signal Section.	-do-	-do-	-do-	-do-
-do-	9th Lancs. Fus.	BONNEVILLE.	RAINCHEVAL.	-do-	To clear BONNEVILLE by 9.15 a.m.
-do-	11th Manchesters.	-do-	-do-	-do-	To follow 9th Lancs. Fus.
-do-	8th North. Fus.	MONTRELET.	-do-	-do-	To clear billets by 9.15 a.m.
-do-	34th L. T. M. B.	-do-	-do-	-do-	To clear billets by 9.30 a.m.
-do-	5th Dorset Rgt.	FIEFFES.	BEAUQUESNE.	-do-	To reach BONNEVILLE by 9.30 a.m. and follow 8th North. Fus.

1st Line Transport will march with the units.

SECRET.   Copy No. 2

34th INFANTRY BRIGADE ORDER No. 53.

Reference map - 57.D - 1/40,000.

1. 8th North. Fus. will march to IInd Corps area on 26th February and return on March 3rd.

2. (a) The Battalion (less two companies) will work with 2nd Division and be billeted in huts at OVILLERS - X.7.d.8.1., where billeting Officer should report to Town Major.
   (b) Two companies will work with 18th Division and will be billeted at DONNETS POST - W.12.d.3.3.

3. Reserve S.A.A. and tools need not be taken.

4. The Battalion will clear billets by 9 a.m. and march Via :- ACHEUX - BOUZINCOURT - AVELUY.

5. ACKNOWLEDGE.

Issued at 9.30 p.m.

February 24th 1917.

Captain,
Brigade Major, 34th. Inf. Brigade

Copy No. 1. Office.
        2. War Diary.
        3. Staff Captain.
        4. 8th North. Fus.
        5. No. 4. Coy. Div. Train.
        6. 33rd Field Ambulance.
        7. 11th Division.
        8. 2nd Division.
        9. 18th Division.

APPENDIX. 11.   FEBRUARY, 1917.

Strength of Units from 1st. to 7th. Feb.

	Off.	O.Ranks.	Casualties Officers K. W. M.	O.Ranks K. W. M.
8th. North. Fusiliers	32.	975.	- - -	- - -
9th. Lancs. Fusiliers	33.	914.	- - -	- - -
5th. Dorset Regt.	42.	860.	- - -	- - -
11th. Manch. Regt.	34.	929.	- - -	- - -
34th. M.G. Company	11.	171.	- - -	- - -

Strength of Units from 8th. to 14th. Feb.

8th. North. Fusiliers	32.	974.	- - -	- - -
9th. Lancs. Fusiliers	33.	895.	- - -	- - -
5th. Dorset Regiment	42	850.	- - -	- - -
11th. Manch. Regiment	34.	931.	- - -	- - -
34th. M.Gun Company	11.	174.	- - -	- - -

Strength of Units from 15th. to 21st. Feb.

8th. North. Fusiliers	32.	970.	- - -	- - -
9th. Lancs. Fusiliers	33.	888.	- - -	- - -
5th. Dorset Regiment	41.	837.	- - -	- - -
11th. Manch. Regiment	34.	950.	- - -	- - -
34th. M Gun Company	10.	174.	- - -	- - -

Strength of units from 21st. to 28th. Feb.

8th. North. Fusiliers	32.	875.	- - -	- 2. -
9th. Lancs. Fusiliers	33.	889.	- - -	- - -
5th. Dorset Regiment	40.	819.	- - -	- - -
11th. Manch. Regiment	34.	951.	- - -	- - -
34th. M Gun Company	11.	175.	- - -	- - -

Reinforcements

	From 1st. to 7th. O. O.R.	From 8th. to 14th. O. O.R.	From 15th. to 21st. O. O.R.	From 22nd. to 28th. O. O.R.
8th. North. Fusr.	---	---	- 8.	---
9th. Lancs. Fusr.	---	---	- 11.	---
5th. Dorset Regt.	---	---	1. --	5. 16.
11th. Manch. Regt.	- 20.	---	1. 14.	1. --
34th. M.G. Company	---	---	1. --	---

Army Form W.3091.

Cover for Documents.

Nature of Enclosures.

24/

62

3w Div

Notes, or Letters written.

Vol. 9.

Headquarters
34th Inf. Bde.
(11th Div)
March 1917.

W A R   D I A R Y.

March 1917.

34th. Infantry Brigade H.Q.

8th. Northd. Fusiliers.
9th. Lancs. Fusiliers.
5th. Dorset   Regt.
11th. Manchester Regt.
34th. M.G. Company.

34th Inf BRIGADE.

WAR DIARY
INTELLIGENCE SUMMARY.

MARCH 1917

Army Form C. 2118.

Place	Date	Hour	Summary of Events and Information	Remarks and references to Appendices
BEAUQUESNE.	1.		11 Manchester Regt. moved from TERRA MESNIL and were disposed as follows:- Head quarters and two Coys at VARENNES two Coys at MAILLY-MAILLET and were employed on making a railway from ACHEUX to BEAUMONT HAMEL.	
	2/3/4.		8 N. Fusiliers marched from FORCEVILLE to BEAUMONT HAMEL and were employed on Road making	
	5th		5 Border Regt moved from RAINCHEVAL to MAILLY MAILET for work on SERRE Road. Whole Brigade on working parties - in a few cases training of specialists was carried on.	
	6th & 9th			
	10th & 13th		Convoy Officers and Regimental Officers and Brigade Staff reconnoitred the forward area between PUISIEUX and MIRAUMONT.	
	13th & 14th		8 N. Fusiliers moved up in support of 15th by Bde at MIRAUMONT. Early on 14th they were moved into the front line and assisted in the attack on ACHIET-LE-PETIT, from which place the enemy finally withdrew	

WAR DIARY
or
INTELLIGENCE SUMMARY.

Army Form C. 2118.

Place	Date	Hour	Summary of Events and Information	Remarks and references to Appendices
BEAUQUESNE	14th & 15th		The fighting during these days was semi open warfare. The enemy was holding a strongly entrenched and heavily wired position, while our troops manoeuvred round the village and finally had nearly surrounded it when the enemy withdrew. The 8th & 9th N. Fusiliers were relieved and marched to BEAUCOURT during the night 15th/16th.	
	16th		8 N. Fusiliers marched to FORCEVILLE. The Div Comdr of 6. 2nd Division wrote very complimentary letters as to the gallantry and excellent behaviour of the 8 N. Fus during the above action. Casualties Killed 1 Off 10 O.R. Wounded 4 + 3 O.R.	
	17th & 23rd		Battalions were on road work and railway work throughout this time.	
	24th		The Brigade concentrated once more in BEAUQUESNE TERRA-MESNIL area - vide APPENDIX I.	

Army Form C. 2118.

WAR DIARY
or
INTELLIGENCE SUMMARY.
(Erase heading not required.)

Place	Date	Hour	Summary of Events and Information	Remarks and references to Appendices
	25th		Sunday Church Services etc -	
	26 to 31st		This time was devoted to training. 1st day Platoon training 2 and 3rd days Coy training 4th and 5th days Battalion " 6th day Brigade Exercise - Although there was snow or rain daily throughout the week, much valuable training was carried out, particularly for semi open-warfare -	

G. SG. Elton Capt.
Bn. 34th Lt BC

1/4/17.

SECRET.   Copy No. 3

34th INFANTRY BRIGADE ORDER No. 34.

Reference map LENS 11.   23 : 3 : 17.

1. The Brigade will be concentrated at BEAUQUESNE and TERRA MESNIL on 24th inst. in accordance with table below.

2. Working parties (except those in 13th Corps Area) will be discontinued after 23rd inst.

3.

Unit.	To.	Route.	Remarks.
8th North Fus.	TERRA MESNIL.	ACHEUX LEALVILLERS. RAINCHEVAL.	To clear FORCEVILLE by 9 a.m. 24th
11th Manchesters.	BEAUQUESNE.	LEALVILLERS.	To clear VARENNES by 9-45 a.m. 24th
5th Dorset Rgt.	BEAUQUESNE.	FORCEVILLE. ACHEUX.	To clear FORCEVILLE by 9-45 a.m. 24th
9th Lancs. Fus.	TERRA MESNIL.		Move to be complete by 12 Noon 24th

4. The usual march intervals will be maintained.

5. Billeting parties to report to Town Major concerned early on 24th inst.

6. ACKNOWLEDGE.

                                                           Captain,
Issued at 9 a.m.   Brigade Major, 34th. Infty. Brigade.

Copy No. 1. Office.   Copy No. 9. 34th M. G. Coy.
        2. Staff Captain.   10. 34th L. T. M. B.
        3. War Diary.   11. 11th Division.
        4. Bde. Signals.   12. No. 4. Coy. Train.
        5. 8th North. Fus.   13. Town Major, BEAUQUESNE
        6. 9th Lancs. Fus.   14.   -do-   TERRA MESNIL.
        7. 5th Dorset Rgt.   15. 32nd Brigade.
        8. 11th Manchesters.   16. 33rd Brigade.

APPENDIX 11.
March 1917.

Strength of Units from 1st. to 7th.

Unit	Officers	Other Ranks	Casualties Officers K.	W.	M.	Other Ranks K.	W.	M.
8th. North.Fus.	33.	966.	-	-	-	-	-	-
9th. Lancs.Fus.	34.	884.	-	-	-	-	-	-
5th. Dorset R.	45.	913.	-	-	-	-	-	-
11th. Manch. R.	33.	929.	-	-	-	-	-	-
34th. M.G. Coy.		Detached.	-	-	-	-	-	-

Strength of Units from 8th. to 14th.

Unit	Officers	Other Ranks	K.	W.	M.	K.	W.	M.
8th. North.Fus.	33.	941.	-	-	-	-	-	-
9th. Lancs.Fus.	33.	875.	-	-	-	-	-	-
5th. Dorset R.	46.	953.	-	-	-	-	-	-
11th. Manch. R.	31.	933.	-	-	-	-	-	-
34th. M.G. Coy.		Detached.	-	-	-	-	-	-

Strength of Units from 15th. to 21st.

Unit	Officers	Other Ranks	K.	W.*	M.	K.	W.	M.
8th. North.Fus.	38.	861.	-	1.	-	5.	34.	-
9th. Lancs.Fus.	35.	887.	-	-	-	-	-	-
5th. Dorset R.	46.	919.	-	-	-	-	-	-
11th. Manch. R.	35.	926.	-	-	-	-	-	-
34th. M.G. Coy.	12.	174.	-	-	-	-	-	-

* Since report died of wounds.

Strength of Units from 21st to 31st.

Unit	Officers	Other Ranks	K.	W.*	M.	K.	W.*	M.
8th. North.Fus.	39.	861.	-	2.	-	-	3.	-
9th. Lancs.Fus.	35.	877.	-	-	-	-	-	-
5th. Dorset R.	46.	917.	-	-	-	-	-	-
11th. Manch. R.	35.	920.	-	-	-	-	-	-
34th. M.G. Coy.	12.	177.	-	-	-	-	-	-

* Accidently. Grenade explosion.

Reinforcements.

Unit	From 1st. to 7th. O.	O.R.	From 8th. to 14th. O.	O.R.	From 15th. to 21st. O.	O.R.	From 22nd to 31st. O.	O.R.
8th. North.Fus	-	-	2.	1.	4.	12.	1.	4.
9th. Lancs.Fus.	-	-	-	-	1.	-	-	-
5th. Dorset R.	-	3.	-	1.	3.	-	1.	-
11th. Manch. R.	-	4.	-	3.	-	-	-	1.

(6339) Wt. W160/M3016 1,500,000 10/17 McA & W Ltd (E1898) Forms W3091.   Army Form W.3091.

Cover for Documents.

Nature of Enclosures.

~~24~~

~~G2~~

~~6th B~~

Notes, or Letters written.

Vol. 10.

Headquarters,
34th Inf. Bde.
(11th Div.)

April 1917

Army Form C. 2118.

WAR DIARY
or
INTELLIGENCE SUMMARY.
(Erase heading not required.) 34th Inf Brigade

APRIL Vol 10

Place	Date	Hour	Summary of Events and Information	Remarks and references to Appendices
BEAUQUESNE	1.		Church Services.	
	2nd		Training chiefly for open warfare.	
	10th			
	11th	3.45 pm	Orders received from Division for the 34th Brigade group (less arty) to move to ACHEUX and LEALVILLERS.	
		5.15 pm	The Brigade marched and were accommodated as follows:— 8 North Fusiliers - 9 Lanc Fusiliers 34th LTMB in LEALVILLERS. Bde HQrs - 5th Tank Regt 11 Manchester Regt 34th MG Coy and 86 R.E. Coy at ACHEUX & the march was carried out in a heavy snow storm and was completed by 9.30 pm.	
	12th		The 5 Tank Regt moved to FORCEVILLE.	
ACHEUX	13		Training continued for two days.	
	14			
	15		Very wet day. — Church services and holiday.	

Army Form C. 2118.

WAR DIARY
or
INTELLIGENCE SUMMARY.
(Erase heading not required.)

Instructions regarding War Diaries and Intelligence Summaries are contained in F. S. Regs., Part II. and the Staff Manual respectively. Title pages will be prepared in manuscript.

Place	Date	Hour	Summary of Events and Information	Remarks and references to Appendices
ACHEUX	16th		Training continued. Brigade attack on trenches practised. Fine day till 4.30pm when rain started.	Appendix I
	17		Same as above —	
	18		Received orders (11 Division Order No 64) to march to Hutments in W10. between BOUZINCOURT and AVELUY. BDE order No 36 issued accordingly — — — —	Appendix I
BOUZINCOURT	19		Brigade move completed by 12.30 p.m. Fine day.	"
		3.30pm	11 Division Order No 65 Received for move to BAPAUNE area	
		7.45pm	34 Brigade order No 37 issued accordingly	
THILLOY	20		34 Brigade move completed by 1pm. Fine day. The Brigade became Reserve to the 1st Anzac Corps and in accordance with the Corps defensive scheme took over the left sector of the 2nd Line system (Appendix III).	
"	21		The whole Brigade was out on working parties. Three Battns on Railways and Ammunition Dumps One Battn digging the defense line referred to above —	

Army Form C. 2118.

WAR DIARY
or
INTELLIGENCE SUMMARY.
(Erase heading not required.)

Place	Date	Hour	Summary of Events and Information	Remarks and references to Appendices
THILLOY.	22.	3 p.m.	Divisional order No 66 received (Appendix I). A warning order re the relief had been received the previous night. So arrangements were made with 3rd Australian Bde for their relief on 24th and	
		7.30 p.m.	Bde order No 38 (Appendix I) published at 7.30 p.m. – Fine day – cold N wind.	
	23.	10 a.m.	A Conference was held at Divisional Hd Qrs at which all Bde Sigs and Commanders of other divisional units were present and commanders of other divisional units were present. All points as to our action in the new area were discussed – i.e. Scheme (Belinus) (recommendents). Sanitation – troops – etc.	
		2 p.m.	Brig. Genl. PEDLEY and his staff reconnoitred portion of the BEAUMETZ – MORCHIES line which the 34 Bde is to take over from the 3 rd A. Bde tomorrow. Fine day – cold N wind.	
	24.		Relief of 3rd Australian Bde by 34th Bde vide Bde order No 38 was complete by 11 p.m. – The Brigade was distributed as per Bde order No 38.	Appendix I.

WAR DIARY
or
INTELLIGENCE SUMMARY.

Army Form C. 2118.

Place	Date	Hour	Summary of Events and Information	Remarks and references to Appendices
FREMICOURT	25 to 29		Battns in the line worked on the defences – Improving the posts and wired the whole front. (May showing BEAUMETZ-MORCHIES line 2 Boxes S.A.A – 2 Boxes of bombs and 100 of Rifle grenades were put into slits in each post.	Appendix III
	27		Divisional Operation order 68 received – ordering 34 Bde to relieve 33rd Bde in left sector of Divisional front – on the night 30 April / 1st May.	Appendix I
			The necessary reconnaissances were made and Bde order number 39 was issued to all concerned.	Appendix II
	28			
	30		Relief was carried out and complete by 1 am May 1st without incident.	
			Weather. The first two weeks were very cold & wet with several snow storms. From 17th the weather improved and from 23 to 30th was fine with sunshine all day and much warmer.	

Casualties and Strength report APPENDIX IV.

APPENDIX 1 for

APRIL 1917.

Headquarters, 34th Infantry Brigade.

SECRET.

COPY No. 4

34th INFANTRY BRIGADE ORDER No. 36.

Reference map - Sheet 57.d. - 1/40,000.   April 18th 1917.

1. (a) 11th Division (less Artillery) will relieve the 5th. Australian Division (less Artillery) in their present positions, the relief being completed on the 21st. April.

   (b) 5th. Australian Division is at present in Reserve to 1st. ANZAC Corps and is located as under :-

Divisional Headquarters.	N.11. Central.
8th. Aust. Brigade.	FREMICOURT.
14th Aust. Brigade.	THILLOY.
15th Aust. Brigade.	N.24. Central.

2. The 34th Infantry Brigade Group (less Artillery) will move on 19th inst. to Huts in W.10. in accordance with attached March Table.

3. Brigade Headquarters will close at ACHEUX at 8 a.m. Destination will be notified later.

4. 1st. and 2nd. Line Transport (less Supply Wagons) will march with units.

5. 5th. Army Area intervals will be maintained. (500 yards between units - 100 yards between Companies.)

6. No. 4. Company, Divsl. Train will move under orders to be issued by the A.A. & Q.M.G.

7. Advanced parties will meet the Staff Captain at BRUCE HUTS in W.10. at 10-45 a.m.

8. ACKNOWLEDGE.

ISSUED AT 6.35 pm

Captain,
Brigade Major, 34th. Infty. Brigade.

Copy No. 1. Bde. Hd. Qrs.	Copy No. 9. 5th Dorset Rgt.
2. -do-	10. 11th Manchesters.
3. -do-	11. 34th M. G. Coy.
4. War Diary.	12. 34th L. T. M. B.
5. -do-	13. 86th Field Co. R.E.
6. Bde. Signals.	14. 34th Field Amb.
7. 8th North. Fus.	15. No.4.Coy.Div.Train.
8. 9th Lancs. Fus.	16. 11th Division.

MARCH TABLE (Issued in conjunction with B.O. 30.)

UNIT.	FROM.	TO.	STARTING POINT.	TIME HEAD WILL PASS S.P.	ROUTE.
Bde. Hd. Qrs.	ACHEUX.	BRUCE HUTS CABSTAND HUTS. MIDLAND HUTS. }W.10.	Railway Crossing in P.14.c.	8-45 a.m.	FORCEVILLE – HEDAUVILLE – BOUZINCOURT.
11th Manchesters.	-do-	-do-	-do-	8-30 a.m.	-do-
34th M. G. Coy.	-do-	-do-	-do-	9- 0 a.m.	-do-
34th M. G. Coy.	-do-	-do-	-do-	9- 8 a.m.	-do-
36th Fd. Co. R.E.	-do-	-do-	-do-	*	-do-
5th. Dorset Rgt.	FORCEVILLE.	-do-	*		
8th North. Fus.	LEALVILLERS.	-do-	CLAIRFAYE X Roads in 0.23.d.	9-20 a.m.	VARENNES – HEDAUVILLE.
9th Lancs. Fus.	-do-	-do-	-do-	9-55 a.m.	-do-
34th L. T. M. B.	-do-	-do-	-do-	9-45 a.m.	-do-
34th Field Amb.	-do-	-do-	-do-	10- 5 a.m.	-do-

Exact clock hour halts to be observed.

* = Tail to clear Battalion Orderly Room at 9 a.m.

S E C R E T.   Copy No. 4.

34th INFANTRY BRIGADE ORDER No. 37.

Reference maps – 1/40,000
Sheets 57.c & d.   April 19th 1917.

1. 34th Infantry Brigade (less Artillery) will march tomorrow in accordance with attached March Table and relieve the 14th Australian Brigade.

2. The following intervals will be maintained :-

    200 yards between Battalions.
    100 yards between Companies.

    There will be no long halts between POZIERES and BAPAUME.

3. Guides will meet advanced parties of units at 11 a.m. as follows :-

    8th North. Fus.)
    5th Dorset Rgt.) At Brigade Headquarters,
    34th M. G. Coy.) M.2.a.66.
    34th L. T. M. B.)

    9th Lancs. Fus.) At Town Majors Office,
    86th Fd. Co. R.E) BAPAUME.

    11th Manchesters.   At H.32.a.98.

4. 1st. and 2nd. Line Transport (less Supply Wagons) will accompany units.

5. ACKNOWLEDGE.

ISSUED AT 7.45 p.m.   [signature] Captain,
Brigade Major, 34th. Infy. Brigade.

Copy No. 1. Bde. Hd. Qrs.   Copy No. 9. 5th Dorset Rgt.
       2.   –do–   10. 11th Manchesters.
       3.   –do–   11. 34th M. G. Coy.
       4. War Diary.   12. 34th L. T. M. B.
       5.   –do–   13. 86th Field Co. R.E.
       6. Bde. Signals.   14. 34th Field Amb.
       7. 8th North. Fus.   15. No.4.Coy.Div.Train.
       8. 9th Lancs. Fus.   16. 11th Division.
           14th Aust. Brigade.

MARCH TABLE (Issued in conjunction with B.O. 37. herewith)

UNIT.	UNIT TO BE RELIEVED.	LOCATION.	STARTING POINT.	TIME HEAD PASSES S.P.	ROUTE.
11th Manchesters.	56th Aust. Infy.	GREVILLERS.	Cross Roads in V.16.b.	7 a.m.	CRUCIFIX CORNER - OVILLERS - Main BAPAUME - ALBERT Road.
34th M. G. Coy.		THILLOY.	-do-	7-12 a.m.	-do-
5th Dorset Rgt.	53rd Aust. Infy.	-do-	-do-	7-18 a.m.	-do-
8th North. Fus.	54th Aust. Infy.	-do-	-do-	7-30 a.m.	-do-
9th Lancs. Fus.	55th Aust. Infy.	BAPAUME.	-do-	7-42 a.m.	-do-
Bde. Hd. Qrs.		THILLOY M.28.a.66.	-do-	8-4 a.m.	-do-
8th Field Co. R.E.	14th Aust. Fd. Co. R.E.	AVESNES.	-do-	8-8 a.m.	-do-
34th L.T.M.B.	14th L.T.M.B.	THILLOY.	-do-	8-14 a.m.	-do-

S E C R E T.　　　　　　　　　　　　　　　　　　　　　　　Copy No. 4.

34th INFANTRY BRIGADE ORDER No. 38.

Reference map – 1/40,000 – Sheet 57.C.　　　　　　　　22nd. April 1917.

1. 11th Division (less Artillery) will relieve the 1st. Australian Division (less Artillery) on the night 23rd/24th and night 24th/25th :-
   (a) 32nd Brigade and 33rd Brigade in the line.

   (b) The 34th Brigade in Reserve.

2. (a) The boundary between 11th Division and 20th Division (on our Right) is line joining K.31.b.5.5. to N.24.b.2.2. on BAPAUME - PERONNE Road.

   (b) The boundary between 11th Division and 2nd Australian Division (on our Left) will be H.23.d.50 - I.14 Central - I.9.d.0.0. - I.10 Central - I.5.d.2.3. - C.30 Central - D.19.b.50.- D.14.d.50. - D.15. b.19.

   (c) The boundary between Sub-Sectors will be J.6.d.2.0 to BEAUMETZ (inclusive to the Right Brigade) and thence a line drawn from J.13. Central to I.31. Central.

3. The 34th Infantry Brigade will relieve the 3rd. Australian Brigade on 24th. as under :-

   (a) 9th Lancs. Fus., 11th Manchester Regt., 34th M. G. Coy. and 34th L. T. M. B. in the MORCHIES - BEAUMETZ Line - The 9th Lancs. Fus. on the Right - 11th Manchester Regt. on the Left.

   (b) The 8th North. Fus. and 5th Dorset Regt. will form Divisional Reserve.

4. (i) 8th North. Fus will relieve 12th. Battn. Australian Infantry at FREMICOURT.

   (ii) 9th Lancs. Fus. will relieve 10th Battn. Australian Infantry with Hd. Qrs. at LEBUCQUIERE.

   (iii) 5th Dorset Regt. will relieve 11th Battn. Australian Infantry at VELU.

   (iv) 11th Manchester Regt. will relieve 9th Battn. Austln Infantry with Hd. Qrs. at I.12.a.5.5.

   (v) 34th M. G. Coy. will relieve 3rd M. G. Coy., Hd. Qrs. at FREMICOURT.

   (vi) 34th L. T. M. B. will relieve 3rd L. T. M. B. at FREMICOURT.

5. (a) The relief by 8th North. Fus. and 5th Dorset Regt. to be complete by 2 p.m.

(2)

5. (b) 9th Lancs. Fus. will NOT move East of FREMICOURT before 4 p.m. and then only by Companies at 5 minutes interval.

   (c) 11th Manchester Regt. will not move East of BEUGNY before 7 p.m.

6. All details of relief to be arranged between Commanding Officers concerned.

7. (a) The 9th Lancs. Fus. and 11th Manchester Regt. will forward to Brigade Headquarters a sketch of their line, showing dispositions of Companies and Lewis Guns by 6 p.m. on 25th.

   (b) 34th M. G. Coy. will forward by the same time a sketch showing location of the guns with their arcs of fire, stating also the nature of the emplacement.

8. Relieving units will take over defence schemes, plans of work, photographs and all huts tents and shelters from the units they are relieving and will send a detail, in duplicate, of everything taken over to Brigade Headquarters by 6 p.m. on 25th inst.

9. Units will march with ammunition Echelons full and will take over all surplus ammunition left by relieved units.

10. Wheeled transport should proceed as far as LEBUCQUIERE only, by day.

11. Completion of reliefs will be reported at once to Brigade Headquarters.

12. Brigade Headquarters will close at THILLOY at 4 p.m. and re-open at FREMICOURT at the same hour.

13. Instructions will be issued later regarding

    (a) Administrative matters.

    (b) Relief of Field Companies and Field Ambulances.

14. ACKNOWLEDGE.

ISSUED AT 7:30 p.m.

(signature) Captain,

Brigade Major, 34th. Infantry Brigade.

Copy No. 1. Office
2. Bde. Hd. Qrs.
3. -do-
4. War Diary.
5. -do-
6. Bde. Signals.
7. 8th North. Fus.
8. 9th Lancs. Fus.
9. 5th Dorset Rgt.

Copy No. 10. 11th Manchesters.
11. 34th M. G. Coy.
12. 34th L. T. M. B.
13. 86th Field Co. R.E.
14. 34th Field Ambulance.
15. 32nd Brigade.
16. 33rd Brigade.
17. 11th Division.
18. 3rd Aust. Brigade.

SECRET.　　　　　　　　　　　　　　　　　　　　　　　　　Copy No. 4

34th INFANTRY BRIGADE ORDER No. 39.

Reference map - 57.C. - 1/40,000.　　　　　　　　　　　28th. April., 17.

1. The 34th Infantry Brigade will relieve the 33rd Infantry Brigade in the Left Sector of the Divisional Front on the night 30th April /1st May, with three Battalions in the Line and one in Reserve.

2. Reliefs will be carried out in accordance with attached table.

3. Detailed arrangements will be made by Commanding Officers concerned.

4. All maps, aeroplane photos and trench stores belonging to the Left Sector will be taken over, and those of the BEAUMETZ - MORCHIES Line handed over. Copies of receipts in each case will be forwarded to Brigade Headquarters by 6 p.m. on 1st. prox.

5. All units will forward by Noon on May 2nd. maps or sketches showing their distributions. (The maps will be copied and returned to units

6. Company Commanders and one N.C.O. per Company and one man per M. G. team will go into the line on the night April 29th.

7. In order to ensure continuity of work, great care will be taken that all work now in progress is taken over and arrangements made for its continuance on the night of relief.

8. The two platoons of the 8th North. Fus and 5th Dorset Rgt. now doing escort to Guns will be taken over by the 6th Border Regt. and 6th Lincoln Regt. respectively.

9. ACKNOWLEDGE.

ISSUED AT 7.0 p.m.

　　　　　　　　　　　　　　　　　　　　　　　　S. A. B__
　　　　　　　　　　　　　　　　　　　　　　　　　　　　　Captain,
　　　　　　　　　　　　　　　　　Brigade Major, 34th. Infantry Brigade.

Copy No. 1. Office.
　　　　2. Bde. Hd. Qrs.
　　　　3.　 -do-　　　　　　　　Copy No. 10. 11th Manchesters.
　　　　4. War Diary.　　　　　　　　　　11. 34th M. G. Coy.
　　　　5.　 -do-　　　　　　　　　　　　12. 34th L. T. M. B.
　　　　6. Bde. Signals.　　　　　　　　13. 86th Field Co. R.E.
　　　　7. 8th North. Fus.　　　　　　　14. 33rd Field Ambulance.
　　　　8. 9th Lancs. Fus.　　　　　　　15. 32nd Brigade.
　　　　9. 5th Dorset Rgt.　　　　　　　16. 33rd Brigade.
　　　　　　　　　　　　　　　　　　　　17. 11th Division.
　　　　　　　　　　　　　　　　　　　　18. 2nd. Aust. Bde.
　　　　　　　　　Copy No. 19. No.4.Coy.Train.

RELIEF TABLE (Issued in conjunction with B.O. No. 39.)

UNIT.	UNIT TO BE RELIEVED.	RELIEVING UNIT OF 33rd Brigade.	DESTINATION.	REMARKS.
8th North. Fus.	9th Shor. Foresters.	6th Border Regt.	G.30.d.5.5. BDE. RESERVE.	1. Each Battalion will leave a representative per Coy. to hand over to the relieving unit. 2. No reliefs N. of BEAUMETZ – MORCHIES line to commence before 8-30 p.m.
9th Lancs. Fus.	8th Lincoln Regt.	7th S. Stafford Regt.	J.4.c.8.1. LINE CENTRE.	
5th Dorset Rgt.	7th S. Stafford Rgt.	6th Lincoln Regt.	J.17.a.8.8. LINE RIGHT.	
11th Manchesters.	6th Border Regt.	9th Shor. Foresters.	D.19.c.5.0. LINE LEFT.	
34th M. G. Coy.	33rd M. G. Coy.	33rd M. G. Coy.	I.12.a.8.8.	
34th L. T. M. B.	33rd L. T. M. B.	33rd L. T. M. B.	I.12.a.6.6.	

APPENDIX 11 for

APRIL 1917.

Headquarters, 34th Infantry Brigade.

APPENDIX 11.

Strength of Units from 1st. to 7th. April.

Unit	Officers	Other Rank	Casualties Officers K.	W.	M.	Other Ranks K.	W.	M.
8/North. Fus.	37.	822.	=	=	=	=	=	=
9/Lancs. Fus.	36.	859.	=	=	=	=	=	=
5/Dorset Rgt.	45.	916.	=	=	=	=	=	=
11/Manch. Rgt.	34.	911.	=	=	=	=	=	=
34/M.G. Coy.	12.	175.	=	=	=	=	=	=

Strength of Units from 8th. to 14th. April.

Unit	Officers	Other Rank	K.	W.	M.	K.	W.	M.
8th. North. Fus.	37.	812.	=	=	=	=	=	=
9/Lancs. Fusr.	37.	849.	=	=	=	=	=	=
5/Dorset Regt.	44.	933.	=	=	=	=	=	=
11/Manch. Regt.	35.	900.	=	=	=	=	=	=
34/M.Gun Coy.	12.	173.	=	=	=	=	=	=

Strength of units from 15th. to 21st. April.

Unit	Officers	Other Rank	K.	W.*	M.	K.	W.*	M.
8/North. Fusr.	38.	812.	=	1	=	=	1.	=
9/Lancs. Fusr.	39.	955.	=	=	=	=	=	=
5/Dorset Regt.	44.	942.	=	=	=	=	=	=
11/Manch. Regt.	35.	900.	=	=	=	=	=	=
34/M.Gun Coy.	12.	172.	=	=	=	=	=	=

Strength of Units from 22nd. to 30th. April.

Unit	Officers	Other Rank	K.	W.	M.	K.	W.	M.
8/North. Fusr.	38.	812.	=	=	=	=	=	=
9/Lancs. Fusr.	39.	955.	=	=	=	=	7.	=
5/Dorset Regt.	44.	942.	=	=	=	1.	2.*	=
11/Manch. Regt.	35.	900.	=	1.	=	2.	5.*	=
34/M.Gun Compy.	12.	172.	=	=	=	1.	=	=

* 1 Officer 3.O.R. wounded accidentally.

REINFORCEMENTS

	From 1st. to 7th. Off.	O.R.	From 8th. to 14th. Off.	O.R.	From 15th. to 21st. Off.	O.R.	From 22nd. to 30th. Off.	O.R.
8th. North. Fusr.	1.	4.	=	7.	3.	=	1.	4.
9th. Lancs. Fusr.	1.	=	=	117.	2.	=	=	=
5th. Dorset Regt.	=	=	=	19.	=	=	=	=
11th. Manch. Regt.	1.	1.	=	=	=	7.	=	7.
34th. M. Gun Comp.	=	=	=	=	1.	3.	=	=

APPENDIX 111 for

APRIL 1917.

==*=*=*

Headquarters, 34th Infantry Brigade.

****

FIFTH ARMY AREA. (B.)
Map showing HINDENBURG LINE from latest available photos (dated 6-3-17.)

Date of Publication 21-3-17.
Scale 1:40,000
Dotted lines indicate work laid out but not then dug

(6339) Wt. W160/M3016 1,500,000 10/17 McA & W Ltd (E 1898) Forms W3091.   Army Form W.3091.

Cover for Documents.

Nature of Enclosures.

~~62~~

~~24/~~

~~Tanks~~

Notes, or Letters written.

Vol. 11.

Headquarters,
34th Inf. Bde.
(11th Div.)
May 1917.

Army Form C. 2118.

WAR DIARY or INTELLIGENCE SUMMARY. No. 34 Inf Bde Vol XI

MAY 1917.

Ref map sheet 57 C 1/40000

Place	Date	Hour	Summary of Events and Information	Remarks
MORCHIES	1.		The Brigade relieved the 33rd Bde in the left sector of the Division from last night relief being completed at 1 a.m.	
	2-6-9th		Very quiet with but little hostile shelling. The weather was brighter and warmer, excepting for one day's rain. Work was carried out continuously on the defensive lines all posts being further improved. The whole front was wired. for method of defence see Defence Scheme Appendix I. Patrols were out along the whole front every night and encountered several enemy patrols. Two prisoners were brought in, one of the 9th Regt of 3rd Guards Division and one of the 209th Regt. The former had lost his way and was caught while carrying rations. The latter was one of three who approached our front posts. He was wounded before capture, and died shortly afterwards.	

Army Form C. 2118.

WAR DIARY
or
INTELLIGENCE SUMMARY.
(Erase heading not required.)

Place	Date	Hour	Summary of Events and Information	Remarks and references to Appendices
	10 and 11th		Passed with nothing of importance to report. The enemy were quiet, apparently busy working on their own defences for many working parties were observed. A man of the 98th Regt. R.I.R. was shot approaching our wire.	
	12th	9.30am	Divisional Order No 74 was received, ordering relief of this Div by 48 Division and this Bde by 143 Inf Bde to be carried out on night 13th/14th B:	Appendix I.
		8pm	Bde Order 42 issued for relief.	
	13th	8.30pm	Relief by 143 Bde commenced	
		4am.	Relief completed. On relief units marched back to FRENICOURT and bivouacs for the remainder of the night. Heavy rain started at 3 a.m. In consequence of the relief not being over until 4 a.m. were the darkness of the night, rain. Each Battn had 14 separate posts to take over. There were no casualties during the relief.	

WAR DIARY
or
INTELLIGENCE SUMMARY.
(Erase heading not required.)

Army Form C. 2118.

Place	Date	Hour	Summary of Events and Information	Remarks and references to Appendices
	14th	12 Noon	The Brigade group marched vide Brigade order No 43 and were billeted in huts between MONTAUBAN and CARNOY.	Appendix I.
		6 p.m.	Move completed.	
	15th	1 a.m.	The move of Bde group to BUIRE area was cancelled.	
	16th	9 a.m.	The Bde Group marched to BUIRE area (vide annexed march table attached to Bde order No 43).	
		4 p.m.	Move completed.	
	17th 11-0 P.M. to 19th 3-0 A.M.		The Brigade Group commenced entraining at BUIRE on the evening of the 17th inst. First train departed at 11-0 P.M., 17th inst. Last train departed the morning of the 19th inst. A particularly smooth move at 3-0 A.M. on the morning of the 19th inst. Detrainment took place at BAILLEUL. Brigade Group proceeded to join 19th Corps - marched to LE ROUKLOSHILLE area, - were billeted in farms, huts, tents. Weather fine throughout.	See Appendix I. R/3046.
	18th 19th			
	20th		Units settling down in new billets. Kit inspections. Weather fine.	
	21st		C.E. Mothd Funk & 9th Lancs. Fuss. proceeded to forward areas to work under 19th Division. Remaining units carried out training. Weather continues fine.	

WAR DIARY
or
INTELLIGENCE SUMMARY.
(Erase heading not required.)

Army Form C. 2118.

Place	Date	Hour	Summary of Events and Information	Remarks and references to Appendices
	22nd		Army Commander (Lieut. General Plumer) visited the Brigade in the ROOKLOSILLE area at 11-30 A.M., & inspected the 5th Dorset Regt. & Officers of the 11th Manchester Regt. Training was continued.	
	23rd		Training continued. 11th Manchester Regt. moved into forward area for work under A.D. Signals, 9th Corps.	
	24th		M.G. Coy. moved to be attached to 19th Division. Training continued.	
	25th		Remainder of Brigade Group moved into 9th Corps Reserve, vide Appendix 1, Bde. Order 45.	
	26th		Weather continued fine. Training continued by remaining Units of Brigade Group.	
	27th		do. do. do.	
	28th		do. do. do.	
	29th		do. do. do.	

Army Form C. 2118.

WAR DIARY
or
INTELLIGENCE SUMMARY.
(Erase heading not required.)

Instructions regarding War Diaries and Intelligence Summaries are contained in F.S. Regs., Part II. and the Staff Manual respectively. Title pages will be prepared in manuscript.

Place	Date	Hour	Summary of Events and Information	Remarks and references to Appendices
May	30th & 31st		Training continued. Months Fust. returned to Bde Group. on completion of attachment to 19th Division. Training continued. Weather fine throughout.	

A.G. Elton Capt
B.M. 3rd Inf Bde

APPENDIX 1 for

MAY 1917

Headquarters, 34th Infantry Brigade.

SECRET.   Copy No. 4

34th INFANTRY BRIGADE ORDER No. 40.

Reference map - 1/20,000 - Sheet 57.C. N.E.   May 1st., 1917.

1. With a view of distracting the enemy's attention from the Division on our Left, the following procedure will be carried out.

2. Three Bangalore torpedoes will be discharged in the enemy wire on the night 2nd./3rd. by the 86th Field Company R.E. in D.17.d.

3. Each torpedo will be carried by sappers.

4. (a) The 11th Manchester Regiment will supply a covering party which will precede the sappers until the wire is reached and the charge laid.

   (b) A Lewis Gun will be pushed well forward to protect each flank.

   (c) When the charge has been laid, the whole party (except two sappers per torpedo) will withdraw a hundred yards. On completion of this movement the sappers will light the fuze and withdraw to the covering party. The whole party will then withdraw to our lines.

5. The sappers will report at Company Headquarters at D.27.c.82 at 9 p.m. and will move forward at a time to be arranged later.

6. The covering party will reconnoitre the ground tonight, and study with glasses tomorrow.

7. Progress of the operation and its completion will be reported to Brigade Headquarters.

8. ACKNOWLEDGE.

ISSUED AT 8 p.m.

                                                          Captain,
                                    Brigade Major, 34th. Infty. Brigade.

Copy No. 1. Bde. Hd. Qrs.   Copy No. 9. 11th Manchesters.
         2.   -do-   10. 34th M. G. Coy.
         3.   -do-   11. 34th L. T. M. B.
         4. War Diary.   12. 86th Field Co. R.E.
         5.   -do-   13. 32nd Brigade.
         6. 8th North. Fus.   14. 11th Division.
         7. 9th Lancs. Fus.   15. 13th A.F.A.
         8. 5th Dorset Rgt.   16. 6th. A.F.A.
                                           17. 2nd. Aust. Bde.

SECRET.

Copy No. 4.

34th INFANTRY BRIGADE ORDER No. 41.

Reference map - 1/20,000 - Sheet 57.C. N.E.   May 4th., 1917.

1. The 8th Northumberland Fusiliers will relieve the 5th Dorset Regiment in the Right Sub-Sector on the night 7th/8th. May.

2. On relief the 5th Dorset Regiment will occupy the positions vacated by the 8th Northumberland Fusiliers and become Brigade Reserve.

3. All details to be arranged between C.O's. concerned.

4. All maps, photos and trench stores concerning each line will be handed over.

5. Completion of relief to be reported to Brigade Headquarters.

6. ACKNOWLEDGE.

ISSUED AT........ 8 p.m.

G.D.G. Elton.   Captain,
Brigade Major, 34th. Infty. Brigade.

Copy No. 1. Bde. Hd. Qrs.
2.   -do-
3.   -do-
4. War Diary.
5.   -do-
6. 8th North. Fus.
7. 9th Lancs. Fus.
8. 5th Dorset Rgt.

Copy No. 9. 11th Manchesters.
10. 34th M. G. Coy.
11. 34th L. T. M. B.
12. 86th Field Co. R.E.
13. 32nd Brigade.
14. 33rd -do-
15. 11th Division.
16. Bde. Sigs. Officer.

SECRET.   Copy No. 4......

34th INFANTRY BRIGADE ORDER No. 42.

Reference maps - Sheet 57.C.)   May 12th. 1917.
                 & ALBERT.) - Scale 1/40,000.
                 (Combined).)
                 LENS 11.   - Scale 1/100,000.

1. The 11th Division (less Artillery) will be relieved in the Right Sector of the Corps Front by the 48th Division (less Artillery) on the nights 13th/14th and 14th/15th. May.

2. The 34th Infantry Brigade will be relieved by the 143rd Infantry Brigade on the night 13th/14th in accordance with attached table.

3. Details of relief to be arranged between C.O's. concerned.

4. Two guides for each Battalion will be at BEUGNY Field Ambu -lance at the following times :-

         8-15 p.m. for the 6th. Battn.
         8-45 "   "   " 7th.   "
         9-15 "   "   " 8th.   "
         9-45 "   "   " 5th.   "
         10-15 "   "   " M. G. Coy.

5. All plans, maps, defence schemes, photographs, trench stores, etc., are to be handed over and copies of receipts, in duplicate, forwarded to Brigade Headquarters by 12 noon on 14th.

6. Units will march with all ammunition echelons full.

7. Brigade Headquarters will close at I.11.c.5.6. on completion of relief and re-open at the same hour at FREMICOURT.

8. Completion of reliefs will be reported in the usual way.

9. ACKNOWLEDGE.

ISSUED AT.. 2. p.m. ....

                                          Captain,
                      Brigade Major, 34th. Infy. Brigade.

Copy No. 1. Bde. Hd. Qrs.   Copy No. 10. 11th Manchesters.
        2.   -do-   12. 34th M. G. Coy.
        3.   -do-   13. 34th L. T. M. B.
        4. War Diary.   14. 86th Field Co. R.E.
        5.   -do-   15. 6th. A.F.A.B.
        6. Bde. Sigs. Officer.   16. 13th A.F.A.B.
        7. 8th North. Fus.   17. 143rd Brigade.
        8. 9th Lancs. Fus.   18. 34th Field Amb.
        9. 5th Dorset Rgt.
             Copy No. 19. No.4.Coy.Divsl.Train.
                     20. 33rd Brigade.
                     21. 32nd Brigade.
                     22. 11th Division.

RELIEF TABLE issued in conjunction with Brigade Order No. 42.

DATE.	UNIT.	RELIEVING UNIT.	FROM	TO.	ROUTE.	REMARKS.
Night 13th/14th May.	8th North. Fus.	6th R. Warwick Regt.	Right Sub Sector.	Bivouacs in I.25.		
-do-	9th Lancs. Fus.	7th R. Warwick Regt.	Centre Sub Sector.	-do-		
-do-	5th Dorset Rgt.	5th R. Warwick Regt.	Brigade Reserve.	-do-		
-do-	11th Manchesters.	8th R. Warwick Regt.	Left Sub Sector.	-do-		
-do-	34th M. G. Coy.	143rd M. G. Coy.	I.12.a.9.6.	-do-		
-do-	34th L. T. M. B.		I.12.a.5.9.	-do-		Will march back to Bivouac Area as soon as it is dark.
14th.	34th Bde. Group.		Bivouacs in I.25.	MONTAUBAN and BERNAFAY.	BEAULENCOURT GUEDECOURT FLERS.	Afternoon move.
15th.	34th Bde. Group.		MONTAUBAN and BERNAFAY.	BUIRE.	HAMETZ 1 MEAULTE.	Morning move.

The following intervals will be maintained on the roads - 200 yards between Battalions
200 yards between transport of units and other units.
100 yards between Companies.

SECRET.　　　　　　　　　　　　　　　　　　　　　Copy No. 4

34th INFANTRY BRIGADE ORDER No. 43.

Reference Map – Sheet 57.C.)　　　　　　　　May 13th. 1917.
　　　　　　　& ALBERT.　　) – Scale 1/40,000.
　　　　　　　(Combined).)

1. The 34th Infantry Brigade Group (less Artillery) will march on 14th and 15th in accordance with attached March Table.

2. A representative from each unit will meet the Staff Captain

　　　On 14th at Town Major's Office
　　　　　　MONTAUBAN at 3-30 p.m.

　　　On 15th at Town Major's Office
　　　　　　BUIRE at 10-30 a.m.

3. Rations will be delivered to units on 14th and 15th by No. 4 Company, Divisional Train.

4. (a) 1st Line Transport will be Brigaded and march under orders of Brigade Transport Officer, Via BAPAUME, POZIERES, CONTALMAISON.
   (b) Orders re lorries will be issued separately.

5. On 15th 1st Line Transport will accompany units.

6. ACKNOWLEDGE.

ISSUED AT ...5-15 p.m.

　　　　　　　　　　　　　　　　　　　　　[signature] Captain,
　　　　　　　　　Brigade Major, 34th. Infantry Brigade.

Copy No. 1. Bde. Hd. Qrs.　　　　　Copy No. 10. 11th Manchesters.
　　　2.　　　-do-　　　　　　　　　　　11. 34th M. G. Coy.
　　　3.　　　-do-　　　　　　　　　　　12. 34th L. T. M. B.
　　　4. War Diary.　　　　　　　　　　13. 86th Field Co. R.E.
　　　5.　　　-do-　　　　　　　　　　　14. 34th Field Amb.
　　　6. Bde. Sigs. Officer.　　　　　15. No.4.Coy.Div.Train.
　　　7. 8th North. Fus.　　　　　　　 16. 33rd Brigade.
　　　8. 9th Lancs. Fus.　　　　　　　 17. 32nd Brigade.
　　　9. 5th Dorset Rgt.　　　　　　　 18. 11th Division.

MARCH TABLE issued in conjunction with Brigade Order No. 43.

DATE.	UNIT.	STARTING POINT.	TIME OF PASSING STARTING POINT.	ROUTE.	DESTINATION.
14th.	5th Dorset Rgt.	CEMETERY in I.31.a.	12 noon.	BANCOURT. RIENCOURT. BEAULENCOURT. FLERS. MONTAUBAN.	Huts in
-do-	11th Manchesters.	-do-	12-15 p.m.	-do-	-do-
-do-	8th North. Fus.	-do-	12-30 p.m.	-do-	-do-
-do-	9th Lancs. Fus.	-do-	12-45 p.m.	-do-	-do-
-do-	34th M.G. Coy.	-do-	1 p.m.	-do-	-do-
-do-	85th Field Coy. R.E.	-do-	1-8 p.m.	-do-	-do-
-do-	34th L.T.M.B.	-do-	1-15 p.m.	-do-	-do-
-do-	34th Field Amb.	-do-	1-20 p.m.	-do-	-do-
-do-	No.4.Coy.Divsl.Train.			Will march independently and clear FREMICOURT by 12 noon.	

MARCH TABLE issued in conjunction with Brigade Order No. 43.

DATE.	UNIT.	STARTING POINT.	TIME OF PASSING STARTING POINT.	ROUTE.	DESTINATION.
15th.	9th Lancs. Fus.	COSY CORNER.	9-5 a.m.	MAMETZ MEAULTE. DERNANCOURT.	BUIRE.
-do-	8th North. Fus.	-do-	9-20 a.m.	-do-	-do-
-do-	11th Manchesters.	-do-	9-35 a.m.	-do-	-do-
-do-	5th Dorset Rgt.	-do-	10 a.m.	-do-	-do-
-do-	34th M. G. Coy.	-do-	10-15 a.m.	-do-	-do-
-do-	34th L. T. M. B.	-do-	10-28 a.m.	n -do-	-do-
-do-	86th Field Coy. R.E.	-do-	10-32 a.m.	-do-	-do-
-do-	34th Field Ambulance.	-do-	11 a.m.	-do-	-do-
-do-	No.4.Coy.Divsl.Train.	Will march independently and be cleared of Camp by 8-30 a.m.			

AMENDED MARCH TABLE for 2nd day's march detailed in Brigade Order No. 43.

DATE.	UNIT.	STARTING POINT.	TIME OF PASSING STARTING POINT.	ROUTE.	DESTINATION.
16th.	Brigade Hd. Qrs.	Turning marked "IN" to watering troughs just S. of CARNOY.	9-5 a.m.	CARNOY. HEAULTE. BERNANCOURT.	BUIRE.
-do-	5th Dorset Rgt.	-do-	9-10 a.m.	-do-	- PIEDMONT.
-do-	11th Manchesters.	-do-	9-22 a.m.	-do-	BUIRE.
-do-	8th North. Fus.	-do-	9-34 a.m.	-do-	-do-
-do-	9th Lancs. Fus.	-do-	9-43 a.m.	-do-	-do-
-do-	34th M. G. Coy.	-do-	10 a.m.	-do-	DERNANCOURT.
-do-	34th L.T.M.B.	-do-	10-5 a.m.	-do-	-do-
-do-	34th Field Amb¹.	-do-	10-15 a.m.	-do-	-do-
-do-	86th Field Co. R.E.	will march independently to DERNANCOURT, but will not leave Camp before 12 noon. These will join in the column behind their respective units.			
-do-	No.4.Coy.Divl.Train.	will march independently to BUIRE and clear COSY CORNER by 8-30 a.m.			

1. Mess carts and cookers will be drawn up in above order on main road S. of CARNOY with head of column 300 yards W. of junction of main road and CARNOY road by 9 a.m.. These will join in the column behind their respective units.

2. The remainder of 1st Line Transport will march under the Brigade Transport Officer - head of column to pass Starting Point at 10-45 a.m.

3. No. 4 Company, Divsl. Train will deliver rations at Unit's destinations tomorrow

4. Baggage wagons are to be ready loaded at 8 a.m. when the Divsl. Train will collect them.

Captain,
Brigade Major, 34th. Infty. Brigade.

15 : 5 : 17.

To O.C.

Reference 11th. Division Entraining Orders No. 80/Q/99 dated May 15th. 1917. These will be strictly adhered to.

In addition the following duties will be found :-

1. (a). The O.C. 86th. Field Company, R.E. will detail one Captain to represent the Brigade, vide para 5 of the above orders.

   (b). 1 Company, 11th. Manchester Regiment 2 Officers and 150 O.R. will report to R.T.O. at 8.p.m. on the 17th. inst.

   1 Company 5th. Dorset Regiment will report to R.T.O. at 4.a.m on 18th. inst. for entraining duties as per appendix attached.

   (c). 1 Company 8th. North. Fusiliers (2 Officers and 150 O.R.) will report on arrival to R.T.O. for detraining duties.

   1 Company 6th. East Yorks Regt. (2 Officers and 150 O.R.) will report on arrival to R.T.O. for detraining duties as per appendix attached.

2. All Units will entrain at EDGE HILL Station on road between BUIRE and DERNANCOURT.

3. Where a Company is detailed from its Battalion, its cooker and tea Team will remain with the Company.

4. The SALVAGE Company will remain attached to the 8th. North. Fusiliers.

May 16th. 1917.

Captain,
Staff Captain, 34th. Infantry Brigade.

APPENDIX.
****

Serial No. of Train.	Units proceeding by the Train.	Time at which train leaves.	Unit responsible for entraining.	Time to report to R.T.O.	Unit responsible for detraining.
1.	Bde.HD.Qrs. 34th.M.G.Coy. M.T.M.By. 1 Coy. North.Fus.	24.00 17 : 5 : 17.	2 Officers 150 O.R. North.R.(a)	20.00 17 : 5 : 17.	2 Off. 150. O.Ranks North.Fus. M.T.M.B.(d)
2.	9th. North. Fusr. less 1 Coy.	4.00 18 : 5 : 17.	-do-	18 : 5 : 17	-do-
7.	9th. Lancs. Fusr. less 1 Coy.	8.00 18 : 5 : 17.	2 Off. 150 O.R. 5th.Dorset R.(a)	4.00 18 : 5 : 17.	-do-
10.	5th. Dorset Regt. less 1 Coy.	12.00 18 : 5 : 17.	-do-	-do-	2 Off. 150 O.Ranks 9th.Lancs.Fusiliers.(c)
13.	11th.Lanch. Regt. less 1 Coy.	16.00 18 : 5 : 17.	2 Off. 150 O.R. 11th. Lanch.R.(a)	12.00 18 : 5 : 17.	-do-
16.	H.Q.Divl.R.E., 1 Coy 8th.E.Yorks H.Q.Divl.Signals. H.Q.Divl.Train and Sanitary Section	20.00 18 : 5 : 17.	-do-	-do-	-do-
19.	1 Coy. 9th. Lan. Fusr., No.4.Coy. Train. and 86th. Fd.Coy.R.E.	24.00 18 : 5 : 17.	2 Off. 150 O.R. 5th.Dorset R.(a)	20.00 18 : 5 : 17.	2 Off. 150 O. Ranks 8th. E. Yorks Regt.
22.	1 Coy. 5th.Dorst R., 1 Coy.Lan. Regt. and 34th. Field Ambulance.	4.00 19 : 5 : 17.	-do-	-do-	-do-

(a).   This Company entrains in Train No. 22.

(b).   This Company detrains from Train No.1.

(c).   This Company detrains from Train No.7.

S E C R E T.   Copy No ...4......

34th INFANTRY BRIGADE ORDER No.44.

Ref. Map Sheets 27 & 28 - 1/40,000.   May 20th. 1917.

1. The 11th Division (less Artillery) will move into 9th. Corps Reserve Area by 25th. inst.

2. The 34th. Brigade Group will move into SUB Area 15 (i.e.R.4.C.& D. 5 C. & D. 10 - 11 - 12 A.& C. - 16 - 17 - 18 A.& C. - 22 a-b- 23)

3. On receipt of orders Units will move to Camps as follows :-

    1. Brigade Headquarters.   R.18.c.3.6.
    2. 8th. North. Fusiliers - Camp   R.16.b.9.5.
    3. 9th. Lancs. Fusiliers -   "   R.18.c.9.3.
    4. 5th. Dorset Regiment -   "   R.10.B.2.4.
    5. 11th. Manchester Regt. -   "   R.16.D.3.3.
    6. 34th. Machine Gun Coy -   R.22.B.5.5.
    7. 34th. L. T. M. B. -   R.22.B.2.2. M.11.a.4.2.
    8. 86th. Field Coy. R.E. -   R.18.A.7.7.
    9. 34th. Field Ambulance -   R.17.B.5.3.

4. Additional tentage has been applied for 5th Dorsets and 11th Manchesters will detail parties to pitch them to-morrow
    The 5th. Dorsets will pitch tents for 1 - 2 - 4 & 9.
    The 11th. Manchesters   "   "   "   3 - 5 - 6 & 7.
    Further details will be issued later.

5. In the case of fields which have not been previously occupied by troops the ground taken up is to be reduced to the absolute minimum and the remainder of the field is to be railed off.

6. In all cases tents, horse standing etc. are to be located as near to the entrance of the field as possible.

7. ACKNOWLEDGE.

ISSUED AT ...7.30.p.m.

G.E.G. Elton. Captain,
Brigade Major 34th Infantry Brigade.

Copy No. 1. Bde Hd. Qrs.
       2. Staff Captain.
       3. War Diary.
       4.   - do -
       5.   - do -
       6. Bde. Sigs. Officer.
       7. 8th North. Fus.
       8. 9th Lancs. Fus.
       9. 5th Dorset Rgt.

Copy No. 10. 11th. Manchesters
       11. 34th. M. G. Cpy.
       12. 34th. L. T. M. B,
       13. 86th. Field Co.R.E.
       14. No.4.Coy.Div.Train.
       15. 34th. Field Ambul.
       16. 11th. Division.
       17. Area Commandant
           BERTHEN.

SECRET.

Copy No. 3.

34th. INFANTRY BRIGADE ORDER No. 45.

Reference Maps - Sheets No.27 & 28)
BELGIUM & FRANCE.) - Scale 1/40,000   24th May 1917.

1. All Units remaining in 34th. Brigade Group will move on the 25th. inst. in accordance with attached March Table.

2. The following intervals will be maintained on the march

    200 yards between Battalions.
    200   "   "   Transport and other Troops.
    100   "   "   Companies.

3. Small parties should be sent on in advance to reconnoitre the camps and to guide their respective units into camp on their arrival.

4. Transport will accompany their Units.

5. Brigade Headquarters will close at X.1.d.3.3. at 2 p.m. and re-open at R.16.c.5.7. at 5.30 p.m.

6. Completion of move to be notified in the usual way.

7. ACKNOWLEDGE.

ISSUED AT 12 noon.

G.F.W. Gatacre
Lieut.
A/Brigade Major 34th. Infantry Brigade.

Copy No. 1. Bde. Hd. Qrs.
       2. Staff Captain.
       3. War Diary.
       4.   - do -
       5.   - do -
       6. Bde. Sigs. Officer.
       7. 8th. North Fus.
       8. 9th. Lancs Fus.
       9. 5th. Dorset Rgt.

Copy No. 10. 11th. Manchesters.
       11. 34th. M. G. Coy.
       12. 34th. L. T. M. B.
       13. 86th. Field Co. R-E.
       14. 34th. Field Amb.
       15. No.4 Coy. Train.
       16. 11th. Division.
       17. 32nd Brigade.
       18. 33rd Brigade.

MARCH TABLE issued in conjunction with Brigade Order No. 45.

DATE.	UNIT.	STARTING POINT.	TIME OF PASSING STARTING POINT.	FROM.	ROUTE.	DESTINATION.
May 25th.	34th. Bde. Hdqrs.	ROAD JUNCTION at R.32.d.10.7. (Sheet 27)	2-30 p.m.	ROUKLOSHILLE AREA.	2nd.Class ROAD through R.33.a -R.27.b.-R.22.c. -R.27.central BERTHEN - R.13. d.6.7.	SUB AREA 15.
- do -	5th Dorset Rgt.	- do -	2-35 p.m.	- do -	- do - do - do - BERTHEN- BOESCHEPE- R.10. c.10.8.	- do -
- do -	Headquarters 85th Field Co R.E.	- do -	2-50 p.m.	- do -	do - do - do BERTHEN-ROAD JUNCTION in R.16.c. - R.17.c.- R.18.a.77.	- do -
- do -	34th L. T. M. B.	- do -	2-53 p.m.	- do -	do - do - do BERTHEN - ROAD JUNCTION in R.13.c. -R.16.d.- R.17.c.a b. -R.12.d.	- do -
- do -	34th Field Amb.	- do -	3 - p.m.	- do -	do - do - do BERTHEN - ROAD JUNCTION in R.16.c. -R.16.d.- R.17.b.5.3.	- do -

APPENDIX 11 for

MAY 1917.

Headquarters, 34th Infantry Brigade.

APPENDIX 11.

Strength of Units from 1st. to 7th. May.

Unit	Officers	O.Ranks	Killed O.	Killed O.R.	Wounded O.	Wounded O.R.	Missing O.	Missing O.R.
8th. North. Fusiliers.	39.	821.	=	=2.	1.	6.	=	=
9th. Lancs. Fusiliers.	38.	948.	=	1.	1.	8.	=	=
5th. Dorset Regiment.	44.	917.	=	7.	=	12.	=	=
11th. Manchester Regt.	36.	902.	=	=	=	6.	=	=
34th. Machine Gun Coy.	12.	173.	=	=	=	=	=	=

Strength of Units from 8th. to 14th. May.

Unit	Officers	O.Ranks	Killed O.	Killed O.R.	Wounded O.	Wounded O.R.	Missing O.	Missing O.R.
8th. North. Fusiliers.	39.	816.	=	1.	=	7.	=	=
9th. Lancs. Fusiliers.	38.	942.	=	=	=	6.	=	=
5th. Dorset Regiment.	44.	916.	=	4.	=	10.	=	=
11th. Manchester Regt.	37.	897.	=	=	=	3.	=	=
34th. Machine Gun Coy.	12.	173.	=	=	=	=	=	=

Strength of Units from 15th. to 21st. May.

Unit	Officers	O.Ranks	Killed O.	Killed O.R.	Wounded O.	Wounded O.R.	Missing O.	Missing O.R.
8th. North. Fusiliers.	39.	936.	=	=	=	1.	==	=
9th. Lancs. Fusiliers.	38.	982.	=	=	=	=	=	=
5th. Dorset Regiment.	44.	900.	=	=	=	=	=	=
11th. Manch. Regiment.	37.	982.	=	=	=	=	=	=
34th. Machine Gun Coy.	12.	172.	=	=	=	1.	=	=

Strength of Units from 21st. to 31st. May.

Unit	Officers	O.Ranks	Killed O.	Killed O.R.	Wounded O.	Wounded O.R.	Missing O.	Missing O.R.
8th. North. Fusiliers.	39.	958.	1.	4.	1.	19.	=	=
9th. Lancs. Fusiliers.	40.	972.	=	=	=	=	=	=
5th. Dorset Regiment.	43.	938.	=	=	=	=	=	=
11th. Manchester Regt.	36.	979.	=	3.	=	4.	=	=
34th. Machine Gun Coy.	12.	172.	=	=	=	=	=	=

REINFORCEMENTS

Unit	From 1st to 7th. May. O.	From 1st to 7th. May. O.R.	From 8th. to 14th. May. O.	From 8th. to 14th. May. O.R.	From 15th. to 21st. May. O.	From 15th. to 21st. May. O.R.	From 22nd to 31st. May. O.	From 22nd to 31st. May. O.R.
8th. North. Fusr.	=	11.	2.	126.	1.	29.	=	7.
9th. Lancs. Fusr.	=	6.	=	37.	=	2.	=	6.
5th. Dorset Regt.	=	23.	=	=	=	49.	1.	11.
11th. Manchester R.	=	4.	=	12.	=	83.	=	6.
34th. M.G.Company.	=	=	1.	1.	=	=	=	=

APPENDIX 111 for

MAY 1917.

Headquarters, 34th Infantry Brigade.

NIL

Army Form W.3091.

Cover for Documents.

~~G.R. 1/5~~

Nature of Enclosures.

~~Miscellaneous~~

Notes, or Letters written.

WAR DIARY for

JUNE 1917.

Headquarters, 34th Infantry Brigade.

WAR DIARY or INTELLIGENCE SUMMARY

34 Bde.

JUNE 1917

Army Form C. 2118.

Place	Date	Hour	Summary of Events and Information	Remarks and references to Appendices
MONT KOKEREELE. R.16.D.65. Ref. map Sheet 27 1/40000.	1st		The Brigade was located as follows:- Bde Hd Qrs MONT KOKEREELE. 8. N. Fusiliers " " (Camp.) 9 Lanc. Fusiliers " " 5th Dorset Regt BOESCHEPE " Lancashire " LOCRE (attached 1 × Corps signals) 34 M.C. Coy M11A (" 16 Division) 34 L.T.M.B. MONT KOKEREELE " 86 R.E. " "	
	2nd to 5th		Training was carried out. All officers reconnoitred the lines of the 36th, 19th and 36th Divns During this period instructions were issued for the coming Offensive.	
	5th	4pm	Capt. G.D.G. ELTON. M.C. Bde. Major awarded D.S.O. in Birthday Honours	
	5th	2pm	Divisional Order No 79 received	
	6th	10 am	Bde order No 46 issued (Appendix I)	
		3pm	Orders issued that in the event of Bde order 46 would be carried out tonight	

WAR DIARY
or
INTELLIGENCE SUMMARY.
(Erase heading not required.)

Army Form C. 2118.

Hour, Date, Place	Summary of Events and Information	Remarks and references to Appendices
5th	At a Divisional conference the plan of attack was explained to all Brigadiers. Similarly a Brigade conference was held and the plan was explained to Commanding Officers – and details etc was discussed and decisions made –	
LA CLYTTE. 7th 12 noon 8/ 7 P.M.	Move of Brigade was complete by 3 A.M. The Brigade remained ready to move at a moments notice until 7 pm when orders were received that the Brigade would not move tonight. 34 MG Coy rejoined the Brigade. Telephone message received that the Brigade would relieve 109 Bde & 36 Division in trenches by 9 am tomorrow and would in support relieving the 4.5th Bde 16 Div in the evening	11 Manchester Regt 34 MG Coy rejoined. Appendix I Bde order No 47 Bde order No 48

Army Form C. 2118.

WAR DIARY
or
INTELLIGENCE SUMMARY.
(Erase heading not required.)

Instructions regarding War Diaries and Intelligence Summaries are contained in F.S. Regs., Part II and the Staff Manual respectively. Title pages will be prepared in manuscript.

Hour, Date, Place		Summary of Events and Information	Remarks and references to Appendices
9th	9.30am	Brigade move completed. Brigade Head Quarters remained for the day at LA CLYTTE.	Ref Map Sheet 28 SW 1/20000
CHINESE WALL N23 B 5.2 10th	8.30pm	Bde H.Q Quarters moved to Strong Point 12 N23 B 5.2.	
	1.30am	Relief reported completed without any incident.	
11th		56th Inf Bde on our left advanced their line East of VAN HOVE Farm – 8 N. Fusiliers advanced their posts E. of TOYE Farm and the TOYE Farm – WAMBEKE Road. No enemy seen or met with.	
12th		Took over positions of the line held by 32 Bde and handed over their positions to 56 Bde 19 Div. On our left, in order to reorganise the line the boundaries laid down in Divisional order	

(73989) W4141—463. 400,000. 9/14. H.&J.Ltd. Forms/C. 2118/10.

Army Form C. 2118.

WAR DIARY
or
INTELLIGENCE SUMMARY.
(Erase heading not required.)

Instructions regarding War Diaries and Intelligence Summaries are contained in F.S. Regs., Part II. and the Staff Manual respectively. Title pages will be prepared in manuscript.

Hour, Date, Place	Summary of Events and Information	Remarks and references to Appendices
13 9.30 P.M.	The Brigadier was called to a conference and told that at 7.30 pm on 14th the 1st Army would attack at various points and on the arrival of the Army to be demonstrations would be made to simulate a general attack. The 11 Division were ordered to send out strong patrols under a barrage to various points on its front.	
14th 12.45 A.M.	B.M. orders were issued to S.N. Fusiliers that they would attack four farms in front of their lines. One platoon to each farm. Owing to the lack of munition brushes to cut forward first, it was impracticable that the assaulting platoons should get into positions before day light. (see appendix II) Walton the Brigadier went up to 140 Gds. N. Lus and explain the orders to the C.O. and Coy Cmdrs.	Appendix I

WAR DIARY
or
INTELLIGENCE SUMMARY.

Army Form C. 2118.

Hour, Date, Place	Summary of Events and Information	Remarks and references to Appendices
14.45 7.30pm	The barrage fires perfectly, the assaulting platoons advanced and took all objectives without opposition.	
10.30pm	The platoons withdrew as ordered. Casualties 10 O.R. & O.R. wounded.	
15th	From 11th to 15th Enemy made no sign of aggressive action. Infantry except for a few snipers. Nothing was seen of him. His artillery however was active and barraged our front lines several times with H.E. He also fired heavily with H.E. He also fired heavily with H.E. on the back areas of the Brigade Sector causing heavy casualties. It is stated that there were no trenches in the area to start with, & also presumably the area Battn were working parties of the Battn were working in that area were in the open) in the (unknown) area.	

Army Form C. 2118.

WAR DIARY
or
INTELLIGENCE SUMMARY.
(Erase heading not required.)

Instructions regarding War Diaries and Intelligence Summaries are contained in F.S. Regs., Part II. and the Staff Manual respectively. Title pages will be prepared in manuscript.

Hour, Date, Place	Summary of Events and Information	Remarks and references to Appendices
16th 12 noon	Nothing of interest to record - Issued orders for relief of 7 N Fusiliers by 11 Manchester Regt on night 18/19th - and 5 Dorset Regt by 9 Lanc Fusiliers on 19/20th -	Bde order No 50 Appendix I.
17th	Quieter day - less enemy shelling -	
18th	Received orders that 3.6 Division will relieve 11th Division at once - Brigadier of 107 Inf Brigade visited our Head Quarters and arranged for relief - Brigade order No 50 cancelled	
12 noon 19th	Brigade order No 51 issued for relief by 10.7 Inf Brigade tonight - Relief continued 12-0 midnight 19th (inst.) Brigade billetted night of 19th/20th in DRANOUTRE.	Appendix I.

8 a.m.

(73989) W4141—463. 400,000. 9/14. H.&J.Ltd. Forms/C. 2118/10.

Army Form C. 2118.

WAR DIARY
or
INTELLIGENCE SUMMARY.
(Erase heading not required.)

Instructions regarding War Diaries and Intelligence Summaries are contained in F.S. Regs., Part II. and the Staff Manual respectively. Title pages will be prepared in manuscript.

Hour, Date, Place	Summary of Events and Information	Remarks and references to Appendices
20th June.	Brigade Group with 6th E.Yorks Regt. (Pioneers) marched to SCHAEXKEN Area. (See Bde.'Order No 51. Appendix I)	
21st "	do do do to MERRIS AREA (See ditto). Capt. G.D.G. ELTON. D.S.O. M.C. 13th Inf. Bn. trans. to take up appointment of G.S.O.2. 13th Division.	(See ditto).
22nd "	do do do to CAESTRE AREA (less 6th E.Yorks Regt. (Pioneers)	(See do)
23rd "	do do do to RENESCURE AREA	(See ditto).
24th "	do do do to HOOLLE AREA. (less 86th Field Coy. R.E).	(See ditto). Weather fine throughout
25th "	Brigade commenced training.	
26th "	Training continued.	
27th "	do do	
28th "	do do	

Capt. F.G. TURNER. M.G. General List. attd. to H.Q. 34th Inf.Bde. Signed F.G. Turner. Capt. 34th Inf.Bde.

Army Form C. 2118.

WAR DIARY
or
INTELLIGENCE SUMMARY.
(Erase heading not required.)

Instructions regarding War Diaries and Intelligence Summaries are contained in F.S. Regs., Part II. and the Staff Manual respectively. Title pages will be prepared in manuscript.

Hour, Date, Place	Summary of Events and Information	Remarks and references to Appendices
29th June	Training continued	
30th "	Training continued hot day	
	Jas Turner Capt	
	R/A Major	

APPENDIX 1 for

JUNE 1917
=*=*=*=*=

Headquarters, 34th Infantry Brigade.
=*=*=*=*=*=*=*=*=*=*=*=*=*=*=*=*=

S E C R E T .   Copy No...4....

34th INFANTRY BRIGADE ORDER No.46.

Reference map - Sheets 27 & 28.- 1/40,000.   June 6th. 1917.

1. The 34th Infantry Brigade (less detached troops) will march on "Y"/"Z" night to LA CLYTTE Area (Squares M.12 & 18) in accordance with attached March Table.

2. 1st Line Transport will accompany Units. (Including Cookers).

3. Completion of move to be reported to B.H.Q. at once.

4. Units will send an N.C.O. to B.H.Q. at 9 p.m. daily until move has been carried out to synchronise watches.

5. Brigade Headquarters will close at R.16.d.6.5. at 11-30 p.m. and re-open at LA CLYTTE at the same hour.

6. When the Brigade moves from LA CLYTTE Area the Officers and men left behind by Battalions will move to DE ZON CAMP without further orders.

7. ACKNOWLEDGE.

ISSUED AT 10 A. M.

G. T. G. Elton
Captain,
Brigade Major, 34th Infantry Brigade.

Copy No. 1. Office.   Copy No. 10. 11th Manchesters.
         2.   -do-   11. 34th M. G. Coy.
         3. Staff Captain.   12. 34th L. T. M. B.
         4. War Diary.   13. 86th Field Co. R.E.
         5.   -do-   14. 34th Field Ambulance.
         6. D/o. Signals.   15. 32nd Brigade.
         7. 8th North. Fus.   16. 33rd Brigade.
         8. 9th Lancs. Fus.   17. No.4.Coy.Div.Train.
         9. 5th Dorset Rgt.   18. Area Commandant.
              Copy No. 19. 11th. Division.

March Table issued in conjunction with 34th Brigade Order No.46.

UNIT.	STARTING POINT.	TIME FOR PASSING STARTING POINT.	ROUTE.	DESTINATION.
Brigade Headquarters.	Brigade Headquarters.	12 Midnight.	M & Z tracks to junction LA CLYTTE with main road at M.23.a.0.8. - HYDE PARK CORNER - LA CLYTTE.	
9th Lancs. Fus.	Junction of tracks at M.19.b.2.8.	12-35 a.m.	-do-	Bivouacs in M.12.d.
8th North. Fus.	Brigade Headquarters.	12-10 a.m.	-do-	-do-
5th Dorset Rgt.	-do-	12-25 a.m.	-do-	DE ZON CAMP.
34th L.T.M.B.		To follow the 5th Dorset Regiment.		
86th Field Co. R.E.	Junction of tracks at M.19.b.2.8.	1-15 a.m.	-do-	Camp in M.12.d.

THE USUAL, HOURLY HALTS WILL BE OBSERVED.

SECRET   Copy No. 2

54th INFANTRY BRIGADE ORDER NO. 47.

Reference maps – TRACK MAP.   June 8th. 1917.
Sheet 28.S.W.– 1/20,000.

1. The 54th. Infantry Brigade will relieve the 109th Infantry Brigade tomorrow.

2. The Brigade will march as follows :–

UNIT.	STARTING POINT.	ROUTE.	REMARKS.
8th N.F.	N.F. Camp.	"Z" TRACK – LA CLYTTE–KEMMEL Road – KEMMEL – LINDENHOEK.	To clear S.P. by 6–15 a.m.
9th L.F.	–do–	–do–	Clear S.P. 6–30 a.m.
L.T.M.B.	–do–	–do–	Clear S.P. 7 a.m.
M.G.Coy.	–do–	–do–	Clear S.P. 7–5 a.m.
5th Dor.	Junction of LOCRE–LA CLYTTE Road with "Y" TRACK.	"Y" TRACK – Junction with LA CLYTTE–KEMMEL Road – KEMMEL – LINDENHOEK.	Head to pass S.P. at 6–45 a.m.
86th R.E.	WILL MOVE UNDER ORDERS OF C.R.E.		

B.H.Q. *Will not move.*

3. Cookers, water carts and Lewis Gun Limbers only will accompany units; the remainder will stay in the present position pending further orders.

4. One mounted Officer per Unit will meet the Brigade Major at LINDENHOEK Cross Roads at 6–45 a.m. tomorrow.

5. ACKNOWLEDGE.

ISSUED AT 12 Midnight.

                                                                Captain,
                                        Brigade Major, 54th. Infty. Brigade.

Copy No. 1. Office.   Copy No. 5. 5th Dorset Rgt.
        2. War Diary. ✓   6. 54th M.G. Coy.
        3. 8th North. Fus.   7. 54th L.T.M.B.
        4. 9th Lancs. Fus.   8. 86th R.E.
                    Copy No. 9. 11th Division.

SECRET.   Copy No....4......

34th INFANTRY BRIGADE ORDER No. 48.

Reference maps - TRENCH MAP, Sheet 28.S.W.   June 9th. 1917.
                 Scale 1/20,000.

1. 34th Infantry Brigade will relieve 48th Infantry Brigade in Support on the night 9th/10th.

2. 5th Dorset Regt. will relieve 8th and 9th Royal Dublin Fus. in the MAUVE LINE - H.Q. at TORREKEN FARM.

   8th North. Fus. will relieve 2nd Royal Dublin Fus. and 7th Royal Irish Rifles in the BLACK & BLUE LINES. - H.Q. at N.19.d.5.9.

   9th Lancs. Fus. will move into dug-outs in CHINESE WALL in N.23.b. and will be in Reserve.

   34th Machine Gun Company will relieve 48th Machine Gun Compy. taking over their present dispositions and barrage lines.

   34th L. T. M. B. will move into CHINESE WALL.

3. The 5th Dorset Regt. will move at 6-30 p.m.
   The 8th North. Fus. and 9th Lancs. Fus. will move at 7-30 p.m.

4. Details of relief will be arranged between C.O's. concerned.

5. Movement West of YORK ROAD will be by platoons at 200 yards interval.

6. Guides for all Battalions will be sent to Brigade Headquarters at N.23.b.5.2. (Strong Point 12.)

7. All units will render sketch maps showing their exact dispositions by Noon on the 10th inst.

8. 11th Manchester Regt. will move into Reserve in the RED LINE tomorrow evening. Reconnoitring parties should report to Brigade Headquarters by 10 a.m. tomorrow.

9. Completion of relief will be reported to Brigade Headquarters in the usual way.

10. Brigade Headquarters will open at Strong Point 12 at 8-30 p.m. tonight.

11. ACKNOWLEDGE.

ISSUED AT 4.30 p.m.   G.D.G. Elton   Captain,
                                       Brigade Major, 34th. Infantry Brigade.

Copy No. 1. Office.   Copy No. 10. 11th Manchesters.
         2. -do-   11. 34th M. G. Coy.
         3. Staff Captain.   12. 34th L. T. M. B.
         4. War Diary.   13. 86th Field Co. R.E.
         5. -do-   14. No.4.Coy.Div.Train.
         6. Bde. Signals.   15. 32nd Brigade.
         7. 8th North. Fus.   16. 33rd Brigade.
         8. 9th Lancs. Fus.   17. 48th Brigade.
         9. 5th Dorset Rgt.   18. 11th Division.

SECRET.

Copy No. 4

34th INFANTRY BRIGADE ORDER No.49.

Reference map - Trench map, WYTSCHAETE,
Sheet 28.S.W.2 - 1/10,000.   June 10th 1917.

1. The 34th Infantry Brigade will relieve the 33rd Infantry Brigade in the Front Line and the 32nd Infantry Brigade in portions of MAUVE LINE on the night 10th/11th in the following Area.

2. Boundaries.

   On the South - O.28.b.3.2. - Building at O.28.a.6.2. (Exclusive) - Road Junction at O.26.b.95.20. - North edge of PETITS PUITS - O.26.2.3. exclusive - N.30.b.8.5. on RED LINE.

   On the North - Junction of Road and track O.22.c.8.9. - MATHIEU FARM exclusive - Junction of Road and train O.21.c.8.9. - O.20.a.4.2. - S. corner of HOSPICE O.19.a.7.7. - N.24.b.9.7.

3. Dispositions. The 32nd Brigade hold the OOSTTAVERNE LINE on our Right and the 56th Brigade on our Left.

4. (a) The 8th North. Fus. will relieve the 6th Lincoln Regt. and 9th Sherwood Foresters in the Front Line - with H.Q. at O.27.a.3.6.

   (b) They will not move East of MAUVE LINE before 9 p.m.

   (c) I. The 5th Dorset Regt. will relieve the 8th Duke of Wellington Regt. in the MAUVE LINE as far as O.27.b.1.2.
   II The 5th Dorset Regt. will hand over portion of MAUVE LINE N. of 21.c.30.95. to the 8th S. Lancs. Regt. of 56th Brigade.

   (d) 9th Lancs. Fus. will relieve 8th North. Fus., 6th Yorks. Regt. and 9th W. Yorks. Regt. in the BLACK & BLUE LINES with H.Q. at O.19.d.5.9.

   (e) 11th Manchester Regt. will be in Reserve in CHINESE WALL.

   (f) I The 34th M. G. Coy. will relieve 33rd M. G. Coy. with two sections forward and two sections behind MAUVE LINE.
   II The 33rd M. G. Coy. will select positions for two sections behind the BLACK LINE and be attached to 34th Infantry Brigade.

   (g) The 34th L. T. M. B. will relieve 33rd L. T. M. B.

5. The details of relief will be arranged between C.O's. concerned.

6. Receipts for all trench stores, etc., taken over will be forwarded to Brigade Headquarters by 8 p.m. 11th.

7. The 8th North. Fus. will forward a sketch map to Brigade Headquarters by 9 a.m. 12th. showing their exact distribution.

8. Completion of relief will be reported by Code Word ARMAGH.

9. Brigade Headquarters will be at S.P.12. O.23.b.5.2.

10. ACKNOWLEDGE.

ISSUED AT 3 p.m.

Captain,
Brigade Major, 34th. Infty. Brigade.

Copy No. 1. Office.	Copy No. 8. 9th L.Fus.	Copy No. 15. 32nd Brigade.
2. -do-	9. 5th Dorsets.	16. 33rd Brigade.
3. Staff Capt.	10. 11th Man' R.	17. 56th Brigade.
4. War Diary.	11. 34th M.G.Coy.	18. 59th F.A.B.
5. -do-	12. 34th L.T.M.B.	19. 35th Fd. Amb.
6. Bde. Sigs.	13. 86th R.E.	20. 11th Division.
7. 8th N.Fus.	14. No.4.Coy.Train.	21.

SECRET.

Copy No. 4

34th INFANTRY BRIGADE ORDER No. 50.

Reference map – Sheet 28.S.W.
Scale 1/20,000.

June 16th. 1917.

1. The 11th Manchester Regiment will relieve the 8th. Northumberland Fusiliers in the Front System on the night 18th/19th.

2. On relief the 8th. Northumberland Fusiliers will move into shelters behind the CHINESE WALL in N.23.d.

3. The 9th. Lancashire Fusiliers will relieve the 5th. Dorset Regiment in the MAUVE LINE on the night 19th/20th.

4. On relief the 5th Dorset Regiment will move to the BLACK LINE.

5. All details of relief to be arranged between C.O's concerned.

6. All maps and photographs of the area and trench stores to be handed over to the relieving unit.

7. The 11th Manchester Regiment will send one Officer per Company in the Front Line and one N.C.O. per post into the line on night 17th/18th.

8. Completion of relief to be reported by Code Word "CHUNKS".

9. ACKNOWLEDGE.

ISSUED AT 12 noon.

Captain,
Brigade Major, 34th. Infty. Brigade.

Copy No. 1. Office.
2. -do-
3. Staff Captain.
4. War Diary.
5. -do-
6. 8th North. Fus.
7. 9th Lancs. Fus.
8. 5th Dorset Rgt.
9. 11th Manchesters.

Copy No. 10. 34th M. G. Coy.
11. 34th L. T. M. B.
12. 58th F. A. B.
13. 11th Division.
14. No.4.Coy.Div.Train.
15. 32nd Brigade.
16. 33rd Brigade.
17. 57th Brigade.
18. 86th Field Co. R.E..

S E C R E T. Copy No. 4

34th INFANTRY BRIGADE ORDER No.51.

Reference maps - Sheets 27 & 28. - 1/40,000.
HAZEBROUCK. 5a. - 1/100,000.   June 19th. 1917.

1. The 11th Division (less Artillery) is being withdrawn from the line and concentrated in the MERRIS AREA prior to moving by road to join the 5th Army in TILQUES North Training Area.

2. The 107th Brigade (36th Division) will relieve the 32nd and 34th Brigades on the 19th and night of 19/20th.

3. The relief will be carried out in accordance with attached table.

4. All details of relief will be arranged between C.O's concerned.

5. All trench stores, photos, trench maps of this area, defence schemes, etc., will be handed over and receipts forwarded to this Office by noon on 20th.

6. No troops will cross the MESSINES-WYTSCHAETE Ridge before 10 p.m.

7. Completion of relief will be reported to B.H.Q. by the Code Word "OPPIT".

8. On the 20th the 34th Brigade Group will move in the evening to No. 16 Area round SCHAEKXEN.

9. On the 21st the 34th Brigade Group and 6th E. Yorks Pioneers will move in the early morning to MERRIS Area.
March tables for these moves will be issued later.

10. ACKNOWLEDGE.

Issued at 8 A.M.

C. K. G. Elton Captain,
Brigade Major, 34th. Infy. Brigade.

Copy No. 1. Office.   Copy No. 7. 9th Lancs. Fus.   Copy No.13. 11th Div.
         2. -do-   8. 5th Dorset Rgt.   14. No.4.Coy.
         3. Staff Captain.   9. 11th Manchesters.   15. 32nd Bde.
         4. War Diary.   10. 34th M. G. Coy.   16. 35th F.A.
         5. -do-   11. 34th L. T. M. B.   17. 107th Bde.
         6. 8th North. Fus.   12. 58th F.A.B.   18. 86th R.E.

RELIEF TABLE issued in conjunction with Brigade Order No. 51.

DATE.	UNIT.	RELIEVING UNIT.	FROM.	TO.	ROUTE.	REMARKS.
19/20th.	11th Manchester Rgt.	-	CHINESE WALL.	Bivouacs in M.35.a.	KEMMEL - N.19.c. - M.30.b.2.7. - Track to M.29. Central.	To clear Camp at 5-30 p.m.
--do--	9th Lancs. Fus.	-	BLACK and BLUE LINES.	--do--	--do--	Not to move before 10 p.m.
--do--	8th North. Fus.	9th Royal I. Rifles.	FRONT LINE.	WAKEFIELD HUTS N.29.c.8.8.	--do--	
--do--	34th M. G. Coy.	107th M. G. Coy.	The LINE.	Camp opposite WAKEFIELD HUTS.	--do--	
--do--	5th Dorset Rgt.	10th. Royal I. R.	MAUVE LINE.	DRANOUTRE.	LINDEHOEK.	
--do--	34th L. T. M. B.	-	CHINESE WALL.	--do--	--do--	To clear Camp at 5 p.m.
--do--	86th Field Co. R.E..	-	N.17.c.1.1.	LURGAN HUTS N.5.b.5.0.	--do--	To move at 6 p.m.
--do--	Brigade Headquarters.	-	S.P.12.	DRANOUTRE.	--do--	

1. The following intervals will be maintained :-
    200 yds. between Battalions.
    200 yds. between transport of units and other troops.
    100 yds. between Companies.

2. The Staff Captain will point out each Unit's Camp.

3. Units should reconnoitre the roads and tracks.

MARCH TABLE for 20th. in continuation of Brigade Order No. 51.

UNIT.	STARTING POINT.	TIME HEAD OF UNIT TO PASS STARTING PT.	HEAD OF DESTINATION.	ROUTE TO STARTING POINT.	ROUTE FROM STARTING POINT.
Brigade Headquarters.	Road junction at R.34.c.2.5.	4-15 p.m.	R.35.c.5.8.	Via KOUDEKOT.	Road through R.35.c. & a. - CROIX DE PEPERINGHE - Road through M.32 central - ST. JANS CAPPEL - SCHAEXKEN.
11th Manchester Regt.	-do-	4-20 p.m.	R.35.a.5.4.	Via Track through M.34.b.	-do-
9th Lancs. Fus.	-do-	4-35 p.m.	R.28.d.3.8.	-do-	-do-
8th North. Fus.	-do-	4-50 p.m.	R.35.a.8.0.	Via Track through M.35.a. and M.34.b.	-do-
5th Dorset Regt.	-do-	5-5/15 p.m.	R.28.b.8.4.	Via KOUDEKOT.	-do-
34th M.G. Coy.	-do-	5-30 p.m.	R.29.c.0.7.	-do-	-do-
34th L.T.M.B.	-do-	5-45 p.m.	R.29.c.0.7.	-do-	-do-
86th Field Co. R.E.	-do-	5-32 p.m.	R.29.c.0.5.	Via DRANOUTRE and KOUDEKOT.	-do-

6th E. Yorks. Regt. (Pioneers) will march independently, leaving their Camp at 4 p.m.
ROUTE :- KEMMEL - DRANOUTRE - CROIX DE POPERINGHE - Road through M.32 central - ST. JANS CAPPEL - SCHAEXKEN.

1. Advanced parties will meet the Staff Captain at SCHAEXKEN X ROADS (R.35.c.O.4.) at 10 a.m. tomorrow 20th. inst.
2. Intervals will be the same as ordered for the 19th inst.
3. First Line Transport will march with Units.
4. Completion of move to be reported as usual.
5. ACKNOWLEDGE.

C.L.Chu.
Captain,
Brigade Major, 34th Infantry Brigade.

MARCH TABLE for 21st. in continuation of Brigade Order No. 51.

UNIT.	STARTING POINT.	TIME HEAD OF UNIT TO PASS STARTING PT.	DESTINATION.	ROUTE.	REMARKS.
Brigade Headquarters.	Cross Roads, SCHAEXKEN. (R.35.a.0.4.)	7 a.m.	MERRIS.	Road through R.34.d. - LES 4 FILS AYMON - METEREN.	
8th North. Fus.	-do-	7-5 a.m.	No. 1 Camp, MERRIS AREA.	-do-	Camp areas as shown to your representative by Staff Capt. on morning of 20th.
11th Manchester Regt.	-do-	7-20 a.m.	No. 2 Camp, MERRIS AREA.	-do-	-do-
9th Lancs. Fus.	-do-	7-35 a.m.	No. 3 Camp, MERRIS AREA.	-do-	-do-
5th Dorset Rgt.	-do-	8 a.m.	No. 4 Camp, MERRIS AREA.	-do-	-do-
6th E. Yorks. Regt.	-do-	8-15 a.m.	MERRIS AREA.	-do-	-do-
34th M.G. Coy.	-do-	8-30 a.m.	MERRIS.	-do-	
34th L.T.M.B.	-do-	8-40 a.m.	MERRIS.	-do-	
86th Field Co. R.E.	-do-	9 a.m.	W.28.b.1.2.	-do-	-do-

No.4.Coy.Div.l.Train. will march independently to E.3.b.5.5., but should clear their Camp by 9 a.m. 21st. inst.
ROUTE :- LES 4 FILS AYMON - METEREN - STRAZELE.

1. Intervals on the march - as on 19th and 20th inst.
2. First Line Transport will march with Units.
3. Completion of move will be reported as usual.

ACKNOWLEDGE.

H. G. Gillen Captain,
Brigade Major, 34th. Infantry Brigade.

MARCH TABLE for 22nd. inst. in continuation of Brigade Order No. 51.

UNIT.	STARTING POINT.	TIME HEAD OF UNIT TO PASS STARTING PT.	DESTINATION.	ROUTE.	REMARKS.
9th Lancs. Fus.	Cross Roads at W.24.b.8.5.	6-30 a.m.	CAESTRE AREA. ("A" Sub area)	Road through W.17.d. and c. - Road junctions at W.13.d.0.3.	
11th Manchesters.	-do-	6-45 a.m.	-do-	-do-	
8th North. Fus.	-do-	7-10 a.m.	-do-	-do-	Route to starting point via Road through X.14.c. - Road junction at X.13.b.0.1. - MOOLENACKER.
5th Dorset Rgt.	Cross Roads at X.10.c.1.9.	6-35 a.m.	-do-	STRAZEELE - PRADELLES - BORRE.	
Brigade Headquarters.	Road Junction at STRAZEELE (W.29.a.6.5.)	7 a.m.	-do-	-do-	Route to starting point via Road through W.30.c. - W.29.●.Central. To join in behind 5th. Dorsets at STRAZEELE.
34th M. G. Coy.	-do-	7-5 a.m.	-do-	-do-	
34th L. T. M. B.	-do-	7-15 a.m.	-do-	-do-	
86th Field Co. R.E.	-do-	7-18 a.m.	-do-	-do-	
34th Field Ambulance.	To march independently via PRADELLES. To be clear of PRADELLES by 8-15 a.m.				
No.4.Coy.Divsl.Train.	-do-	-do-	-do-	-do-	7-45 a.m.

1. The STRAZEELE-ROUGE CROIX ROAD is not to be crossed until 7-5 a.m.
2. The 6th E. Yorks. Regt. (Pioneers) will be attached to 33rd Infantry Brigade from 22nd inst. inclusive.
3. Representatives to meet their respective Units under arrangements made by Staff Captain.
4. Intervals to be as previously ordered.
5. First Line Transport will accompany Units.
6. Completion of move to be reported to B.H.Q. in the usual way.
7. Brigade Headquarters will close at MERRIS at 6 a.m. 22nd and re-open at BORRE at 9-30 a.m. 22nd.

Duplicate

MARCH TABLE for 23rd inst. in continuation of Brigade Order No. 51.

UNIT.	STARTING POINT.	TIME HEAD OF UNIT TO PASS STARTING PT.	DESTINATION.	ROUTE.	REMARKS.
8th North. Fus.	Cross Roads at V.22.b.0.2.	4-45 a.m.	REMESCURE AREA ("Y" Area)	HAZEBROUCK STATION - VALLO" - CAPPEL - LYNDE - WARDRECQUES STATION.	
9th Lancs. Fus.	- do -	5-5 a.m.	- do -	- do -	Route to starting point via LA KREULE V.15.b.7.4.)
11th Manchesters.	- do -	5-20 a.m.	- do -	- do -	
34th L.T.M.B.	- do -	5-35 a.m.	- do -	- do -	
Brigade Headquarters.	Junction of HAZEBROUCK - LA KREULE and HAZEBROUCK - BORRE Roads in HAZEBROUCK (V.28.a.6.9.)	5-48 a.m.	- do -	- do -	
5th Dorset Rgt.	- do -	6-5 a.m.	- do -	- do -	
34th M.G. Coy.	To join in behind 5th Dorset Rgt. as latter pass 34th M.G.Coy's Camp on Road through V.23.C.				
34th Field Ambulance.	Will march in rear of the column passing the starting point at Cross Roads V.22b.0.2.- 6.20 a.m				
No.4 Coy.Divl.Train.	Will march independently by same route, but will not clear their camp until 5 a.m.				
86th Field Co. R.E.	Will move under orders of the C.R.E. 11th. Division.				

1. Representatives to meet their respective Units under arrangements made by Staff Captain.
2. Intervals to be as previously ordered.
3. First Line Transport will accompany Units.
4. Completion of move to be reported to B.H.Q. in the usual way.
5. Units (less L.T.M.B.) will be preceded by 1 mounted officer at sufficient distance to give warning traffic control posts of the approach of a column(To be detailed by Units concerned).

Acknowledge.

J.J. Lloyd Lieut
Brigade Major 34th Infty Brigade.

MARCH TABLE for 24th. inst. in continuation of Brigade Order No. 51.

UNIT.	STARTING POINT.	TIME HEAD OF UNIT TO PASS STARTING PT.	DESTINATION.	ROUTE.	REMARKS.
Brigade Headquarters.	Junction of ARQUES-RACQUING-HEM Road and tracks immediately south of the P in CAMPAGNE.	5-45 a.m.	HOULLE AREA.	BLEUDEQUES - Road junction immediately North of the O in WESTOVE - Cross Roads ¾ mile South of ST. OMER - ST. MARTIN - TILQUES - MOULLE.	
11th Manchester Rgt.	-do-	6 a.m.	-do-	-do-	
5th Dorset Regt.	-do-	6-15 a.m.	-do-	-do-	
8th North. Fus.	-do-	6-30 a.m.	-do-	-do-	
9th Lancs. Fus.	-do-	6-45 a.m.	-do-	-do-	
34th M. G. Coy.	-do-	7-10 a.m.	-do-	-do-	
34th T. M. B.	-do-	7-20 a.m.	-do-	-do-	
34th Field Ambulance.	-do-	7-27 a.m.	-do-	-do-	
No.4.Coy.Divsl.Train.	-do-	7-45 a.m.	-do-	-do-	

1. Representatives to meet their respective units at MOULLE under arrangements made by Staff Captain.
2. Intervals to be as previously ordered.
3. First Line Transport will accompany units.
4. Completion of relief to be reported to B.H.Q. in the usual way.
5. Brigade Headquarters will close at CAMPAGNE at 5 a.m. and re-open at EPERLEQUES at 12 noon.
6. ACKNOWLEDGE.

F. J. W. Gaith
Lieut.
A/Brigade Major, 34th. Infantry Brigade.

APPENDIX 11 for

JUNE 1917.

Headquarters, 34th. Infantry Brigade.

APPENDIX 11

June 1917.

Strength of Units from 1st. to 7th.

Unit	Officers	Other Ranks	Casualties Officers K.	W.	M.	Other Ranks K.	W.	M.
8th. North.Fus.	37.	925.	-	-	-	-	-	-
9th. Lancs.Fus.	43.	926.	-	-	-	-	*10.	-
5th. DorsetReg.	43.	951.	-	-	-	-	2.	-
11th. Manch.Reg.	36.	933.	-	-	-	6.	11.	-
34th. M.G. Coy.	12.	176.	-	-	-	-	4.	-

Strength of Units from 8th. to 14th.

Unit	Officers	Other Ranks	K.	W.	M.	K.	W.	M.
8th. North.Fus.	31.	845.	1.	5.	-	16	60.	1.
9th. Lancs.Fus.	43.	928.	-	-	-	2.	5.	-
5th. DorsetReg.	42.	882.	-	2.	-	14.	25.	1.
11th. Manch.Reg.	36.	926.	-	-	-	3.	2.	-
34th. M.G. Coy.	12.	163.	-	-	-	4.	10.	-

Strength of Units from 15th. to 21st.

Unit	Officers	Other Ranks	K.	W.	M.	K.	W.	M.
8th. North.Fus.	29.	972.	1.	2.	-	9.	66.	-
9th. Lancs.Fus.	41.	874.	-	1.	-	2.	21.	-
5th. DorsetReg.	40.	871.	1.	1.	-	1.	7.	-
11th. Manch.Reg.	36.	931.	-	-	-	-	-	-
34th. M.G. Coy.	12.	179.	-	-	-	-	-	-

Strength of Units from 22nd. to 30th.

Unit	Officers	Other Ranks	K.	W.	M.	K.	W.	M.
8th. North.Fus.	30.	902.	-	-	-	-	-	-
9th. Lancs.Fus.	39.	931.	-	-	-	-	-	-
5th. DorsetReg.	39.	860.	-	-	-	-	-	-
11th. Manch.Reg.	35.	947.	-	-	-	-	-	-
34th. M.G. Coy.	12.	187.	-	-	-	-	-	-

* Accidentally. Grenade explosion.

Reinforcements.

Unit	From 1st. to 7th. O.	O.R.	From 8th. to 14th. O.	O.R.	From 15th. to 21st. O.	O.R.	From 22nd. to 30th. O.	O.R.
8th.North.Fus.	2.	7.	-	-	2.	-	1.	140.
9th.Lancs.Fus.	6.	-	-	6.	-	-	-	6.
5th.Dorset.R.	-	7.	1.	6.	-	-	-	2.
11th.Manch.R.	-	-	-	-	-	4.	-	49.

APPENDIX 111 for

JUNE 1917.

Headquarters, 34th Infantry Brigade.

War Diary

34th INFANTRY BRIGADE.

Narrative of operations - 7th - 15th June.

Prior to the operations, the Brigade (less 11th Manchester Regiment and Machine Gun Company) was billetted in the BERTHEN Area.

The 11th Manchester Regt., encamped near LOCRE, were employed, under orders of the IX Corps, in digging and placing the cable line towards WYTSCHAETE.

The 34th Machine Gun Company, under orders of the 19th. Division, were employed in making emplacements for their guns between VIERSTRAAT and BRYKERIE FARM from which position they were to join in the creeping barrage of the Artillery covering the front of the 19th. Division.

On the night of the 6/7th June the Brigade (less 11th. Manchester Regt. and M. G. Coy.) moved to LA CLYTTE.

7th. June. The Brigade (less 11th Manchester Regt. and M. G. Coy.) remained at LA CLYTTE.

The 11th Manchester Regt. at ZERO plus 4 hrs. (7-10 a.m.) moved from their Camp near LOCRE to BOARDMAN Trench which was reached at 8-45 a.m. The Battalion was extended along the projected cable line from about N.30.a.3.8. to SCOTT FARM - dug a trench - 6' deep laid the cable and filled in, returning to Camp at 3 p.m.

The 34th Machine Gun Coy. opened fire at ZERO - 10 Guns joining the creeping barrage, 6 Guns searching special points beyond the first and second objectives. Soon after the Infantry had reached the BLUE LINE, their role being at an end, they received their orders to rejoin the Brigade. They reported arrival about 1 p.m.

8th. June. The Brigade (less 11th Manchester Regt.) remained at LA CLYTTE.

The 11th Manchester Regt. completed laying of cable from SCOTT FARM to O.26.a.2.8. and returned to Camp at LOCRE.

9th. June. The Brigade (less 11th Manchester Regt.) moved to VROILANDHOEK in relief of the 109th. Brigade. Relief was complete by 9 a.m.

On the night of the 9/10th. the 8th Northumberland Fusiliers and 5th Dorset Regiment relieved two Battalions of the 48th. Brigade, in the MAUVE LINE. Relief complete at 1-30 a.m. on the 10th.

10th June. The 11th Manchester Regt. rejoined the Brigade.

On the night of the 10/11th. two Battalions and the Machine Gun Company took over the Northern portion of the OOSTTAVERNE LINE held by the 33rd Brigade, the other two Battalions moving to the BLACK and BLUE LINES in Support. Relief was complete by 2 a.m.

11th June. The 56th Brigade, on our Left, advanced their line East of VAN HOVE FARM: the 8th Northumberland Fusiliers conformed by moving their Posts to the Line just E. of JOYE FARM - O.28.b.7.3.

12th June. Portions of the line were taken over from the 32nd Brigade and other portions handed over to the 56th Brigade (19th. Division) in order to adjust the boundaries as laid down in Divisional Orders.

13th June. At 10 p.m. a conference was held at the 32nd. Brigade H.Q. to arrange for an operation to be carried out on the day following.

14th June. Four Platoons of the 8th Northumberland Fusiliers took part in the demonstration carried out at 7-30 p.m. on our Divisional Front in conjunction with operations North and South. Advance was made under Artillery barrage at the hour assigned; the objective was reached without opposition and the platoons were withdrawn to our lines by 10-30 p.m. Casualties during the operation - one Officer and eight other ranks wounded.

15th June. No special incident.

From 10th to 15th the enemy has made no sign of aggressive action, but his Artillery has been very active during the period especially upon our Front and Support Lines.

Casualties during the period reported upon :-

	KILLED.	WOUNDED.	MISSING.
Officers,	1.	8.	-
Other Ranks.	39.	154.	2.

June 18th. 1917.

Brigadier General,
Commanding 34th. Infantry Brigade.

SECRET.   Copy No. 3

PROVISIONAL DEFENCE SCHEME.

Reference map - WYTSCHAETE - 28.S.W.2.
            Scale 1/10,000.   June 12th 1917.

1.   The Brigade Front is 900 yards.

   BOUNDARIES.

   Northern.

      Junction of road and track O.22.c.8.9. - MATHIEU FARM
      exclusive - Junction of road and train O.21.c.85.90. -
      O.20.a.45.25. - South corner of HOSPICE O.19.a.7.7. -
      N.24.b.9. - 7. on RED LINE.

   Southern.

      O.28.b.3.2. - Building at O.28.a.6.2. exclusive - Road
      junction at O.26.b.9.2. - North edge of PETITS PUETS -
      O.26.a.25.35. exclusive - N.30.b.8.5. on RED LINE.

2.   System of defence.

   (a) The Front System consisting of a line of posts with Support
       Line and Strong Posts.

   (b) The Reserve Line. (MAUVE LINE).

   (c) The Second Line of Defence. (BLACK LINE).

3.   Dispositions.

   (a) The Front System is held by one Battalion and seven
       Vickers' Guns.

   (b) The Reserve Line is held by one Battalion and seven
       Vickers' Guns.

   (c) The Second Line of Defence is held by one Battalion and
       eight Vickers' Guns of 33rd M. G. Coy.

   (d) The fourth Battalion remaining in Brigade Reserve in the
       CHINESE WALL.

4.   Action in case of attack.

   (a) In the event of an attack by the enemy, the Front System
       is to be held.

   (b) The O.C. of the Supporting Battalion in the Reserve Line
       will at once get into communication with the O.C. of the
       Front System and be ready to counter attack at once on his
       own iniative, should the enemy gain a footing at any point.

   (c) The Second Line of Defence is to be highly organised for
       defence and the garrison will not be moved.

   (d) The Battalion in Brigade Reserve will at once form up ready
       to move and the C.O. will report to Brigade Headquarters.

5. Artillery.

The Brigade Front is covered by two Brigades of Field Artillery - the 58th. and 175th. Brigades.

6. Brigade Headquarters will move to Forward Report Centre in SCOTT FARM O.25.a.4.7.

7. ACKNOWLEDGE.

G.F.G. Elton Captain,

Brigade Major, 34th. Infantry Brigade.

DISTRIBUTION :-

    Copy No. 1. Office.
            2. -do-
            3. War Diary.
            4. -do-
            5. 8th North. Fus.
            6. 9th Lancs. Fus.
            7. 5th Dorset Rgt.
            8. 11th Manchesters.
            9. 34th M. G. Coy.
          10. 34th L. T. M. B.
          11. 11th Division.
          12. 32nd Brigade.
          13. 58th F. A. B.
          14. 175th F. A. B.

July 1917.

WAR DIARY.

34th Infantry Brigade.
H.Q.
8th North'd Fusiliers.
9th Lancs. Fusiliers.
5th Dorset Regt.
11th Manchester Regt.
34th M.G. Coy.

WAR DIARY
of
INTELLIGENCE SUMMARY.

Army Form C. 2118.

68th Infy Brigade
34 (Infy Brigade)

Hour, Date, Place	Summary of Events and Information	Remarks and references to Appendices
EPERLECQUES July 1st	Sunday. 8th NORTHUMBERLAND FUSILIERS firing on range. 9th LANC. FUS. moved to MENTQUE. 11th MANCHESTER REGT. to NORTBECOURT and 34th L.T.M.B. to WINDSKI. These moves were made to bring the units nearer the training area.	
" 2nd	Training continued	
" 3rd	Training continued. During the afternoon and evening a Brigade Tactical Exercise was carried out, the Brigade practising passing through known objectives already gained and attacking a further.	
4th	Before dawn the Brigade practised a Night Scheme, this idea being the same as for the Tactical Exercise the previous day, but the advance	

WAR DIARY
INTELLIGENCE SUMMARY.
(Erase heading not required.)

Army Form C. 2118.

of 3rd Inf. Bde.

Place	Date	Hour	Summary of Events and Information	Remarks and references to Appendices
EPERLECQUES	5th		was made in a different direction. Training continued.	
"	6th		1/A MANCHESTER Regt carried out a scheme in conjunction with the Manchester Regt Bn. Owing to them being used for other purposes 5th DORSET Regt main HQ and 2 Coys to NORTBECOURT, the other 2 Coys and Transport to BARLINGHEM, CUSHINGHEM, and CULEM.	
"	7th		Training continued in the morning Bde. Horse Shows held in the afternoon. Fine and hot day.	
"	8th		Sunday. Church Parades & holiday.	
"	9th		Training continued. G.O.C. lectured to the Officers of the Bde.	
"	10th		Training continued	
"	11th		Training continued. Brigade Day: a scheme of attacking two objectives with 2 Bns. Capturing first objective and the other two Bns. passing through and capturing the second was practised.	
"	12th		Training continued. G.O.C. gave to a lecture on "Role of	

Army Form C. 2118.

WAR DIARY
or
INTELLIGENCE SUMMARY.
(Erase heading not required.)

Instructions regarding War Diaries and Intelligence Summaries are contained in F. S. Regs., Part II. and the Staff Manual respectively. Title pages will be prepared in manuscript.

Place	Date	Hour	Summary of Events and Information	Remarks and references to Appendices
EPERLECQUES	13th		11th Div: in coming operations given by the XVIII Corps Commander at the Corps School	
"	14th		Training continued.	
			Training continued. 73th Bde. Day. The scheme was for the Bde. after great successes by other troops, to push forward so an advanced guard and drive the demoralised enemy out of a village, semi-open warfare then being practised. The Commander-in-Chief with his Chief of Staff visited the Bde. and watched these operations	
"	15th		Sunday. Church Parade.	
"	16th		Training continued	
"	17th		Training continued. Order received from Div. that Bde. will march to XVIII Corps area starting on 24th inst.	
"	18th		Training continued. 73th Bde. Day. The scheme being for Bdes. on "Z"+4 day to advance from objectives already captured and attack the next line of	

WAR DIARY
or
INTELLIGENCE SUMMARY.
(Erase heading not required.)

Army Form C. 2118.

Place	Date	Hour	Summary of Events and Information	Remarks and references to Appendices
EBERLECQUES	19th 20th		Parades. The practice attack was carried out on a course laid out to represent the probable scene of future operations. Extracts from "XVIII Corps Instructions for the offensive" issued to units.	
"	20th		Training continued. Training continued. Divisional Day. 23rd Bn. 24th Bn. and 14th Bn. Madrid the scene of operations on the 18th, and 23rd Bn. passed through them to explore the ground beyond. Bn. order No. 52. On the 24th inst. was sent to units to inform the parties on completing concentration at G.H.Q. before the proposed operations.	
"	21st		Training continued. 23rd again practised the proposed attack over the laid out course.	
"	22nd		Sunday. A Brigade Parade in the morning for presentation	

Army Form C. 2118.

WAR DIARY
or
INTELLIGENCE SUMMARY.

(Erase heading not required.)

Instructions regarding War Diaries and Intelligence Summaries are contained in F. S. Regs., Part II. and the Staff Manual respectively. Title pages will be prepared in manuscript.

Place	Date	Hour	Summary of Events and Information	Remarks and references to Appendices
EPERLECQUES	23rd		of medal ribbons by G.O.C. Division, followed by Divine Service with an address by the Bishop of Khartoum. Training continued. The Brigade prepares to move.	
"	24th	4.30 a.m.	Bat. leave EPERLECQUES and marches to RUBROUCK. See appendix for march-table.	
RUBROUCK				
RUBROUCK	25th	5.15 a.m.	Bdr. leaves RUBROUCK and marches to WORMHOUDT. See appendix for march-table. Order received from 11th Div. postponing the move to ST. JANS TER BIEZEN	
WORMHOUDT			from 26th to 29th inst. Some training done, but Bde. mostly visiting G.O.C. visits the probable flanking Bdes. in coming operations for purposes of liaison.	
"	26th			
"	27th		Route march by each unit.	
"	28th		Training continued.	
"	29th	4.35 a.m.	The Bde. marches to "G" Camp ST. JANS-TER-BIEZEN. See appendix for march-table. Very heavy thunderstorm breaks as	
ST. JANS-TER-BIEZEN				

Army Form C. 2118.

WAR DIARY
or
INTELLIGENCE SUMMARY.
(Erase heading not required.)

Place	Date	Hour	Summary of Events and Information	Remarks and references to Appendices
ST JANSTER-BIEZEN	30th	9 p.m.	The last Bn. marches into the new camp. The Bde. marches to a more forward camp at A.17.d WINDMILL CAMP (sheet 28) See appendix for March Table.	
A.17.d	31st	3.50 a.m.	The attack on the Germans begins. In most places all their objectives are taken. In the late afternoon heavy rain begins & continues all day. G.O.C. reconnoitres the route up to our new front line. The Bde. is still kept in reserve and awaits further orders.	

J.S. Tarn. Capt.
Brigade Major
34th Inf. Bde.

SECRET.

Copy No. 5

34th INFANTRY BRIGADE ORDER No.52.

Reference maps - HAZEBROUCK - 1/100,000. July 19th., 1917.
      Sheet 27. - 1/40,000.

1. The 34th Infantry Brigade will march to XVIII Corps area, starting on 24th. inst.

 March Table No. 1 is attached.

 The other March Tables will be issued later.

2. Special attention is called to the following XVIII Corps March Regulations :-

 (a) All units will be preceded at sufficient distance by a mounted Officer to give warning to Traffic Control Posts of the approach of a column.

  When marching by night, in the back area, the head and tail of columns will be marked by lamps.

 (b) Times and routes when laid down will be rigidly adhered to.

  The following distances will be maintained :-

  (i) East of the RENINGHELST - POPERINGHE - PROVEN Road, 200 yards between Companies.

  (ii) West of the above Road and East of the CASSEL - WORMHOUDT Road, 500 yards between Battalions.

  (iii) West of the CASSEL - WORMHOUDT Road, no restrictions.

3. Completion of each move will be reported by Special D.R.

4. ACKNOWLEDGE.

Issued at ....

              Captain,

     Brigade Major, 34th Infantry Brigade.

Copy No. 1. Office.	Copy No. 9. 11th Manchesters.
2. -do-	10. 34th M. G. Coy.
3. Staff Captain.	11. 34th L. T. M. B.
4. War Diary.	12. 11th Division.
5. War Diary.	13. No.4.Coy.Div.Train.
6. 8th North. Fus.	14. 32nd Brigade.
7. 9th Lancs. Fus.	15. 34th Field Amb.
8. 5th Dorset Rgt.	16. 68th Field Co. R.E.

MARCH TABLE for 24th. July, 1917, issued in conjunction with O.O. 52.

UNIT.	STARTING POINT.	TIME HEAD OF UNIT TO PASS STARTING Pt.	DESTINATION.	ROUTE.	REMARKS.
Bde. Hd. Qrs.	EPERLECQUES CHURCH.	4-30 a.m.	RUBROUCK AREA.	HELLEBROUCQ - WATTEN - LEDERZEELE.	B.H.Q. will close at EPERLECQUES at 4. 0 a.m. and open at RUBROUCK at 9-30 a.m.
68th Field Co. R.E.	-do-	4-31 a.m.	-do-	-do-	
34th Field Amb.	-do-	4-36 a.m.	-do-	-do-	
8th North. Fus.	-do-	4-40 a.m.	-do-	-do-	
9th Lancs. Fus.	-do-	4-48 a.m.	-do-	-do-	
5th Dorset Rgt.	-do-	5-6 a.m.	-do-	-do-	
11th Manchesters.	-do-	5-14 a.m.	-do-	-do-	
34th L. T. M. B.	-do-	5-22 a.m.	-do-	-do-	

1. Intervals bwteen Units will be as laid down in F.S.R. Part I, Chapter 3, Section 25.
2. 1st Line Transport will accompany Units.
3. There will be the usual Regulation halts from 10 minutes before the hour till the hour.

* * * * * * * *

MARCH TABLE for 25th. July 1917, issued in continuation of Brigade Order 52.

UNIT.	STARTING POINT.	TIME HEAD OF UNIT TO PASS STARTING PT.	DESTINATION.	ROUTE.	REMARKS.
Bde. Hd. Qrs.	Cross Roads at H.4.a.3.4.	5-15 a.m.	WORMHOUDT Area.	BUSCH HOUCK.	B.H.Q. will close at RUBROUCK at 4-30 a.m. and open at WORMHOUDT at 6-30 a.m.
34th Field Amb.	- do -	5-16 a.m.	- do -	- do -	
5th Dorset Rgt.	- do -	5-21 a.m.	- do -	- do -	
9th Lancs. Fus.	- do -	5-29 a.m.	- do -	- do -	
8th. North. Fus.	- do -	5-37 a.m.	- do -	- do -	
11th Manchesters.	- do -	5-45 a.m.	- do -	- do -	
34th L.T.M.B.	- do -	6-3 a.m.	- do -	- do -	

1. No. 4 Coy. Divsl. Train will join on to the tail of the column at B.29.d.3.5. at 6-30 a.m. and march in rear of, 34th. L.T.M.B.

2. 68th. Field Coy. R.E. will join on to the tail of the column at B.30.b.6.4. at 6-45 a.m. and march in rear of No. 4 Coy. of the train.

3. Intervals between units will be as laid down in F.S.R., Part I, Chapter 3, Section 25.

4. 1st Line Transport will accompany Units.

5. There will be the usual regulation halts from 10 minutes before the hour till the hour.

6. ACKNOWLEDGE.

Captain,
Brigade Major 34th Infantry Brigade.

July 22nd., 1917.

MARCH TABLE for 29th. July, 1917, issued in continuation of Bde. Order 52.

UNIT.	STARTING POINT.	TIME HEAD OF UNIT TO PASS STARTING Pt.	DESTINATION.	ROUTE.	REMARKS.
Bde. Hd. Qrs.	Cross roads at C.12.d.9.1.	4-35 a.m.	ST. JANS-TER-BIEZEN Area.	HOUTKERQUE - WATOU.	B.H.Q. will close at WORMHOUDT at 3 a.m. and open at ST. JANS -TER-BIEZEN at 8-30 a.m.
9th. Lancs. Fus.	-do-	4-43 a.m.	-do-	-do-	
11th Manchesters.	-do-	4-57 a.m.	-do-	-do-	
68th Field Co. F.E.	-do-	5-11 a.m.	-do-	-do-	
34th L. T. M. B.	-do-	5-25 a.m.	-do-	-do-	
5th. Dorset Rgt.	-do-	5-41 a.m.	-do-	-do-	
8th. North. Fus.	-do-	5-55 a.m.	-do-	-do-	
34th Field Amb.	-do-	6-19 a.m.	-do-	-do-	
No. 4. Coy. Train.	-do-	6-29 a.m.	-do-	-do-	

1. Intervals of 500 yards between Units will be kept.
2. 1st Line Transport will accompany Units.
3. There will be the usual regulation halts from 10 minutes before the hour till the hour.
4. ACKNOWLEDGE.

July 24th., 1917.

F. Austin, Captain,
Brigade Major, 34th. Infantry Brigade.

MARCH TABLE for 30th. July, 1917, issued in continuation of Bde. Order 52.

UNIT.	STARTING POINT.	TIME HEAD OF UNIT TO PASS STARTING Pt.	DESTINATION.	ROUTE.	REMARKS.
Bde. Hd. Qrs.	F.27.c.9.6. 2/	9 p.m.	"D" Bde. Group Area. ELVERDINGHE.	VOGELTJE - Switch road N. of POPERINGHE - POPERINGHE- ELVERDINGHE Road.	B.H.Q. will close at ST. JANS TER BIEZEN at 9 p.m. and open at ELVERDINGHE at Midnight 30th/31st.
9th Lancs. Fus.	-do-	9-8 p.m.	-do-	-do-	
11th Manchesters.	-do-	9-30 p.m.	-do-	-do-	
34th L. T. M. B.	-do-	10-2 p.m.	-do-	-do-	
5th Dorset Rgt.	-do-	10-11 p.m.	-do-	-do-	
8th North. Fus.	-do-	10-33 p.m.	-do-	-do-	
34th Field Amb.	-do-	11-5 p.m.	-do-	-do-	
No.4.Coy.Div.Train.	-do-	11-15 p.m.	-do-	-do-	

1. Intervals of 500 yards between Battns. and 200 yards between Companies will be kept.
2. 1st Line Transport will accompany Units and for purposes of intervals will count as Companies.
3. There will be the usual regulation halts from 10 minutes before the hour till the hour.
4. ACKNOWLEDGE.

H. Turner, Captain,
Brigade Major, 34th. Infantry Brigade.

July 28th., 1917.

APPENDIX 11.

Strength of Units from 1st. to 7th. July.

Unit	Officers	O. Ranks	Casualties Officers K.	W.	M.	Other Ranks K.	W.	M.
8th. North. Fusiliers.	30.	901.	=	=	=	=	=	=
9th. Lancs. Fusiliers.	39.	925.	=	=	=	=	=	=
5th. Dorset Regiment.	39.	858.	=	=	=	=	=	=
11th. Manchester Regt.	35.	946.	=	=	=	=	=	=
34th. Machine Gun Coy.	12.	187.	=	=	=	=	=	=

Strength of Units from 8th. to 14th. July.

Unit	Officers	O. Ranks	K.	W.	M.	K.	W.	M.
8th. North. Fusiliers.	34.	965.	=	=	=	=	=	=
9th. Lancs. Fusiliers.	36.	924.	=	=	=	=	=	=
5th. Dorset Regiment.	38.	925.	=	=	=	=	=	=
11th. Manchester Regt.	35.	942.	=	=	=	=	=	=
34th. Machine Gun Coy.	12.	187.	=	=	=	=	=	=

Strength of Units from 15th. to 21st. July.

Unit	Officers	O. Ranks	K.	W.	M.	K.	W.	M.
8th. North. Fusiliers.	37.	957.	=	=	=	=	=	=
9th. Lancs. Fusiliers.	36.	921.	=	=	=	=	2*	=
5th. Dorset Regiment.	38.	916.	=	=	=	=	=	=
11th. Manch. Regiment.	35.	971.	=	=	=	=	=	=
34th. Machine Gun Coy.	12.	185.	=	=	=	=	=	=

Strength of Units from 22nd. to 31st. July.

Unit	Officers	O. Ranks	K.	W.	M.	K.	W.	M.
8th. North. Fusiliers.	39.	962.	=	=	=	=	=	=
9th. Lancs. Fusiliers.	36.	914.	=	=	=	=	2*	=
5th. Dorset Regiment.	38.	914.	=	=	=	=	=	=
11th. Manchester Regt.	36.	955.	=	=	=	=	1	=
34th. Machine Gun Coy.	12.	176.	=	=	=	1	2	=

* accidentally.

REINFORCEMENTS.

UNIT	From 1st. to 7th. O.	O.R.	From 8th. to 14th. O.	O.R.	From 15th. to 21st. O.	O.R.	From 22nd to 31st. O.	O.R.
8th. North. Fusr.	4.	80.	3.	==	2.	6.	=	==
9th. Lancs. Fusr.	=	==	1.	==	1.	==	1.	4.
5th. Dorset Regt.	=	85.	1.	2.	=	10.	=	=
11th. Manchester R.	=	==	=	30.	1.	2.	2.	=
34th. M.G.Company.	=	==	=	==	=	==	1.	=

Vol 14. August '17

Confidential

War Diary

of

34th Infantry Brigade

From 1st To 31st August 1917.

August 1917

WAR DIARY
INTELLIGENCE SUMMARY. 34th Inf. Bde
(Erase heading not required.)

Army Form C. 2118.

Place	Date	Hour	Summary of Events and Information	Remarks and references to Appendices
A.17.c.d (Shst 28), Windmill Camp	1st August		The heavy rain which began on the afternoon of the previous day fell continuously until this short break about 9 p.m. The Camp rapidly became a quagmire and floated in many places. The Bde. still awaits orders, but the offensive begun the day before is hampered by the wet weather and constant condition of the ground.	
"	2nd.		Heavy rain continued till about 8 a.m., and the condition of the ground became appalling. The rain ceased for a while in the morning, but fell again in the afternoon, finally stopping about sunset. The Bde. went into a Rest March by Coys., and is still held in reserve.	
"	3rd.		Rain fell again in the night and most of the day. The condition of the ground becoming deplorable and bringing active operations to a standstill. G.O.C. holds a conference of C.O.s to discuss the number of personnel available for fighting with the actual platoons.	

WAR DIARY
or
INTELLIGENCE SUMMARY.

(Erase heading not required.)

Army Form C. 2118.

Place	Date	Hour	Summary of Events and Information	Remarks and references to Appendices
A.17.d (Sheet 28) WINDMILL CAMP	4th		Rain again in the early morning, fine between showers and 1 p.m. & then heavy showers at intervals for the rest of the day. G.O.C. and Bde. Major attend a Divisional Conference at which G.O.C. Division states that owing to the wet a change of plans is necessary. 11th Div. will relieve 51st Div. in the line on 7th/8th, but no any further attack is impossible before 15th. 32nd Bde. will hold the line first and 34th Bde. come in on the night of 13th/14th previous to attacking on 15th inst.	
	5th		Sunday. Church Parade. G.O.C. holds a Conference of C.O.s and explains the change of plans. As at present arranged 34th Bde. will only attach PHEASANT TRENCH and not ROSE TRENCH as will. Order received from Div. that Bde. will move forward as far as SIEGE CAMP (B.21.c) on 8th inst. A fine hot day, and the ground begins to dry out. The conditions are still no good for all movement.	

WAR DIARY or INTELLIGENCE SUMMARY

Army Form C. 2118.

Place	Date	Hour	Summary of Events and Information	Remarks and references to Appendices
A.17.d (Sheet 28)	6th		This day Training carried on around camp. Bde. Order No. 53 (see appendix 1) issued for move of Bn. on 8th inst. A letter	Appendix 1
HINDMUCH CAMP			of thanks from G.O.C. 51st Div. for the good work done by 34th M.G. Coy while it was attached to that Div. from the operations on July 31st, is forwarded to the Bde. from the Div. Date of attack advanced to 13th inst.	
"	7th		This day & conditions for transport & movement are greatly improved. Training carried on.	
"	8th	8 a.m.	The Bde. move three miles towards the canal to SIEGE CAMP in accordance with Order No. 53 issued on 6th inst. Very heavy rain storm for two hours in the evening.	
B.21.c SIEGE CAMP	9th		This day C.R.A. 11th Div. lectures to all officers of the Bde. on the barrage in the coming operations. The plan of attack is also explained by G.O.C. 11th Div. also says a few words. Date of attack postponed till 14th inst. Operation Order for the attack received from 11th Division. Training continued.	

WAR DIARY
INTELLIGENCE SUMMARY

(Erase heading not required.)

Place	Date	Hour	Summary of Events and Information	Remarks and references to Appendices
B.21.C (Sheet 28)	10th		Fine day and a good drying wind. Bde. Order 54 (see appendix) issued for the attack. The attack is again postponed 24 hours, the date now proposed being the original one of 15th inst. Order for relief of 32nd Bde in the line by 34th Bde on X/Y night issued from 11th Division. Training continued.	Appendix 1.
SIEGE CAMP	11th		Bde. Order No. 55 issued ordering relief of 32nd Bde. by 34th Bde. in the line (see appendix). G.O.C. holds a conference of all O.C. units to discuss the forthcoming operations. Training continued. Fine morning, but shower in the afternoon, and heavy rain began falling at 10 p.m. The attack is postponed till 16th inst. Training continued.	Appendix 1
"	12th		Fine day with a few showers in the afternoon. Training continued.	
"	13th		Fine day. G.O.C. reconnoitres approaches to front line in early morning.	

WAR DIARY or INTELLIGENCE SUMMARY

Army Form C. 2118.

Place	Date	Hour	Summary of Events and Information	Remarks and references to Appendices
B.21.C (Sheet 28) SIEGE CAMP.	14th		8th North. Fus. and 5th DORSET Regt. and 34th M.G. Coy. in the morning in accordance with Bde. Order 57, and at night move on and relieve 2 Bns. of 32nd Bde. in the Line	
"	15th		Very heavy rain from 3-4 a.m. Condition of ground bad again	
EACH FARM		8 a.m.	Bde. H.Q. open at EACH FARM and G.O.C. 34th Bde. takes over command of Line from G.O.C. 32nd Bde. 9th Loyal Fus. 11th MANCHESTER Regt. and 3/6th L.F. M.G. move up to CANAL BANK, and at night move up to positions for attack.	
		4.45 a.m.	The attack began under a heavy barrage on the whole of the Fifth Army Front. As laid down in Bde. Order 57, it had been intended that the two leading Bns. — 8th NORTH Fus. on the right and 5th DORSET Regt. on left — should form up prior to the attack East of the STEENBEEK, but a previous operation by 32nd Bde. and 20th Div. on our left having failed to push back the enemy, hence the line	

WAR DIARY
or
INTELLIGENCE SUMMARY.
(Erase heading not required.)

Army Form C. 2118.

Place	Date	Hour	Summary of Events and Information	Remarks and references to Appendices
			supporting Coys of the 5th DORSET Regt had to form up West of the STEENBEEK in front of 9th LANCASHIRE FUS. The forming up was done on tapes and was still carried out. The 8th NORTH. FUS were heavily shelled just before starting but nevertheless both bodies advanced well against the first objective. Unfortunately the Div on our right flank was held up and this left our flank exposed to the enemy, opened heavy MG enfilade fire from MONT DU HIBOU NORTH WEST of that road, with Fair right counter attack and was unable to push their Fus suffered severe casualties and attack past the LANGEMARCK - ZONNEBEKE Road and dug in West of that road. Meanwhile on the left 5th DORSET Regt. reached their objective with little difficulty and consolidated posts as laid down in S.O.55 both in advance of and behind the LANGEMARCK - ZONNEBEKE Road. After a pause of 1 hr 55 mins on the line gained the two Bns. / 11th MANCHESTER Regt on the right and 9th LANC.	

Fus. on the left passed through the leading Bns and advanced towards the second objective. 1st MUNCH Regt at once suffered from the enemy's enfilade fire from the right and inclined in their advance towards the left, this made the gap considby the further of the Divn on our left to get on on all the greater. At BULOW FARM the advance came hill up, and being fired on from the flank and strongly resisted in front the MUNCH Regt was forced back on to the LANGEMARCK Road, while the right flank was refused to make a defensive flank. On the left 9th LANC Fus pushed on on reach by their right flank lying in the air on the MUNCH Regt being pushed back, were unable to advance any further. Dublins this their left reached their final objective and also occupied WHITE HOUSE.

For some hours the actual position of our troops was very obscure, but on the situation being cleared up it was found that the line held

WAR DIARY or INTELLIGENCE SUMMARY

Army Form C. 2118.

(Erase heading not required.)

Place	Date	Hour	Summary of Events and Information	Remarks and references to Appendices

by a S par on the right from C.S.d.7.4. through the gap/lk at C.S.d.7.7., CEMETERY at C.S.b.9.9. to LEKKERBOTERBEEK at V.29.d.9.5.5.5. This right sub-sector was held by the NORTH. FUS. and MAN. Regt. who had both suffered heavy losses and their men were in many places mingled together. The left sub-sector was held by LANC.FUS. with DORSET Regt. in support on both sides of LANGEMARCK Road from LEKKERBOTERBEEK at V.29.d.9.5.55. then west at RAT HOUSE through V.29.b.7.4. and PHEASANT Trench at V.30.a.2.8. to a point just west of WHITE HOUSE from which it had been shelled. At this point touch was kept with the 20 R. Div. During the afternoon several attempts at counter-attack by the enemy were reported, but none materialised. The enemy was active with snipers and M.G.'s from MONT DU HIBOU and the vicinity, and he kept up a continuous shelling on the ridge west of the STEENBEEK. The night of 16th/17th passed without any change in the situation.

Army Form C. 2118.

WAR DIARY
or
INTELLIGENCE SUMMARY.
(Erase heading not required.)

Place	Date	Hour	Summary of Events and Information	Remarks and references to Appendices
ELCH. EINH	17th		After a quiet night the day was spent in keeping touch with the flanks and adjusting the line ready to straighten it for defence. In the morning an order was received from the Div. ordering the relief of 34th Bde (less MGs Coy) by 33rd Bde on the following night (17th/18th.) Before this relief could be effected RAT HOUSE ought to be occupied by the Bn. to straighten the defensive flank. The Lanc. Fus. were ordered to carry this out. They occupied RAT HOUSE after dusk without opposition and issued the copse east of it at several snipers. This enabled more forward posts to be dug and the line thus ran from LEKKERBOTERBEEK to U.30.a.0.1 and thence to WHITE HOUSE which was again occupied by us without opposition from the enemy. This relief was carried out without incident after dusk	Appendix 1

WAR DIARY
or
INTELLIGENCE SUMMARY.
(Erase heading not required.)

Army Form C. 2118.

Instructions regarding War Diaries and Intelligence Summaries are contained in F. S. Regs., Part II. and the Staff Manual respectively. Title pages will be prepared in manuscript.

Place	Date	Hour	Summary of Events and Information	Remarks and references to Appendices
			Prisoners taken by the Bde. amounted to 290, whilst 5th Dorset Regt captured 2 Field guns and 2 M.G.s	
			The total casualties in the Bde. during these operations totalled:-	
			Officers Killed 12 Wounded 19 Missing 1	
			O.R. " 155 " 687 " 125	
			A fuller account of operations forms appendix 5	
FOUKA FILEH	18th		The relief had reported completed at 6 a.m. and the Brigade (less M.G. Coy) moved back to SIEGE CAMP (T.32.c.)	
SIEGE CAMP T.32.c.			The Brigadier visited for the remainder of this day	
"	19th		Sunday. Church Parades. At 5.30 p.m. G.O.C. held a conference of C.O.s and had several officers and N.C.O.s give their account of various incidents in the operations. By this means various points were cleared up and the correction of views made clear.	
"	20th		The Brigade is engaged in washing and reorganising. A full report of operations is written for the Division - for 34th M.G. Coy & 32nd M.G. Coy. This day.	
			Copy see appendix 3	
			The Line by 32nd M.G. Coy on return is referred to appendix 3	

WAR DIARY
or
INTELLIGENCE SUMMARY.
(Erase heading not required.)

Army Form C. 2118.

Place	Date	Hour	Summary of Events and Information.	Remarks and references to Appendices
SIEGE CAMP (B.21.C)	21st		34th M.G. Coy. took SIEGE CAMP on relief from the Line. Reorganisation of Battalions & completed on arrival.	
"	22nd		"B" Echelon and reinforcements join and hot day marred by shrivelled sky. Brig-General S.H. PEDLEY, C.B., relinquishing command of the Bde. and Brig-General B.G. CLAY, D.S.O., 7th DRAGOON GUARDS, assumed command. Coy. training began by Bns.	Appendix B
"	23rd		Three Bns. of the Bde. engaged on working-parties — making roads and tracks to the front line, erecting a new winter-camp, constructing 30 yards range and layout tracks by BRIELEN training area. Coy. training continued by remaining Bn.	
"	24th		Working-parties for most of Bde., training for the rest.	
"	25th		Working-parties and training. Some shelling near the camp about 9 p.m., & two shells into the camp — but no damage done. 34th M.G. Coy. gone into the line to assist in the attack.	
"	26th		Sunday; Church Parade for 2 B., working parties for rest of	

WAR DIARY or INTELLIGENCE SUMMARY

(Erase heading not required.)

Army Form C. 2118.

Place	Date	Hour	Summary of Events and Information	Remarks and references to Appendices
SIEGE CAMP (B.21.C.)	27th		Bdes. Heavy rain from 10 p.m. onwards.	
			Heavy rain on and off till 6.30 a.m. Three Bns of the Bde. still on working-parties and the fourth training. At 1.30 p.m. the rain began again and the strong wind which had been blowing for some days became a gale. At 1.55 p.m. 11th Div. attacked again, both 32nd & 73rd Bdes, but the weather conditions and ground were appalling and the attack failed. The rain and gale continued throughout the night. Div. Order received that 11th Div. would be relieved in the Line by 51st Div. on night 29th/30th and that 34th Bde. would move to DIRTY BUCKET CAMP (A.30. Central) on 30th inst.	
"	28th		The rain continued till midday and the gale till sunset. Two Bns. on working parties, the other two training Bdes. Order 58 issued ordering move to DIRTY BUCKET CAMP on 30th inst.	Appendix 1

Army Form C. 2118.

WAR DIARY
or
INTELLIGENCE SUMMARY.
(Erase heading not required.)

Instructions regarding War Diaries and Intelligence Summaries are contained in F. S. Regs., Part II. and the Staff Manual respectively. Title pages will be prepared in manuscript.

Place	Date	Hour	Summary of Events and Information	Remarks and references to Appendices
SIEGE CAMP (B.21.C)	29th		The Bns training and the rest on working parties 34th M.G. Coy came out of the line and rejoins the Bde at SIEGE CAMP. Heavy showers during the day and very cold.	
	30th	8 a.m.	The Bde marches to DIRTY BUCKET CAMP (A.30. central-E)	
DIRTY BUCKET CAMP (A.30. central)	31st		Heavy showers, cold and overcast. The Bde carries out training. Heavy showers during the morning but fine afterwards.	

W. Turner Capt.
B.M. 34th Inf Bde.
34th

Appendix 1.

SECRET.   Copy No. 5

War Diary.

34th. INFANTRY BRIGADE ORDER No. 53.

Reference 1/40,000 map – Sheet 28.   August 6th., 1917.

1. 11th Division (less Artillery) will relieve 51st. Division (less Artillery) in the Left Sector of the XVIII Corps front by the morning of 8th. inst., by which time the 32nd Inf. Brigade will have relieved the 154th. Inf. Brigade in the Line.

2. The 34th Infantry Brigade will move on the morning of 8th. inst. from their present Camp to SIEGE CAMP (B.21.c.). The times of march for each Unit will be in accordance with the attached table.

3. 1st. Line Transport will move with Units.

4. Intervals of 200 yards between Companies, (and the same distance between Battalions) will be kept. For the purpose of intervals each Unit's transport will count as a Company.

All Units will be preceded at sufficient distance by a mounted Officer to give warning to Traffic Control Posts of the approach of a column.

5. Brigade Headquarters will close at WINDMILL CAMP at 7-30 a.m. and open at SIEGE CAMP at 9 a.m.

6. ACKNOWLEDGE.

ISSUED AT 1 P.M.

F.G. Turner,
Captain,
Brigade Major, 34th Infantry Brigade.

Copy No. 1. Office.
       2. -do-
       3. -do-
       4. War Diary.
       5. -do-
       6. Bde. Sigs.
       7. 8th North. Fus.
       8. 9th Lancs. Fus.
       9. 5th Dorset Rgt.
      10. 11th Manchesters.

Copy No. 11. 34th M. G. Coy.
      12. 34th L. T. M. B.
      13. No.4.Coy.Div.Train.
      14. 34th Field Amb.
      15. 11th Division.
      16. Area Commandant, WINDMILL CAMP.
      17. Area Commandant, SIEGE CAMP.
      18. 32nd Brigade.

Copy No. 19. 33rd. Inf. Brigade.

MARCH TABLE issued in conjunction with 34th INFANTRY BRIGADE ORDER No. 55 of 6/8/17.

UNIT.	STARTING POINT.	TIME TO PASS STARTING PT.	ROUTE.	DESTINATION.	REMARKS.
Brigade H.Q.	DROMORE CORNER.	8 a.m.	Via. HOSPITAL FARM.	SIEGE FARM (B.21.c.)	
8th North. Fus.	-do-	8-3 a.m.	-do-	-do-	
5th Dorset Regt.	-do-	8-18 a.m.	-do-	-do-	
34th T.M.B.	-do-	8-33 a.m.	-do-	-do-	
34th M.G. Coy.	-do-	8-37 a.m.	-do-	-do-	
9th Lancs. Fus.	-do-	8-42 a.m.	-do-	-do-	
11th Manchesters.	-do-	8-57 a.m.	-do-	-do-	

N.B. There will be no halt at 8-50 a.m.

* * * * * * *

SECRET

War Diary

Copy No....5......

34th INFANTRY BRIGADE ORDER No. 54.

Reference maps - 1/20,000 - Sheets 28.N.W. & 20.S.W.
and special POELCAPELLE Map - 1/10,000.   AUG. 10th. 1917.

1.   On a date and at an hour to be detailed later the Fifth Army will attack the enemy on its front.   All preparations will be completed by August 12th.

2.   The 11th Division will attack on the Left of XVIII Corps with the 145th Brigade (48th Division) on its Right and the 60th Brigade (20th Division) on its Left.

3.   The 11th Division attack will be carried out by 34th Brigade.

4.   The Objectives and Boundaries of Brigade and Battalions are shown on the attached map "A"; the first objective will be the GREEN LINE, the second objective the RED LINE.
   The Right portion of the 145th Brigade will pause for 20 minutes on the GREEN LINE and assault the RED LINE as far to the Left as C.12.b.8.9. simultaneously with the XIX Corps on its Right.
   The 34th Brigade will pause for one hour and 55 minutes on the GREEN LINE and assault the RED LINE simultaneously with the 60th Brigade on its Left and the Left portion of the 145th Brigade on its Right.
   On arrival at the GREEN LINE and until such time as the 60th Brigade has captured ALOUETTE FARM the Left flank of the 5th Dorset Regt. will be refused as shown on the attached map "A", care being taken that house at U.29.d.1.9. is occupied.

5.   ZERO Hour will be communicated to all concerned later.

6.   The two Bns. holding the Line will lead the attack - 8th Northumberland Fusiliers on the Right, 5th Dorset Regiment on the Left, followed by 11th Manchester Regt. on the Right and 9th Lancs. Fus. on the Left.
   After the pause on the GREEN LINE, 11th Manchester Regt. and 9th Lancashire Fus. will leap-frog and carry on the attack against the RED LINE.   8th North. Fus. and 5th Dorset Regt. will remain on the GREEN LINE and consolidate as laid down below in para 10.

7.   Each Battalion will attack in the following formation :-
Each Battalion in 2 waves consisting of 2 Companies per wave, all four Platoons in the line, each Platoon in formation for attack as laid down in S.S. 143, Appendix 1.
   The distance between lines will be 25 yards, between waves 100 yards.

8.   The two Battalions holding the line will close up just East of the STEENBEEK, so as to be in position of readiness to attack at ZERO minus 2 hours.   The other two Battalions will move from the Canal bank at ZERO minus 5 hours, and form up about 100 yards West of the STEENBEEK, in lines of Platoons in file, ready to cross at ZERO
   A party under an Officer per Battalion will be detailed to mark out the frontage of each Battalion with tapes and discs and in the case of 9th Lancs. Fus. and 11th Manchester Regt. to lead forward tape lines to the bridges across the STEENBEEK.   These parties will move forward at dusk on "Y"/"Z" Night.
   The approaches from the BLACK LINE to the STEENBEEK will be marked with tapes and direction posts.   A pair of trained guides from Corps Cavalry or Divisional Scouts will be told off to each Company Commander of the two Supporting Battalions to lead him to the forming up point.   In addition the two leading Battalions will each detail four guides for their Supporting Battalion

(2)

9. At ZERO Hour the two leading Battalions will close up to the barrage and the two Supporting Battalions close up to the STEENBEEK.

Assaulting troops will follow the barrage closely, and 5th Dorset Regt. will ensure that all ranks understand the refusing of their Left flank on the GREEN LINE as laid down in para 4.

Definite Units (usually a Platoon) will be detailed to deal with and mop up suspected enemy Strong Points. These are :-

    (a) Up to the 1st. objective -

        At C.5.b.05.05.
        HAANIXBEEK FARM.
        COCKCROFT.
        House U.29.d.40.55.

    (b) Between first and second objectives -

        BULOW FARM.
        RAT FARM.

These parties, after mopping up and detailing escort for prisoners taken, rejoin their Battalions.

In addition to the above, after the capture of the RED LINE, special parties, detailed beforehand from 9th Lancs. Fus., will move forward close to the barrage to attack PHEASANT FARM and WHITE HOUSE.

10. On the main objective being gained consolidation will be carried out on the following lines (for approximate positions of posts see map "A".) :-

    (a) The Outpost Line and first line of resistance consisting of eight posts Nos. 1 to 8.

    (b) The 2nd Line of resistance consisting of eight posts Nos. 9 to 16.

    (c) The LANGEMARCK - WINNIPEG Road line consisting of eight posts Nos. 17 to 24 and including RAT HOUSE.

    (d) A Support Line to (c) of eight posts Nos. 25 to 32, including Strong Points at enclosure C.5.b.6.0. - COCKCROFT - U.29.d.1.9. - HAANIXBEEK FARM.

Work on (c) and (d) will begin directly the Green Line is taken.

The object in view is to consolidate the RED ~~DOTTED~~ and GREEN LINES so that they can eventually be held by two Battalions disposed in depth.

The Outpost Line will be especially sited and prepared with a view to a further advance.

R.E. personnel will assist in the consolidation, see appendix 3.

11. As soon as the posts have been established, and during ~~while~~ they ~~are~~ digging in, four arrowhead patrols from each Battalion are to be sent forward as close to the protective barrage as they can get, to ascertain (1), If there are any enemy posts within the area enclosed by our protective barrage and (2), When our protective barrage dies down, the three patrols nearest to the following tactical points to move forward and occupy them viz., 11th Manchester Regt. to
CEMETERY on Western slope of hill 19 (V.25.c.)
MALTA HOUSE at V.25.a.15.55.
        9th. Lancashire Fus. to
CEMETERY 200 yards N.E. of PHEASANT FARM.

12. In order to ensure close touch with the flanking Brigades one Section will be detailed to meet similar parties of 145th and 60th Brigades at each of the following places as under :-

(3)

To meet.	To be detailed by.	Place.	Time.
145th Brigade.	O.C. 8th North. Fus.	MON DU HIBOU.	Zero plus 30 min.
-do-	-do-	COCKCROFT.	Zero plus 70 min.
-do-	O.C. 11th Manch Rgt.	Cross roads, C.6.b.1.5.	Zero plus 2 hours 50 minutes
-do-	-do-	NEW HOUSES.	Zero plus 3 hrs. 10 mins
60th. Brigade.	O.C. 5th Dorset Rgt.	Cross roads, U.29.c.3.8.	Zero plus 15 min. [20]
-do-	-do-	Cross roads, U.29.b.0.2.	Zero plus 70 min. [1hr 15 mins]
-do-	O.C. 9th Lancs. Fus.	WHITE HOUSE.	Zero plus 3 hrs. 40 mins

The object of these posts is to find out if the troops on their flanks are up in line with ours. As soon therefore as they have learnt the position of those troops 2 men of the section should be sent back with the information to their Battalion H.Q. The remainder of the section rejoin their Unit as soon as the next liaison post in front of them has been established.

13.   The attack will be made under :-

   (a) An Artillery barrage - See Appendix 1.

   (b) A Machine Gun barrage - See Appendix 2.

The Artillery barrage will come down 300 yards East of the STEENBEEK. It will lift at ZERO plus 5 minutes and will advance at the rate of 100 yards in 5 minutes.
There will be a smoke barrage during the pause on the GREEN LINE. Details will follow.

14.   Eight tanks have been allotted to assist the 34th Brigade in the attack. Four will operate on the Right and four on the Left of the attack. The Tanks will assemble in the STEENBEEK VALLEY by ZERO minus 2 hours. *Cancelled owing to wet weather*

15.   A contact aeroplane will be in the air during the attack on each objective. The leading troops only will mark their position by flares to the Contact Aeroplane when asked for by either (a) KLAXON HORN or (b) a series of White Lights.

16.   Situation reports will be sent by Battalions to Brigade H.Q. every 2 hours after ZERO.

17.   At ZERO Hour H.Q. will be as under :-

   34th Brigade H.Q.   FOCH FARM.
   Adv. Report Centre.   GOURNIER FARM.

   8th North. Fus.   )   VANACKERT
   11th Manchesters.)   FARM.

   5th Dorset Rgt.   )   FRANCOIS
   9th Lancs. Fus.   )   FARM.

After the capture of the GREEN LINE H.Q. of 11th Manchester Rgt. and 9th Lancs. Fus. will move forward to HAANIXBEEK FARM.

(4)

18. On Y/Z Night 34th Machine Gun Company will move to CANE AVENUE, C.9.a.6.4. Four guns will be detailed for the consolidation of the GREEN LINE and four guns for the consolidation of the RED LINE. These guns will be allotted positions designed particularly to cover POELCAPELL - ST. JULIEN Road, the flanks of PHEASANT FARM and WHITE HOUSE and the Valley of the LEKKERBOTERBEEK. They will move forward about ZERO plus one hour.

19. On Y/Z Night two guns of 34th L. T. M. B. will be detailed to follow up behind the rear Company of 8th North. Fus. and two guns behind the rear Company of 5th Dorset Rgt. to their forming up place East of the STEENBEEK. After ZERO Hour these guns will follow up, 2 behind the last wave of the Left Company of 8th North. Fus. and 2 behind the last wave of the Left Company of 5th Dorset Rgt. During the advance to the RED LINE they will follow behind the Left Companies of 11th Manchester Rgt. and 9th Lancs. Fus.

Their probable targets will be for the Right pair of guns (a) COCKCROFT (b) BULOW FARM ; for the Left pair (a) Houses on LANGEMARCK Road about U.29.Central (b) RAT HOUSE (c) PHEASANT FARM.

On consolidation the Right pair will take up a position about No.? Post (See map "A"), and the Left pair about 200 yards West of PHEASANT FARM.

20. An orderly with a signaller's watch will be sent to all Battalion H.Q. at noon and 11 p.m. on X and Y Days for the purpose of synchronising watches.

21. The following Appendices will be issued with this Order :-

1. R.A. Programme and Barrage map.
2. Machine Gun Programme.
3. R.E. Instructions.
4. Administrative Instructions.
5. Medical Instructions.
6. Arrangements for "Contact" and "Infantry Protection" Aeroplanes.
7. Intercommunication.

Nos. 2, 3, 5 and 6 & 7 are forwarded herewith.

22. ACKNOWLEDGE.

ISSUED AT...... 8. P.M.

F.G. Turner, Captain,
Brigade Major, 34th. Infantry Brigade.

Copy No. 1. Office.
2. -do-
3. Staff Captain,
4. War Diary.
5. -do-
6. 8th North. Fus.
7. 9th Lancs. Fus.
8. 5th Dorset Rgt.
9. 11th Manchesters.
10. 34th M. G. Coy.
11. 34th L. T. M. B.
12. Bde. Signals.
13. 11th Division.

Copy No. 14. 86th Field Co. R.E.
15. 34th Field Ambulance.
16. No.4.Coy.Div.Train.
17. 32nd Brigade.
18. 33rd Brigade.
19. 145th Brigade.
20. 60th Brigade.
21. 20th Coy."G"Bn. Tank Corps.
22. Liaison Officer.
23. C.R.A. 11th Divn.
24.
25.
26.

To *War Diary*

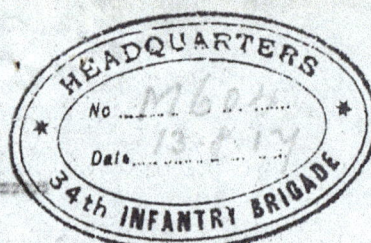

SECRET.

Reference 34th Infantry Brigade Order No. 54 dated 10th instant, para 17.

Brigade Report Centre (Advanced) will be at MINTY FARM, and not as previously stated.

K. Turner, Captain,

August 13th., 1917.   Brigade Major, 34th. Infty. Brigade.

SECRET.

To: War Diary

Reference 34th Infantry Brigade Order No. 54 dated 10th. August, para. 17.

H.Q. of 8th North. Fus. will be at FERDINAND FARM, and H.Q. of 11th Manchester Regt. will be at RED FARM, and NOT as previously stated.

Captain,

August 11th., 1917. Brigade Major, 34th. Inf. Brigade.

SECRET.

To

O.C. War Diary

Reference 34th Infantry Brigade Order No. 54 dated August 10th., 1917, para 14.

Owing to the wet state of the ground the eight Tanks alloted to this Brigade will not form up prior to ZERO on the Brigade front, but S.W. of ST. JULIEN.

They will cross the STEENBEEK by the ST. JULIEN Road, advance along the POELCAPPELLE Road, and turning to the Left at the LANGEMARCK Road will move along that Road.

It is improbable therefore that the Tanks will be in time to help in the taking of the GREEN LINE, but they should be able to assist the attack against the RED LINE.

Captain,

August 13th., 1917. Brigade Major, 34th. Inf Brigade.

S E C R E T.

ADMINISTRATIVE INSTRUCTIONS

(in connection with 11th. Divn. Order No. 95.)

****

War Diary

1. **PRISONER OF WAR CAGE.** The Divisional P.O.W. Cage is situated at B.28.a.4.2. CHATEAU TROIS TOURS.
   All prisoners of War will be marched down to Bridge 4 (C.25.a. 5.9.) under escort which will be as small as is feasible. Here they will be taken over by Officer in charge of P.O.W. Collecting Station.

2. **CASUALTIES.** Estimated casualties will be reported early in accordance with the scheme previously issued. Actual numbers will be sent in as soon as verified. Names of Officer casualties will be carefully checked before report is made.

3. **BURIALS.** The dead should be buried in recognised cemeteries only. It is however, often necessary for sanitary reasons that they should be buried by troops practically in the firing line- when this is done care should be taken that all details of men so buried, and the exact sites, are reported direct to Divisional Burial Officer.

4. **AMMUNITION.** Brigade Dumps of S.A.A. and Bombs are being established at FRANCOIS FARM and VON WERDEN FARM. Ammunition and bombs can be issued to Units upon application direct to 2/Lieut. GREGG at FRANCOIS FARM,

5. **HOT MEALS.** O's.C. Units will be responsible that the troops under their command are provided with a Hot Meal before the attack. For this purpose and for use during the operations 140 tins Solidified alcohol are being issued to each Battalion, 30 to 34th. M.G.Company and 10 to 34th. L.T.M.Battery.

   15 hot food containers each are also being issued to 9th. Lancashire Fusiliers and 11th. Manchester Regiment. 8th. North. Fusiliers and 5th. Dorset Regt. will each take over about a similar number from 32nd. Brigade in the Line.

   The Hot meals should be provided from these if possible, and the solidified alcohol should be carefully husbanded.

6. **RATIONS AND WATER.** Rations and water for 2 days will have been issued and carried on the man in action.

   Instructions for issue of rations for "Z" plus 1 day will be issued later.

   A reserve supply of rations and water is at each of the Dumps mentioned in paragraph 4. These can be drawn in case of necessity on application to 2/Lieut. GREGG as above.

7. Two water lorries of 500 and 400 gallons respectively will report to the Brigade Transport Officer at the transport lines on "X" day. He will arrange for the distribution of water from them

8. **SALVAGE.** Every effort will be made to salvage Arms, Equipment, Ammunition, Shrapnel shell bodies and shell cases.

   Each Unit will establish a salvage dump of its own to which all individuals or parties returning should bring some article of salvage.

/A Brigade

(2).

A Brigade Dump will be established, the location of which will be notified later. Salvage will be returned to this dump by means of returning ration transport, etc.

Salvage Dumps should be clearly labelled " SALVAGE".

9. R.E. MATERIAL. It is hoped to establish a R.E. Dump in the neighbourhood of HAANIXBEEK FARM directly transport conditions permit of it. For the present, Units will have to depend mainly upon what they can salvage.

10. PETROL TINS. Units will ensure that all petrol tins sent up with water are returned the following night with stoppers complete.

11. STRAGGLERS POSTS. Stragglers posts will be established along the Canal Bank. All stragglers will be collected and those fit to return will be sent to Brigade Headquarters and returned to their Battalions.

12. ACKNOWLEDGE.

                                              Cichult Captain,

11-8-17.   Staff Captain, 34th. Infantry Brigade.

Copy No.		Copy No.	
1.	Office.	15.	86th. Field Coy.R.E.
2.	-do-	16.	34th. Field Ambulance.
3.	-do-	17.	No.4.Coy. Dvl.Train.
4.	Bde. Major.	18.	32nd. Brigade.
5.	War Diary.	19.	33rd. Brigade.
6.	-do-	20.	145th. Brigade.
7.	8th. North.Fus.	21.	60th. Brigade.
8.	9th.Lancs.Fus.	22.	20th. Coy."G" Bn Tanks.
9.	5th. Dorset R.	23.	Liason Officer.
10.	11th.Manch.R.	24.	C.R.A. 11th. Divn.
11.	34th.M.G.Coy.	25.	B.T.O.
12.	34th.L.T.M.B.	26.	D.S.O.
13.	Bde. Signals.	27.	Bombing Officer.
14.	11th. Division.	28.	

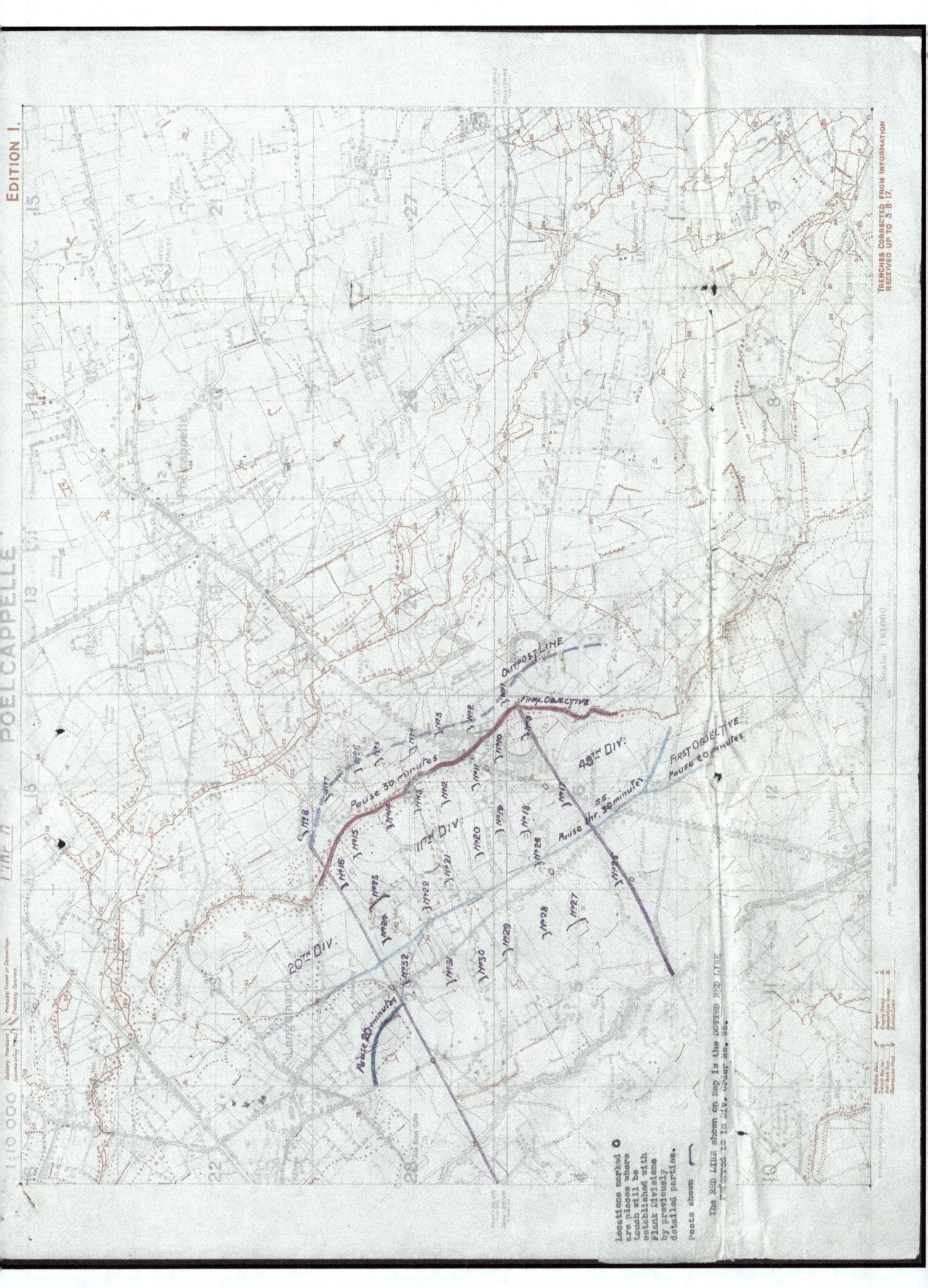

SECRET. Copy No. 5

34th INFANTRY BRIGADE ORDER No. 55.

Reference maps - Sheets 28.N.W. and 20.S.W. - 1/20,000. Aug. 11th.
Special POELCAPELLE Map - 1/10,000.

1. 34th Infantry Brigade will relieve 32nd Infantry Brigade in the line by 8 a.m. "Y" day.

2. Moves will take place in accordance with the attached movement table.

3. Units of 34th Brigade will take over all necessary trench maps, photographs, stores and appliances connected with the defence of the line from the Units which they relieve.

4. All details for relief will be arranged between Os.C. Battalions concerned.

5. Reconnaissances of the tracks from the Canal to the STEENBEEK will be carried out daily by Officers and N.C.Os.

6. One Officer per Company and one per Battalion H.Q. of 8th North. Fus. and 5th Dorset Rgt. will go into the line on "W"/"X" Night.

7. Completion of all moves will be reported to Brigade Hd. Qrs. by the Code "NIL RETURN".

8. Brigade Headquarters will close at SIEGE CAMP at 6-30 a.m. on "Y" Day and open at FOCH FARM at 8 a.m. the same day, at which hour the Command of the Line passes to G.O.C. 34th Infantry Brigade.

9. ACKNOWLEDGE.

ISSUED AT... 8 p.m.

F.G. Turner, Captain,
Brigade Major, 34th. Infty. Brigade.

* * * * * *

Copy No. 1. Office.
2. -do-
3. Staff Captain.
4. War Diary.
5. -do-
6. Bde. Signals.
7. 8th North. Fus.
8. 9th Lancs. Fus.
9. 5th Dorset Rgt.
10. 11th Manchesters.
11. 34th M. G. Coy.

Copy No. 12. 34th L. T. M. B.
13. 11th Division.
14. 32nd Brigade.
15. 33rd Brigade.
16. 86th Field Co. R.E.
17. No.4.Coy.Div.Train.
18. 34th Field Ambulance.
19. 60th Brigade.
20. 145th Brigade.
21. Camp Commandant, SIEGE CAMP.
22. ~~Liaison Officer.~~ Camp Commandant 18th Corps Area Canal Bank

MOVEMENT TABLE issued with 34th Brigade Order No. 55.

DATE.	Serial No.	UNIT.	From.	To.	Route.	Remarks.
"X" Day.	1.	8th North. Fus.	Present Camp.	Canal Bank. C.25.a.6.5. Relieving 6th York & Lancs.	BRIELEN - B.29. d.7.5. - ESSEX FARM.	To clear present Camp by 6-30 a.m. To come under orders of G.O.C. 32nd Bde. on arrival.
-ditto-	2.	5th Dorset Rgt.	-ditto-	Canal Bank. C.25.a.8.7. Relieving 6th Yorks. Regt.	-ditto-	To clear present Camp by 6-45 a.m. To come under orders of G.O.C. 32nd Bde. on arrival.
-ditto-	3.	34th M. G. Coy.	-ditto-	Canal Bank.	-ditto-	Clear present Camp 7 a.m. To come under orders of G.O.C. 32nd Bde. on arrival.
Night of "X"/"Y" Day.	4.	8th North. Fus.	Canal Bank.	Line. (Relieve 9th W. Yorks.)		Under orders of G.O.C. 32nd Brigade.
-ditto-	5.	5th Dorset Rgt.	-ditto-	Line. (Relieve 8th D. of W. Rgt.)		-ditto-
-ditto-	6.	34th M. G. Coy.	-ditto-	Line.		-ditto-
"Y" Day.	7.	Bde. Hd. Qrs.	Present Camp.	FOCH FARM.	As in No. 1.	Clearing present Camp 6-25 a.m.
-ditto-	8.	9th Lancs. Fus.	-ditto-	Canal Bank. C.25.a.8.7. (Relieve 8th D. of W. Rgt.)	-ditto-	Clearing present Camp at 6-30 a.m.

(2)

DATE.	Serial No.	UNIT.	From.	To.	Route.	Remarks.
"Y" Day.	9.	11th Manch. Rgt.	Present Camp.	Canal Bank. C.25. a.6.5. (Relieving 9th West Yorks R.)	As in No. 1.	Clearing present Camp at 6-45 a.m.
-ditto-	10.	34th L.T.M.B.	-ditto-	Canal Bank.	-ditto-	Clearing present Camp at 7 a.m.

NOTES : (1) Dates will be communicated secretly.

(2) Intervals of 200 yards will be kept between Companies.

FG Turner, Captain,

Brigade Major, 34th. Infy. Brigade.

August 11th., 1917.

"A" Form.
MESSAGES AND SIGNALS.

Army Form C. 2121.
(In pads of 100.)

Prefix	Code	in	Words.	Charge	This message is on a/c of:	Recd. at .... m.
Office of Origin and Service Instructions.			Sent			Date............
War Diary			At............m.		.................Service.	From............
			To............			By............
			By............		(Signature of "Franking Officer.")	

TO — All Units.

Sender's Number.	Day of Month.	In reply to Number.	A A A
B.M. 397.	17.		

ORANGE will be relieved in the line tonight by OBLIGE aaa ORDEAL and ORIGIN will be relieved by OBEY aaa ORGAN and ORIENT by OBSERVE aaa All details concerning guides, times, etc., will be arranged direct between Os.C. Units concerned aaa During today all 4 Bns. will adjust the line, organise a proper system of defence and ensure touch with flanking Units is maintained aaa ORGAN in conjunction with ORIENT's Post at U.29.b.8.4 will occupy RAT HOUSE aaa ORBIT will be attached to OBLIGE for defence of line and will arrange to relieve eight guns of OBVIATE with his Reserve guns aaa All carrying parties will rejoin their Units aaa Lorries will convey the Bde. from Canal Bank to SIEGE CAMP aaa Hour of starting from Canal Bank will be notified later aaa Completion of relief in line will be reported to Bde. H.Q. by Code Word "BULLY".

From ORANGE.

Place

Time

Captain.

The above may be forwarded as now corrected. (Z)

.... Censor. Signature of Addressee or person authorised to telegraph in his name.

* This line should be erased if not required.
(3796.) Wt. W 492/M1647. 650,000 Pads. 5/17. H. W. & V., Ld. (E. 1187.)

```
**************
S E C R E T .                                            War Diary         Copy No...5....
**************
```

34th INFANTRY BRIGADE ORDER No. 56.

Reference map - Sheet 28 - 1/40,000.   August 28th., 1917.

1. The 51st Division will relieve the 11th Division in the line on the night 29th/30th. August up to the original Southern Boundary.

2. After relief the 11th Division will be concentrated in the OOSTHOEK Area with Divisional H.Q. at "X" Camp (A.16.c.2.3.)

3. The 34th Infantry Brigade will move to DIRTY BUCKET CAMP (A.30.Central) on 30th. inst. in accordance with the attached Table.

4. 1st Line Transport will march with Units, falling in behind the rear Company on passing HOSPITAL FARM.

5. Intervals of 200 yards between Companies (and the same distance between Battalions) will be kept. For the purpose of intervals each Unit's transport will count as a Company.
   All Units will be preceded at sufficient distance by a mounted Officer to give warning to Traffic Control Posts of the approach of a column.

6. Brigade Headquarters will close at SIEGE CAMP at 7-30 a.m. and open at DIRTY BUCKET CAMP at 9 a.m.

7. ACKNOWLEDGE.

ISSUED AT. 2.p.m.

                                                        Captain,
                                    Brigade Major, 34th. Infy. Brigade.

                            * * * * *

DISTRIBUTION.

    Copy No. 1. Office.
           2.   -do-
           3. Staff Captain.
           4. War Diary.
           5.   -do-
           6. Bde. Signals.
           7. 8th North. Fus.
           8. 9th Lancs. Fus.
           9. 5th Dorset Rgt.
          10. 11th Manchester Regt.
          11. 34th M. G. Coy.
          12. 34th L. T. M. B.
          13. 11th Division.
          14. 32nd Brigade.
          15. 33rd Brigade.
          16. 86th Field Co. R.E..
          17. No.4.Coy.Div.Train.
          18. 34th Field Ambulance.
          19. Camp Commandant, SIEGE CAMP.
          20.   -do-   DIRTY BUCKET CAMP.

MOVEMENT TABLE issued with 34th Brigade Order No. 56.

UNIT.	STARTING POINT.	TIME TO PASS STARTING Pt.	ROUTE.	DESTINATION.
Brigade Hd. Qrs.	SIEGE JUNCTION.	8 a.m.	HOSPITAL FARM.	DIRTY BUCKET CAMP.
11th Manchesters.	-do-	8-3 a.m.	-do-	-do-
5th Dorset Rgt.	-do-	8-18 a.m.	-do-	-do-
8th North. Fus.	-do-	8-33 a.m.	-do-	-do-
34th L. T. M. B.	-do-	8-48 a.m.	-do-	-do-
34th M. G. Coy.	-do-	8-52 a.m.	-do-	-do-
9th Lancs. Fus.	-do-	8-57 a.m.	-do-	-do-

N.B. There will be no halt at 8-50 a.m.

Appendix 2

APPENDIX 11.

Strength of Units from 1st. to 7th. Aug.

Unit	Officers	O.Ranks	Casualties Officers K	W	M	O. Ranks K	W	M
8th. North. Fusiliers.	40.	962.	=	=	=	=	=	=
9th. Lancs. Fusiliers.	41.	912.	=	=	=	=	=	=
5th. Dorset Regiment.	38.	908.	=	=	=	=	=	=
11th. Manchester Regt.	38.	938.	=	=	=	=	1	=
34th. M.G. Company.	12.	175.	=	=	=	1	2	=

Strength of Units from 8th. to 14th. Aug.

Unit	Officers	O.Ranks	K	W	M	K	W	M
8th. North. Fusiliers.	40.	1015.	=	=	=	=	1	=
9th. Lancs. Fusiliers.	41.	902.	=	=	=	=	2	=
5th. Dorset Regiment.	38.	958.	=	=	=	=	1	=
11th. Manchester Regt.	39.	934.	=	=	=	=	1	=
34th. M.G. Company.	12.	170.	=	=	=	=	=	=

Strength of Units from 15th. to 21st. Aug.

Unit	Officers	O.Ranks	K	W	M	K	W	M
8th. North. Fusiliers.	39.	1059.	6	4	=	47.	231.	30.
9th. Lancs. Fusiliers.	40.	893.	1	9	=	33.	174.	33.
5th. Dorset Regiment.	37.	961.	=	3	=	25.	114.	6.
11th. Manchester Regt.	39.	938.	4	4	1.	45.	150.	56.
34th. M.G. Company.	12.	165.	=	=	=	7.	19.	=

Strength of Units from 22nd. to 31st. Aug.

Unit	Officers	O.Ranks	K	W	M	K	W	M
8th. North. Fusiliers.	29.	754.	=	=	=	=	=	=
9th. Lancs. Fusiliers.	29.	655.	=	=	=	=	6	=
5th. Dorset Regiment.	34.	834.	=	=	-	=	2	=
11th. Manchester Regt.	30.	687.	=	=	=	=	=	=
34th. M.G. Company.	12.	151.	=	=	=	1	3	=

REINFORCEMENTS.

Unit.	From 1st. to 7th. O.	O.R.	From 8th. to 14th. O.	O.R.	From 15th. to 21st. O.	O.R.	From 22nd. to 31st. O.	O.R.
8th. North. F.	2.	68.	=	59.	2.	=	2.	176.
9th. Lancs. F.	1.	=	=	=	=	=	1.	117.
5th. Dorsets.	=	51.	=	=	1.	2.	=	55.
11th. Manchesters.	1.	5.	=	7.	=	=	1.	60.
34th. M.G.Company.	=	1.	=	=	2	8	1.	30.

Appendix 3.

SPECIAL ORDER OF THE DAY.
=================================

The G.O.C., 11th. Division wishes to thank the
34th. Infantry Brigade for the very fine fighting qualities
that they showed on the 16th. August. Though all objectives
were not gained, the G.O.C. thoroughly realizes the difficulties that were encountered and congratulates all troops of
the Division who took part in the attack.

The continuous hard work under fire, of the Royal
Artillery, Royal Engineers, Signal Company and 6th. East
Yorks Pioneer Battalion contributed largely to the success
that was gained.

The 32nd. Infantry Brigade by the attacks they made
on August 10th. and 13th. ensured a forming up place for the
attacking troops, and so demoralised the enemy in that part
of the line, that he offered little resistance on 16th. August.

The work of the R.A.M.C. was most efficiently and
quickly carried out.

The G.O.C. XVIII Corps has expressed his opinion
that the 33rd. Infantry Brigade by holding the line under
most difficult circumstances for a fortnight before the attack
of 31st. July, contributed as much as any Brigade in the
Corps to the success on that day.

T. D. Coleridge Lieut. Colonel,
20th. August 1917.   General Staff, 11th. Division.

Copies to: 32nd. Inf. Bde.
             33rd. "   "
             34th. "   "
             C.R.A.
             C.R.E.
             A.D.M.S.
             6th. E. Yorks.

Fifth Army.
G.A. 790/9.
19th. Aug, 1917.

XVIII Corps.

1. The attached copy of a letter received by the Army Commander from the Commander-in-Chief is forwarded for your information.

2. The Army Commander wishes it to be published for the information of all ranks, and at the same time to express his congratulations to Commanders, Staffs, and the troops under their command, on the successes gained on the 16th. inst.

3. He particularly wishes to express his deep admiration of the gallant determination and great spirit shown by the troops under the recent trying conditions of bad weather, and in face of stubborn resistance by the enemy. It is this splendid spirit of determination to win which is fast contributing to the defeat of our enemy.

(Sd) N. MALCOLM,
Major General, G.S.

11th. Division No. G.S. 409.

34th. Inf. Bde.
33rd. " "
32nd. " "
C.R.A.
C.R.E.
A.D.M.S.
6th. E.Yorks Regt.

For information and communication to all ranks.

20th. August 1917.

[signature] Major,
General Staff, 11th. Division.

No. O.A. 830/12.

General Headquarters,
British Armies in France,
17th August 1917.

General Sir H. de la P. Gough, K.C.V.O., K.C.B.,
Commanding Fifth Army.

      I wish to congratulate you personally, as well as the Commanders, Staffs and troops under your command, most warmly on the successes gained by the Fifth Army yesterday, under conditions of great difficulty and in the face of the most determined opposition.

      The bad weather which delayed the continuance of our offensive enabled the enemy to bring up and concentrate considerable forces in reserve and to make careful preparations to meet our attack yesterday. In spite of this the determination and gallantry of the troops under your command succeeded in striking another of the successful blows, the cumulative effects of which are shattering the enemy's power of resistance and will ultimately lead to his complete defeat.

(Sd). D. HAIG,
Field Marshal.

Copy :-
  M.S.

War Diary

Report on the operations of the 34th Infantry Brigade on
August 16th., 1917.

1. In order to carry out the attack ordered for 16th. inst., it was necessary for the Brigade to form up astride the STEENBEEK.
The original plan was for the two leading Battns. (8th North. Fus. on the Right and 5th Dorset Rgt. on the Left) who had gone into the line on the night of 14th/15th. and were holding posts East of the STEENBEEK to close up behind these posts and be all formed up East of the STEENBEEK. But, owing to the failure of a previous attempt by the 32nd Brigade and by the Division on our Left to drive back the existing enemy posts, only the two lead -ing Companies of 5th Dorset Regiment were able to form up East of the STEENBEEK, and the Supporting Companies lined up on the West side. The 8th Northumberland Fusiliers formed up on the East side without much difficulty. Behind these leading Battns. the two rear Battns. (11th Manchester Regt. on the Right and 9th Lancashire Fusiliers on the Left) were formed up West of the STEENBEEK.
To carry out the operation of forming up the I.O. of each Battn. with a specially selected party laid out tapes. This diffi -cult operation was successfully accomplished, as a daylight ins- pection subsequently proved, and all the Battns. formed up as plan ned, though a patrol of the enemy from near MON BULGARE noticed and bombed the tape of 8th North. Fus., and one of the Supporting pla- toons of 5th Dorset Regt. was thrown into confusion by a shell, which caused 6 to 8 casualties, and for a considerable time lost touch with the leading platoons.

At Midnight there was touch with the Division on each flank At that time a Sergt. of the Glosters came from the Right flank and informed 8th North. Fus. that other Battns. were to pass through that night. Shortly after Midnight 2nd Lieut. McDINE, 8th North. Fus., patrolled to the Right, East of the STEENBEEK, but could find none of the troops of the Right Brigade there, and later at 3-15 a.m. 2nd Lieut. THOMPSON, 8th North. Fus., also patrolled to the Right, but he too found no one in touch with us, though he went at least 100 yards outside the Divisional Boundary to find them.

During the period from ZERO to ZERO plus 5 mins., while the leading Battns. were closing up to the barrage and the Supporting Battns. were pushing up to and across the STEENBEEK, the 11th Manchester Regt. (Right Support Bn.) suffered heavy losses from the enemy shell fire. In fact 8 out of their 12 Company Officers became casualties when only just across the STEENBEEK. The 9th Lancs. Fus. (Left Support Bn.) on the other hand met with no casualties from the enemy barrage, which came down on the STEEN -BEEK on our Right; thus catching 11th Manchester Regt., but then ran N.W. to about COMEDY FARM thereby missing 9th Lancs. Fus.

At ZERO plus 5 mins. (4-50 a.m.) the barrage moved forward followed closely by the leading Battns.
The trouble of 8th North. Fus. was all in the first 100 yards. Heavy enfilade Machine Gun fire was opened on them from their Right flank which was exposed; both the Company Commanders of the Leading and Supporting Right Companies were killed and many other Officers became casualties. The barrage in front of the two Right platoons was very thin and the enemy was seen to fire from loopholes through the barrage. At 5 a.m. 2nd Lieut. THOMPSON, 8th North. Fus., noticed the Brigade on the Right was only 50 yards across the STEENBEEK. He states he signalled to them to come on, and two men advanced but were at once killed and no further advance was seen on that flank. At this point 2nd Lieut. CHEESEWRIGHT was Commanding both the Right Companies, and Sergt. BARLOW the two Left Companies of 8th North. Fus. The first obstacle met with was a series of sniper's posts arranged in three lines parallel to and about 100 yards in front of the gun positions at C.5.d.6.7. These held in all about 100 men, who

were nearly all killed. The gun positions at C.5.d.6.7. then held up the Right Companies and by the time 2nd Lieut. CHEESEWRIGHT had captured this strong point, by putting Lewis Guns on both flanks, bombarding with Rifle Grenades and rushing the position, the barrage had already passed beyond the first objective to its protective line. Sergt. BARLOW Commanding the two Companies on the Left had difficulty in overcoming the block-house at C.5.d.6.9. and thereby also lost the barrage. He, however, pushed on with the Left front Company and dug in 100 yards West of LANGEMARCK Road with his Left on CEMETERY at C.5.b.8.8. Four guns, he states, of the protective barrage firing short prevented his digging in East of the Road. Owing to the heavy fire from MONT DU HIBOU and the TRIANGLE on the exposed Right flank the Right Companies who had suffered very heavily were unable to advance past the line C.5.d.6.7. - C.5.d.6.9. The Right flank, therefore, was already refused, forming a defensive flank on the exposed Right.

Meanwhile on the Left 5th Dorset Regt. had advanced without much difficulty. As the Commanding Officer suspected strong points at the start between his men and the barrage, he had ordered the two leading Companies to push out Lewis Gun Posts to assist the advance at ZERO Hour up to the barrage. This proved a most wise and necessary step and materially assisted the advance, the garrisons of the posts being rushed and dealt with, under the fire of the Lewis Guns. Touch was kept throughout the advance with the Brigade on the Left, but the party detailed on the Right for liaison with 8th North. Fus. failed to make touch and another party at once detailed also failed. The LANGEMARCK Road was reached up to time and consolidation began at once on both sides of the Road. The Right leading Company finding their Right exposed at once seized the huts at U.29.d.9.2. and took prisoners from there. This Company refused its flank back to the LANGEMARCK Road, while the Right Support Company, seeing the position on the Right, made a defensive flank to South side of HAANIXBEEK FARM - a fine bit of tactical work. Within an hour all the posts were well on their way to completion, having been well sited and giving good mutual support.

11th Manchester Regt., the Right Support Bn., detailed to leapfrog the 8th North. Fus. and to advance on the RED LINE, had suffered heavily immediately after ZERO. They had only 3 Company Officers Left when they began their advance, and owing to the heavy fire directed upon their Right flank from MON DU HIBOU and the TRIANGLE only a portion on the extreme Left of the Battalion was in time.

The COCKCROFT was found to be unoccupied, and the advancing troops passed through. Then Lieut. FALCONER, Commanding the Right leading Company, finding no one on his Right flank and seeing no sign of the Brigade on the Right attacking there, and also owing to heavy Machine Gun fire from MON DU HIBOU and his Right flank, decided to go off left-handed to get round. The Commanding Officer of the Battn. seeing this movement himself and not understanding the cause, sent a runner to him with an order to keep to his Right. At the same time he ordered Captain BLEAKLEY, Commanding the Right Support Company to go up and fill the gap on the Right. He shortly afterwards received a message from Captain BLEAKLEY from the work at C.5.d.5.9. stating he could not get on on the Right flank, owing to heavy fire from the direction of MON DU HIBOU. The C.O. then went to the spot himself to find out the exact position of affairs and found Captain BLEAKLEY's report was correct. MON DU HIBOU was not captured by 145th Brigade, from where the fire was coming. The C.O. therefore ordered Captain BLEAKLEY to stay where he was and to form a defensive flank. Meanwhile Lieut. FALCONER, on receiving the order from his C.O., swung back towards the Right and captured the work at C.6.a.55.50. with 40 prisoners. They then came under heavy fire from BULOW FARM and the Right front, and having only a few men left Lieut. FALCONER decided to go back himself and try to collect some more men, but this post owing to the heavy enemy fire was unable to stop there.

The Left leading Company and Supporting two platoons crossed the LANGEMARCK road on the Left and advanced till they came under

(3)

flanking fire from BULOW FARM, and seeing no further advance of 9th Lancs. Fus. on their Left stayed where they were. Later, seeing some men retire on their Left, they too withdrew to the huts at U.30.d.90.35. The C.O. of the 11th Manchester Regt., himself seeing this retirement, also seeing some men retiring past these huts, sent his Adjutant to the spot to push them forward again to the huts and to form a defensive flank so as to join up with 9th Lancs. Fus. on his Left. This was done and these positions were held till the Brigade was relieved.

On the Left the 9th Lancs. Fus. leap-frogged the 5th Dorset Regt. on the GREEN LINE and went forward with the barrage at the right time. The advance went well till the Right Company came under heavy enfilade fire from BULOW FARM and also from the work on their front at U.30.c.2.8. At this point Captain GRAINGER, Commanding the Right Leading Company was killed and the Company after holding on for a time eventually fell back in line with the 11th Manchester Regt.

Meanwhile the Left leading Company pushed on and though one platoon lost 18 men going from RAT HOUSE to PHEASANT TRENCH the objective was gained. The Left Support Company had closed up owing

Touch had been lost with the Right Companies when they were held up, so Lieut. HAYES, now Commanding the two Left Companies, hoping the Right Companies might have reached the trench more to the Right

GOSS, whose platoon had been detailed to take WHITE HOUSE, occupied this point; subsequently he was heavily shelled, 8 of his platoon being killed and he himself wounded. It was then agreed with the Right Company of the Right Battalion (K.S.L.I.) of 60th Brigade to withdraw and hold 2 posts 50 yards West of WHITE HOUSE, which was visited by patrols periodically and never re-occupied by the enemy. Throughout 2nd Lieut. INGLIS kept touch with the Brigade on our Left, and Lieut. HAYES refused his Right flank to get touch with the Right Companies, the line running from PHEASANT TRENCH West of RAT HOUSE and then joining up with 11th Manchester Regt. on the LEKKERBOTER-BEEK at U.29.d.99.45.

This was the position during the night of Z/Z plus 1. On Z plus 1 day it was decided RAT HOUSE must be re-occupied to straighten the line at that point and to strengthen the defensive flank. 9th Lancs. Fus. were ordered to carry out this minor operation. After dusk Lieut. HAYES sent out a patrol which reported RAT HOUSE unoccupied by the enemy, but snipers in the COPSE East of it. A platoon then advanced in extended order, occupied RAT HOUSE and passing on mopped up and killed 8 enemy snipers who were scattered in shell holes in the COPSE East of RAT HOUSE. New posts were then dug so that the line ran from WHITE HOUSE, which was again occupied without opposition, through PHEASANT TRENCH at U.30.a.3.8., 2.7., 1.4., 0.1., U.29.d.9.9., 9.7. to the Battalion Boundary on the LEKKERBOTER-BEEK at U.29.d.99.45. This line was handed over to 33rd Brigade on relief on night Z plus 1/Z plus 2.

The 20th Division also dug a defensive line from the salient in PHEASANT TRENCH at U.23.d.9.0. due South. The 5th Dorset Regt. therefore dug a post about U.29.b.85.55. to join up the existing post at U.29.b.8.4. to the Divisional Boundary at U.29.b.8.7. This post was dug about 3'6" deep before relief and was then handed over to the relieving Company of 9th Sherwood Foresters.

O.C. 34th Machine Gun Company had 4 guns detailed for the consolidation of the GREEN LINE and four for the consolidation of the RED LINE. These guns crossed the STEENBEEK about 5-45 a.m. The guns detailed to help the Right got into action to try and assist the attack when held up, and remained in position here, one being subsequently knocked out. On the Left the two guns helping the consolidation of the 5th Dorset Regt. got into position about 6-5 a.m., while the two detailed to help the 9th Lancs. Fus. moved on and finding the Right of 9th Lancs. Fus. was held up came into action behind RAT HOUSE to protect the Right flank. About 4 p.m. these guns withdrew and took up positions in front of the LANGEMARCK Road on the line of the Dorset forward posts.

O.C. 34th Light Trench Mortar Battery detailed two guns to assist each flank. The two guns on the Right advanced behind 8th North. Fus. to C.5.d.5.9. and the Infantry being held up, a gun was got into action and with one man holding it between his legs, 2nd Lieut. JONES fired at the COCKCROFT and continued till M. G. firing from COCKCROFT ceased. No ammunition was left. The carriers were either wounded or had gone forward with the Infantry, and it was therefore decided to go into Reserve. The two guns on the Left crossed the STEENBEEK behind 5th Dorset Regt. but were not called on during the advance to the LANGEMARCK Road. Following on behind the 9th Lancs. Fus. they reached a position about 100 yards West of RAT HOUSE, but the position of our troops being uncertain, were unable to fire from there. They withdrew later and took up a psoition near one of the 5th Dorset Regt. posts, where they remained till the relief.

Communications during operations were difficult owing to the heavy shell fire that the enemy kept up on the rising ground West of the STEENBEEK. As soon as lines were laid across that area they were immediately cut. But great credit is due to 5th Dorset Regt. who got continual messages back to Brigade H.Q. from the very outset, mostly by runner. A detailed report on Inter-communication has already been submitted by Bde. SIG. Officer to O.C. 11th Division Signal Company.

Casualties were heavy in three out of the four Battns., all three losing very severely in Officers, but 8th North. Fus. casualties were the heaviest of all, and the loss of all their four Company Commanders very soon after ZERO was a great handicap to them. The total casualties are shown below :-

	Officers.			Other ranks.		
	K.	W.	M.	K.	W.	M.
8th North. Fus.	6.	5.	-	~~50.~~ 46	~~222.~~ 231	~~45.~~ 30
9th Lancs. Fus.	1.	9.	-	~~36.~~ 33	~~148.~~ 174	~~60.~~ 33
5th Dorset Rgt.	-	3.	-	~~19.~~ 25	~~79.~~ 114	~~15.~~ 6
11th Man'. Rgt.	4.	4.	1.	45.	145.	55.
34th M. G. Coy.	NIL.			Total 24.		
34th L. T. M. B.	NIL.			1.	8.	1.
Brigade H.Q.	NIL.			-	8. 1	2. 0

August 20th., 1917.

S. Sedley Brigadier General,
Commanding 34th. Infantry Brigade.

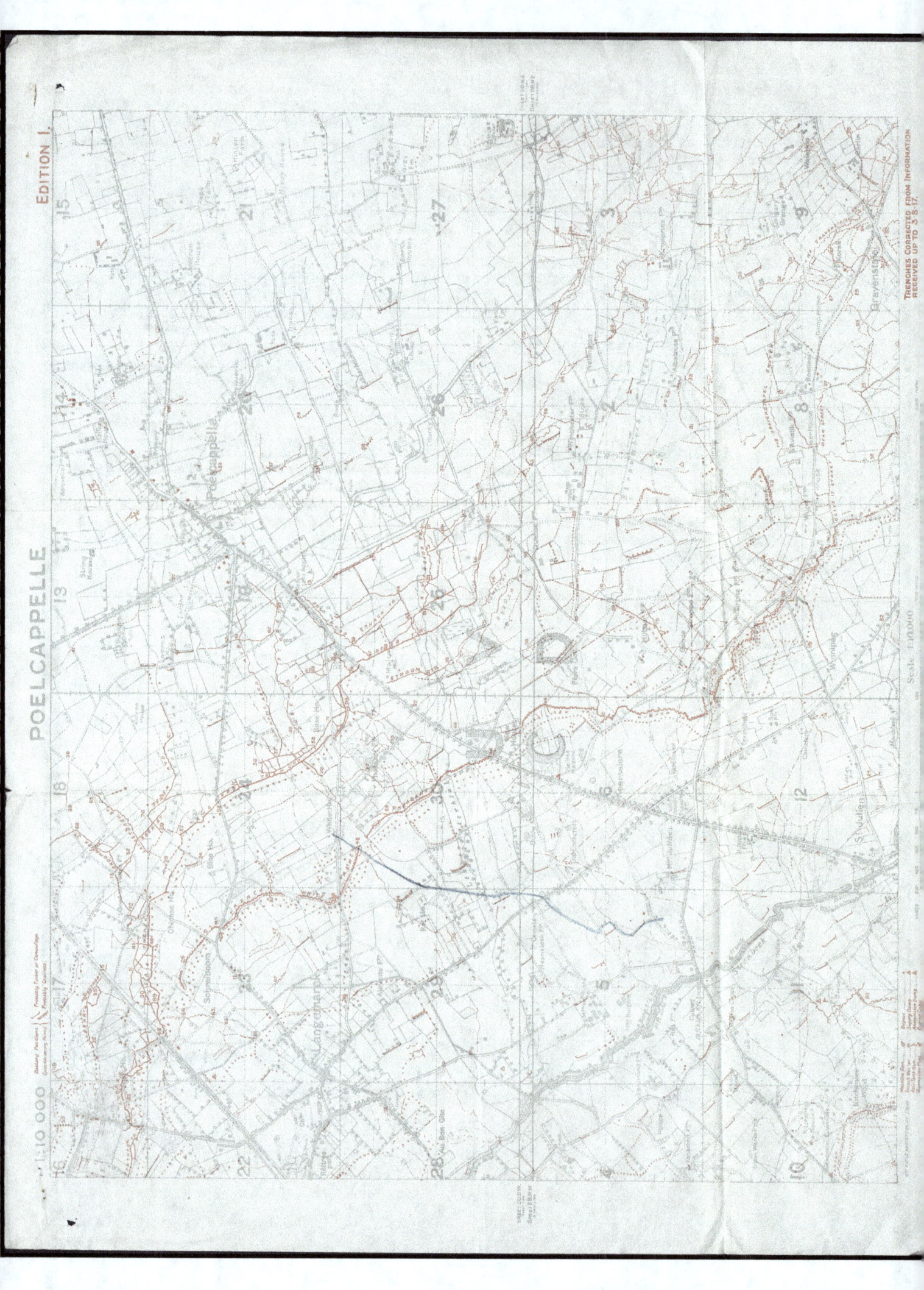

28031 W3125/M2250 1000m 6/17 M.R.Co.,Ltd. (1367) Forms W3091   Army Form W.3091.

Cover for Documents.

Nature of Enclosures.

Notes, or Letters written.

28031 W3125/M2250 1000m 6/17 M.R.Co.,Ltd. (1367) Forms W3091   Army Form W.3091.

Cover for Documents.

Confidential

Nature of Enclosures.

War Diary

Headquarters 34th Infantry Brigade

From 1st To 30th September

Vol 15

Notes, or Letters written.

WAR DIARY / INTELLIGENCE SUMMARY

Army Form C. 2118.

Sept 1917 of 34th Inf. Bde.

Place	Date	Hour	Summary of Events and Information	Remarks and references to Appendices
DIRTY BUCKET CAMP (A.30.c.60.60)	1st		Training carried out. Showery day.	
"	2nd		Sunday. Church Parades. G.O.C. Div. holds a conference at D.H.Q. to discuss various points raised by recent operations. Showers again during the morning, but fine in afternoon and evening.	
"	3rd		Fine day. Training continued. Order received from the Division ordering the move of the Bde. to WATOU Training Area to-morrow, 4th inst. Order issued accordingly (see Appendix 1) for the Bde. to move.	Appendix 1
"	4th	4:30 a.m.	A German aeroplane flying over the camp at 4.30 a.m. dropped 6 bombs amongst the tents of 9th Lan. Fus., killing 16 and wounding 71 men of that Battalion. Owing to the early start which the Bde. was ordered to make for its march, fires had been lighted in the "cookers" and in the bivouacs before dawn & these lights probably attracted & hostile	
		5.45 a.m.	aeroplane flying back home from a raid. The Bde.	

Army Form C. 2118.

WAR DIARY
or
INTELLIGENCE SUMMARY.
(Erase heading not required).

Instructions regarding War Diaries and Intelligence Summaries are contained in F. S. Regs., Part II. and the Staff Manual respectively. Title pages will be prepared in manuscript.

Place	Date	Hour	Summary of Events and Information	Remarks and references to Appendices
L.13 Central (Sheet 27)	4th (continued)	9.30 a.m.	marches to Matou Training Area, Bde H.Q. opens at L.13 Central (Sheet 27) at 9.30 a.m. This unit of the Bde are distributed in K.12.d, L.1.b, L.7.a, L.8.c, L.13.c, and L.14.b. Fine day, very warm.	
"	5th		Fine day. Training carried on.	
"	6th		Training continued. The Corps Commander, Lieut-Gen Sir Ivor Maxse, came to Bde H.Q. and met all the C.O.s He asked questions about the operations on Aug 15th and makes suggestions for the future. Fine morning but heavy rain in the evening and at night.	
"	7th		Training continued.	
"	8th		Training continued.	
"	9th		Sunday. Church Parades. Firing on ranges. Fine day. Order received from Div. that Bde. will move on 11th to LE NOUVEAU MONDE area.	
"	10th		Bde. Order No. 57 (see Appendix I) issued ordering move to LE NOUVEAU Appendix I.	

WAR DIARY
or
INTELLIGENCE SUMMARY.

(Erase heading not required.)

Army Form C. 2118.

Place	Date	Hour	Summary of Events and Information	Remarks and references to Appendices
L.13.central	11th	7 a.m	MONDE area. Training continued. Fine day	
			Bdes. H.Q. closes at L.13 Central at 7 a.m. and opens at	
D.7.c.5.1.		11.30 a.m	D.7.C.5.1 at 11.30 a.m. The Bde. marches by route march	
(Sheet 27)			to LE NOUVEAU MONDE area. Fine day, cloudless sky and	
			hot.	
	12th		Training carried on	
	13th		Training continued	
	14th		Training continued	
	15th		Training continued	
	16th		Sunday. Church parade & presentation of medal-ribbons	
			won in recent operations to each Bn. by Div. General	
	17th		Training continued	
	18th		Training continued	
	19th		Training continued	
	20th		Training continued. Inter-Battalion shooting competition for team	
			of 8 in the morning — won by 9th L.N.L. Fus. Bde. Sports	

WAR DIARY
or
INTELLIGENCE SUMMARY.
(Erase heading not required.)

Army Form C. 2118.

Instructions regarding War Diaries and Intelligence Summaries are contained in F.S. Regs., Part II. and the Staff Manual respectively. Title pages will be prepared in manuscript.

Place	Date	Hour	Summary of Events and Information	Remarks and references to Appendices
D.7C.5/21st			held in the afternoon.	
(Sheet 27) 22nd			Training continued. Bde. Route March. Orders received that Bde. will remain in this area for about another week & continue training for the proposed operations. 9th R.W.Fus. bring the Bn. allocated for Bde. Reserve, will go forward on 25th to make forward dumps.	
"	23rd		Church Parades. Conference at Div. H.Q. at 3 p.m. to discuss coming operations. Fine day	
"	24th		Training continued. Weather still hot and fine.	
"	25th		Training continued. Bde. practice attack over laid-out course.	
"	26th		Training continued. Bde. practice attack rehearsed. Conference at Div. H.Q. at 4.30 p.m. 9th R.W.Fus. will move forward to take part in attack	
"	27th		Training continued.	
"	28th		Training continued. Corps Commander watches Bde. practice attack. Weather still fine and hot.	

Army Form C. 2118.

WAR DIARY
or
INTELLIGENCE SUMMARY.
(Erase heading not required.)

Instructions regarding War Diaries and Intelligence Summaries are contained in F. S. Regs., Part II. and the Staff Manual respectively. Title pages will be prepared in manuscript.

Place	Date	Hour	Summary of Events and Information	Remarks and references to Appendices
D.7C.5.1. (Sheet 27)	29th		Training continued. Div Order for move preparatory to operations issued, and Bde. Order 58 issued in accordance	Appendix I
"	30th		Sunday. Church Parades. Bde. Order 59 for the afternoon issued. G.O.C. visits 32nd 73rd H.Q. in line to arrange taking over. Weather fine, and very hot by day but cold at night.	Will be included in book. 2/Windsor I

Secret.

To O.C. War Diary

[Stamp: HEADQUARTERS 34th INFANTRY BRIGADE No. 1613 Date 3/9/17]

Reference this Office No. M. 67 of today's date.

March Table is as under.

UNIT.	STARTING POINT.	TIME HEAD OF COLUMN TO PASS STARTING POINT.	ROUTE.	DESTINATION.
Brigade Hd. Qrs.	Junction of CHEMIN MILITAIRE and POPER-INGHE – ELVERDINGHE Road.	5-45 a.m.	SWITCH ROAD North of POPERINGHE – ST. JANS TER BIEZEN.	L. 13. Central. (Sheet 27)
9th Lanc. Fus.	–do–	5-48 a.m.	–do–	L.8.c.6.6.
5th Dorset Rgt.	–do–	6-13 a.m.	–do–	L.14.b.8.4.
11th Man'. Rgt.	–do–	6-28 a.m.	–do–	L.13.c.4.4.
34th L.T.M.B.	–do–	6-43 a.m.	–do–	L.1.d.4.3.
34th M.G. Coy.	–do–	6-47 a.m.	–do–	K.12.d.7.8.
8th North. Fus.	–do–	7-2 a.m.	–do–	L.7.a.9.6.

1. Brigade Headquarters will close at DIRTY BUCKET CAMP at 5 a.m. and open at L.13. Central at 9-30 a.m.

2. There will be the regulation halts of 10 minutes before the hour to the hour.

3. ACKNOWLEDGE.

Captain,
Brigade Major, 34th Inf. Brigade.

September 3rd., 1917.

War Diary

S E C R E T.   Copy No...4......

34th INFANTRY BRIGADE ORDER No.57.

Reference map - Sheet 27 - 1/40,000.   September 10th.

1. The 34th Infantry Brigade will move on September 11th by route march to LE NOUVEAU MONDE Area in accordance with the attached March Table.

2. First Line Transport will march with Units.

3. Intervals of 500 yards between Battalions and 10 yards between Companies will be kept.
   There will be the usual halts at regulation times, with the exception that there will be NO halt in either WATOU or HOUTKERQUE. Any Unit, therefore, which finds in approaching either of those Villages that it cannot clear the place before 10 mins. to the hour must halt outside till the column starts again at the hour.

4. Brigade Headquarters will close at L.13. Central at 7 a.m. and open at D.7.c.5.1. at 11-30 a.m.

5. ACKNOWLEDGE.

ISSUED AT. 2. p.m.

R. Turner,
Captain,
Brigade Major, 34th. Infy. Brigade.

DISTRIBUTION.

Copy No. 1. Office.
    2. -do-
    3. Staff Captain.
    4. War Diary.
    5. -do-
    6. Bde. Signals.
    7. 8th North. Fus.
    8. 9th Lancs. Fus.
    9. 5th Dorset Regt.

Copy No. 10. 11th Manchesters.
    11. 34th M. G. Coy.
    12. 34th L. T. M. B.
    13. 11th Division.
    14. 33rd Brigade.
    15. No.4.Coy.Div.Train.
    16. 34th Field Amb'.
    17. Area Commandant,
        No.2.Area, WATOU.

MARCH TABLE issued with 34th Brigade Order No.57.

UNIT.	STARTING POINT.	TIME HEAD OF COLUMN TO PASS STARTING POINT.	ROUTE.	DESTINATION.
Brigade Hd. Qrs.	Cross-roads at K.12.c.6.3.	7-55 a.m.	WATOU – HOUTKERQUE – thence shortest route to respective billets.	D.7.c.5.1.
34th M. G. Coy.	-do-	8-1 a.m.	-do-	D.15.a.3.5.
34th L. T. M. B.	-do-	8-7 a.m.	-do-	D.20.b.6.3.
8th North. Fus.	-do-	8-15 a.m.	-do-	D.19.c.7.0.
9th Lancs. Fus.	-do-	8-26 a.m.	-do-	D.8.c.1.4.
11th Man'. Rgt.	-do-	8-37 a.m.	-do-	D.16.c.1.9.
5th Dorset Rgt.	-do-	8-48 a.m.	-do-	D.17.b.4.1.

SECRET.   Copy No. 4

34th. INFANTRY BRIGADE ORDER No. 58.

Reference maps - 1/10,000 POELCAPPELLE.
                 1/10,000 PILCKEM.
                 1/40,000 Sheet 27.
                 1/40,000 Sheet 28.

1. The 34th Infantry Brigade will relieve the 32nd Infantry Brigade in the Right Sector of their front in accordance with the attached table.

2. Especial attention is drawn to the following :-

   EMBUSSING AND DEBUSSING ROUTINE.

   (a) Each bus will hold 25 men and personnel will be told off into parties of 25 before arriving at the embussing point.

   (b) Immediately on arrival at the debussing point, Companies will march off independently as soon as formed up. It is most important that there should be no delay in marching off, so that busses can move away from debussing point and thus prevent congestion of traffic.

   (c) In the forward area at least 200 yards will be maintained between Companies.

   (d) Busses for moving 34th. Brigade will assemble with tail of column just clear of HERZEELE on the HOUTKERQUE - HERZEELE Road.

3. Transport will march on the same day as that on which its unit moves, route - ST. JANS TER BIEZEN - SWITCH ROAD North of POPERINGHE.

4. ACKNOWLEDGE.

ISSUED AT... 9. P.M.

                                             F.G. Turner, Captain,
29th. September, 1917.   Brigade Major, 34th. Infy. Brigade.

DISTRIBUTION.

Copy No. 1. Office.	Copy No. 10. 11th. Manchesters.
2. -do-	11. 34th. M. G. Coy.
3. Staff Captain.	12. 34th L. T. M. B.
4. War Diary.	13. 11th. Division.
5. -do-	14. 32nd. Brigade.
6. Bde. Sigs.	15. 33rd. Brigade.
7. 8th North. Fus.	16. No.4 Coy. Div. Train.
8. 9th. Lan' Fus.	17. 34th Field Ambulance.
9. 5th Dorset Rgt.	18. Area Comdt. D.B. Camp.

Copy No. 19. Area Commandant, LE NOUVEAU MONDE Area.

MOVEMENT TABLE to accompany 34th Brigade Order No. 58.

Serial No.	Unit.	Date.	From.	Via.	To.	Remarks.
1.	Brigade H.Q. 9th. Lan'. Fus. 11th Man'. Rgt. 34th M. G. Coy.	Oct. 1st.	NOUVEAU MONDE AREA.	VLAMERTINGHE.	DIRTY BUCKET CAMP.	(a) Busses for 1750. Embus at 9 a.m. (b) Route March from VLAMERTINGHE to Dirty Bucket Camp.
2.	1 Company, 11th Manchester Rgt.	Oct. 2nd.	D. B. Camp.		CANE TRENCH.	To arrive at CANE TRENCH by 8 a.m. and come under orders of G.O.C. 32nd Bde
3.	9th. Lan'. Fus. (less 2 Coys.). 11th Man'. Rgt. (less 2 Coys.). 34th M. G. Coy.	Oct. 2nd.	D. B. Camp.		CANAL BANK.	To arrive on CANAL BANK at 10 a.m. and come under orders of G.O.C. 32nd Bde
4.	One Company, 9th. Lan'. Fus.	Oct. 2nd.	D. B. Camp.		MURAT SHELTERS.	To arrive at MURAT SHELTERS at 10 a.m. and come under orders of G.O.C. 32nd Brigade.
5.	8th North. Fus. 5th Dorset Rgt. less Dump parties.	Oct. 2nd.	NOUVEAU MONDE AREA.	VLAMERTINGHE.	DIRTY BUCKET CAMP.	As in Serial No. 1.
6. (a)	9th. Lan'. Fus. (less 2 Coys.). 11th Man'. Rgt. (less 2 Coys.). 34th M. G. Coy.	Night 2nd /3rd Oct.	CANAL BANK.		(a) LINE.	Relief of Right Sector of Divisional Front.
(b)	One Company, 9th. Lan'. Fus.		MURAT SHELTERS.		(b) MON DU RASTA.	

(2)

Serial No.	Unit.	Date.	From.	Via.	To	Remarks.
7.	One Company, 9th. Lan'. Fus. One Company, 11th Man'. Rgt.	Oct. 3rd.	Dirty Bucket Camp.		CANAL BANK.	To arrive on Canal Bank at 11-30 a.m.
8.	8th North. Fus. 5th Dorset Rgt. (less Dump Parties).	Oct. 3rd.	Dirty Bucket Camp.		SIEGE CAMP.	

One Company, 8th Northumberland Fus. and one Company, 5th Dorset Regt. employed on making dumps will rejoin their units on completion of duties.

*0*0*0*0*0*0*

35807. W16879/M1879 500,000 3.17 R.T. (1074) Forms/W3091/3   Army Form W.3091.

Cover for Documents.

Confidential

Nature of Enclosures.

War Diary.

of

34th Infantry Brigade Headquarters

From 1st October 1917
To   1st October 1917

Notes, or Letters written.

Army Form C. 2118.

WAR DIARY

Oct. 1917 INTELLIGENCE SUMMARY. of 34th Inf. Bde.

(Erase heading not required.)

Instructions regarding War Diaries and Intelligence Summaries are contained in F. S. Regs., Part II. and the Staff Manual respectively. Title pages will be prepared in manuscript.

Place	Date	Hour	Summary of Events and Information	Remarks and references to Appendices
D76.b.1 (Sheet 27)	Oct 1		Bde. Order 57.A. for the attack issued and attention to Order 57 (see Appendix I).	Appendix I
DIRTY BUCKET CAMP	"	2.30 p.m.	Bde. H.Q. moves to DIRTY BUCKET CAMP, also 9th Lanc. Fus. 11th MANCHESTERS	Appendix I
			Regt. and M.G. Coy. Bde. Order 60 for the relief at portion of	
			32nd Inf. Bde. in right sector of Div. front issued (see Appendix I)	
			Weather still hot and fine. Bomb dropped by hostile aircraft	
			in camp at 9.45 p.m. but no casualties.	
"	2nd		9th Lanc. Fus. (less 1 Coy) + 11th MANCHESTER Regt. (less 1 Coy) and M.G. Coy move	
			on to the Line, and 5th DORSET Regt. and 8th NORTH FUS. move	
CAMP POST		6 p.m.	to DIRTY BUCKET CAMP. Bde. H.Q. moves to CAMP POST at	
			6 p.m.	
"	3rd	12.5 a.m.	Relief in Line completed at 12.5 a.m. & G.O.C. 34th Inf. Bde.	
			assumed command of the right sector of Divisional front	
			The weather breaks at 1.30 a.m. and rain falls gently till	
			6 a.m., & then weather clears again. Notification received that	
			ZERO HOUR will be 6 a.m. tomorrow. 8th NORTH FUS. and	

Army Form C. 2118.

WAR DIARY
or
INTELLIGENCE SUMMARY.
(Erase heading not required.)

Instructions regarding War Diaries and Intelligence Summaries are contained in F. S. Regs., Part II. and the Staff Manual respectively. Title pages will be prepared in manuscript.

Place	Date	Hour	Summary of Events and Information	Remarks and references to Appendices
MAISON BULGARE		2.30 a.m.	5th DORSET Regt. moved to SIEGE CAMP in the morning, and 5th DORSET Regt. on to MURAT SHELTERS by 7 p.m. Bde. HQ. moved forward to MAISON BULGARE at 2.30 p.m. The afternoon was fine but the night was cloudy and very dark. The Coys. for the assaulting Bno. to form up on was laid as soon as it was dark and the Bussex Coys of the assaulting Bno. began to move up.	
"	4th		The forming-up was completed successfully before ZERO. Shortly before ZERO a drizzling rain began to fall and this made ZERO hour darker than it would ordinarily have been.	
		6 a.m.	At 6 a.m. under a splendid artillery barrage, reinforced for 3 mins. by rapid fire from 4 guns of 34th LTMB. firing at thirty strong-points close up to the starting-point, the 9th LAN. FUS. on the right and 11th MAN. FUS. on the left began the assault. The going at first was very heavy especially about the STROOMBEEK, but little resistance was	

units by this time, and the DOTTED RED LINE was captured up to time. Already heavy losses had been incurred among officers, 11th Man R suffering severely in this respect.

After an interval of 1 hour, when the advance was resumed against the RED LINE again the resistance was not stubborn, the only concrete building on the whole Bde-front being GLOSTER FARM. Here the enemy made some stand but ward was sent back to 9 & R & LT & B for gun got rapidly into action with good effect. Two Tanks hit here approaching and a party of MANCHESTERS rushed the building, either killing or capturing the whole garrison — about in all.

By this whole objective was captured. Consolidation at once began, and while the protective barrage was down no patrols were pushed out, but as far as the barrage would permit the MEBUS at V.20.a.3.6 was captured and hld, and both BEEK HOUSES and MEUNIER HOUSE appear to have been vacated by the enemy.

WAR DIARY
or
INTELLIGENCE SUMMARY.
(Erase heading not required.)

Army Form C. 2118.

Place	Date	Hour	Summary of Events and Information	Remarks and references to Appendices
			but our troops were unable to occupy them owing to the protective barrage, and by the time that it had lifted the enemy had reoccupied them. 10th M.M.R. at one time pushed a post as far forward as V.20.C.9.7., but being isolated this had subsequently to be withdrawn in a line with the other posts, which ran from V.26.a.6.6. to GLOSTER FARM inclusive to V.20.C.1.9. Meanwhile Major MILNER, commanding 9th LANCERS, had 4 of their Coy. commdrs., and three of the Coy. comdrs. of 11th M.M.R. had all been hit, and both Bns. had suffered considerable casualties, though their majority were walking cases, and the number of killed very slight. About 6.30 p.m. 300 to 400 Germans were seen to come over the ridge South-East of BEER HOUSES to counter-attack, but in answer to a S.O.S. signal the artillery barrage was put down and completely dispersed them. Gunfire	

Army Form C. 2118.

WAR DIARY
or
INTELLIGENCE SUMMARY.
(Erase heading not required.)

Place	Date	Hour	Summary of Events and Information	Remarks and references to Appendices
			party at 50. Germans had been seen coming from behind MEUNIER HOUSE about 4 p.m., but they were dealt with by rifle and m.g. fire. The consolidation of the front system was completed by night and a support line constructed in front of the DOTTED RED LINE with Strong-points constructed at V.26.a.0.b and at V.19.d.5.2. Meanwhile two coys of 5th DORSET Regt had followed up in close support and one in about V.25.a and b., whilst the other two coys took up a position in C.T.S.d. The HQ of the Bn was at BULOW FARM, both of the assaulting Bns having moved their HQ forward from there to about V.25.6.6.37. The operations having been so successful an order was issued at 1.30 p.m. for the 5th DORSET Regt to pass through at 5 p.m. and capture BEEK HOUSES and MEUNIER HOUSE, but at 3.30 p.m. this order was cancelled, owing to 4th Div. on the left of 11th Div. having been counter-attacked	

WAR DIARY or INTELLIGENCE SUMMARY

Army Form C. 2118.

Place	Date	Hour	Summary of Events and Information	Remarks and references to Appendices
			by the enemy.	
			During the night a patrol passed through the MESU at K.20.a.3.9., which was fired upon. The boundary of 33rd Bde. was handed over to 7th SUFFR Regt. Major MENGEN'S command 11th Mar. Regt., was hit by a sniper after dark and had to	
MINSON BULGARE	5th		leave the 13th. The following morning The situation remained unchanged. The following day an order was received from the Div. stating that the opposing force would be learned at an early date. and that 32nd Bde. with 33rd Bde. 150th relief 34th Bde. on night 7th/8th. 5th NORTH FUS. and 33rd Bde. in Divisional Rose.	
			Order No. 61 was issued accordingly (see Appendix I) and also Appendix I	
			BM 858 was sent out ordering 5th DORSET Regt. to relieve 7th LAN. FUS. and 11th MAN. Regt. in the line on the night 5th/6th. (See Appendix I)	
			Heavy rain fell during the day & the conditions became most trying. The relief ordered in BM 858 was carried out successfully during the night.	

WAR DIARY
or
INTELLIGENCE SUMMARY.
(Erase heading not required.)

Army Form C. 2118.

Place	Date	Hour	Summary of Events and Information	Remarks and references to Appendices
MAISON BULGARE	6th		and 4th MAN. Regt. came back to an support position in K.25.a and b + while 9th LAN. FUS. were in reserve in C.5.d. In the afternoon 9th LAN. FUS. were withdrawn further back to HURST PARK area and one Coy of 4th MAN. Regt. took their place in E.S.A. Bde Order No. 62 (Appendix I) was issued ordering relief at 3 A.M. Bdn by a portion of 32nd Bde. on night 7th/8th. Heavy rain fell during the day and the weather became cold. During the night there was heavy shelling at the 11th MAN. R in V.25.a. and b., but no attempt to counter-attack was made by the enemy. Vigorous patrolling 1530 carried out by us, and it was discovered that the enemy was holding a line of snipers posts 100 to 150 yds in front of our line.	
"	7th		The position still unchanged. Heavy rain again fell and at noon a message was received from the Div. saying	

A6945 Wt. W11422/M1160 350,000 12/16 D. D. & L. Forms/C./2118/14

WAR DIARY
or
INTELLIGENCE SUMMARY.
(Erase heading not required.)

Army Form C. 2118.

Instructions regarding War Diaries and Intelligence Summaries are contained in F. S. Regs., Part II. and the Staff Manual respectively. Title pages will be prepared in manuscript.

Place	Date	Hour	Summary of Events and Information	Remarks and references to Appendices
			the relief that night might be cancelled. The question for the relieving units had been ordered to be met. Bde. H.Q. at 5 p.m. but only at 7 p.m. was it finally decided to carry out the relief, so that the leading platoons of the relieving units did not pass Bde. H.Q. till 11.30 p.m. This made the relief very late	For further account see Appendix III.
MAISON BULGARE	8th		and when day broke two platoons of 5th DORSET Regt. in this front posts though relieved were unable to get away. On relief the units moved to	
SIEGE CAMP		9 a.m.	SIEGE CAMP, where they rested till noon and then marched	
		2 p.m.	to DIRTY BUCKET Station to entrain. The Bde. trained	
			HATTON Station at 10 p.m. and went into billets in the	
EPERLECQUES		11 p.m.	EPERLECQUES area.	
	9th		The Bde. rests. The two platoons of 5th DORSET Regt. still in the line on the right 7/8th from their unit. 32nd Bde.	
			relieve the attack in and south of POELCAPELLE with little success.	

Army Form C. 2118.

WAR DIARY
or
INTELLIGENCE SUMMARY.
(Erase heading not required.)

Instructions regarding War Diaries and Intelligence Summaries are contained in F. S. Regs., Part II. and the Staff Manual respectively. Title pages will be prepared in manuscript.

Place	Date	Hour	Summary of Events and Information	Remarks and references to Appendices
EPERLECQUES	10th		8th NORTH. FUS. who had been held in Div. reserve are not used except on req. for carrying and stretcher-bearing	
HOULLE	"	11 a.m.	The Bde. move from EPERLECQUES area to HOULLE area Bde. H.Q. closed at EPERLECQUES and opens at HOULLE	
"	11th		8th NORTH. FUS. and 34th M.G. Coy. rejoin the Bde. The Bde. washed, reorganise and begin training	
"	12th		Reorganisation and training continued. G.O.C. sees the men of 9th LAN. FUS. and 11th MAN. Regt. who took part in the recent battle and congratulates them on their great success. A warning order received from Div. that the Div. will be transferred to First Army and move on 15th inst. by train to ST. HILAIRE area. M.283 issued to units accordingly (see Appendix I.)	Appendix I
	13th		Training carried on. Brig. Gen. CLAY goes on leave and Lt. Col. C. C. HANNAY, 5th DORSET Regt. assumes temporary command of the Bde. Heavy rain. Move to ST. HILAIRE area postponed till 18th inst.	

Army Form C. 2118.

WAR DIARY
or
INTELLIGENCE SUMMARY.
(Erase heading not required.)

Place	Date	Hour	Summary of Events and Information	Remarks and references to Appendices
HOUCHIN	14th		Sunday. Church parades. Fine day, but rain again at night.	See Appendix
"	15th		This day Training carried on in all Bns. Firing on ranges.	for Operation Order of Day
"	16th		Training continued. A conference held at 3.30 p.m. at Div. H.Q. to discuss lessons learnt from recent operations and training programme. Bde. Order No. 63 ordering move to ST. HILAIRE area on 18th inst. issued (see Appendix I)	Appendix I
"	17th		Training continued. Order for move to ST. HILAIRE area cancelled, and Div. Order for move to AMES area and then into line in relief of 6th Div. issued. Bde. Order No. 64 issued to units accordingly (see Appendix I)	Appendix I
"	18th		This Bde. marched to billets in AMES area. Bde. H.Q. opens at 8 p.m. then marches to WATTEN station, proceeds to LILLERS and at ECQUEDECQUES.	
ECQUEDECQUES		6 p.m.	Then marches to billets to HOUCHIN - VAUDRICOURT - NOEUX area. 1 Bn. This Bde. moves by bus to HOUCHIN - VAUDRICOURT - NOEUX area.	
VAUDRICOURT	19th	1.30 a.m.	H.Q. closing at ECQUEDECQUES at 9 a.m. and opening at VAUDRICOURT at 1.30 p.m. Bde. Order No. 65 issued ordering relief of	Appendix II

WAR DIARY
or
INTELLIGENCE SUMMARY.
(Erase heading not required.)

Army Form C. 2118.

Place	Date	Hour	Summary of Events and Information	Remarks and references to Appendices
VAUDRICOURT	20th		71st Inf. Bde. & 34th Inf. Bde. on nights 20th/21st and 21st/22nd. Move in accordance carried out in accordance with Bde. Order 20.	
NOEUX-LES-MINES		12 noon	65 Bde H.Q. Close at VAUDRICOURT at 11 a.m. and open at NOEUX-LES-MINES at noon. 8th North. Fus. relieve 9th NORFOLKS in support, 5th DORSETS relieve 1st LEICESTERS in reserve and 34th L.T.M.B. relieve 71st L.T.M.B. in the line.	
"	21st		Relief of 71st Inf. Bde. in the line completed, 5th DORSET Regt. relieving 2nd SHERWOOD FORESTERS on the right front and 8th NORTH FUS. 9th SUFFOLKS on left front, while 9th LON. FUS. and 11th Manch. Regt. move up to support and reserve respectively. The relief is completed by 9.45 p.m., when command of sector passes to G.O.C. 34th Bde. 65 Bde. H.Q. open at CITÉ ST. PIERRE (M.11.a.6.2 - sheet LENS 36 C.S.W.)	
CITÉ ST. PIERRE	22nd		One deserter of 1st Guards R.I.R. is taken by 5th DORSET Regt. He states enemy will probably raid in N.8.d on night 23rd/24th. 34th M.G. Coy. relieve 71st M.G. Coy. in the line. Units trained of this.	

WAR DIARY
or
INTELLIGENCE SUMMARY.
(Erase heading not required.)

Army Form C. 2118.

Place	Date	Hour	Summary of Events and Information	Remarks and references to Appendices
CITE ST PIERRE	23rd		The situation is unchanged. All efforts concentrated on digging, especially on the left front, where trenches it situated are very shallow. Rain all the morning.	
"	24th		Situation unchanged. Front line 6 trench mortars on Bn left front during night 23-24. Fine day.	
"	25th		Showery day. Trenches in bad condition. Bn continued digging and deepening. Coy "B" CLAY returns from leave.	
"	26		Situation unchanged. Rainy day. Enemy T.M's fired on our Left Bn in b/Coy ar our artillery retaliated successfully.	
"	27		Showery. Trenches very muddy - no special actions.	
"	28		Situation unchanged. Brigade Defence scheme issued.	
"	29		3 Privates of 5 Gren.R.R. brought in by Dispatch-bearer. Left Bn was on patrol. 5 Dispatch successfully hostile enemy tours up the front sporting it is weak - B.N.F. attempted similar work on right, but found enemy working parties & posts in front of wire.	

Army Form C. 2118.

WAR DIARY
or
INTELLIGENCE SUMMARY.
(Erase heading not required.)

Instructions regarding War Diaries and Intelligence Summaries are contained in F. S. Regs., Part II. and the Staff Manual respectively. Title pages will be prepared in manuscript.

Place	Date	Hour	Summary of Events and Information	Remarks and references to Appendices
Ch'lu Pent Estate			Bgde HQrs moonlight infantry with winter and patrols — E. Co. A. whit carried out — 9 L.F. relieving D.L.F. in left subsector, and 11 Manchesters r. Dorsets in Rt. subsector. B.M.G. and r. Dorsets coming into support and reserve respectively. Relief complete 6. 7.30 P.M. M/p. c	
	Nov 31		Very fine day. Considerable enemy aeroplane activity & desultary shelling of communication trenches etc — helped repetition of gas at 6 P.M. but tend owing to unfavourable wind	

1.XI.17.

A Chichester
M/ Brigade Major
3u Inf. Bde

S E C R E T.   Copy No........

34th INFANTRY BRIGADE ~~INSTRUCTIONS~~ ~~ORDER No. 59.~~ ORDER No. 59.

Reference special POELCAPPELLE Map - 1/10,000.   29th. Sept., 1917.

1.   On a date and at an hour to be detailed later the Fifth Army will attack the enemy on its front. All preparations will be completed by October 3rd.

2.   11th Division will attack on the Left of XVIII Corps with 143rd Brigade (48th Division) on its Right.

3.   11th Division attack will be carried out by 34th Brigade on the Right and 33rd Brigade on the Left.

4.   The objectives and boundaries of Brigade and Battalions are shown on the attached map; the objective will be called the RED LINE, and there will be a pause on the DOTTED RED LINE during the advance to the RED LINE.

5.   The Brigade will attack with two Battalions - 9th Lancashire Fus. on the Right, and 11th Manchester Regt. on the Left.   5th. Dorset Regt. will be held in Reserve to counter the counter-attack.
        The exact role of 8th Northumberland Fus. will be ~~decided~~ later.   **notified**

6.   The attack will be made in accordance with the principles laid down during training.

7.   The Battalions in the Line will be formed up for attack by ZERO minus 1 hour.
        5th Dorset Regt. will move in suitable formation at an hour to be settled later from vicinity of HURST PARK so as to occupy our present front line as it is vacated. Close liaison with the assaulting Battalions is necessary to ensure this being done.

8.   Os.C. 9th Lan'. Fus. and 11th Man'. Regt. will ensure that their forming-up lines are laid out on X/Y Night, so that they can be checked on Y Day. The tapes and discs for forming-up will not be finally placed in position until Y/Z Night.
        O.C. 5th Dorset Regt. will ensure that the approaches to the present front line are thoroughly reconnoitred and arrangements made for guides, so that his Battalion can begin to move up during the hours of darkness.

9.   Definite units will be detailed to deal with all known or suspected Strong Points. These are :-

        (a) For Right Assaulting Battalion.

            (1) MEBU at V.25.c.75.90.
            (2) M.G. at V.25.d.7.8. (If not dealt with by flank unit)
            (3) Huts and Shell-holes at V.26.a.1.9.
            (4) TERRIER FARM. (If not dealt with by flank unit)
            (5) Shell-holes at V.26.a.4.6.
            (6) Shell-holes at V.26.a.30.75.
            (7) Gun-pit at V.26.a.6.8.
            (8) Shell-holes at V.20.c.6.0.

(2)

(b) For Left Assaulting Battalion.

(1) MALTA HOUSE.
(2) M.G. at V.25.b.05.50.
(3) Shell-holes at V.25.a.7.8.
(4) MEBU at V.19.c. 65.10. (If not dealt with by flank unit)
(5) Gun-pit at V.25.a.8.9.
(6) Gun-pit at V.25.b.3.8.
(7) MEBU at V.20.c.1.0.
(8) GLOSTER FARM.
(9) Gun-pit at V.19.d.9.5.
(10) Gun-pit at V.20.c.2.7.

The parties detailed for mopping up these points will garrison and consolidate them, and will remain there until definitely relieved.

10. After the capture of the RED LINE the ground will be consolidated for defence, the object in view being to hold the ground in depth. Further instructions will be issued in Appendix 6. The out-post line will be selected with a view to assisting a further advance.

11. On the capture of the RED LINE and as soon as the protective barrage permits, patrols previously detailed will be sent to the following points :-

By Right Battalion to BEEK HOUSES and to shell-holes at V.20.c.(8.4

By Left Battalion to MEBU at V.20.a.35.00.

They will ascertain whether these are held by the enemy. If found vacated, they will be occupied. The patrol to BEEK HOUSES will be supported by a Lewis Gun.

A patrol will also be sent by 11th Manchester Regt. to MEUNIER HOUSE to ascertain whether this is occupied by the enemy or not.

12. Liaison will be established by units as under :-

Detailed by	To meet	Place
9th. Lan'. Fus.	143rd Brigade.	TWEED HOUSE.
-do-		TERRIER FARM.
11th Man'. Rgt.	7th S. Staffs. Rgt.	RETOUR Cross-roads.
		Road junction at V.19.d.95.(90.

The object of these posts is to find out if the troops on their flanks are up in line with ours. As soon therefore as they have learnt the position of those troops, 2 men of the Section should be sent back with the information to their Company H.Q. The remainder of the Section rejoin their unit as soon as the next liaison post in front of them has been established.

13. The attack will be made under :-

(a) An Artillery Barrage. (See Appendix 1).
(b) A Machine Gun Barrage. (See Appendix 2).

14. Tanks will probably take part in the attack. Definite information on this point will be given later in Appendix 4.

(3)

15. A contact aeroplane will be in the air during the attack. The leading troops *only* will mark their position to the contact aeroplane by flares when asked for.
Flares should be lit in small clusters and not singly. Further instructions will be issued in Appendix 5.

16. Situations reports will be sent by Battalions to Brigade H.Q. every two hours after ZERO.

17. At ZERO Hour H.Q. will be as under :-

34th Brigade H.Q.	MAISON BULGARE.
9th. Lan'. Fus.) 11th Man'. Rgt.)	BULOW FARM.
5th. Dorset Rgt.	FERDINAND FARM.
8th. North. Fus.	CANAL BANK.

18. One gun of 34th Machine Gun Company is allotted to each assaulting Battalion for the attack. The remaining guns will be utilised for holding the ground gained, in accordance with instructions to be issued in Appendix 2.

19. Six guns of the 34th L.T.M.B. will be in position to bombard the enemy's positions before ZERO. The two remaining guns will be ready to move forward at ZERO to a position from which fire can be brought to bear on GLOSTER FARM.

20. Full use must be made of compasses for keeping direction. The true bearing to the RED LINE from the Right flank is 60 degrees, from the Left flank 57 degrees.

21. Os.C. units will ensure that no orders, Secret maps, documents or letters containing information of value to the enemy are carried by any Officers or men of the assaulting troops.

22. Arrangements as to the synchronisation of watches will be issued later.

23. ZERO Hour will be notified later.

24. The word "retire" does not exist. Anyone using it is to be shot or bayoneted at once. Should it be necessary to withdraw from any position, an order to that effect will be issued only by an Officer, who will be called upon to justify his action.

25. The following Appendices will be issued to these instructions :-

    Appendix 1. Artillery Arrangements.
    -do- 2. Machine Gun Arrangements.
    -do- 3. Signal Arrangements.
    -do- 4. Tanks.
    -do- 5. Contact Aeroplanes.
    -do- 6. R.E. Arrangements.
    -do- 7. Intelligence.

26. ACKNOWLEDGE.

ISSUED AT............

F. Turner,
Captain,
Brigade Major, 34th. Infty. Brigade.

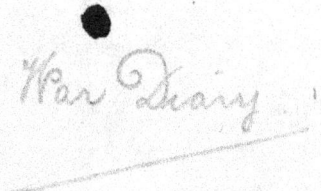

SECRET.

APPENDIX 2.

MACHINE GUN ARRANGEMENTS.

The disposition of the 34th Machine Gun Company will be as follows : three guns will follow the Assaulting Battalions as closely as is practicable and will take up positions for consolidating the Final Objective as shown below :-

(a)   V.20.c.1.9.
(b)   GLOSTER FARM.
(c)   V.26.a.55.60.

To consolidate the RED DOTTED LINE three guns will be utilised about :-

(a)   V.19.d.2.3.
(b)   V.25.b.55.60.
(c)   V.25.b.90.01.

Two guns will be allotted to 5th Dorset Regt. in case of their counter-attacking and they will be in a position of readi-ness about HAANIXBEEK FARM and will automatically move forward in rear of the 5th Dorset Regt. when they advance to counter-attack.

Two guns will be in Reserve in CANE TRENCH.
Six guns will be in Reserve in Canal Bank.

APPENDIX 3.   *War Diary*   SECRET.

To 34th Brigade Instructions issued under this Office No. M. 246, dated 30th. September, 1917.

COMMUNICATIONS.

1. H.Q.

At ZERO Brigade H.Q. will be at MON BULGARE and Brigade Forward Station will be at NEW HOUSES (U.30.d.7.2.).

2. LINES.

There will be two pairs (Nos. 3 & 4) on the Right route of the DIVISIONAL CABLE SCHEME available, between MON BULGARE and BULOW FARM. These pairs will be used by 9th Lancashire Fus. and 11th Manchester Rgt. respectively. This route will be carried forward as soon after ZERO as is practicable.

When Battalions move their H.Q. forward they will keep in touch as far as possible with Bde. Froward Stn. by Visual and when their H.Q. are fixed they will at once notify Brigade of the location and send back 2 Signallers to act as guides to Cable Parties. These guides will assist in laying of cable.

3. VISUAL.

There will be Visual Stations at Bde. Forward Stn. and at HAANIX-BEEK FARM. While at BULOW FARM Battalions will keep Visual communication open with the latter Station and when they move forward they must open up communication with the former as soon as possible; messages to this Station will probably be DD.DD and if so are to be sent through complete once and then repeated in their entirety.

There will also be Divisional Visual Stations at MINTY FARM and CANE POST and if it is impossible to signal to NEW HOUSES communication should be opened with either of these.

4. PIGEONS.

The exact allottment will be notified later. It is expected that there will be two pairs for each attacking Company and 2 pairs for each Battalion H.Q. One pair of each attacking Company is for release as soon as Final Objective is reached. The second pair should be reserved for emergency. Special attention should be paid to putting time of release on the message. Special "Map" Pigeon Message Forms have already been issued.

Pigeons will be drawn from Brigade H.Q. by Battalion Pigeoneers at 6 p.m. on Y Day.

5. ROCKETS.

The exact allottment will be notified later. It is expected that there will be 2 rockets for each attacking Company and 2 for Battalion H.Q. One rocket per attacking Company should be fired on reaching Final Objective and the remaining one reserved for emergency. Rockets should be fired at nearest formation behind i.e. Company to Battalion H.Q. and Battalion H.Q. to Brigade Forward Station or Brigade H.Q.

Stands for firing rockets will be issued. These should be laid in the side of a shell-hole with the spikes on end firmly fixed in the ground. The rocket must rest its whole length in the groove and should be laid flat against it, fuze on top. To obtain maximum range (1,300 yards) stand should be set at an angle of 65 to 70 degrees. Rocket must be aimed at its objective. When all rockets are fired stands should be recovered and returned to Brigade H.Q.

6. POWER BUZZERS AND AMPLIFIERS.

There will be a Power Buzzer and Amplifier at BULOW FARM working to MON BULGARE. There will be two operators from Brigade Section with these instruments. There will be one Power Buzzer at Brigade Forward Stn. working to BULOW FARM and one Power Buzzer spare.

(2)

As soon as the situation allows the Power Buzzer and AMPLIFIER at BULOW FARM will be moved to Bde. Forward Stn. and one Power Buzzer will be moved to each Battalion H.Q. and will work to Bde. Forward Stn. These Power Buzzers will then be manned by Battn. Signallers. Direction of bases will be notified later.

7. WIRELESS.
Brigade Wireless Station will be at RED FARM.

8. RUNNERS.
At ZERO there will be a system of runner relay posts between Bde. H.Q. and Brigade Froward Stn. These will be pushed forward towards Battalion H.Q. as soon as possible.
Messages should not be sent by runner if other suitable means are available. Battalion runners should not be sent direct to Brigade H.Q. but advantage should be taken of the Bde. Relay System which saves time and reduces chances of runners becoming casualties. All runners will carry their messages in the Right-hand breast pocket of their tunics.

9. GENERAL.
The preamble will be included in ALL messages except those sent by Power Buzzer.
The attention of all Officers should be drawn to the importance of putting the time at the foot of every message they write. This especially applies to Pigeon messages which are often quite valueless unless this is done as otherwise there is no means of knowing how long the bird has taken in its flight.
Pigeons must be released in pairs only. Only the authorised Pigeon Message form should be used and it should always be enclosed in a clip. These are issued with the birds. Messages should be sent in duplicate - one copy with each bird.
There will be an issue of cable on Y Day probably 1½ miles D.II on reels to each Battalion. As this is all that will be available it should be used carefully.
Aeroplane shutters, strips and panels will be used at Brigade and Battalion H.Q. Brigade Dropping Ground will be at MON BULGARE.

The following Code Calls and Names will be in use for all means of communication :-

	CODE NAME.	CODE CALL.
34th Inf. Brigade.	ORANGE.	ORZ
-do- (Forward Stn.).	ORANGE ADVANCED.	AORZ
8th North. Fus.	ORDEAL.	ORH
9th. Lan'. Fus.	ORGAN.	ORI
5th Dorset Rgt.	ORIENT.	ORK
11th Man'. Rgt.	ORIGIN.	ORL
34th M.G. Coy.	ORBIT.	ORM
34th L.T.M.B.	ORCHARD.	ORT

*O*O*O*O*O*O*O*

SECRET.

APPENDIX 4.

TANKS.

Four Tanks, "D" Battalion, Tank Corps, will operate on the Brigade's Front, but the objective of two of these is TERRIER FARM.

At ZERO 4 Tanks will advance on RETOUR CROSS ROADS, dealing with DELTA HOUSE on the way if necessary. When our Infantry are at RETOUR CROSS ROADS these four Tanks will turn South along the TERRIER FARM ROAD and proceed as far as possi-ble, according to the position of the protective Artillery barrage.

When the protective barrage lifts, 2 of these Tanks will move forward to deal with TERRIER FARM, the other 2 will have as their Objective GLOSTER FARM.

All ranks must be warned that they should never follow Tanks : Tanks have to reach their Objectives often by devious routes so as to make use of the best roads; men following them will therefore lose direction.

It must be clearly understood that the plan of operations is framed independently of the Tanks, and on no account are Infantry to await the arrival of Tanks.

Attention is called to Signals to Tanks. (See S.S.148, Section VI.).

War Diary

SECRET.

APPENDIX 5.

CONTACT AEROPLANES.

1. A contact aeroplane will fly over the objectives at :-

    ZERO plus 1 hour and 30 minutes -
    ZERO plus 3 hours and 30 minutes -
    and
    when ordered by Corps H.Q.

    Infantry will be ready to light RED Flares at these hours, but will NOT do so unless called for by KLAXON Horn or by the dropping of White lights.

2. Counter-attack Machine.

    (a) An aeroplane will be up continuously during daylight, from ZERO onwards, whose mission will be to detect the approach of enemy counter-attacks.

    (b) Whenever this patrol observes hostile parties of 100 or more moving to counter-attack it will drop a smoke bomb over that portion of the front to which the enemy is moving. The smoke bomb will burst about 100 feet below the machine, into a white parachute flare, which descends slowly leaving a long trail of brown smoke about one foot broad behind it.

3. No troops will fire at low flying aeroplanes on ZERO Day except the Lewis or Vickers Guns especially detailed for that purpose.

SECRET.

APPENDIX 6.

To 34th Brigade Instructions issued under this Office No. M. 246 dated 30th. September, 1917.

After capture of RED LINE the 9th Lancashire Fus. and 11th. Manchester Regt. will each construct 6 strong points, three of them 50 to 100 yards in front of and three 50 to 100 yards behind the RED LINE. The Posts of 9th Lan'. Fus. will be numbered 1, 2, 3 and 7, 8, 9, the posts of 11th Man'. Regt. 4, 5, 6, and 10, 11, 12.

To form the basis of a definite supporting position strong points will be constructed about :-

      V.26.a.00.63. (To be called A).

      V.19.d.74.21. (To be called B).

These will be constructed by 2 Platoons of 8th Northumberland Fus. under orders of C.R.E. and assisted in the case of A by one Platoon of 9th Lancashire Fus. and in the case of B by one Platoon of 11th Manchester Regt.; these Platoons will be definitely detailed beforehand for the purpose. On completion these posts will be garrisoned by these platoons of 9th Lan'. Fus. and 11th Man'. Regt.

The two platoons of 8th North. Fus. mentioned above will not move forward until definite information is received from Brigade H.Q. that the RED LINE is captured and that work of consolidation is in progress. Information as to the time they may advance will be sent to R.E. from Brigade H.Q.

In addition, Strong Points will be dug -

by 9th. Lan'. Fus. about V.25.b.8.2. (To be called No. 13.)

by 9th. Lan'. Fus. about V.25.b.65.65. (To be called No. 14.)

by 11th Man'. Rgt. about V.25.b.6.9. (To be called No. 15.)

by 11th Man'. Rgt. about V.19.d.4.2. (To be called No. 16.)

APPENDIX 7.

To 34th Brigade Instructions issued under this Office No. M.246 dated 30th. September, 1917.

INTELLIGENCE.

The 10th Ersatz Division is at present opposite the Divnl. Sector.

This Division is fresh and up to strength: probably good quality: last reported in BRUGES Area.

It consists of the 369th., 370th. and 371st I.Rs. (Prussians) and has twice been engaged in severe fighting: South of the SOMME in September, 1916, and in CHAMPAGNE in May, 1917. During June and July, 1917 this Division has been in a quiet Sector on the French Front where it was relieved early in August. It is, therefore, fresh and up to strength. It has not the reputation of being a 1st class Division, but may put up a good defence as it is composed of WESTPHALIANS and THURINGIANS, who usually fight well.

ORDER OF BATTLE.

North to South.
- 371 I.R.
- 369 I.R.
- 370 I.R.

Three Battalions in the line - one Battalion reinforcing at night.

370th. I.R. Company strength 95 men (7th Company) and 25 Company Carrying Party.

III Battalion went into the line night 22nd/23rd.
I Battalion went into the line night 23rd/24th.
II Battalion went into the line night 24th/25th.

HOSTILE ATTITUDE.

The enemy force opposite the Divisional Sector are distributed in depth, one Battalion holding a system of organised shell-holes in the Front Line, a second Battalion in close support and the third in Reserve.

In the event of an advance by us a counter-attack would be delivered within a very short space of time by elements of the counter-attacking Division now situated in the WESTROOSBEKE Area.

This attack may be expected to develop from two to three hours after ZERO.

The enemy is making far less use of his concrete dug-outs, as in several instances the occupants have all been knocked out by direct hits. The men now consider themselves safer in shell-holes.

Counter-attacks. Information gathered from a captured sketch indicates that counter-attacks may be expected from direction of V.14.d.3.3. (NOBLES FARM) and V.21.a.1.8. Also from V.21.c.1.8. and V.26.b.1.9. (BEEK HOUSES).

SECRET.

Order No. 59.a.

34th Infantry Brigade

The following "Instructions" issued under M.246 are cancelled :-

No. 7. para. 2.
No. 8. para 2.
No. 11.
No. 12 as regards places for Liaison.
No. 17. as regards 5th. Dorset Regt. H.Q.
No. 18.

1. 5th Dorset Regt. will move from SIEGE CAMP so as to arrive at MURAT SHELTERS by 7 p.m. on Y Day.
    5th Dorset Regt. less two Companies will move so as to be in HURST PARK area by ZERO plus 2 hours, and they will reach our present Front Line at ZERO plus 4 hours. The remaining two Companies will move from MURAT SHELTERS so as to reach HURST PARK area by ZERO plus 3 hours.
    The routes and approaches to HURST PARK area and from there to our Front Line are to be carefully reconnoitred in advance.
    The 5th Dorset Regt. will be employed solely for countering hostile counter-attacks. They will not be used to reinforce the assaulting Battalions in the Firing Line.
    Orders for their employment will be given by Brigade H.Q.
    The O.C. is empowered to deal with an enemy counter-attack on his own initiative should the reserves of the Assaulting Battalion have failed to dislodge the enemy. Such action is to be at once reported to Brigade H.Q.
    Close touch must be kept by this Battalion with the situation in front and an Officer with runners should be sent to assaulting Battalion H.Q. for this purpose.

2. 8th Northumberland Fus. less one Company will reach Canal Bank from SIEGE CAMP at ZERO plus 6 hours and will be in Divisional Reserve.
    Reference above Company -

    (a) 2 Platoons will report to C.R.E., 11th. Division on Oct. 2nd and will work under his orders.

    (b) 2 Platoons will move to CANE POST at a time to be notified later to form carrying parties as required.
    They will be under the orders of the Staff Captain.

3. On the capture of the RED LINE patrols will be pushed forward, under cover of the foremost posts, as far as the protective barrage permits to discover the enemy's dispositions.
    Patrols will also be sent forward, as soon as the protective barrage permits, to shell-holes at V.26.a.9.9., trench at V.20.c.8.4., MEBU at V.20.a.3.0., to ascertain whether these points are held by the enemy.

4. Liaison will be established by units as under :-

Detailed by	To meet	Place.
9th. Lan'. Fus.	143rd Brigade.	Bridge at V.25.b.75.35 over LEKKERBOTERBEEK.
-do-	-do-	TERRIER FARM.
11th Man'. Regt.	7th S. Staffs. Regt.	On road at V.19.d.2.2.
-do-	-do-	On road at V.20.c.12.86.

The meeting of the above liaison parties will be especially reported.
Other meeting-places may be arranged, if wished, direct between Os.C. Battalions concerned.

5. ARTILLERY. The initial Artillery barrage will come down on the line V.25.c.98.58 - V.25.a.05.55 - U.24.d.15.50. - 150 yards in front of the leading lines of the forming up Infantry.

    The barrage will lift at ZERO plus 3 minutes and move forward for the first 200 yards at the rate of 50 yards in 2 minutes.

    After the first 200 yards and up to the protective barrage for the RED DOTTED LINE it will move at the rate of 50 yards in 6 minutes.

    It will lift off the RED DOTTED LINE at ZERO plus 47 minutes and will reach a protective line from V.26.a.30.30. to V.19.a.85.65. at ZERO plus 59 minutes, where it will remain until ZERO plus 2 hours and 10 minutes.

    The barrage will move forward again from this protective line at ZERO plus 2 hours and 10 minutes at the rate of 50 yards in 4 minutes, until it clears the RED LINE at about 2 hours and 34 minutes and becomes protective on the line V.26.b.13.82 - V.20.a.00.70 - V.13.d.42.05 at ZERO plus 2 hours and 46 minutes, where it remains for 2 hours.

    All lifts will be of 50 yards.

    Smoke. During the pause on the RED DOTTED LINE, the high ground about MEUNIER HOUSE will be masked by a smoke screen.

6. 34th L. T. M. B. will bombard with a burst of fire from ZERO to ZERO plus 3 minutes. (NOT before ZERO as previously stated).

7. Attention is drawn to Divisional Standing Battle Orders.

8. An orderly will be sent round to units to synchronise watches on Y Evening.

9. ACKNOWLEDGE.

F.G. Turner, Captain,

1st. October, 1917.   Brigade Major, 34th. Infantry Brigade.

*O*O*O*O*O*O*O*O*O*

Copies to all recipients of M. 246 of 30/9/17.

*O*O*O*O*O*O*O*O*O*

To -

SECRET.

Reference 34th Brigade Order No. 59.a.

Cancel para. 1 and substitute the following -

5th Dorset Regt. will move from SIEGE CAMP so as to arrive at MURAT SHELTERS by 7 p.m. on Y Day.

5th Dorset Regt. less two companies will move so as to be in HURST PARK Area by ZERO and they will reach our present front line by ZERO plus two hours. The remaining two companies will move from MURAT SHELTERS so as to reach HURST PARK Area by ZERO plus 1 hour, and they will move on so as to be East of the STEENBEEK (about C5.d.55) by ZERO plus two hours. The exact location of these two companies must be at once notified to Brigade H.Q.

O.O. 5th Dorset Regt. will move forward in time to open his H.Q. at BULOW FARM at ZERO.

5th Dorset Regt. will be employed for countering hostile counter-attacks.

Orders for their employment will be given by Brigade H.Q.

The O.C. is empowered to deal with an enemy counter-attack on his own initiative should the Reserves of the assaulting battalions have failed to dislodge the enemy. Such action is to be at once reported to Brigade H.Q.

The O.C. is also empowered to employ not more than two companies of his battalion should all Reserves of assaulting Battalions have been employed in the task of capturing the Final Objective and the situation is such that an attack launched at once by two fresh companies would probably succeed in capturing the Final Objective.

ACKNOWLEDGE.

Captain,
Brigade Major, 34th. Infy. Brigade.

2nd. October, 1917.

H.Q.
34TH INFANTRY BDE.
No. CJ/26
Date 30/9/17

=*=*=*=*=*=
S E C R E T
=*=*=*=*=*=

War Diary

ADMINISTRATIVE INSTRUCTIONS.

FOR MOVE OCTOBER 1st.-2nd. 1917.
===

(1). Transport wagons of Units will report to them on Sept. 30th. and will be available for move to DIRTY BUCKET CAMP. One Lorry will also be at the disposal of each Infantry Unit, and one for Brigade Headquarters and Machine Gun Company. These will be able to do two journeys. They will report at 6 am. on day of move. The Lorry for Machine Gun Company should return and report to them at 1 pm.

(2). All Bombs for carriage on the man will be issued at DIRTY BUCKET CAMP, also 5 Sandbags per. man, S.O.S.Signals, and the following petrol tins:-

Northd. Fusiliers.	130.
Lancas. Fusiliers.	81.
Dorset Regt.	80.
Manchester Regt.	110.
Machine Gun Company.	12.

(3). The Store Tent at present with 11th. Manchester Regt. will be erected at DIRTY BUCKET CAMP for storage of Greatcoats and Blankets of all Units.

(4) A Bus to convoy billeting parties of 9th. Lancashire Fusiliers, 11th. Manchester Regt., and 34th. Machine Gun Company will be at Brigade Headquarters at 7 am. on October 1st. for 9th. Lancashire Fusiliers and Machine Gun Company and at HERZEELE CHURCH for 11th. Manchester Regt. at 7-15 am. Lancashire Fusiliers and Manchester Regt. will each include 1 Officer and 8 men in their party and 34th. Machine Gun Company 1 Officer and 2 men. 11th. Manchester Regt. will also send a senior officer to reconnoitre transport lines which will probably be at HOSPITAL FARM.
    Billeting Parties of 8th. Northumberland Fusiliers and 5th. Dorset Regt. will be attached to 9th. Lancashire Fusiliers and 11th. Manchesters for movement on 1st. and will embus with them, taking rations for one day.

(5). Busses will be drawn up in two columns on 1st. and 2nd., head of 1st. Column about D.18.a.0.9., rear of 2nd. Column E of HERZEELE. On Oct. 1st. 11th. Manchester Regt. and 34th. Machine Gun Company will proceed in 1st. Column, 11th. Manchesters leading. Lancashire Fusiliers and Brigade Headquarters in 2nd. Column, Lancashire Fusrs. leading. On Oct. 2nd. 34th. Field Ambulance and 5th. Dorsets in 1st. Column, 5th. Dorsets leading; and 8th. Northd. Fusrs. in the 2nd. Column. 11th. Manchester Regt. will detail a Senior Officer to represent the Brigade Staff and superintend the embussing and debussing on Oct.1st., and 8th.Northd.Fusrs. on Oct 2nd.

- 2 -

(6). The 4 men left behind in charge of surplus stores will draw rations from XVIII Corps Rest Station, HERZEELE, for consumption on and after October 4th. and not Oct. 7th. as stated.

(7). Preserved rations for consumption on Oct. 3rd. and 4th. will be issued to 9th. Lancashire Fusrs. and 11th. Manchesters on Oct. 2nd., and for consumption on the 5th. on Oct. 3rd.
Preserved rations for consumption on 4th. Oct. and onwards will be issued to all units and to 34th. Machine Gun Coy. from 3rd. Oct.

(8). All tents and Area Stores in this Area, except tents and bivouacs for use in transport lines and Store tents, will be handed over to the Area Commandant who will give a certificate that all tentage and other Camp stores have been satisfactorily handed over and camps left in a clean and sanitary condition.

(9). Receipts for all Trench Stores and ammunition taken over in the line will be sent to Brigade Headquarters as soon as possible.

(10). Brigade Bomb Dump is established at BULOW FARM under the charge of 2/Lieut. PEGGS, 5th. Dorset R. and Bombing Corporal. They will be accommodated and rationed on and after Oct. 4th. by 9th. Lancashire Fusrs.
The contents of the Dump will be as shown in the schedule and will be issued on demand.

(11). It is hoped to provide a carrying party of not more than 2 Platoons to carry forward ammunition on Z day - detail as to this later.

(12) Units will make their own arrangements for delivering rations to their men each night.

(13) ACKNOWLEDGE.

                    C. Chute   Captain,
30/9/17.   Staff Captain, 34th. Infantry Brigade.

Copy to/
- No.1. Office.
- 2. -do-
- 3. Brigade Major.
- 4. War Diary.
- 5. -do-
- 6. 8th. Northd. Fusrs.
- 7. 9th. Lancs. Fusrs.
- 8. 5th. Dorset R.
- 9. 11th. Manch. Regt.
- 10. 34th. M.G. Coy.
- 11. 34th. L.T.M. Batty.
- 12. 11th. Division.
- 13. No. 4 Coy Div. Train.
- 14. 34th. Field Ambulance.
- 15. Area Commandant, Dirty Bucket Camp.
- 16. Area Commandant, Nouveau Monde Area.

SCHEDULE.

BULOW FARM.

COMMODITY.	ESTABLISHMENT.
Rations.	1,500.
Water Tins.	400.
S.A.A.Boxes.	250.
Do.(for M.Guns) boxes.	200.
Mills, No. 23.	1,500.
Rifle Grenades, No. 24.	1,000.
S.O.S. Sets.	100.
Ground Flares, Red.	300.
Very Lights, 1".	300.
Stokes, 3".	750.
Sand Bags.	10,000.
Barbed Wire Coils.	50.
French Wire.	30.
Pickets.	200.
Picks.	300.
Shovels.	1,000.
Duckboards.	50.

SECRET.

Copy No. 3....

War Diary

34th Infantry Brigade Order No. 60.

Reference map - 1/10,000 - POELCAPPELLE.   Oct. 1st./17.

1. 34th Infantry Brigade will relieve a portion of 32nd. Infantry Brigade in the Right Sector of the 11th. Divisional Front on night of October 2nd/3rd.

2. All maps, aeroplane photos and documents referring to the front will be taken over on relief.

3. The completion of reliefs will be reported to Brigade H.Q. by wiring the Serial No. as shown in Movement Table accompanying 34th Brigade Order No. 58 and the time of completion of relief.

4. Reference Serial No. 6. of Movement Table with 34th. Brigade Order No. 58. 32nd Brigade will provide 2 guides each for 9th. Lancashire Fus. and 11th Manchester Regt. to be at Canal Bank at 6-15 p.m. Intervals of 200 yards will be kept between Platoons. One guide per Battalion H.Q., per Company H.Q. and per Platoon will meet the Battalions at MON DU RASTA and guide them to their positions.

5. 11th Manchester Regt. will take over the portion of the line in Left Sector now held by 9th W. Yorkshire Regt.; this will be taken over from 11th Manchester Regt. by 33rd Infantry Brigade after relief is complete.

6. H.Q. of both 9th Lancashire Fus. and 11th Manchester Regt. will be at BULOW FARM.

7. O.C., 34th Machine Gun Company will arrange guides direct with O.C., 32nd Machine Gun Company.

8. Brigade H.Q. will close at DIRTY BUCKET CAMP at 4 p.m. and open at CANE POST on completion of relief, when Command of Right Sector will pass to G.O.C. 34th Infantry Brigade.

9. ACKNOWLEDGE.

ISSUED AT.. 10.30 p.m.

F.G. Turner, Captain,
Brigade Major, 34th Infantry Brigade.

DISTRIBUTION.

Copy No. 1. Office.	Copy No. 10. 11th Man'. Regt.
2. -do-	11. 34th M. G. Coy.
3. War Diary.	12. 34th L. T. M. B.
4. -do-	13. 11th Division.
5. Bde. Sigs.	14. 32nd Brigade.
6. Staff Captain.	15. 33rd Brigade.
7. 8th North. Fus.	16. 143rd Brigade.
8. 9th Lan'. Fus.	17. No. 4 Coy. Train.
9. 5th Dorset Rgt.	18. 34th Field Amb.

TO				
	~~ORGAN~~	~~ORDEAL~~	~~OBLIGE~~	
	~~ORIENT~~	ORIGIN	~~PRAIN~~	
Sender's Number	Day of Month	In reply to Number.		AAA
B.M. 856.	5			

ORIENT will relieve ORGAN and ORIGIN in the line tonight under arrangements to be made direct between C.Os. aaa ORIENT will hold the line with 2 Coys. in front system and 2 Coys. in Support aaa ORIGIN after relief will be in Support about V.25.a. and b. aaa ORGAN will be in Reserve about C.5.d. aaa ORDEAL will remain in Div. Reserve aaa ACKNOWLEDGE

Place: ORANGE.

F. Turner, Captain.

==*=*=*=*=*
SECRET.
==*=*=*=*=*

Copy No. 4

34th Infantry Brigade Order No. 61.

Reference maps - POELCAPPELLE - 1/10,000 - Edn. 3.
             Sheet 28.   - 1/40,000.   Oct. 5th./17.

1. The Offensive will be resumed at a very early date which will be secretly notified to all concerned.

2. (a) The 32nd. Infantry Brigade will carry out the attack on the 11th. Division Front.

   (b) 8th Northumberland Fus. and one Battalion of 33rd. Infantry Brigade will be in close Support.

3. All ground gained yesterday must be consolidated and the defensive system improved as much as possible.

4. The 34th Infantry Brigade will be relieved in the line by a portion of the 32nd Infantry Brigade on night 7th/8th. October.

5. The 32nd Infantry Brigade will be attacking on a three-Battalion front, with boundaries between Battalions as under ;-

   Between Right and Centre Battalions - V.20.c.35.45.
   Between Centre and Left Battalions - V.19.b.8.3.

   The O.C., 5th Dorset Regt. will therefore make dispositions on night of 6th/7th. October for flanks of forward Companies to rest on V.20.c.35.45. so as to facilitate relief.

6. ACKNOWLEDGE.

ISSUED AT 4 p.m.

                                          , Captain,
                            Brigade Major, 34th. Infty. Brigade.

==*=*=*=*=*
DISTRIBUTION.
==*=*=*=*=*

Copy No. 1. Office.   Copy No. 10. 11th Man'. Rgt.
         2.   -do-   11. 34th M. G. Coy.
         3. Staff Captain.   12. 34th L. T. M. B.
         4. War Diary.   13. 11th Division.
         5.   -do-   14. 32nd Brigade.
         6. Bde. Signals.   15. 33rd Brigade.
         7. 8th North. Fus.   16. Right Flank Bde.
         8. 9th Lan'. Fus.   17. No. 4 Coy. Train.
         9. 5th Dorset Rgt.   18. 34th Field Amb.

==*=*=*=*=*

War Diary.

SECRET.   Copy No...4...

34th Infantry Brigade.

DEFENCE SCHEME.
(Provisional)

Reference map - 1/10,000 - POELCAPPELLE.   6th. Oct., 1917.

1. <u>Brigade Area and Boundaries.</u>

    (a) The Brigade holds the Right Sector of the 11th. Divisional Front.

    (b) The Brigade Boundaries are as follows :-

   <u>On the Right</u> - LEKKERBOTERBEEK at V.26.a.7.5.
                                          V. 25.b.9.0.
                  STEENBEEK at   V.25.c.7.5.
                  ST. JULIEN-   )
                  POELCAPPELLE Rd.) at V.6.b.1.5.
                  STEENBEEK at   - V.5.d.0.2.

   <u>On the Left</u> - S.E. of POELCAPPELLE CHURCH at V.20.c.10.87.
                 Near RETOUR X Roads at V.19.d.27.20.
                 On ST. JULIEN-)
                 POELCAPPELLE Rd.) at U.30.b.90.35.
                 On LANGEMARCK Road at U.29.d.80.15.
                 On STEENBEEK at C.5.a.15.10.

    (c) The 143rd Infantry Brigade (48th. Division) is on our Right and 33rd Infantry Brigade is on our Left.

2. <u>Front Line Area.</u>

    Our Front Line (RED LINE) runs from V.26.a.7.5. - V.20.c.1.9.
    The area between the front line and the RED DOTTED LINE is known as the front line area.

3. <u>Support Area.</u>

    The area between the RED DOTTED LINE and the WINNIPEG-LANGEMARCK Road is known as the Support Area.

4. <u>Method of holding.</u>

    (a) The Front Line is held by one Battalion - 2 Coys. in Front Line and 2 Coys. in Support - with Battalion H.Q. at V.25.b.4.7.

    (b) One Battalion is in Bde. Support - 3 Coys. in the area BAVARIOSE HOUSE-MALTA HOUSE and 1 Coy. in C.5.d. - with Battalion H.Q. at BULOW FARM.

    (c) One Battalion is in Bde. Reserve in the HURST PARK Area with Battalion H.Q. at PALACE FARM, C.4.d.4.5.

5. <u>Vickers Machine Guns.</u>

    6 guns are allotted to the Front Line Battalion and are under the orders of that Battalion Commander.
    2 guns are held back to replace casualties.
    8 guns are in Brigade Reserve in the Canal Bank.

(2)

6. Trench Mortars.

   34th L.T.M. Battery is in Brigade Reserve in the Canal Bank.

7. ARTILLERY.

   The Brigade is covered by the Right Group, 11th Divisional Artillery (Commander Lt.Col. WINTER, C.M.G., D.S.O.). Headquarters CANE POST.
   Liaison Officers live at Brigade and Front Line Battn. H.Q.

8. Communications.

   Battalion H.Q. are connected to Brigade H.Q. by telephone wire and Visual Signalling.
   Brigade H.Q. are connected to Right Artillery Group H.Q. by wire (direct line).

9. Action in case of attack.

   (a) Front Line Battalion. The Front Line Battalion will be disposed so as to hold strong posts arranged in depth and constructed for all-round defence. These posts will break up by rifle and machine gun fire any hostile attack. Should the enemy succeed in penetrating our line at any point, he will be driven out at once by local counter-attack.
   Local Commanders must all clearly understand what action is expected of them in case of attack.

   (b) Brigade Support Battalion. The Support Battalion will be used for counter-attack. The O.C. Support Battalion will, if he considers the urgency of the situation demands it, counter-attack without waiting for orders from Brigade H.Q. He will report his action to Brigade H.Q. at once. This Battalion will not be used to reinforce the Front Line Battalion.

   (c) Brigade Reserve Battalion. The Reserve Battalion will be in readiness to move forward into the Support Battalion Area on receipt of orders to that effect from Brigade H.Q.

10. ACKNOWLEDGE.

F.G. Turner, Captain,

Brigade Major, 34th. Infantry Brigade.

==*=*=*=*=*=*
DISTRIBUTION.
==*=*=*=*=*=*

Copy No. 1. Office.
        2. -do-
        3. Staff Captain.
        4. War Diary.
        5. -do-
        6. Bde. Signals.
        7. 8th North. Fus.
        8. 9th Lan'. Fus.
        9. 5th Dorset Rgt.

Copy No. 10. 11th Man'. Rgt.
        11. 34th M.G. Coy.
        12. 34th L.T.M.B.
        13. 11th Division.
        14. 32nd Brigade.
        15. 33rd Brigade.
        16. 143rd Brigade.
        17. Right Group, 11th Divnl. Arty.

*0*0*0*0*0*

SECRET.

Copy No. 4

34th Infantry Brigade Order No. 62.

Reference map - 1/10,000 - POELCAPPELLE.   6th. Oct. 1917.

1. The 34th Infantry Brigade will be relieved in the line by a portion of the 32nd Infantry Brigade on the night 7th/8th. Oct.

2. 6th York and Lancs. Regt. will relieve the Right Front and Support Companies of 5th Dorset Regt., i.e. from the Divisional Boundary on the Right as far as V.20.c.35.45., O.C. 5th Dorset Regt. making his dispositions for that night so that the boundary between his forward Companies rests on this point - as ordered in B.O. No.61, para. 5.

   6th York and Lancs. Regt. will also relieve Right Company of 11th Manchester Regt. and the Company in C.5.d.

   9th West Yorks. Regt. will relieve the Left Front and Support Companies of 5th Dorset Regt. and the Centre and Left Companies of 11th Manchester Regt.

3. Os.C. 5th Dorset Regt. and 11th Manchester Regt. will provide one guide from each Company H.Q. and Platoon to be relieved by 6th. York and Lancs. Regt. to be at MON DU RASTA at 5 p.m. (WINTER TIME, which comes into operation on 7th. inst. at 1 a.m.) ; and similarly one guide from each Company H.Q. and Platoon to be relieved by 9th West Yorks. Regt. to be at MON DU RASTA at 5-45 p.m.

   In addition, 5th Dorset Regt. will provide one guide for Bn. H.Q. of 6th York and Lancs. Regt. to be at MON DU RASTA at 5 p.m.

   All other details of relief to be arranged direct between Os.C. concerned.

4. 34th Machine Gun Company will be relieved by 32nd Machine Gun Company. Guides will be arranged direct between Os.C.

5. 34th L.T.M.B. will be relieved on Canal Bank by 32nd L.T.M.B.

6. All maps, papers, etc. referring to the defence of the line will be handed over to relieving units.

7. The completion of reliefs will be reported to Brigade H.Q. by the Code Word "CHEERY" and the time of completion of relief.

8. 9th Lancashire Fusiliers will move off independently after dusk, avoiding the BOUNDARY Road.

9. 8th Northumberland Fusiliers will remain in Divisional Reserve at their present location.

10. On relief units will proceed to SIEGE CAMP. Transport arrangements will be notified later.

11. Brigade H.Q. will close at MON BULGARE on completion of relief and open at SIEGE CAMP three hours later.

12. ACKNOWLEDGE.

ISSUED AT 11. p.m.

F. Turner, Captain,
Brigade Major, 34th. Infantry Brigade.

Copy No. 1. Office.	Copy No. 7. 8th N. Fus.	Copy No. 13. 11th Divn.
2. -do-	8. 9th L. Fus.	14. 32nd Bde.
3. Staff Capt.	9. 5th Dorsets.	15. 33rd Bde.
4. War Diary.	10. 11th Man. R.	16. 143rd Bde.
5. -do-	11. 34th M.G.Coy.	17. R. Group D.A.
6. Bde. Sigs.	12. 34th L.T.M.B.	18. No.4 Coy.

Table to be read in conjunction with 34th Brigade Order No. 62.

Serial No.	Unit.	Date.	From.	To.	Remarks.
1.	8th North. Fus.	7th Oct.	MURAT SHELTERS.	CANAL BANK.	To arrive CANAL BANK by 6 p.m.
2.	34th Brigade, less 34th M.G. Coy. and 8th North. Fus.	Night 7th/8th.	LINE.	SIEGE CAMP.	
3.	6 guns 34th M.G. Coy.	-do-	LINE.	IRISH FARM.	
4.	34th Brigade, less 34th M.G. Coy. and 8th North. Fus.	8th Oct.	SIEGE CAMP.	EPERLECQUES AREA. by train.	Details of trains and exact destinations will be issued separately by "Q".
5.	8th North. Fus.	8th Oct.	CANAL BANK.	HURST PARK AREA.	To be clear of Canal Bank by 6 p.m.
6.	34th M.G. Coy.	Night 10/11th.	LINE.	IRISH FARM SHELTERS.	After relief by Unit of 18th. Division.
7.	34th M.G. Coy.	11th Oct.	IRISH FARM SHELTERS.	EPERLECQUES AREA. by train.	As in Serial No. 4.

NOTE: Orders regarding moves of transport, and details of units from HOUTKERQUE, will be issued separately by "Q".

*O*O*O*O*O*O*O*

34th Infantry Brigade.

REPORT ON RECENT OPERATIONS.

On the night 2nd/3rd. the Brigade, with the two assaulting Battalions (9th Lancashire Fusiliers on the Right and 11th Manchester Regiment on the Left) in the front line relieved a portion of the 32nd Brigade. As soon as the relief was complete, the lines for forming-up on the following night were laid out with string. These were checked the following day, and having been found correct the actual tapes were put in their place on the night 3rd/4th. While this was being done active patrolling was carried out to ensure that the enemy did not observe anything unusual and later to prevent his noticing any movement during the forming-up of the assaulting troops. The STROMBEEK was a considerable obstacle, but duckboards laid across it overcame the difficulty.

The forming-up was completed without incident by 4-45 a.m. and the Battalions remained in position concealed in shell-holes till ZERO Hour.

At ZERO (6 a.m.) the assaulting troops closed up to the opening barrage in perfect order. From ZERO to ZERO plus 3 minutes 4 guns of the 34th L. T. M. B. opened rapid fire on MALTA HOUSE and other likely points, and appear to have done good work against the enemy in shell-holes near our front line.

During the first advance to the DOTTED RED LINE little opposition was met with and the first objective was reached accg according to time-table.

The pause on the DOTTED RED LINE enabled the leading companies of each Battalion to re-organise, and 11th Manchester Rgt. corrected a slight deviation to the Right. While the protective barrage was on, there was considerable enemy activity : some of them attempted a very feeble counter-attack against 11th Manchester Regt., who disposed of it with Lewis Gun and Rifle fir fire, and during the last few minutes of the protective barrage we inflicted heavy casualties on the enemy as they ran away. Both Battalions had already suffered severe losses in Officers, especially 11th Manchester Regt., who appear to have kept too close to our barrage.

The second advance, to the RED LINE, was begun punctually. 9th Lancashire Fus. encountered little resistance and reached the Final Objective in excellent order. 11th Manchester Regt. were hampered for a while by Machine Gun fire from POELCAPPELLE, first from the direction of the Church and then from the BREWERY, but this did not hold up the attack. There was a slight check at GLOSTER FARM, and a message was sent back to one gun of 34th. L. T. M. B. advancing in close support. This gun got rapidly into action with good effect and GLOSTER FARM was easily rushed by 11th Manchester Regt., just as two Tanks were coming to their assistance.

Consolidation at once began on the plan laid down in orders. By this time, 9th Lancashire Fus. had suffered 10 casualties in Officers, including the Commanding Officer Major MILNES and all 4 Company Commanders, Major MILNES although badly hit about the time that the DOTTED RED LINE was captured remained in Command at his Forward H.Q. near the STROMBEEK till the capture of the Final Objective. The Officer casualties in the 11th Manchester Regt. to this time numbered 11, including 3 Company Commanders.

After the capture of the RED LINE patrols were sent out uncover of the protective barrage to clear the ground immediately in front of our posts. At this time BEEK HOUSES and MEUNIER HOUSE both appeared to have been vacated by the enemy, but owing to our own protective barrage it was impossible for our men to occupy them though Sergt. COVERDALE, 11th Manchester Regt., with a patrol attempted to do so, but he had several casualties from our guns and had to abandon the attempt. By that time our protective barrage had lifted both BEEK HOUSES and MEUNIER HOUSE had been re-occupied in strength by the enemy.

The H.Q. of both Battalions were by now established well forward about V.25.b.4.7. and V.25.b.3.8., the 9th Lancashire Fus. being Commanded by the Adjutant, Lieut. PEMBERTON.

Meanwhile, 5th Dorset Regiment had been in close support and ready to counter any enemy counter-attack. Two Companies moved up to our original forming-up line by ZERO and the other two Companies to C.5.d. The leading Companies got in the enemy's barrage, but the Artillery formation proved its value and casualties were light.

About 1-30 p.m. an order was received for the success of the morning to be followed up : 5th Dorset Regt. were to pass through the front Battalions and at 5 p.m. under an Artillery barrage advance in conjunction with troops on both flanks and capture BEEK HOUSES and MEUNIER HOUSE. Orders were issued to this effect, and the two rear Companies of Dorsets began to close up to the STROOMBEEK to take the place of the two front Companies who were to carry out the attack. At 3-40 p.m., however, the order was cancelled, and the two rear Companies of Dorsets who had by that time reached the STROOMBEEK were again withdrawn to C.5.d. They passed through heavy Artillery fire both in going and coming back, but owing to the skilful handling by Lt.Col. STEPHENSON - 2nd in Command of the Battalion - only 25 casualties were incurred.

During the afternoon and evening the enemy made three attempts to counter-attack - two feeble ones from MEUNIER HOUSE, one of which was dealt with by the Artillery and the other by M.G. and Rifle fire. The other came from the Ridge N.E. of BEEK HOUSES where 300 to 400 of the enemy were seen to be massing. In answer to our S.O.S. the Artillery barrage dropped right on the place where the enemy were, and they were quickly dispersed.

During the consolidation 3 guns of 34th Machine Gun Company who were detailed to cover the front line did good work, especially the one at GLOSTER FARM, where two captured M.G's were also turned against the enemy with excellent effect. Three other guns of 34th M.G. Coy. covered the Support Line.

Soon after dark Major MEUGENS, Commanding 11th Manchester Regt. was sniped at GLOSTER FARM while going round his front posts, but though shot through the arm he continued at duty most ably assisted by his Adjutant 2nd Lt. KELSEY till 10 a.m. the next day when Captain AIRY, who had been ordered up from the Transport Lines relieved him. During the night 4th/5th. active patrolling was carried out and several small encounters took place. The enemy had a line of sniper's posts along our front about 100 yards in front of our line. They made any approach to GLOSTER FARM very difficult, and once attempted to bomb it, but were driven off by Lewis Gun fire.

Lieut. CLAYTON, 11th Manchester Regt. with his H.Q. at GLOSTER FARM superintended the defence of his Battalion's front in a most able and fearless manner.

On the morning of the 5th. Captain WARD McQUAID, who was sent for from the Transport Lines, took over Command of 9th Lancashire Fus. from Lieut. PEMBERTON, who had done admirable work in re-organising the Battalion and superintending the consolidation of his front. Heavy rain fell during the day and made the ground very bad.

On the night 5th/6th. 5th Dorset Regt. relieved both 9th. Lancashire Fus. and 11th Manchester Regt. in the front line, 11th. Manchester Regt. going into Support in the positions vacated by the Dorsets and 9th Lancashire Fus. being in Reserve in C.5.d. On the afternoon of the 6th. 9th Lancashire Fus. were withdrawn further to HURST PARK area, and one Company of 11th Manchester Regt. took their place in C.5.d. The day passed without incident for the front line.

On the night 6th/7th. vigorous patrolling was again carried out by the 5th Dorset Regt. and attempts to approach BEEK HOUSES and MEUNIER HOUSE were prevented by strong resistance by the enemy. The three Companies of 11th Manchester Regt. in Support were heavily shelled during the night, but no casualties were received.

The situation on 7th. was again unchanged, but heavy rain fell during the morning, and at noon a message was received from the Division that the relief by 32nd Brigade ordered for the following night might be cancelled. At 7-15 p.m. another message was received that the relief would be carried out after all. Guides had been ordered to be at MON DU RASTA for relieving Units at 5 p.m., but as the decision to carry out the relief was not made till 7-15 p.m. the leading Platoons of the relieving Battalions (6th. York and Lancs. Regt. and 9th. W. Yorks. Regt.) did not reach MON DU RASTA till 11-45 p.m. This made the relief very late, and though tapes had been laid right up to the front to avoid any chance of losing the way and causing delay daylight prevented 2 platoons of 5th Dorset Regt., who had been relieved, from getting away, and these platoons had therefore to remain till the following night. The relief of the rest of the Battalion was completed by 4-30 a.m. on 8th.

Throughout this time 8th Northumberland Fus. had been held in Divisional Reserve, but two platoons had been used to dig strong points under R.E. on Z Day and 2 platoons carried up ammunition, water, etc. that day. Also, on night 6th/7th. 2 platoons carried up rations to the 5th Dorset Regt. in the line.

The communications throughout the operations were good, despite the fact that the Signalling Officers of both Assaulting Battns. became casualties early on, and great credit is due to the Brigade Signalling Officer, Lieut. SINCLAIR, and his section for their work. A wire was run from Brigade H.Q. at MAISON BULGARE to BULOW FARM, and then to the Forward Battalion H.Q. The wire as far as BULOW FARM held most of the time, and when it was out Power Buzzer and Amplifier worked with good effect between these places. The line on to the front Battalion was more often than not cut owing to the heavy Artillery fire frequently placed on the STROOMBEEK valley and on the POEL-CAPPELLE Road; but when this line was cut visual was almost always working direct from the front Battalion H.Q. to Brigade H.Q., and both on night 4th/5th. and night 5th/6th. messages came through in this way with commendable regularity. Altogether the number of telephone and visual messages received was much above the average and extremely creditable to all signallers concerned. When other means of communication failed or the nature of the message prohibited visual signalling, runners as usual did gallant and invaluable work. Pigeons were useful, one message coming through in 20 minutes, but only one message-rocket was fired and that was not picked up.

The casualties during these operations were as under :-

Unit.	Officers.			Other Ranks.		
	K.	W.	M.	K.	W.	M.
8th North. Fus.	-	-	-	3.	40.	1.
9th. Lanc. Fus.	4.	9.	1.	15.	119.	73.
5th Dorset Rgt.	2.	2.	-	24.	96.	33.
11th Manc. Rgt.	1.	11.	-	38.	252.	26.
34th M. G. Coy.	1.	1.	-	4.	19.	-
34th L. T. M. B.	-	-	-	2.	1.	1.
TOTAL.	8.	23.	1.	86.	527.	134.

12th. October 1917.

F.G. Turner, Captain,
Brigade Major 34th Infty. Bde.

11th Division No G.S.110.

SPECIAL ORDER OF THE DAY.

The G.O.C. wishes to congratulate the 33rd and 34th Infantry Brigades and all Troops of the Division who took part in the action on the great success of the attack of 9th October in which all Objectives were taken and held.

The G.O.C. wishes also to thank the 32nd Infantry Brigade for the attack they made under most difficult circumstances on 9th October. In spite of extremely bad weather this resulted in the capture of important ground on the left.

The thanks of the whole Division are due to the Divisional Artillery and it is well recognised by all how much the success of our operations owes to their splendid work. During many months, almost continuously in action under constant shell fire they have well maintained their high reputation.

The G.O.C. wishes to record his warm appreciation of the devotion to duty of the Royal Engineers, 6th East Yorks (Pioneers), and of the Royal Army Medical Corps.

H.Q. 11th Division.
14th October, 1917.

J. D. Coleridge Lieut-Colonel,
General Staff 11th Division.

War Diary.

To:—................   11th. Division No. G.S. 1157
   ....

The following correspondence is forwarded for information and communication to all ranks :—

(1)

From GENERAL SIR H. de la P. GOUGH., K.C.B., K.C.V.O.
     Commanding Fifth Army, to MAJOR GENERAL H.R.DAVIES., C.B.,
     Commanding 11th. Division.

15/10/17.
          After nearly four months in the Fifth Army the 11th. Division is leaving my command, and I cannot let the occasion pass without sending them my best wishes for the future and best thanks for the past.
          Their invariable staunchness and gallantry, especially during the general engagements they took part in during August and on October 4th. and 9th. has been beyond praise.
          The Division may well be proud of the distinguished part they have played in the third battle of YPRES.

(2)

From MAJOR GENERAL H.R.DAVIES., C.B., Commanding 11th.Division,
     to GENERAL SIR H. de la P GOUGH, K.C.B., K.C.V.O.
     Commanding the Fifth Army.

15/10/17.
          All Ranks of the 11th. Division much appreciate your message.

15th.October 1917.   T. D. Coleridge   Lieut.Colonel,
                                      General Staff, 11th. Division.

SECRET.

War Diary

Copy No. 4

34th Infantry Brigade Order No. 63.

Reference map - 1/100,000 - HAZEBROUCK.   16th. Oct./17.

1.   34th Brigade Group (~~less 86th Field Coy. R.E.~~) will move to ST. HILAIRE Area in accordance with the attached Movement Table.

2.   Advanced parties for billets will report to the Area Commandant of their Area on the day previous to the movement of their units.

3.   First Line Transport will move tomorrow, 14th. inst. by road to THEROUANNE and will rejoin their units on 15th.

4.   A distance of 500 yards will be maintained between all units, and between First Line Transports of units when moving separate from xxxxxxxx their units.

5.   Units will report the completion of all moves by S.D.R.

6.   ACKNOWLEDGE.

ISSUED AT... 2 p.m. ......

F.G. Turner, Captain,
Brigade Major, 34th Inf. Brigade.

Copy No. 1. Office.   Copy No. 9. 5th Dorset Regt.
        2. -do-   10. 11th Manchesters.
        3. Staff Captain.   11. 34th M. G. Coy.
        4. War diary.   12. 34th L. T. M. B.
        5. -do-   13. 11th Division.
        6. Bde. Signals.   14. 32nd Brigade.
        7. 8th North. Fus.   15. 33rd Brigade.
        8. 9th Lanc. Fus.   16. 34th Field Ambulance.

SERIAL No.	Unit.	Date.	From.	To.	Remarks.
1.	Brigade H.Q.	Oct. 18th.	Present billets.	FONTAINE-Lez-HERMAS.	Train from WATTEN to LILLERS and then march independently to billets.
2.	8th North. Fus.	-do-	-do-	PELY.	-do-
3.	9th. Lan'. Fus.	-do-	-do-	AUCHY-Au-BOIS.	-do-
4.	5th Dorset Rgt.	-do-	-do-	LIGNY-lez-AIRE.	-do-
5.	11th Man'. Rgt.	-do-	-do-	WESTREHEM.	-do-
6.	34th M. G. Coy.	-do-	-do-	La TINPAUD.	-do-
7.	34th L. T. M. B.	-do-	-do-	FLECHINELLE.	-do-
8.	88th Field Co. R.E.	-do-	-do-	FLECHINELLE.	
9.	34th Field Amb.	-do-	-do-	REDONCHELLE.	
10.	No.4.Coy.A.S.C.	-do-	-do-	FONTAINE-Loz-HERMAS.	

Times for march to WATTEN will be notified later.

Serial No.	Unit.	Date.	From.	To.	Remarks.
11.	Brigade H.Q.	Oct. 19th.	FONTAINE-Lez-HERMANS.	FLECHIN.	March off at 10 a.m.
12.	8th North. Fus.	-do-	RELY.	LAIRES.	-do-
13.	9th. Lan'. Fus.	-do-	AUCHY-Au-BOIS.	PALFART.	-do-
14.	5th Dorset Rgt.	-do-	LIGNY-les-AIRE.	FEBVIN PALFART.	-do-
15.	11th Man'. Rgt.	-do-	WESTREHEM.	FLECHIN.	March off at 9 a.m.
16.	34th M. G. Coy.	-do-	La TIRMAND.	PIPPEMONT.	March off at 10 a.m.
17.	34th T. M. B.	-do-	FLECHINELLE.	PALFART.	-do-
18.	34th Field Amb.	-do-	NEDONCHELLES.	LAIRES.	March off at 9-30 a.m.
19.	No.4.Coy.A.S.C.	-do-	FONTAINE-Lez-HERMANS.	FEBVIN PALFART.	After refilling.
20.	86th Field Co RE	do	FLECHINELLE	LAIRES	March off 10 a.m.

Brigade Headquarters will close at FONTAINE-Lez-HERMANS at 10 a.m.
and open at FLECHIN at 11-30 a.m.

SECRET.

War Diary

Copy No. ......

34th Infantry Brigade Order No. 64.

Reference maps – YPRES./ HAZEBROUCK. } 1/100,000/   19/10/17.

1. 34th Infantry Brigade Order No. 63 is cancelled.

2. 11th Division will relieve 9th Division in the line and will come under the orders of the I Corps.

3. 34th Brigade Group will move in accordance with attached Table.
   March table with fuller details for moves on 19th., 20th., and 21st. inst. will be issued later.

4. A distance of 500 yards will be maintained between units on the march.

5. Advance parties for billets will report to the Area Commandant of their area on the day previous to the movement of their units.

6. Completion of each move will be reported by S.D.R.

7. ACKNOWLEDGE.

ISSUED AT 11 p.m.

F.G. Turner,
Captain,
Brigade Major, 34th. Inf. Brigade.

Copy No. 1. Office.
     2. -do-
     3. Staff Captain.
     4. War Diary.
     5. -do-
     6. Bde. Signals.
     7. 8th North. Fus.
     8. 9th. Lan'. Fus.

Copy No. 9. 5th Dorset Rgt.
     10. 11th Manchesters.
     11. 34th M. G. Coy.
     12. 34th L. T. M. B.
     13. 11th Division.
     14. 32nd Brigade.
     15. 33rd Brigade.
     16. 34th Field Amb.

Table to accompany Brigade Order No. 64

Unit	Sept 13/14th	Sept 19/20th	Sept 20/21st	Sept 21/22nd
8th North Staff 2nd Devon Regt	AMES Area	HOUCHIN –	} Support and } Reserve	} Front line } (Right)
9th Lancashire Fusiliers		VAUDRICOURT	} MAZINGARBE } LES BREBIS	} Support } and
11th Royal Regt		NOEUX Area	} BULLY GRENAY } Area	} Reserve

Notes:
(1) No 6 Coy returns 24 hours after the Brigade has taken over the line
(2) Moves from WATTEN to LILLERS could be by train althro moves by march

SECRET.
Copy No. 4

34th Infantry Brigade Order No. 65.

Reference maps – HAZEBROUCK – 1/100,000.
Sheet 36.c. S.W.1. –1/10,000.   Oct. 19th/17.

1. – 34th Infantry Brigade will relieve 71st Infantry Brigade in the Right Sector of the Divisional front on nights 20th/21st and 21st/22nd.

2. – Moves and reliefs will be carried out in accordance with the attached Movement Table.

3.   Guides will be arranged direct between Os.C. concerned.

4. – All maps, aeroplane photographs, papers, etc. referring to the defence of the line will be taken over from units relieved.

5.   Completion of relief will be notified to Brigade H.Q. by wiring the Serial No. and time of completion of relief.

6.   Brigade H.Q. will close at NOEUX-LES-MINES at 4-30 p.m. on 21st. inst. and open at M.11.a.6.1. on completion of relief when command of the Right Sector will pass to G.O.C. 34th Inf. Brigade.

7.   ACKNOWLEDGE.

ISSUED AT 9.30 p.m.

H. Turner, Captain,
Brigade Major, 34th. Inf. Brigade.

DISTRIBUTION.

Copy No. 1. Office.	Copy No. 11. 34th M.G. Coy.
2. –do–	12. 34th L.T.M.B.
3. Staff Captain.	13. 11th Division.
4. War Diary.	14. 32nd Brigade.
5. –do–	15. 33rd Brigade.
6. Bde. Signals.	16. 71st Brigade.
7. 8th North. Fus.	17. 86th Field Co. R.E.
8. 9th. Lan'. Fus.	18. 34th Field Amb.
9. 5th Dorset Regt.	19. No.4. Coy. A.S.C.
10. 11th Man'. Regt.	20.

MOVEMENT TABLE issued in conjunction with B.O. 35.

Serial No.	Unit.	Date.	From.	To.	Remarks.
1.	Brigade Hd. Qrs.	20th.	VAUDRICOURT.	NOEUX-LEZ-MINES.	Close at VAUDRICOURT at 11 a.m. and open at NOEUX-LEZ-MINES at 12 noon.
2.	9th. Lan'. Fus.	-do-	HOUCHIN.	BULLY-GRENAY.	Clear present billets at 10 a.m.
3.	11th Man'. Rgt.	-do-	VAUDRICOURT.	LES-BREBIS.	-do-
4.	34th M. G. Coy.	-do-	NOEUX-LEZ-MINES.	BULLY-GRENAY.	-do-
5.	8th North. Fus.	Night 20/21st.	-do-	Support. (relieving 9th Norfolk Rgt.)	To come under orders of G.O.C. 71/Bde.
6.	5th Dorset Rgt.	-do-	-do-	Reserve. (relieving 1st Leicester Rgt.)	-do-
7.	34th L. T. M. B.	-do-	-do-	Line. (relieving 71st L.T.M.B.)	-do-
8.	Brigade Hd. Qrs.	Night 21/22nd.	-do-	Line.	G.O.C. 34th Bde. assumes Command of Sector on completion of relief.
9.	9th. Lan'. Fus.	-do-	BULLY GRENAY.	Support. (relieving 8th North. Fus.)	
10.	11th Man'. Rgt.	-do-	LES BREBIS.	Reserve. (relieving 5th Dorset Rgt.)	
11.	8th North. Fus.	-do-	Support.	FRONT-LINE - Left. (relieving 9th Suffolk Rgt.)	
12.	5th Dorset Rgt.	-do-	Reserve.	FRONT-LINE - Right. (relieving 2nd Shor. For.)	
13.	34th M. G. Coy.	Night 22/23rd.	BULLY GRENAY.	Line. (relieving 71st M. G. Coy.)	

SECRET.

Copy No. 4

34th Infantry Brigade.

DEFENCE SCHEME.
(Provisional)

Reference map - Sheet 36.C. S.W.1. - 1/10,000.   28th. Oct., 1917.

1. The 34th Infantry Brigade holds the front line from N.13.b.30.00. (Railway exclusive) to F.8.b.40.15. (CANTEEN ALLEY inclusive).

Boundary with the Brigade on our Right is :-

N.13.b.65.00. along Railway to N.18.d.30.50. - N.18.d.26.78. - N.18.c.23.56. - N.18.a.56.30.

Boundary with the Brigade on our Left is :-

CANTEEN ALLEY (inclusive to 34th Infantry Brigade) as far as N.8.a.50.45. - thence to junction of CONGRESS & CONTRACT (N.7.a.95.55.) - thence along trench at N.7.a.00.50. (trench inclusive to 34th Infantry Brigade) - Road junction at M.12.b.05.75. - thence along Road to CITE ST. PIERRE CHURCH - M.11.a.85.75. - along DOUBLE CRASSIER.

2. The Section is held by two Battalions in Front Line with one Battalion close Support and one Battalion Reserve.

Boundary between Front Line Battalions is :-

N.8.c.70.10. (CONDUCTOR to Right Battalion) - N.8.c.50.40. - N.8.c.20.50. - F.7.d.70.90.
Headquarters Right Battalion at HOSPITAL N.7.c.00.75.
Headquarters Left Battalion N.7.b.60.10.

Close Support Battalion.

Headquarters at M.11.d.90.50.
One Company at M.12.b.9.2. (at the disposal of O.C. Left Front Battalion for operations).
Two Companies North and South of Road near M.12.a.6.2. (one at the disposal of Right Front Battalion for operations).
One Company at M.12.c.00.

Reserve Battalion.

Headquarters at M.11.c.30.10.
Four Companies in Houses CITE ST. PIERRE in area between points M.11.c.85.00. - M.11.c.75.18. - M.12.a.20.10. - M.12.c.50.60.

34th Machine Gun Company.

Headquarters at M.12.b.02.60.

34th Light Trench Mortar Battery.

Headquarters at M.12.b.10.30.

(2)

3. Lines of resistance.

(1) Front Line. CHICORY TRENCH, NABOB ALLEY, CARP TRENCH - with Posts in front.

(2) Intermediate Line. COWDRAY, COMMOTION, CUT-OFF, COWLEY, DOUGLAS - with Posts in front where required owing to limited field of fire from the trench.

(3) Reserve Line. To be constructed as shown on tracing ~~issued herewith.~~ to follow

4. Disposition of Battalions in the Line.

The Front Line System will be held by each Battalion with two Companies. Each of these Companies will have at least one Platoon and Company H.Q. disposed between the Front and Intermediate Lines.

The Intermediate Line System. will be held by each Battalion with one Company which will be disposed in the Intermediate System.

The remaining Company of each Battalion will be in the neighbourhood of Battalion H.Q.

5. Action in case of attack.

In the event of attack the Front Line System will be defended to the last by its garrison.
The Platoon in Company Commander's Reserve will be available for Support or local counter-attack.

The Intermediate Line System will be manned by its garrison, and must be held at all costs.

The rear Company of each Battalion will stand-to and will be used for regaining by counter-attack any ground lost in the Front Line System, under orders of the Battalion Commander.

The Companies of the Support Battalions allotted to Battalions in the Front Line will fall in on their alarm positions prepared to move up, and an Officer from each will report to the H.Q. of the Battalion concerned.
The other two Companies will move up and occupy respectively ~~CYDER~~ Crecest and CHARLIE trenches.

The Reserve Battalion will stand-to in its alarm positions and await orders.

Working parties from Support and Reserve Battalions will stand-to in the nearest suitable positions clear of the main communication trenches, and send a representative to the nearest Battalion H.Q. to report their position and obtain instructions.
They should be sent to their allotted positions as soon as possible.

8. ACKNOWLEDGE.

C. Chute Captain,

A/Brigade Major, 34th. Infy. Brigade.

For distribution P.T.O.

DISTRIBUTION.

```
Copy No. 1. Office.
         2.   -do-
         3. Staff Captain.
         4. War Diary.
         5.   -do-
         3. Bde. Signals.
         7. 8th North. Fus.
         8. 9th. Lan'. Fus.
         9. 5th Dorset Rgt.
        10. 11th Man'. Rgt.
        11. 34th M. G. Coy.
        12. 34th L. T. M. B.
        13. 11th Division.
        14. 32nd Brigade.
        15. 33rd Brigade.
        16. 173rd Brigade.
        17. Arty. Liaison Officer.
        18. 86th Field Co. R.E.
        19. Bde. Intell. Officer.
```

WAR DIARY

SECRET.

WARNING ORDER.

Ref. map. - HAZEBROUCK - 1/100,000.

1. 11th. Div. will be transferred to First Army and will be accommodated in the St. HILAIRE Area.

2. 34th. Bde. will move by tactical train on 15th. inst.

3. First line transport will proceed by march route on 14th. inst.

   Detailed orders will follow.

4. On arrival in St. HILAIRE Area 11th. Div. will be posted to V Corps.

5. ACKNOWLEDGE

12/10/17.

F.G. Turner, Captain,
Bde. Major, 34th Brigade.

War Diary

SECRET.

SCHEDULE No. 1.

(Issued in continuation of 34th Brigade Defence Scheme)

ARTILLERY.

1. The 34th Infantry Brigade Front is covered by the 5th. Canadian Divnl. Artillery. There are 18 18-pdrs. and three 4.5" Howitzers allotted to the 34th Infantry Brigade frontage. Certain Batteries of the 11th Divnl. Artillery are also in position and some of their guns manned by 5th Canadian Divnl. Artillery will be used to re-inforce the defensive barrage if required.

2. Five 6" Mortars (NEWTON) are in action on the Brigade front. It is hoped that two 9-45" Heavy T.Ms. will shortly be in position.

3. Liaison Officers of 5th Canadian Divnl. Artillery are attached to Brigade H.Q. and to Battalions in the line.

4. The S.O.S. Signal will only be sent up in the event of actual attack by enemy Infantry. Every available means of communication will be used.
    The present Signal is a succession of GREEN Rockets or Very Lights and should be known to all.

    On the S.O.S. Signal being received firing will be -

    3 minutes intense
    7 minutes normal,

    it will then cease unless the S.O.S. Signal is repeated.

5. Retaliation is given on the request of the Infantry which may be transmitted by visual signal (succession of Red - White - Red Rockets or Very Lights) or by telephone.

6. Trench Mortars should open retaliatory fire automatically in reply to enemy bombardment.

    Their assistance and that of Heavy Artillery may be obtained through the Brigade Liaison Officer on application to 34th Brigade.

7. The Code numbers of targets were issued under 34th Brigade No. M. 335 of 23th. October, 1917, and should be used in calling for retaliatory fire.

==*=*=*=*=*

War Diary.

SECRET.

SCHEDULE No. 2.

(Issued in continuation of 34th Brigade Defence Scheme)

MACHINE GUNS and TRENCH MORTARS.

1. The 34th Machine Gun Company has 12 guns in the Line, of which two are covering the 11th Division's Left Brigade Front, and the remainder the front occupied by the 34th Infantry Brigade. It has also two guns in position for harassing fire.

2. The front is also covered by barrage fire of 13 guns from N.2.b. which can be called for by S.O.S. Signal or Telephone message.

3. Group H.Q. are at M.12.b.8.0., N.13.b.5.8. and N.8.a.5.4. Close liaison should be maintained between Group Commanders and Company Commanders in the Line.

4. Three Stokes' Mortars are in position at N.13.b. 35.75. - N.14.a.23.92. - N.8.c.40.70. - a fourth gun will be placed in the Left Sector.

    Full use should be made of these by Infantry Commanders for retaliatory fire, etc.

==*=*=*

War Diary   No 4

H.Q.
84th INFANTRY BDE.
CS/50

SCHEDULE 3.

S. A. A. and BOMB STORES.

The following are the dumps in the right Brigade Area
The establishments shown in each dump will be kept up.

Brigade Main Dump - M.11.b.60.35.

S. A. A.	200,000.
Grenades, Mills No. 5	12,000.
" No. 20	3,000.
" No. 23	3,000.
" No. 24	3,000.
Rods	5,000.
M. S. K.	200.
Ground Flares, Red	2,000.
Rockets, Red	100.
" Green	100.
" Sticks	200.
Very Lights, 1" White	5,000.
" " 1" Red	50.
" " 1¼" White	1,500.
" " 1¼" Red	1,500.
" " 1¼" Green	100.
"P" Bombs	200.

Brigade Right Advanced Dump - M.12.d.80.90.

S. A. A.	100,000.
Grenades, Mills No. 5	5,000.
" No. 20	2,000.
" No. 23	2,000.
" No. 24	1,000.
Rods	500.
Rockets, Red	20.
" Green	30.
" Sticks	50.
Very Lights, 1" White	4,000.
" " 1¼" White	2,000.
" " 1¼" Red	100.

Brigade Left Advanced Dump - M.7.a.50.60.

S. A. A.	150,000.
Grenades, Mills No. 5	8,000.
" No. 20	2,000.
" No. 23	3,000.
" No. 24	1,000.
"P" Bombs	500.
Ground Flares, Red	1,000.
Rockets, Red	50.
" Green	30.
" Sticks	1,000.
Very Lights, 1" White	4,000.
" " 1¼" White	1,000.
" " 1¼" Red	360.
" " 1¼" Green	200.

Brigade Corkscrew Dump - M.12.c.25.35.

S. A. A.	200,000.
Grenades, Mills No. 5	1,000.
" No. 23	1,000.

Indents for S.A.A. etc. will be rendered by Units to Brigade
Headquarters. In cases of urgency issues will be made on the
Signature of an Officer.

War Diary

SECRET.

SCHEDULE No. 4.

(Issued in continuation of 54th Brigade Defence Scheme.)

COMMUNICATIONS.

1. **H.Q. and Station Calls.**

Brigade H.Q. M.11.a.6.1.	AI 15
Brigade Forward Station. M.12.b.4.3.	AI 19
Right Battalion. N.7.c.0.7.	AI 39
Left Battalion. N.7.b.6.1.	AI 21
Support Battalion. M.11.d.9.5.	AI 23
Reserve Battalion. M.11.c.45.05.	AI 38
Machine Gun Company. M.12.b.0.7.	AI 56.

2. **Telephone lines.**

   Each Battalion in the line has a buried line back to Brigade H.Q.

   Artillery Liaison Officers have their own lines.

   Support Battalion has buried line back to Brigade H.Q. except for about 200 yards.

   Reserve Battalion has buried line back to Brigade H.Q.

   Machine Gun Company has buried line back to Brigade H.Q. except for about 300 yards.

3. **Visual.**

   Brigade Visual Station is at M.11.b.2.4. and can receive from both Battalions in the line and Support Battalion, and also from one Company of each Battalion in the line.

   Visual is also working between Left Battalion H.Q. and Support Company of Right Battalion. This Company can work to both Right Battalion H.Q. and Brigade Visual Station.

   Stations are manned at arranged hours and test messages sent.

   In event of an emergency all visual stations will be constantly manned.

4. **Runners.**

   There is a runner relay post at Brigade Forward Station (M.12.b.4.3.).

5. **Power Buzzer and Amplifier.**

   There are no Power Buzzers or Amplifiers installed in the area.

6. **Pigeons.**

   Two pairs of pigeons are issued daily to each Battalion in the line.

   ==*=*=*

SCHEDULE 5.

EVACUATION OF WOUNDED.

LINE.

Right Battalion R. A. P. - N.7.c.10.70.

Short carry of 50 yards to Light Railway running to Junction Post (M.12.a.95.45) Evacuation carried out on trolleys.

Left Battalion R. A. P. - N.8.c.10.90.

Hand carry along Trench to Counter Trench Relay Post (N.7.b.60.10) Relay carries by "C" Route to EDDY POST (N.7.a.30.60.) Evacuation from EDDY POST to JUNCTION POST along Light Railway on trolleys.

Evacuation from JUNCTION POST to St. PIERRE A.D.S. by Light Railway, by wheeled stretchers, and walking cases along "C" Route.

Support Battalion.- R. A. P. - M.12.b.40.40.

Short carry of 50 yards to JUNCTION POST; further evacuation as above.

Reserve Battalion R. A. P. - M.11.c.30.40.

Short hand carry of 100 yards, approximately, to St. PIERRE A. D. S.

ST. PIERRE A. D. S. - M.11.c.75.95.

Evacuation by rail to FOSSE 11 de BETHUNE by rail. If the rail is out of action, Ambulance Cars are used, travelling by double Crassier Road and MAROC to Main Dressing Station and Divisional Gas Centre at NOEUX LES MINES or to Special C. C. S's for Special Cases.

FOSSE 11 de BETHUNE - M.8.b.20.20.

Evacuation by Ambulance Cars to Main Dressing Station, NOEUX LES MINES, or special C.C.S's.

Besides R.A.M.C. Squads from Field Ambulance to R. A. P. and Relay Posts, there are 3 Reserve Squads at EDDY POST, 6 at JUNCTION POST and 4 at ST. PIERRE A. D. S.

Reference Map:- LOOS 36 N.W.3. 1/10,000.
                  LENS 36 S.W.1. 1/10,000.

SECRET. Copy No. 4

34th Infantry Brigade Order No. 46.

Reference map - Sheet 36.C. S.W.1. - 1/10,000.   28th. Oct./17.

1.   On the night 30th/31st. October 11th Manchester Regiment will relieve 5th Dorset Regiment in the Right Sector of the Brigade Front and 9th Lancashire Fusiliers will relieve 8th Northumberland Fusiliers in the Left Sector.

         Details of relief to be arranged between Os.C. Units concerned.

2.   On relief, 8th Northumberland Fusiliers will go into Support and 5th Dorset Regiment into Reserve.

3.   All trench stores, defence schemes, log books, etc. will be handed over.

4.   Completion of relief will be reported to this Office by the Code Signal "HOT BATHS PREFERRED" and time.

5.   ACKNOWLEDGE.

ISSUED AT 6 p.m.

                                                          Captain,
                                     A/Brigade Major, 34th Inf. Brigade.

DISTRIBUTION.

Copy No. 1. Office.   Copy No. 11. 34th M. G. Coy.
        2.   -do-   12. 34th L. T. M. B.
        3. Staff Captain.   13. 11th Division.
        4. War Diary.   14. 32nd Brigade.
        5.   -do-   15. 33rd Brigade.
        6. Bde. Signals.   16. 176th Brigade.
        7. 8th North. Fus.   17. 86th Field Co.
        8. 9th Lan. Fus.   18. 34th Field Amb.
        9. 5th Dorset Rgt.   19. No.4.Coy.A.S.C.
       10. 11th Man. Rgt.   20. Arty. Liaison Offr.

Secret  No 4
War Diary

ADMINISTRATIVE INSTRUCTION
TO ACCOMPANY 34th. INFANTRY BRIGADE ORDER No. 36.

1. Copies of receipts for trench stores will be rendered to this Office by 12 noon 1st. November, together with consolidated list by relieving units.

2. Hot Food Containers will be handed over as trench Stores, and receipts given.

                                                Captain,

28/10/17.   A/Staff Captain, 34th. Infantry Brigade.

Copy No.
1. Office.
2. Office.
3. Brigade Major.
4. War Diary.
5. -do-
6. Bde. Signals.
7. Northd. Fus.
8. Lan. Fus.
9. Dorset R.
10. Manch. R.
11. M.G. Coy.
12. L.T.M.B.
13. 11th. Division.
14. 32nd. Brigade.
15. 33rd. Brigade.
16. 178th. Brigade.
17. 88th. Field Coy.
18. 34th. Field. Amb.
19. No. 4 Coy A.S.C.
20. Arty. Liaison Offr.

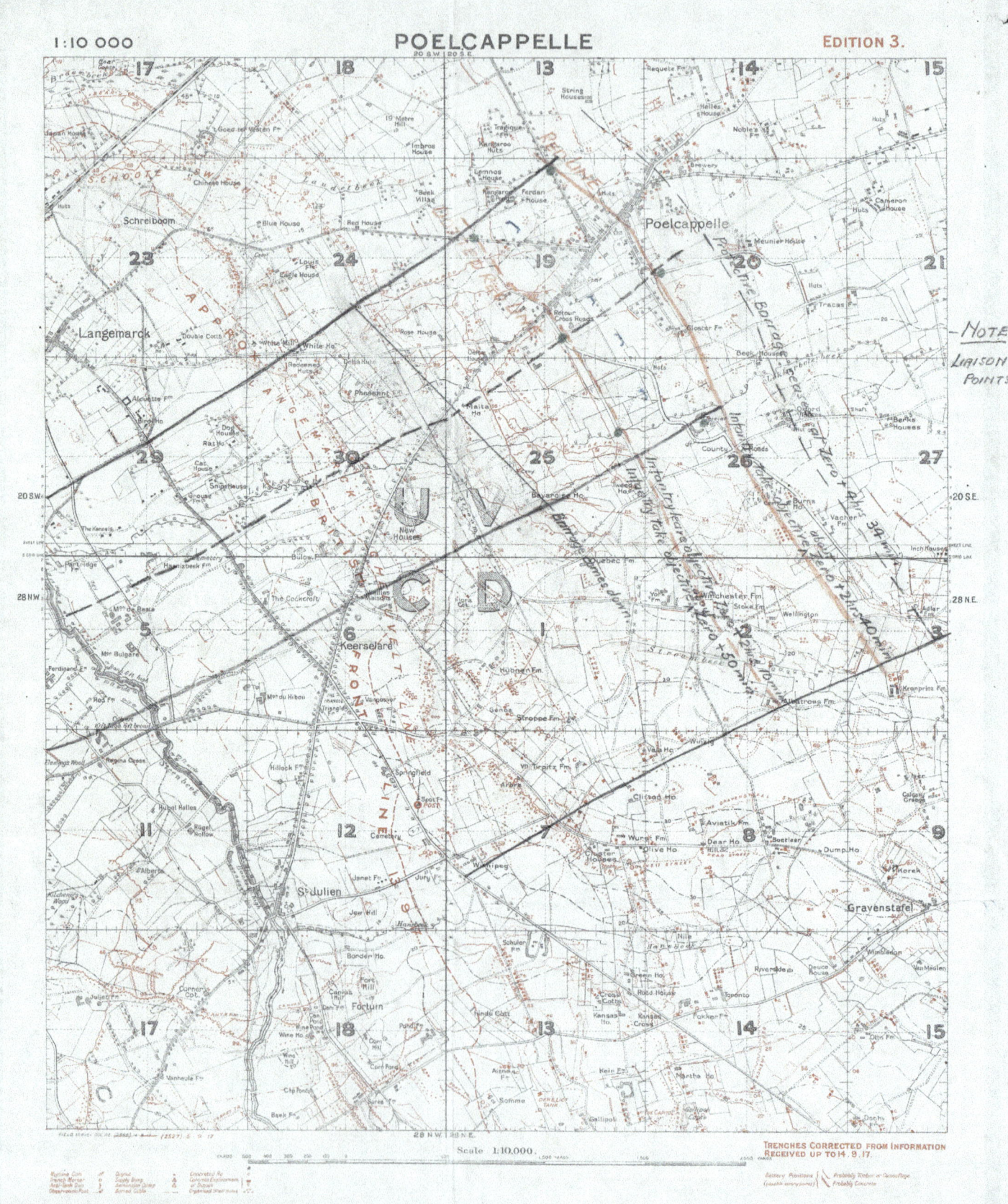

Army Form W. 3091.

Cover for Documents.

Nature of Enclosures.

CONFIDENTIAL.

WAR DIARY

of

Headquarters 34th INFANTRY BRIGADE

From 1st Nov to 30th Nov

Notes, or Letters written.

WAR DIARY
INTELLIGENCE SUMMARY

(Erase heading not required.)

Army Form C. 2118.

Place	Date	Hour	Summary of Events and Information	Remarks and references to Appendices
Cte St PIERRE	Nov 1st		Uneventful day. Fine. Digging of main reserve line commenced.	
M.I.A.d.1 (Map 36c)	Nov 2nd		Heavy spirt. Lois evidence of gas to have projected from R' 5½ area. No immediate effect.	
	Nov 3rd		Very quiet day. Misty & few minshells. Not extended at N8d.5-9. Manned	
	Nov 4th		Fine but rain at midnight. Enemy aircraft patrols to left of "D" indicated CO's seen thorough occupation of enemy front line. Machineguns &	Sent 4/11/17
	Nov 5th		Defence scheme issued. A few gas shells on C "B" at night.	
	6th		Visibility again fair. Some shelling of C & D at PIERRE. Intelligence learned how 11 Div Corps enemy might be fostering attack on	2
			our front. Bth tactical scheme C. which was issued	As appendix 5
	6th		Attendance to Defence scheme issued. Suffolk's relieve B'th Btn	
			relieved by 2D & 10th	
	7th		Uneventful day. Relief in the Line by 33rd Bde completed	
			by 10.30 p.m. Bth. HQ. open at VAUDRICOURT at midnight	
VAUDRICOURT	8th		Moves in accordance with relief orders completed	
	9th		Training begun	

WAR DIARY
INTELLIGENCE SUMMARY
(Erase heading not required.)

Army Form C. 2118.

Place	Date	Hour	Summary of Events and Information	Remarks and references to Appendices
VAUX MARICOURT	10th		Training carried on. Patrols reconnoitre routes up to Line to be held in event of Bde. moving up to counter an enemy attack. Wet day.	
"	11th		G.O.C. reconnoitres route to Line for Bde. in Div Reserve in case of alarm. Defence scheme for Bde. in Div Reserve issued. Training continued.	Appendix I
"	12th		Training continued. Fine day.	
"	13th		Div. Order issued that Bde. relieve 32nd Bde. in Line on left sector of Div. front by 6 p.m. on 15th inst. Bde. Order No. 68 issued to that effect. Training continued. Fine day.	Appendix I
"	14th		First part of relief as ordered in Bde. Ordr. No. 68 completed by 11 p.m. Training continued by other units of Bde. Fine hot day but rain after dark.	
"	15th	11.10 p.m.	Relief completed and command of left sector of Div. Front assumed by G.O.C. 34th Bde. at 11.10 p.m. Fine day.	
ELVASTON CASTLE G.34.a.9.3 (M.1.36c)				

A6945 Wt. W14422/M1160 350,000 12/16 D.D. & L., Forms/C./2118/14.

Army Form C. 2118.

WAR DIARY
or
INTELLIGENCE SUMMARY.
(Erase heading not required.)

Instructions regarding War Diaries and Intelligence Summaries are contained in F. S. Regs., Part II. and the Staff Manual respectively. Title pages will be prepared in manuscript.

Place	Date	Hour	Summary of Events and Information	Remarks and references to Appendices
ELMSTON CASTLE G.3.A.9.3 (Sheet 36c)	16th		This day. Very quiet, artillery on both sides being extremely quiet.	
	17th		No change in the situation. Quiet day and fine. Bn. Order No. 69 issued ordering relief of front line Bn. on night 19th/20th	Appendix I
	18th		Fine day. Situation unchanged. Artillery on both sides quiet.	
	19th		Situation unchanged. Quiet day. Instructions in the event of an enemy retirement issued. Fine day.	2Lt/14A/24.2
	20th		Relief in accordance with Bn. Order No. 59 completed by 1.32 a.m. Quiet day and situation unchanged.	
	21st	4.10 a.m.	At 4.10 a.m. four of enemy rushed our Lewis gun post at N.2.6.50.75. Killing one man of 11th MANCHESTER Regt. and capturing the Lewis Gun. The post was at once re-established, but the enemy escaped.	
		6.15 a.m.	At 6.15 a.m. the 33rd Bn. on our right attempted to raid	

A6945 Wt. W14422/M1160 350,000 12/16. D. D. & L. Forms/C./2118/14.

Army Form C. 2118.

WAR DIARY
or
INTELLIGENCE SUMMARY.
(Erase heading not required.)

Instructions regarding War Diaries and Intelligence Summaries are contained in F. S. Regs., Part II. and the Staff Manual respectively. Title pages will be prepared in manuscript.

Place	Date	Hour	Summary of Events and Information	Remarks and references to Appendices
ELVASTON CASTLE G.34.a.9.3 (Sheet 36 c)	22nd	6 a.m.	a portion of the enemy's front system, but the enemy apparently suspected the attack and it failed. 3th L.T.M.B. cooperated in the attempted raid by rapid fire with 2 guns on suspected enemy M.G. positions. The enemy's artillery in retaliation damaged NUNS ALLEY and LOST TRENCH with shell-fire, but for the rest of the day all was quiet. A wet day, and trenches became very muddy. At 6 a.m. the enemy 300 strong successfully raided the 138th Bde. on our left. Our barrage was put down, and in retaliation the enemy shelled NETLEY TRENCH but otherwise 7 a.m. all was quiet. Dull day and poor visibility. Bde. Order No. 70 altering the 13th Bn. boundary on the 13th Bn. front issued. Bde. Order No. 71 issued, arranging relief of front line Bns. on night 23rd/24th.	Appendix I Appendix I
	23rd		No change in the situation. Rain in the morning. Quiet day.	

Army Form C. 2118.

WAR DIARY
or
INTELLIGENCE SUMMARY.
(Erase heading not required.)

Instructions regarding War Diaries and Intelligence Summaries are contained in F. S. Regs., Part II. and the Staff Manual respectively. Title pages will be prepared in manuscript.

Place	Date	Hour	Summary of Events and Information	Remarks and references to Appendices
ELVASTON CASTLE G.34.d.9.3 (Sheet 36c)	24th		Relief ordered in Bde Order No.71 completed by 1.15 a.m. Situation unchanged. Fine day and high wind. Quiet day.	
"	25th		Order from Div. received that Div. frontage will be extended Northwards. The necessitation all Bns. Bttns. being continually in the Line. B.O. 72 issued accordingly. B.O. 73 also issued ordering Batt relief on night 27th/28th. Fine day. Hostile artillery active during the morning on Road about M.S.A. and C. Otherwise quiet	Appendix 1 Appendix 2
"	26th		and BETHUNE-LENS Road about unchanged.	
"	27th		day, and situation unchanged. Rain up till noon. Quiet day. Situation unchanged Relief ordered in B.O. 73 completed by 2 a.m.	
"	28th		Fine day and good visibility. Hostile artillery activity greatly increased on and behind Reserve line. Gas projectors discharged by 18th Bn. left at 10.30 pm and enemy retaliated with vigourous artillery fire behind our Front and Reserve Lines for an hour, but only caused fear	

Army Form C. 2118.

WAR DIARY
or
INTELLIGENCE SUMMARY.
(Erase heading not required.)

Instructions regarding War Diaries and Intelligence Summaries are contained in F.S. Regs., Part II. and the Staff Manual respectively. Title pages will be prepared in manuscript.

Place	Date	Hour	Summary of Events and Information	Remarks and references to Appendices
ELVERTON CAMP G.34.d.9.3 (Sheet 36)	29th		Casualties — all to 1/4th Batt. Fine day with excellent visibility. Hostile artillery very active during the day + especially in evening N.6. Brigade Order No. 74 issued for Batt. relief on night 1st/2nd Dec.	Appendix I
"	30th		Fine day with excellent visibility and hostile artillery again very active during the day. Situation unchanged.	

N Turner Capt.
A/Adjt 34th to 1/4 Bn.
KRM

SECRET.

Copy No. 4

34th Infantry Brigade Order No. 67.

Reference maps — LENS 36.c. S.W.1. — 1/10,000.
                  LENS 11 — 1/100,000.

5th Nov. 1917.

1. The 33rd Infantry Brigade will relieve the 34th Infantry Brigade on the nights 6th/7th. and 7th/8th. November.

    Details of relief to be arranged between units concerned.

2. On relief the 34th Infantry Brigade will proceed into billets in accordance with accompanying March Table.

3. Each Battalion will detail one Company (not less than 130 diggers) to relieve similar parties of 33rd Infantry Brigade engaged in burying cable. There must be no cessation of work on the bury which should be completed by 10th. inst. when those parties will rejoin their units. Parties of 8th North. Fus. and 5th Dorset Regt. will report on night of 6th/7th. November, and of 9th Lan. Fus. and 11th Lan. Regt. on night of 7th/8th. Nov.

4. All trench stores, S.A.A., Bombs, maps, log books, etc. will be handed over on relief.

5. Completion of relief will be reported to Brigade H.Q. by wiring Serial No. on the Table and time.

6. Brigade H.Q. will close at CITE ST. PIERRE on completion of relief and open at VAUDRICOURT CHATEAU at 12 midnight 7th/8th November.

7. ACKNOWLEDGE.

ISSUED AT 2 P.M.

                                        Captain,
                A/Brigade Major, 34th. Inf. Brigade.

DISTRIBUTION.

Copy No. 1. Office.	Copy No. 11. 54th M. G. Coy.
2. -do-	12. 34th L. T. M. B.
3. Staff Captain.	13. 11th Division.
4. War Diary.	14. 32nd Brigade.
5. -do-	15. 33rd Brigade.
6. Bde. Signals.	16. 177th Brigade.
7. 8th North. Fus.	17. 86th Field Co. R.E.
8. 9th Lan'. Fus.	18. 34th Field Amb.
9. 5th Dorset Rgt.	19. No.4.Coy.A.S.C.
10. 11th Lan'. Rgt.	20. Arty. Liaison Offr.

MARCH TABLE.

Serial No.	Date.	Unit.	Relieved by.	Proceeds to.	Remarks.
1.	Nov. 5th.	8th North. Fus.	8th Border Regt.	BULLY-GRENAY.	) Night working par-
2.	-do-	5th Dorset Rgt.	9th Sherwood Fors	-do-	) ties to proceed on
3.	-do-	34th L. T. M. B.	53rd L. T. M. B.	-do-	) completion of work
4.	Nov. 7th.	8th North. Fus.		NOEUX-les-MINES.	) Arriving
5.	-do-	5th Dorset Rgt.		-do-	) after
6.	-do-	34th L. T. M. B.		-do-	) 12 noon.
7.	-do-	34th Brigade H.Q.	53rd Brigade H.Q.	VAUDRICOURT CHATEAU.	
8.	-do-	9th Lan. Fus.	9th Sherwood Fors	BULLY-GRENAY.	
9.	-do-	11th Lan. Rgt.	8th Border Regt.	-do-	
10.	Nov. 8th.	9th Lan. Fus.		VERQUIN, DROUVIN, VAUDRICOURT.	) As
11.	-do-	11th Lan. Rgt.		VAUDRICOURT.	) above.
12.	-do-	34th M. G. Coy.	53rd M. G. Coy.	NOEUX-les-MINES.	

Intervals of 100 yards will be maintained between Companies.

* * * * * * * * *

SECRET.

War Diary

Copy No. 3

34th Infantry Brigade Order No. 68.

Reference maps - Sheet 36.b. - 1/40,000.
Sheet 36.c.S.W.1. - 1/10,000.
Sheet 36.c.N.W.3. - 1/10,000.

Nov. 13th/17.

1. 34th Infantry Brigade will relieve 32nd Infantry Brigade in the line in the Left Sector of the Divisional Front on nights 14th/15th. and 15th/16th. inst.

2. All moves to be carried out in accordance with attached Table.

3. Details of relief, guides etc. will be arranged direct between O.C. Units concerned.

4. All trench stores, S.A.A., Bombs, Defence Schemes, Log-books, aeroplane photos, etc. will be taken over on relief.

5. Schedule of Working Parties will be taken over from relieved Units, and will remain in force till further orders.

6. The Cable Burying Parties of 8th Northumberland Fus. and 5th. Dorset Regt. will be relieved on night 14th/15th. and of 9th Lancashire Fus. and 11th Manchester Regt. on night 15th/16th.

    There will be no work for either relieved or relieving parties on their respective nights of relief.

    Arrangements will be made for the relieved parties to proceed to MAZINGARBE for baths on the night of relief. They will return to the line on the following night.

    Parties will work as follows :-

Unit.	14th/15th.	15th/16th.	16th/17th.
8th N.F. & 5th Dor.	To baths.	To Line.	-
9th L.F. & 11th Man.	At work.	To baths.	To Line.

7. Completion of relief will be reported to Brigade H.Q. by wiring Serial No. of Table and time.

8. Brigade H.Q. will close at VAUDRICOURT at 5 p.m. on 15th. inst. and open at G.34.d.7.4. on completion of relief when Command of the Left Sector will pass to G.O.C. 34th Infantry Brigade.

9. ACKNOWLEDGE.

ISSUED AT... 8 p.m

H.T. Turner, Captain,
Brigade Major, 34th. Infantry Brigade.

DISTRIBUTION.

Copy No.1. Office.	Copy No.8. 9th. Lan'. Fus.	Copy No.15. 33rd Bde.
2. -do-	9. 5th Dorset Regt.	16. Left Bde.
3. War Diary.	10. 11th Man'. Rgt.	17. 86th R.E.
4. -do-	11. 34th M. G. Coy.	18. No.4.Coy. Div.Train.
5. Staff Capt.	12. 34th L. T. M. B.	
6. Bde. Sigs.	13. 11th Division.	19. 34th F.A.
7. 8th North. Fus.	14. 32nd Brigade.	20. Bde. I.O.

Relief Table issued in conjunction with 54th Brigade Order No. 68.

Serial No.	Date.	Unit.	To.	Relieving.	Remarks.
1.	14th/15th. Night.	5th Dorset Rgt.	Support. H.Q. N.1.a.0.1.	8th W. Riding Regt.	On completion of relief to come under orders of G.O.C. 32nd Inf. Bde.
2.	-do-	8th North. Fus.	Reserve. H.Q. G.56.d.7.0.	6th Yorks & Lancs. R.	-do-
3.	-do-	54th L. T. M. B.	Line. H.Q. QUARRY. M.6.a.	32nd L. T. M. B.	-do-
4.	15th/16th. Night.	11th Lan'. Regt.	Support. H.Q. N.1.a.0.1.	5th Dorset Regiment.	
5.	-do-	9th. Lan'. Fus.	Reserve. H.Q. G.56.d.7.0.	8th North. Fus.	
6.	-do-	8th North. Fus.	Line (Right). H.Q. N.7.b.7.8.	9th West Yorks. Regt.	
7.	-do-	5th Dorset Rgt.	Line (Left). H.Q. N.1.b.0.2.	6th Yorkshire Regt.	
8.	-do-	54th Bde. H.Q.	Line. H.Q. G.54.d.7.4.	32nd Brigade H.Q.	
9.	16th/17th. Night.	54th M. G. Coy.	Line. H.Q. QUARRY. M.6.a.	32nd M. G. Coy.	

War Diary

SECRET.   Copy No. 4

34th Infantry Brigade Order No. 69.

Reference maps - Sheet 36.c.S.W.1. - 1/10,000.
Sheet 36.c.N.W.3. - 1/10,000.   Nov. 17th. 1917.

1. 9th Lancashire Fusiliers will relieve 8th Northumberland Fusiliers in the Right Sector, and 11th Manchester Regiment will relieve 5th Dorset Regiment in the Left Sector of the Brigade Front on the night 19th/20th. November.

2. On relief 8th Northumberland Fus. will go into ~~Support~~ *Reserve* and 5th Dorset Regt. into ~~Reserve~~ *Support*.

3. All details for above reliefs will be arranged direct between Os. C. concerned.

4. All Working-party schedules, Maps, Defence Schemes, Log-books etc. will be handed over on relief.

5. All dumps of R.E. material, S.A.A. Rockets, Grenades and Trench stores will be handed over and signed receipts forwarded by relieved units to this office by noon 20th. inst.

6. The relief must not interfere with Working-parties.
All working parties will be at their rendezvous at 4-30 p.m. on evening of 19th. inst. and work must be completed before relief begins.

7. Completion of relief will be reported to Brigade Headquarters in "B.A.B." Code.

8. ACKNOWLEDGE.

Issued at......10 PM......   Turner, Captain,
Brigade Major 34th Infantry Brigade.

DISTRIBUTION.

Copy No. 1 Office.	Copy No. 10 Manchester Regt.
" " 2 "	" " 11 34th M. G. Coy.
" " 3 Staff Captain.	" " 12 34th L. T. M. B.
" " 4 War Diary.	" " 13 11th Division.
" " 5 "	" " 14 32nd Brigade.
" " 6 Brigade Signals.	" " 15 33rd Brigade.
" " 7 8th North. Fus.	" " 16 138th Brigade.
" " 8 5th Dorset Regt.	" " 17 86th Field Co. R.E.
" " 9 9th Lan. Fus.	" " 18 Bde. Intell. Officer.

SECRET.   Copy No. 4

34th Infantry Brigade Order No. 70.

Reference map - HILL 70 - 1/10,000.   21st. Nov/17.

1.   The boundary between Battalions will be moved Northwards, so that NORMAN TRENCH, with the posts at N.2.d.4.8. and N.2.d.35.75., included in the Right Battalion's Sector.

2.   O.C. 9th. Lancashire Fusiliers will arrange to take over the additional frontage from O.C. 11th. Manchester Regiment at dusk tomorrow, 22nd. inst., and will report that this has been done by wiring to Brigade Headquarters the Code Word "KISMET".

3.   The dug-out recently completed at the junction of NORMAN and HAPPY TRENCHES N.2.d.07.73. will be occupied by 9th. Lancashire Fusiliers.

4.   ACKNOWLEDGE.

ISSUED AT......10.p.m.....

F.G. Turner, Captain,
Brigade Major, 34th. Infty. Brigade.

DISTRIBUTION.

Copy No. 1. Office.   Copy No. 9. 5th Dorset Regt.
         2. -do-   10. 11th Manchester Regt.
         3. Staff Captain.   11. 34th Machine Gun Coy.
         4. War Diary.   12. 34th L. T. M. B.
         5. -do-   13. 11th Division.
         6. Bde. Signals.   14. 32nd Brigade.
         7. 8th North. Fus.   15. 33rd Brigade.
         8. 9th. Lan'. Fus.   16. 138th Brigade.
              Copy No. 17. 86th Field Co.R.E.

==*=*=*=*=
S E C R E T.
==*=*=*=*=

Copy No. 4

War Diary

34th Infantry Brigade Order No. 71.

Reference maps - Sheet 36.C.S.W.1. - 1/10,000.
Sheet 36.C.N.W.3. - 1/10,000.

Nov. 21st./17.

1. 8th Northumberland Fusiliers will relieve 9th Lancashire Fusiliers in the Right Sector, and 5th Dorset Regiment will relieve 11th Manchester Regiment in the Left Sector of the Brigade Front on the night 23rd/24th. November.

2. On relief 9th Lancashire Fus. will go into Reserve and 11th. Manchester Regt. into Support.

3. All details for above reliefs will be arranged direct between Os.C. concerned.

4. All working party schedules, maps, Defence Schemes, Log-books etc. will be handed over on relief.

5. All dumps of R.E. material, S.A.A., Rockets, Grenades and Trench stores will be handed over and signed receipts forwarded by relieved units to this Office by noon 24th. inst.

6. The relief must not interfere with working parties, and work must be completed before relief begins, but relieving Battalions should keep off work on evening of 23rd. all men going on Sentry duty first in the Front Line and their first reliefs, so that those men may be fresh for sentry duty.

7. Completion of relief will be reported to Brigade Headquarters by Code Word "CASCARA".

8. ACKNOWLEDGE.

ISSUED AT...11.P.M...

F.G. Turner, Captain,

Brigade Major, 34th Inf. Brigade.

==*=*=*=*=
DISTRIBUTION.
==*=*=*=*=

Copy No. 1. Office.	Copy No. 10. 11th Man'. Rgt.
2. -do-	11. 34th M. G. Coy.
3. Staff Captain.	12. 34th L. T. M. B.
4. War Diary.	13. 11th Division.
5. -do-	14. 32nd Brigade.
6. Bde. Signals.	15. 33rd Brigade.
7. 8th North. Fus.	16. 138th Brigade.
8. 9th. Lan'. Fus.	17. 86th Field Co.
9. 5th Dorset Rgt.	18. Bde. INT. Off.

*0*0*0*0*0*

War Diary

SECRET.

Copy No. 4

34th Infantry Brigade Order No. 72.

Reference maps – Sheet 36.C. S.W.1. – 1/10,000.
Sheet 36.C. N.W.3. – 1/10,000.   25th Nov. 1917.

1. The frontage of the 11th. Division will be extended Northwards, and the 32nd. Infantry Brigade will relieve the 138th. Inf. Brigade in the Right Section of the 46th. Division Front on HILL 70 on the night 26th/27th.

2. On completion of this relief the following will be the boundaries :-

   (a) Between Right Section and Centre Section, N.8.b.57.57. to N.8.a.60.42. thence as at present.

   (b) Between Centre Section and Left Section, H.32.d.40.10. to H.31.d.72.00. to H.31.c.00.60. to G.30.c.00.00.

3. O.C. 8th. Northumberland Fusiliers will adjust his Right Boundary accordingly by arrangements direct with O.C. 9th. Sherwood Foresters. This adjustment will be completed by 6 a.m. 27th. inst. and a report to this effect wired to Brigade Headquarters by the Code phrase "CARRIED OUT".

4. A Battalion relief (orders to be issued later) will be carried out on the night 27th./28th.
   After the completion of this relief the Battalion in Brigade Reserve will be billeted at LES BREBIS.
   The following Battalion relief will be on the night Dec. 1st/2nd., but after that Battalion reliefs will take place every six days instead of four.

5. ACKNOWLEDGE.

ISSUED AT....8.p.m...

F.G. Turner, Captain,
Brigade Major, 34th. Infantry Brigade.

DISTRIBUTION.

Copy No. 1. Office.
2. -do-
3. Staff Captain.
4. War Diary.
5. -do-
6. Brigade Signals.
7. 8th North. Fus.
8. 9th. Lan'. Fus.
9. 5th Dorset Rgt.

Copy No. 10. 11th Man'. Rgt.
11. 34th M. G. Coy.
12. 34th L. T. M. B.
13. 11th Division.
14. 32nd Brigade.
15. 33rd Brigade.
16. 138th Brigade.
17. 86th Field Co. R.E.
18. Bde. Intell. Offer.

Copy No. 19. Arty. Liaison Officer.
20. 13th. Canadian Brigade.

SECRET.

War Diary

Copy No. 4

34th Infantry Brigade Order No. 73.

Reference maps - Sheet 36.C. S.W.1. - 1/10,000.
Sheet 36.C. N.W.3. - 1/10,000.

25th. Nov., 1917.

1. 9th. Lancashire Fusiliers will relieve 8th. Northumberland Fusiliers in the Right Sector, and 11th. Manchester Regiment will relieve 5th. Dorset Regiment in the Left Sector of the Brigade Front on the night 27th./28th. November.

2. On relief 5th. Dorset Regiment will go into Support and 8th. Northumberland Fusiliers into Brigade Reserve at LES BREBIS.

3. All details for above reliefs will be arranged direct between Os.C. concerned.

4. All maps, Defence Schemes, Log-books, etc. will be handed over on relief.

5. All dumps of R.E. material, S.A.A., Rockets, Grenades and trench stores will be handed over and signed receipts forwarded by relieved units to this Office by noon 28th. inst.

6. The relief must not interfere with working parties, and work must be completed before relief begins, but relieving Battalions should keep off work on evening of 27th. all men going on Sentry duty first in the Front Line and their first reliefs, so that those men may be fresh for sentry duty.

7. Completion of relief will be reported by wire to Brigade H.Q. by the Code Word "CAESAR".

8. ACKNOWLEDGE.

ISSUED AT...11.p.m...

F.G. Turner, Captain,

Brigade Major, 34th Infantry Brigade.

DISTRIBUTION.

Copy No.		Copy No.	
1.	Office.	11.	34th M. G. Coy.
2.	-do-	12.	34th L. T. M. B.
3.	Staff Captain.	13.	11th Division.
4.	War Diary.	14.	32nd Brigade.
5.	-do-	15.	33rd Brigade.
6.	Brigade Signals.	16.	86th Field Co. R.E.
7.	8th North. Fus.	17.	Bde. Intell. Offcr.
8.	9th. Lan'. Fus.	18.	13th Canadian Bde.
9.	5th Dorset Rgt.	19.	Arty. Liaison Offcr.
10.	11th Man'. Rgt.	20.	Town Major, LES BREBIS.

Copy No. 21. No.4.Coy. A.S.C.

※=※=※=※=※=※
SECRET.   *War Diary*   Copy No. 4....
※=※=※=※=※=※

34th Infantry Brigade Order No. 74.

Reference maps - Sheet 36.C. S.W.1. - 1/10,000.
Sheet 36.C. N.W.3. - 1/10,000.   29th Nov. /17.

1. 8th Northumberland Fusiliers will relieve 9th Lancashire Fusiliers in the Right Sector, and 5th Dorset Regiment will relieve 11th Manchester Regiment in the Left Sector of the Brigade Front on the night 1st/2nd. December, 1917.

2. On relief 11th Manchester Regiment will go into Support and 9th Lancashire Fusiliers into Brigade Reserve at LES BREBIS.

3. All details for above reliefs will be arranged direct between Os.C. concerned.

4. All maps, defence schemes, log-books, working party schedules etc. will be handed over on relief.

5. All dumps of R.E. material, S.A.A., Rockets, Grenades and trench stores will be handed over and signed receipts forwarded by relieved units to this Office, by noon 2nd December.

6. The relief must not interfere with working parties, and work must be completed before relief begins, but relieving Battalions should keep off work on evening of 1st. December all men going on sentry duty first in the Front Line and their first reliefs, so that those men may be fresh for sentry duty.

7. Attention is called to this Office No. M.685 of 28th. inst. Battalions going to and coming from LES BREBIS must observe those distances.

8. Completion of relief will be reported by wire to Brigade H.Q. by the Code "O.K."

9. ACKNOWLEDGE.

ISSUED AT....6-30.p.m.

F.G. Turner,
Captain,
Brigade Major, 34th. Infty. Brigade.

※=※=※=※=※=※
DISTRIBUTION.
※=※=※=※=※=※

Copy No. 1. Office.
   2. -do-
   3. Staff Captain.
   4. War Diary.
   5. -do-
   6. Brigade Signals.
   7. 8th North. Fus.
   8. 9th. Lan'. Fus.
   9. 5th Dorset Rgt.
   10. 11th Man'. Rgt.

Copy No. 11. 34th M. G. Coy.
   12. 34th L. T. M. B.
   13. 11th Division.
   14. 32nd Brigade.
   15. 33rd Brigade.
   16. 86th Field Co. R.E.
   17. Bde. Intell. Offcr.
   18. 13th Canadian CFA.
   19. Arty. Liaison Offr.
   20. Town Major, LES BREBIS

Copy No. 21. No.4.Coy.A.S.C.

※=※=※=※

S E C R E T.   War Diary.   Copy No...4......

INSTRUCTIONS IN EVENT OF AN ENEMY RETIREMENT.
34th Infantry Brigade No. M. 576.

Reference map - 1/20,000 - Sheets 36.C., N.W. & S.W.   19th. November/17.

1.   The forward Boundaries of the Divisional Area in the event of an enemy retirement will be :-

   (a) Between 11th. and 46th. Divisions. :-
        HYMAN TRENCH (inclusive to 11th. Division).

   (b) Between 11th. and Division on its Right. :-
        From FOSSE 1 - Railway (inclusive to 11th. Division)
        to N.15.a.5.8. - N.10.b.0.1. - thence LENS-CARVIN Road
        (exclusive to 11th. Division).

2.   The Boundary between the Right and Left Brigades will be :-

   Present point of junction in Front Line - Southern Corner of Railway Triangle, N.9.b.10.85. - Road junction N.4.c.90.75. (inclusive to Left Brigade) - along POST ROAD to bridge over Railway at H.35.c.75.70. (inclusive to Right Brigade).

3.   The Boundary between Battalions on the Left Brigade Front will be :-

   Present point of junction in Front Line - Road junction at N.3.a.9.0. (inclusive to Right Battalion) - H.34.d.5.4., i.e. a point 350 yards due South of Railway running from CITE ST. AUGUSTE to VENDIN.

4.   Infantry Brigades will always maintain close touch with, and observation of, the enemy to ensure the earliest possible intimation of a withdrawal.

5.(a)   The principle on which the advance will be conducted will be to advance by bounds to points of tactical importance and to make them good before moving on.

   (b) This will be effected by pushing forward strong patrols, followed up by Companies, who will secure each successive objective by consolidating, whilst the patrols are pushing forward to the next objective.

   (c) Strong Patrols will consist of platoons who will send forward reconnoitring patrols.

   (d) Signallers will accompany strong patrols and will establish Visual Stations.

6.   The first bound of the Division will be the line N.9.c.80.00. - Railway cutting - N.3.d.25.40. - N.3.Central - N.3.a.90.70. - H.33.c.55.38.
   Brigades will not advance beyond this line till they are in touch, but reconnoitring patrols will go forward.

   The next bound will be   to the line :-

PUITS No. 2 TER - FOSSE 8, reconnoitring patrols being pushed out as before.

7.   The Battalions in the Front Line will be used for the advance.

   Each Battalion will advance on a front of 2 Companies. Each Company will send forward a Platoon. Each Platoon will send forward a Section - preferably under an Officer - supported by a Lewis Gun Section. The remainder of the Platoon will follow in close Support and will make good ground gained by the reconnoitring patrol.
   A sketch showing suggested formation for the advance of a leading Company is attached.

   The Support Battalion will cover the whole Brigade Front and will occupy each consolidated position as it is vacated by either of the leading Battalions.

   The Battalion in Brigade Reserve will not move till it receives orders from Brigade H.Q.

(2)

8.   Until the guns are moved forward, movement cannot be supported beyond the line PUITS 2 TER in N.10.b. - FOSSE 8 de LENS in N.4.b.
    No large bodies of Infantry will move beyond this line until the guns have been moved up into positions from which the further advance can be supported.

9.   Battalions must be prepared to form a defensive flank should the neighbouring ~~Division~~ unit be held up.

10.   ACKNOWLEDGE.

ISSUED AT..............

                                                Captain,

                            Brigade Major, 34th. Infty. Brigade.

DISTRIBUTION.

        Copy No. 1. Office.
                 2. -do-
                 3. Staff Captain.
                 4. War Diary.
                 5. -do-
                 6. Brigade Signals.
                 7. 8th North. Fus.
                 8. 9th. Lan'. Fus.
                 9. 5th Dorset Rgt.
                10. 11th Manchester Regt.
                11. 34th Machine Gun Coy.
                12. 34th L. T. M. B.
                13. 11th. Division.
                14. 33rd. Brigade.
                15. 138th Brigade.
                16. 86th. Field Coy. R.E.

==*=*=*=*=*
S E C R E T.
==*=*=*=*=*

War Diary.

34th Infantry Brigade No. M. 636.

In continuation "INSTRUCTIONS IN EVENT OF AN ENEMY RETIREMENT" issued under this Office M. 576 of 19th. November, 1917. :-

11.   O.C. Machine Gun Company will move up two guns to Support the first bound, one gun taking up a position about the Railway Triangle in N.3.c. and d., and the other gun in H.33.c.
        He will detail two more guns to Support the second bound, one gun moving to FOSSE 8, and the other to the Railway Embankment in H.34.c.
        The remaining 12 guns will be ready to form a protective barrage from positions about NOGGIN and HELEN TRENCHES.
        Of these barrage guns four will be held in readiness to move further forward at short notice.

        The four guns of the Reserve Brigade attached to the Left Brigade will move to the present Machine Gun Company H.Q. in the QUARRY (M.6.a.9.3.).

        The Battalion in Brigade Reserve, on receipt of news that an advance is being made, will detail a carrying party of at least 32 men (complete units to be taken) to report at once to Machine Gun Company H.Q. in the QUARRY (M.6.a.9.3.).

12.   O.C. Light Trench Mortar Battery will attach one gun to each of the two leading Battalions.

        A party of at least 30 carriers (complete units to be detailed) will be detailed by the Reserve Battalion to report to the present L.T.M.B. H.Q. in the QUARRY (M.6.a.9.3.). This party will carry 60 rounds for each gun.

        The other guns will remain in their present positions till further orders are received.

13.   Battalions will ensure that every man (except Lewis Gunners) carries 170 rounds of S.A.A.
        One bomb per man will be carried, a proportion being rifle grenades (Hale's pattern).
        50% of men will carry a tool, in a proportion of 4 shovels to one pick.
        Overcoats will be dumped under Battalion arrangements.

14.   Liaison Officers from the Support Battalion will be with each of the leading Battalions, and a liaison Officer from the Reserve Battalion will be with the Support Battalion.

        ACKNOWLEDGE.

                                        H. Turner, Captain,
                                Brigade Major, 34th Inf. Brigade.
==*=*=*=*=*=*=*=*=*=*=*=*=*=*
Copies to all recipients of M. 576.
==*=*=*=*=*=*=*=*=*=*=*=*=*=*

WAR DIARY

SECRET.   34th Infantry Brigade No. M. 711.

AMENDMENTS AND ADDITIONS TO "INSTRUCTIONS IN EVENT OF AN ENEMY RETIREMENT".

Reference para: 1. (a) - Cancel this and substitute :-

> Between 11th. Division and Division on its Left. :-
> HOBBS ALLEY to H.20.d.8.9. - H.21.a.4.5. - HIVE ALLEY, all inclusive to Left Division.

Reference para: 2. :-

> Where "Left" occurs substitute "Centre".
>
> Add :-
>
> "The Boundary between Centre and Left Brigades will be :-
> HYMAN TRENCH (inclusive to Left Brigade)."

Reference para: 3. :-

> For "Left Brigade" substitute "Centre Brigade".

Add :-

15. CONTACT AEROPLANE PATROLS.

No. 2 Squadron have been ordered to be ready to send out Contact Patrols. These patrols will call for flares to be lit by sounding KLAXON Horns, and firing WHITE Very Lights.
A supply of flares will be kept at each Battalion Headquarters. The Infantry must be warned to respond to the aeroplane calls.

16. ENEMY TRAPS AND RUSES.

(a) A party of 1 Officer and 12 Tunnellers (parties A, B, & C. with Right, Centre and Left Brigades respectively) from the 3rd Australian Tunnelling Company will be attached to each Brigade. 40 O.R. of those attached to 86th Field Co. R.E. from Battalions will be kept detailed by O.C. 86th Field Co. R.E. to accompany 3rd Australian Tunnelling Company.
This party will only move forward on the order of the Brigade Commander, who will give that order when he is satisfied that the line ahead is held by posts and protected. Investigation will first be made of main roads, road junctions, railway embankments, bridges, tunnels and squares, and afterwards in detail of cellars and dug-outs.

(b) The party will wear a distinguishing badge, consisting of a strip of RED cloth, one inch wide and extending the length of the sleeve, on both arms.

The following marks will be used :-

      (Green chalk) .... Examined.
      .... Coy. R.E.

      Considered safe. (White tin sign)............. Considered safe.

      (Red chalk).............. Dangerous.

(2)

Roads will be marked as follows :-

| DANGER. | When road has not been examined or is found mined. | SAFE | When road has been inspected and found fit for traffic. |

17. **SIGNAL COMMUNICATIONS.**

    (a) <u>Buried Cable.</u> Cable Heads on the Corps Buried System are established as follows :-

        N.8.a.9.1........30 pairs.   Direct lines can be provided on this route to Brigade H.Q. ELVASTON CASTLE (G.34.d.9.2.

        N.2.a.6.5........28 pairs.   Connected to ELVASTON CASTLE.

    (b) <u>Pigeons.</u> Carrier pigeons will be issued as required. Application should be made through O.C. Brigade Signals.

    (c) <u>Visual.</u> Schemes should be prepared in advance and as far as possible suitable Signal Stations in the enemy's lines decided upon. The new Stations should be permanently manned until telephonic communication is established.

        Centre Brigade Visual Station for forward communications will be established at N.2.a.00.75.
        This point is situated on the cable bury.
        Signallers will accompany patrols.

18.   The line to which the enemy would probably withdraw in the first place may be taken to be :-

        VITRY-EN-ARTOIS - DROCOURT - MONTIGNY - HARNES - ANNAY - VENDIN-LE-VIEIL - HAISNES - AUCHY or HAISNES-LA-BASSEE.

    Battalions will be on the alert to notice any sign of hostile withdrawal. They will be constantly prepared to follow up any withdrawal immediately by advanced guards preceded by patrols.
NOTE: The general line of our advance to the first bound will be on a bearing of 75 degrees T.B.
ACKNOWLEDGE.

                                    F.G. Turner, Captain,
1st. December, 1917.   Brigade Major, 34th. Inf. Brigade.

Copies to all recipients of
"INSTRUCTIONS IN EVENT OF ENEMY RETIREMENT".

SECRET.   Copy No. 4

WAR DIARY

DEFENCE SCHEME
for
Brigade in Divisional Reserve

Reference maps – Sheet 36.b. – 1/40,000.
                   "   36.c. –   "
                   "   36.c.S.W.1. – 1/10,000.
                   "   36.c.N.W.3. –   "

1. **LOCATION.** The Brigade in Divisional Reserve is located as follows :-

       Brigade H.Q.   VAUDRICOURT.
       "A" Battalion.   NOEUX-les-MINES.
       "B" Battalion.   NOEUX-les-MINES.
       "C" Battalion.   VAUDRICOURT.
       "D" Battalion.   VERQUIN.
       Machine Gun Coy.   NOEUX-les-MINES.
       L. T. M. B.   NOEUX-les-MINES.

2. **ACTION.** The Brigade in Divisional Reserve will be used to make an organised counter-attack if such action should become necessary, in order to ~~establish~~ re-establish any part of our line temporarily captured by the enemy.

   In case of alarm "A" and "B" Battalions will move off from their billets, marching via –

       (a) cross-roads at L.19.a.2.8.
       (b) road junction at L.13.d.2.5.
       (c) road South of FOSSE 3 de NOEUX.
       (d) MAZINGARBE.
       (e) Les BREBIS.
       (f) GRENAY.
       (g) FOSSE 11 de BETHUNE.

   and will assemble, "A" Battalion in the trench running East and West from M.4.Central, "B" Battalion in the trench between M.9.b.6.2. and M.3.d.9.5.

   I Corps will provide on demand lorries as under for the conveyance of "C" and "D" Battalions :-

Unit.	From.	Lorries.	Rendezvous. Head of Column.	To.	Route.
"C" Bn.	VAUDRICOURT.	20.	Cross roads at K.10.b.2.8.	11th Div. Hd. Qrs.	NOEUX-les-MINES
"D" Bn.	VERQUIN.	23.		BRAQUEMONT.	

Battalions will not necessarily move in the order given above, and if sufficient lorries are not available in the first instance for the conveyance of both Battalions the column conveying the first Battalion will, on completion of that journey, proceed with the transport of the other.

11th Division will arrange to meet lorries in NOEUX-les-MINES if they are to be re-directed from that point. Otherwise these Battalions will move – probably by 'bus as far as GRENAY CHURCH if the situation admits, following the same route as "A" and "B" Battalions; or, if marching, via –
    (a) cross roads at PETIT-SAINS.
    (b) road junction at L.28.c.1.3.
    (c) Les BREBIS.
    (d) GRENAY.

(2)

and will assemble, "C" Bn. in the sunken railway and open ground in North East of Square M.8.a., and "D" Battalion in cellars in SOUTH MAROC.

The Machine Gun Company and L. T. M. B. will march in rear of "A" and "B" Battalions following the same route and will assemble about M.3.d.1.5. under cover of the SPOIL HEAP.

The completion of assembly will be at once reported to Brigade Headquarters which will have been moved forward to SOUTH MAROC, M.2.c.4.2.

The Brigade will probably be employed North of the railway running from DOUBLE CRASSIER to CITE ST. AUGUSTE, and after assembly a further advance as far as the RIAUMONT - LOOS Line, from N.1.c.5.4. through N.1.a.0.5. and M.6.b.5.9. to G.33.c.5.6., will be probable.
The routes to be followed to this line are :-

(1) for "A" Battalion - along the valley in M.4.b., M.5.a. and b., between the old wire on the right and the light Left railway on the Left. (movement just North of DOUBLE CRASSIER is impossible owing to shell-holes and wire).

(2) for "B" Battalion - the line of the track from M.3.d. 9.1. through M.10.a. and b., crossing the DOUBLE CRASSIER at M.11.a.8.8., thence just North of the DOUBLE CRASSIER - CITE ST. AUGUSTE Railway.

If the enemy artillery is active on our Battery positions South of the DOUBLE CRASSIER, "B" Battalion will follow in rear of "A" Battalion branching off about M.5.b.9.6. in a S.E. direction.

All Officers and Platoon Commanders of the Brigade in Divisional Reserve will make a thorough reconnaissance of both the routes to the places of assembly and the routes thence to RIAUMONT - LOOS Line, and will also fully acquaint themselves with the exact positions of that line.

3. ACKNOWLEDGE.

Captain,

11th. November, 1917.　　　　　　　　Brigade Major, 34th. Infty. Brigade.

==*=*=*=*=*
DISTRIBUTION.
==*=*=*=*=*

Copy No. 1. Office.
2. -do-
3. Staff Captain.
4. War Diary.
5. -do-
6. Brigade Signals.
7. 8th North. Fus.
8. 9th Lan. Fus.
9. 5th Dorset Rgt.

Copy No. 10. 11th Manchester R.
11. 34th M. G. Coy.
12. 34th L. T. M. B.
13. 11th Division.
14. 32nd Brigade.
15. 33rd Brigade.
16. 86th Field Co. R.E.
17. Brigade I.O.
18.

*0*0*0*0*0*

War Diary

S E C R E T .

AMENDMENT No. D.S./1. to

Copy No. 4....

34th Infantry Brigade

DEFENCE SCHEME.
(Provisional)

The following amendment will be made to

Paragraph 5 :-

(1) After "the Platoon in Company Commander's Reserve" read "will be used for immediate counter-attack should any of the Front Line Posts be temporarily occupied by the enemy" instead of as previously written.

(2) After "CYCLIST and CHARLIE trenches" read the former proceeding direct to CYLIST trench, and the latter via COWDEN and COW trenches to CHARLIE trench between N.7.d.0.0. and N.7.d.9.7.

(3) After "The Reserve Battalion" read "will remain in cellars but will be prepared to move off instantly" instead of as previous-ly written.

Please acknowledge receipt.

4th. November, 1917.

Captain,
A/Brigade Major, 34th. Infy. Brigade.

Army Form W.3091.

Cover for Documents.

CONFIDENTIAL.

Nature of Enclosures.

WAR DIARY

of

Headquarters 34th Infantry Brigade

FROM 1st DEC. 17
TO 31st DEC. 17

Notes, or Letters written.

Army Form C. 2118.

WAR DIARY
INTELLIGENCE SUMMARY of 34th Inf Bde

(Erase heading not required.)

Place	Date	Hour	Summary of Events and Information	Remarks and references to Appendices
ELVERTON CASTLE S.3 and 9.2 (Sheet 36 c)	Dec 1917 1		Fine day with excellent visibility. Enemy artillery less active than during past few days. Situation unchanged.	
"	2		Batt. Reliefs completed in accordance with Relief Order No. 74 by 12.30 a.m. Fine day and good visibility again but	
		5.30 p.m.	artillery on both sides quiet. At 5.30 p.m. Lieut Thompson M.C. 8th North Fus. and 2/Lt MASTERS R.E. with 5 O.R. 8th NORTH FUS.	
			went out from No 5 BRUSTREN at N 29 d 47 to blow up a German bomb-store in No. 4 BRUSKTEN at N 28 d 52.75. They	
		6.10 p.m.	blew up a stack of 24 lb explosives put in and the store was successfully blown up at 6.10 p.m. See appendix I for Sketch and fuller report of the enterprise.	Appendix I
"	3		Fine day with hard frost early in the morning. Excellent visibility but artillery very quiet. Situation unchanged.	
"	4		Fine day and frost. Situation unchanged and quiet.	
"	5		Fine day and frost. Quiet day. 9th Lan. Fus. march up from LES BREBIS in the evening in order to take over from	

Army Form C. 2118.

WAR DIARY
or
INTELLIGENCE SUMMARY.
(Erase heading not required.)

Place	Date	Hour	Summary of Events and Information	Remarks and references to Appendices
ELMSTON CASTLE G.34.d.9.3 (Sheet 36.c.)	6		Line the same on which was bivouac'd	
	7		Again fine and frosty and quiet day. Bde Order No.75 issued ordering Battn. relief on night 7th/8th.	Appendix I
			Centre Bde. Defence Scheme (11th Division sector) issued to all concerned. This alters the dispositions, thinning out the front line, withdrawing most of the front Bns. to Reserve line and support Bns. approximately to positions originally held by Reserve Bns. when the Bde. had all four Bns. up at the same time.	Appendix I
			The front turns to a thaw early in the day.	
			Relief as ordered in Bde. Order No.75 completed by 12.15 a.m. Quiet day, poor visibility and some mud.	
	8		Just day and quiet. Situation unchanged.	
	9		Fine day. Situation still unchanged and quiet.	
	10		Fine but dull day. Very quiet. Bde Order No.76 issued ordering Battn. relief on night 13th/14th inst.	Appendix I
	11			

Army Form C. 2118.

WAR DIARY
or
INTELLIGENCE SUMMARY.
(Erase heading not required.)

Place	Date	Hour	Summary of Events and Information	Remarks and references to Appendices
ELVASTON CASTLE G.34.d.9.3 (Sheet 26 c)	12		Fine but dull day. Little artillery activity and situation unchanged.	
"	13		Weather still dull but fine. Quiet day. Relief ordered in Bde. Order No. 74 completed by 9.15 p.m.	
"	14		Weather unchanged. Quiet day. No change in situation.	
"	15		Fine day and good visibility, but artillery on both sides quiet. Bde. Order No. 77 issued to all concerned.	Appendix I
"	16		Dull day. Situation unchanged and still quiet.	
"	17		Snow during early morning and hard frost. Quiet day. Bde. Order No. 77 successfully carried out in this respect. Being completed by 11.15 p.m. About 7 p.m. a little stir at the junction of HELEN - NOGGIN Trenches (M.2.6.4.7) was being filled, the enemy from his trench 40 yards away shouted out pacific wishes. A Cpl. Lander of 5th DORSET Regt. jumped out of our trench with 6 men and opened with fire. The enemy replied with a M.G. and unfortunately killed the Cpl. Lander.	

Army Form C. 2118.

WAR DIARY
or
INTELLIGENCE SUMMARY.
(Erase heading not required.)

Place	Date	Hour	Summary of Events and Information	Remarks and references to Appendices
ELVASTON CASTLE G.34.d.3.3 (Sheet 36c)	18th		Information received from the Div that it is about to be relieved by 3rd Canadian Div.	
	19th		Hard frost continues. Quiet day and situation unchanged. Frost still holds. Div Order No. 123 with details of relief by 3rd Canadian Div received and Bde Order No. 78 issued to units accordingly. Quiet day	See Appendix I
"	20th		Hard frost. News received that No.4026 Sgt COVERDALE 11th MANCHESTER Regt. is awarded the V.C. for his gallantry during the operations south of POELCAPPELLE on Oct 4th. Quiet day. 11th Manr. Regt. move to VENDIN in accordance with Bde Order No. 78	
"	21st		Still hard frost. Very quiet day. 5th Dorset Regt relieved by 5th C.M.R.	
"	22nd		Still very cold. Quiet day despite improved visibility. Relief as detailed in Bde Order No. 78 completed by 7.30 p.m. Bde H.Q. closed at ELVASTON CASTLE at 7.30 p.m. & opened at NOEUX- LES-MINES at 8.30 p/m.	
NOEUX-LES-MINES				

WAR DIARY or INTELLIGENCE SUMMARY.

Army Form C. 2118.

Instructions regarding War Diaries and Intelligence Summaries are contained in F. S. Regs., Part II. and the Staff Manual respectively. Title pages will be prepared in manuscript.

(Erase heading not required.)

Place	Date	Hour	Summary of Events and Information	Remarks and references to Appendices
NOEUX-LES-MINES	23rd	10 a.m.	Bat. H.Q. close at NOEUX-LES-MINES at 10 a.m. and	
BURBURE		1 p.m.	open at BURBURE at 1 p.m. Weather fine and cold. Frost continues.	
"	24th		Very cold and a fall of snow. The Btn. is engaged in clearing up.	
"	25th		Xmas Day. A thaw during the day, but more snow and frost again at nightfall. Div. order received that Div. must be ready to entrain at 48 hours notice. Units accordingly warned to be ready at 36 hours notice.	
"	26th		Heavy fall of snow during the night. Frost again.	
"	27th		Hard frost. Training carried on. VILLAGE LINE in 42nd Div. area reconnoitred by G.O.C. in accordance with I Corps "Preparatory Measures to meet a Hostile Attack."	
"	28th		Frost continues & more snow falls. Training carried on.	
"	29th		Frost continues & training continued.	

Army Form C. 2118.

WAR DIARY
or
INTELLIGENCE SUMMARY.
(Erase heading not required.)

Place	Date	Hour	Summary of Events and Information	Remarks and references to Appendices
BURBURE	30th		Sunday. Church Parade. Those not in Village Hut in 46th Div. area reconnoitred by G.O.C.	
"	31st		Frost again during the night followed by thaw during the day. Training continued.	

A.E. Turner. Capt.
Brigade Major 113th
Inf Bde
34

SECRET.   Copy No. 4

War Diary

34th Infantry Brigade Order No. 75.

Reference maps - Sheet 36.C. S.W.1. - 1/10,000.
Sheet 36.C. N.W.3. - 1/10,000.   8th. Dec., 1917.

1. 9th. Lancashire Fusiliers will relieve 8th Northumberland Fusiliers in the Right Sector, and 11th Manchester Regiment will relieve 5th Dorset Regiment in the Left Sector of the Brigade Front on the night 7th/8th. December, 1917.

2. On relief 8th Northumberland Fusiliers will go into Support and 5th Dorset Regiment into Brigade Reserve at LES BREBIS.

3. All details for above reliefs will be arranged direct between Os.C. concerned.

4. All maps, defence schemes, log-books, working party schedules etc. will be handed over on relief.

5. All dumps of R.E. material, S.A.A., Rockets, Grenades and trench stores will be handed over and signed receipts forwarded by relieved units to this Office by noon 8th December.

6. The relief must not interfere with working parties, and work must be completed before relief begins, but relieving Battalions should keep off work on evening of 7th. December all men going on sentry duty first in the front line and their first reliefs, so that those men may be fresh for sentry duty.

7. Attention is called to this Office, No. M.685 of 28th. Nov. Battalions going to and coming from LES BREBIS must observe these distances.

8. Completion of relief will be reported by wire to Brigade H.Q. in B.A.B. Code.

9. ACKNOWLEDGE.

ISSUED AT....1 p.m.

F. Turner,
Captain,
Brigade Major, 34th. Infy. Brigade.

DISTRIBUTION.

Copy No. 1. Office.
2. -do-
3. Staff Captain.
4. War Diary.
5. -do-
6. Bde. Signals.
7. 8th North. Fus.
8. 9th. Lan'. Fus.
9. 5th. Dorset Regt.
10. 11th Man. Regt.

Copy No. 11. 34th M. G. Coy.
12. 34th L. T. M. B.
13. 11th. Division.
14. 32nd. Brigade.
15. 33rd. Brigade.
16. 86th. Field Co.
17. Bde. Intell. Off.
18. Centre Group Arty.
19. Arty. Liaison Off.
20. Town Major, LES BREBIS

Copy No. 21. No. 4. Coy. A.S.C.

※※*※*※*※*
S E C R E T.   Copy No. 4....
※※*※*※*※*

War Diary

CENTRE BRIGADE DEFENCE SCHEME.
(11th. Division Sector)

1. **BOUNDARIES, etc.**

    (a) The front of the Brigade (known as ST. AUGUSTE) section, extends from N.8.b.57.57. to H.32.c.38.05, a frontage of 1,200 yards. This is the Centre Sector of the 11th. Divisional Front. *[margin: N.2.b.40.95]*

    (b) The Boundary with the 33rd Brigade on the Right is N.8.b. 57.57. to N.8.a.60.42. - thence to junction of CONGRESS and CONTRACT (N.7.a.85.55.) - thence along trench to N.7.a.00. 50. (trench inclusive to Right Brigade) road junction at M.12.b.05.75. - thence along road to CITE ST. PIERRE CHURCH - M.11.a.65.75. along DOUBLE CRASSIER.

    (c) The Boundary with the 32nd Brigade on the Left is H.32.c.38 .05. to H.31.d.72.00. to H.31.c.00.60. to G.30.c.00.00. *[margin: N.2.b.40.95]*

    (d) The Front Line is held by two Battalions; the Boundary between them is, NORMAN TRENCH (inclusive to Right Battalion). **From NORMAN TRENCH Westwards the boundary between Front Line Battalions is "E" Route (inclusive to Right Battalion).**

2. **DISTRIBUTION OF TROOPS.**

    Brigade H.Q.   ELVASTON CASTLE. (G.34.d.9.3.)
    Advanced Report Centre QUARRY. M.6.a.9.3.

    (a) Right Battalion - Front Line.

    Battalion H.Q.   N.7.b.7.9.

    1 Company. H.Q. COB TRENCH.
    　　(1 Platoon - COMMOTION SAP AREA.
    　　(1 Platoon - East end of COSY AREA.
    　*(1 Platoon - Junction of COSY & HARPY,
    　(for close Support.
    　　(1 Platoon - COB, for counter-attack.

    * Till accommodation has been made this Platoon will live in the Front Line with a Post near junction of COSY and HAPPY.

    1 Company. H.Q. COB TRENCH.
    　　(1 Platoon - BRICKSTACKS AREA.
    　　(1 Platoon - NORMAN, for close support.
    　　(2 Platoons- Cellars off COD, for counter-attack.

    1 Company. H.Q. CATAPULT. N.1.d.9.3.
    　　Whole Company in CATAPULT, permanent garrison of Reserve Line.

    1 Company. H.Q. N.7.b.5.9.
    　　(2 Platoons-CATAPULT, permanent garrison of
    　(Reserve Line.
    　　(2 Platoons-N.7.b., in Support of Reserve Line.

(2)

(b) **Left Battalion - Front Line.**

Battalion H.Q.   N.1.b.05.

4 Platoons. :-
- (1 Platoon - NUNS ALLEY, Front Line.
- (1 Platoon - QUADRILATERAL Area.
- (1 Platoon - NOGGIN.
- (1 Platoon - Junction of NOGGIN and HELEN.

4 Platoons. :-
- (2 Platoons - NUNS ALLEY C.T., in close support.
- (2 Platoons - NUNS ALLEY locality, permanent garrison.

NOTE: It is left to Battalion Commanders whether they have one Company in the Front Line and one Company in NUNS ALLEY C.T. or have two half-companies in the Front Line and two half-companies in NUNS ALLEY C.T.

1 Company. H.Q. CATAPULT. N.1.d.9.9.
Whole Company in CATAPULT, permanent garrison of Reserve Line.

1 Company. H.Q. NETLEY. N.1.b.5.8.
- (2 Platoons - NETLEY, for counter-attack in aid of Front Line system.
- (2 Platoons - NASH ALLEY, in Support of Reserve Line.

(c) **Support Battalion.**

Battalion H.Q.   N.1.a.0.1.

1 Company. H.Q. N.1.d.2.5.   NARWAL.
1 Company. H.Q. M.6.d.3.7.   Old Reserve Trench.
2 Companies H.Q. M.6.c.3.5. HARRISONS CRATER.

(d) **Reserve Battalion.**   LES BREBIS.

3. **LINES OF RESISTANCE.**

(a) Front Line.
(b) Reserve Line.

These are ~~being~~ held by two Battalions, each Battalion holding one Company back in immediate Support.

(a) The Front Line is held by a Picquet Line with picquets, each of one Platoon, holding the Eastern end of the main communication trenches, and other vulnerable points, the Front Line between these posts being kept up as a communication trench.
In close support of these picquets are Platoons having fire positions from which they can bring fire to bear on the flanks of the picquet positions, and to be used, if necessary, for counter-attack.
Three Platoons of the Right Battalion (being in COB TRENCH) and two Platoons of the Left Battalion (living in NASH ALLEY) are for counter-attack in Support of the Front Line.

(b) Six Platoons of the Right Battalion and four Platoons of the Left Battalion will form the garrison of the Reserve Line. The Picquet Line is the Line of resistance and will be held to the last by the garrison and the troops told off for its support.

The Reserve Line will be held at all costs. Its garrison will not be used for relieving pressure on the Front Line by counter-attack.

In addition, the Left Battalion will hold NUNS locality as a retrenchment opposite the gap between NOGGIN and HELEN with a permanent garrison of 2 Platoons. These Platoons will on no account be used for relieving pressure on or making counter-attacks in aid of the Front Line.

Every Section and every man of the garrison of the Reserve Line must know exactly the part of the line that they have to defend and must be able to find their way to their Posts by day or night. All garrisons will always stand-to at the exact spot which they have to defend.

NOTE: On the Artillery opening in response to S.O.S. Signals, the Platoons of Front Line Battalions attached to 86th. Field Co. R.E. will move up and report at once to their Battalion H.Q. These Platoons will be reckoned as the troops (or part of the troops) told off in Support of the Reserve Line. The Platoon of the Support Battalion will report to its Battalion H.Q. The Platoon of the Reserve Battalion will stand-by till further orders.

4. ACTION OF TROOPS IN CASE OF ATTACK.

"In case of attack the Company of the Support Battalion in NARWAL will stand-to, the two Companies in HARRISONS CRATER will move up to BUGS ALLEY, and the Company in the old Reserve Line to the Cutting M.6.b.7.0."

Working parties will move to the allotted positions as soon as possible.

The Support Battalion will be used for counter-attack. All Officers and N.C.Os. therefore must be acquainted with all routes (both overland and G.T.) to any part of the Brigade Sector.

5. THE RESERVE BATTALION.

The Battalion in Brigade Reserve will be used for counter-attack on the Reserve Line.

On receipt of orders from Brigade H.Q. the Battalion will march up from LES BREBIS Via FOSSE 11 de BETHUNE, West of the DOUBLE GRASSIER, then either along the valley in M.4.b., M.5.a. and c. (keeping between the old wire on the Right and the Light Railway on the Left) or making use of the trench system, and just North of the QUARRY in M.6.a. It will assemble in the trench between M.6.b.5.1. and M.6.b.2.4. and in O.G.1 from its junction with that trench to N.1.a.0.5. Battalion H.Q. will move forward to the QUARRY (M.6.a.9.3.) and will report the completion of assembly to Brigade H.Q. without delay.

The Battalion must be prepared to make this move by night, and therefore all Officers and Platoon Commanders will acquaint themselves thoroughly with the routes to the assembly positions.

NOTES: (1) Every Company and Platoon Commander on taking over any Sector, must know what action the troops in that Sector perform, in case of attack; if this action includes movement, he must personally reconnoitre his route. He must know beforehand how he would dispose his troops, what their fields of view and fire would be, and how they could use those to the nest advantage of the Sector.

(2) Men must not be allowed to remain in any Sector ignorant of their positions; sentries when questioned, should know the names of neighbouring trenches and the routes to them.

(3) In case of attack on the troops on either flank, companies in the Front Line, the Machine Gun Company and the Trench Mortar Battery may be able to help the troops on the flank by fire. Dangerous points to the flank must be noted, and the fields of fire by which they can be covered.
Platoon and Company Commanders on the flanks of units should visit Commanders of units on their flank.

6. ARTILLERY.

(1) Field Artillery.

The Artillery covering the front of the Centre Brigade consists of three eighteen pounder Batteries and one 4.5 Howitzer Battery forming the Centre Group, 11th. D.A.

Counter-Battery Work.

Requests for neutralization or destruction of Active Hostile Batteries will normally be forwarded through Brigade H.Q. or Liaison Officers.

NOTES: (1) To make neutralising fire effective the following information is promptly required :-

    (a) Exact time of opening and ceasing fire of enemy batteries.

    (b) Approximate direction of fire (on a bearing if possible).

    (c) Calibre of enemy guns.

(2) Instances of short shooting should be sent with calibre and direction of shooting, and to be effective, must be sent <u>immediately</u>.

(2) T.Ms.

Four 6" T.Ms. at present in action in the Centre Brigade Area located at :-

    N.2.a.34.80.
    N.2.a.64.70.
    N.8.a.00.55.
    N.7.b.96.72.

Two 9.45" Heavy T.Ms. are in action near the inter-Brigade Boundary at :-

    N.7.b.20.50.
    N.7.b.33.55.

(5)

(3) S.O.S. Signals.

The S.O.S. Signal will only be sent up in the event of actual attack by enemy Infantry. Every available means of communication will be used.

The present S.O.S. Light Signal in use on the Brigade Front is a succession of GREEN Rockets or Very Lights. This signal should be known by all ranks.

If an S.O.S. is sent up by any other means, simplicity will be resorted to and the S.O.S. will have priority over all other messages.

On the S.O.S. Signal being received, the Artillery will open fire on their S.O.S. lines, the rate of firing being :-

      3 minutes at INTENSE rate
      7 minutes at NORMAL rate.

It will then cease unless the S.O.S. Signal is repeated. Should the Signal be repeated, the rates of fire will be a repitition of the above. If communications have broken down, the Artillery will continue firing at a slow rate until communications have been re-established. The Artillery should be informed immediately its fire is no longer required.

(4) Retaliation.

Retaliation is given on the request of the Infantry, which may be transmitted by visual signal, telegraph or telephone through the Artillery Liaison Officer attached to Battalions or Brigade H.Q. The present retaliation Signal is RED-WHITE-RED Rockets or Very Lights.

Trench Mortars should open retaliatory fire automatically in reply to enemy bombardments.

The Code Numbers of targets have already been issued to those concerned.

(5) Heavy Artillery Action.

The assistance of the Heavy Artillery may be obtained through the Brigade Liaison Officer at Centre Brigade H.Q.

(6) GAS.

Warning of the approach of gas.

On an alarm of gas being given in the Front Trenches, alarm signals will be sounded and in addition the alarm will be passed by telephone. This message will take "PRIORITY" and wire will be sent in the following matter :-

    "GAS" followed by name of Battalion opposite whose Sector
    the Gas is discharged, and time.

If alarm is heard and gas is not approaching on the immediate front, the following message will be sent :-

    "GAS ALARM FROM" (Name and direction from which heard).

Artillery Action.

Should the Gas cloud be unaccompanied by an Infantry attack no S.O.S. Signal will be sent, but one of the following messages :-

    "GAS" followed by name of Battalion opposite whose Sector
    the gas is discharged.

All Howitzers will be turned on the enemy's trenches from where the gas is being discharged and on his second and third line trenches.

A light barrage of Field Guns will be put up in front of our trenches to prevent hostile patrols from following up the Gas. No intense S.O.S. barrage will be employed at this stage.

The enemy's trenches on the flanks of the gas discharge will be kept under fire, and ground near the hostile front line will be shelled by bursts of fire by 18 pdrs.

Gas Shell or T.M. Bombardment.
In addition to the methods of conveying the alarm as given in S.S.193 warning will also be conveyed by telegraphing or telephoning the word "POISON" followed by the map reference of the position where shells are falling, e.g. -

"POISON N.1.b."

(7) Tests.

Frequent S.O.S. and Gas Tests will be carried out and will originate from Company H.Q. in the front line.

A telephonic message as under will be sent "PRIORITY" and on receipt of same, the Artillery will fire two rounds.

The following times will be noted and forwarded immediately after each test to Brigade H.Q.

(a) Time of giving message to Signallers at Company H.Q.

(b) Time the two rounds reach the German Lines.

Wording of messages to be as follows :-

S.O.S. Test.   DENMARK AUGUSTUS   (Right
                                           (or
                                           (Left.

Gas Test.

The code message of B.A.B. Trench Code with days' correction for -

"GAS APPROACHING FROM FRONT" preceded by the word TEST.

This opportunity will be taken by Company Officers to inspect small box respirators or helmets, see that they are properly adjusted and also that gas-proof blankets for dugouts have been lowered.

Gas alarms, Strombos Horns, Gongs, etc. will NOT be sounded and Rockets will NOT be fired.

(7)

7. **MACHINE GUNS.**

The Centre Brigade Front is covered by one Machine Gun Coy. (H.Q. in the QUARRY, M.6.a.9.3.).
The guns are disposed as follows :-

(a)　One defensive gun covering NUNS ALLEY locality.

(b)　Four defensive guns in Reserve Line.

(c)　Two defensive guns behind Reserve Line.
　　　1st. Echelon.

(d)　Five defensive guns behind Reserve Line.
　　　2nd. Echelon.

(e)　Four barrage guns in M.6.b.

Three M.Gs. of the Right Brigade also fire on the front of the Centre Brigade. Two of these situated in COB TRENCH, are defensive guns and cover the extreme Right of the Centre Brigade Front.
The third is a defensive gun and forms an S.O.S. block opposite the extreme Right of the Centre Brigade Front.

Harassing fire is carried out nightly.

Two 2nd. Echelon guns are used for sniping by day, firing from alternate positions.

8. **STOKES MORTARS.**

(1)　Six Stokes Mortars emplacements are in the Front Line system

　　　(a) N.8.b.47.80.
　　　(b) N.8.b.40.75.
　　　(c) N.2.d.25.15.
　　　(d) N.2.d.10.60.
　　　(e) N.2.d.12.70.
　　　(f) N.2.a.60.35.

Guns are at present in positions ((c), (d) and (f).

(2)　Their policy is both Offensive and Defensive. Fire is directed on vulnerable points in the enemy's lines, and retaliation and S.O.S. fire is opened if called for.

Please acknowledge.

ISSUED AT *8. a.m.*

　　　　　　　　　　　　　　　　　　　　　　　　Captain,

7th. December, 1917.　　　　　　Brigade Major, 34th Infantry Brigade.

Copy No. 1. Office.　　　　　　　Copy No. 10. 11th Man'. Rgt.
　　　　2. -do-　　　　　　　　　　　　11. 34th M. G. Coy.
　　　　3. Staff Captain.　　　　　　　12. 34th L. T. M.B.
　　　　4. War Diary.　　　　　　　　　13. 11th Division.
　　　　5. -do-　　　　　　　　　　　　14. 32nd Brigade.
　　　　6. Bde. Signals.　　　　　　　15. 33rd Brigade.
　　　　7. 8th North. Fus.　　　　　　16. 86th Field Co. R.E.
　　　　8. 9th. Lan'. Fus.　　　　　　17. Centre Group Arty.
　　　　9. 5th Dorset Rgt.　　　　　　18. Arty. Liaison Offr.

*0*0*0*0*0*0*

SECRET.

APPENDIX 1.
to Centre Brigade Defence Scheme.
================================

COMMUNICATIONS.

1. **Lines.**

    Lines from Brigade are all on 1st Corps Buried Cable System, which is maintained by Area Signal Officer: Captain HUME, R.E. in North area and Lieut. STEVEN, R.E. in South area. Both Front Line Battalions and Support Battalion are connected direct to Brigade on this system.
    Battalions are connected laterally by buried lines, and flank Battalions of Right and Left Brigades are also in touch.
    Right and Left Brigades are connected direct with Brigade H.Q.
    Front Battalions have direct lines to supporting Artillery Group.

    Left Battalion has buried lines to within 100 yards of front Company, line direct to NETLEY Company is entirely buried, and to CATAPULT Company buried to within 200 yards.

    Right Battalion has no buried lines to Companies.

    Support Battalion has no buried lines to Companies.

    Reserve Battalion and Brigade Transport Officer have lines to Division Advanced Exchange.

2. **Visual.**

    Right Battalion has Visual communication with their forward Company H.Q.
    Left Battalion has Visual communication with their Right Company.

3. **Pigeons.**

    One pair of pigeons are issued daily to Each Battalion in the line and 8 pairs are kept in Reserve at Brigade H.Q.
    These are flown only in case of emergency. Ordinarily they are returned to loft in baskets.

4. **Power Buzzer.**

    Each Battalion in the line has an Amplifier installed at Battalion H.Q.

    On the Right there is a Power Buzzer at Forward Company H.Q. and at Telephone Post in NUNS ALLEY.

    On the Left there is a Power Buzzer at Forward Company H.Q. and at Telephone Post.

    Test messages are sent at irregular times daily.

5. **Runners.**

    There is a regular Runner Service between Brigade H.Q. and all Battalion H.Q.

6. Attached diagram illustrates telephone system in use.

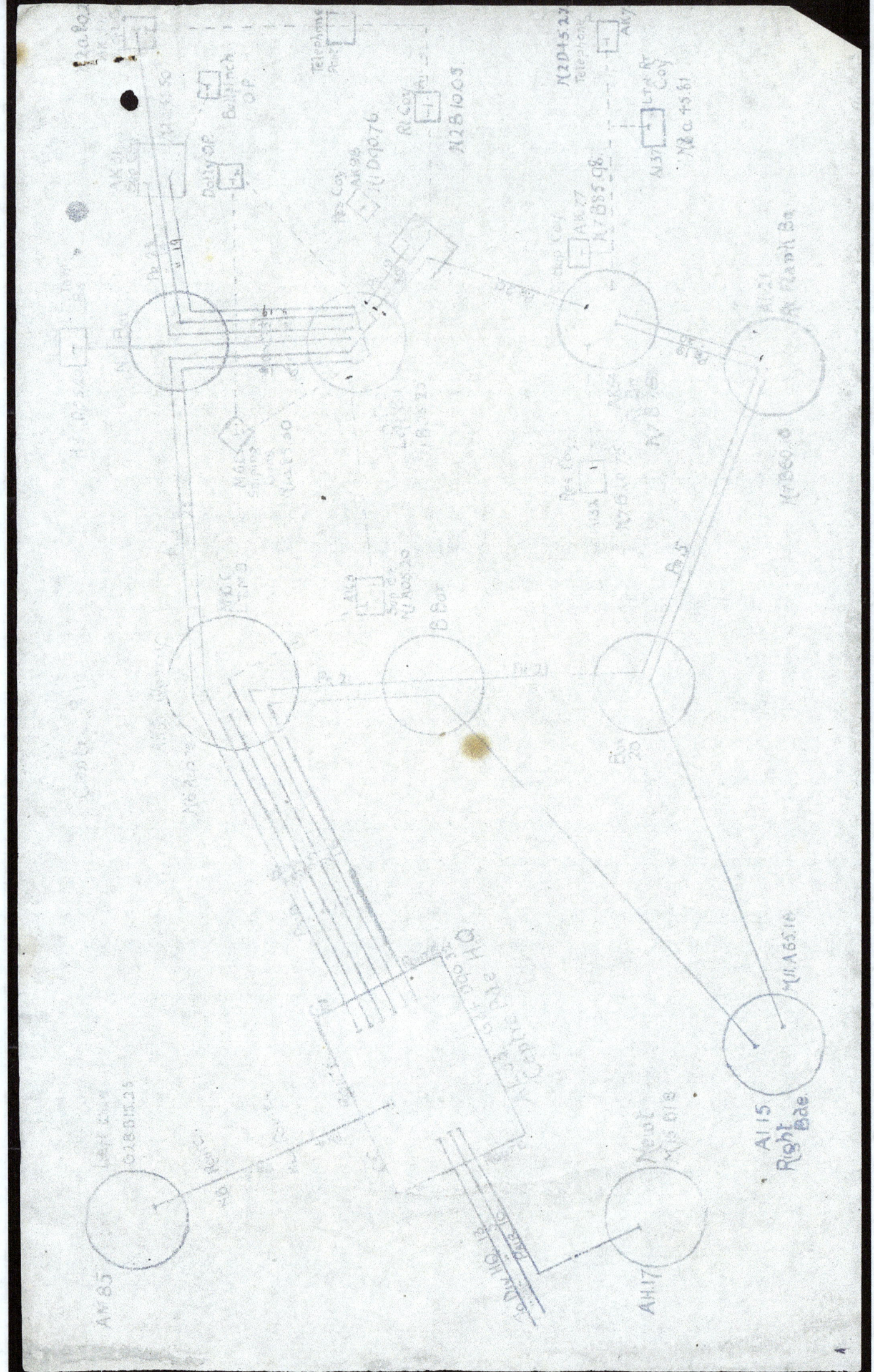

SECRET.

= APPENDIX II =
To CENTRE BRIGADE DEFENCE SCHEME.

RATIONS:-
    <u>Right Battalion</u>:- Limbers to OPERA HOUSE, ST. PIERRE, thence by trolley to COUNTER DUMP.
    <u>Left and Support Battalions</u>:- Limbers to M.6.c.5.5., thence by trolley to Battalion Headquarters.
    <u>H.G.Coy, L.T.M.B., and Brigade H.Qrs</u>:- Limbers to H. Qrs.

R. E. MATERIAL:-
    Right, Left and Support Battalions indent on Staff Captain by 11-30 A.M., who sends consolidated indent to R.T.O., OSTLER SIDING by 12 noon.
    By truck to COUNTER DUMP, N.7.a.30.40. for Right Battalion, and Battalion Headquarters for Left and Support Battalions.
    Special arrangements for other Units.

BOMBS AND AMMUNITION.
    By Limber to HARTS CRATER or trolley to COUNTER DUMP (Right Battn.). Units draw thence by indent on Staff Captain.

LIGHT RAILWAYS.
    Right, Left and Support Battalions each have 4 trucks permanently at their disposal kept at Battalion Headquarters of Left and Support Battalions, and at COUNTER DUMP for Right Battalion.

(NOTE:- at present all trolleys on the HILL 70 LINE must be cleared off the line by 8 P.M.).

SALVAGE.
    Collected by Units and unserviceable sent back in ration limbers direct to HILL TOP SIDING, Units obtaining receipts. Consolidated statement and copies of receipts to be sent to Brigade Headquarters at end of tour.
    Serviceable material collected into recognised dumps, certified statement of amount so collected to be sent to Brigade Headquarters at end of tour.
    Amounts so collected by Units will be published in Brigade Orders.

GUM BOOTS.
    Drying room at HARTS CRATER from which issue will be made to Battalions and to which wet boots and soles will be returned. Dry soles for wet can be issued as required.
    Units in the line make their own arrangements for storing gum boots on their charge when not required, but are responsible for keeping them available in case of need.

BRIGADE SOUP KITCHEN.
    AT HARRISONS DUMP - Units supply Tea, Sugar and bones. Free Tea and Soup are supplied to the Brigade.

BATHS.
    Baths will be available for the Support Battalion in LOOS - G.35.a. 75.95 (12 sprays) from the 8th. December. Application should be made to the Staff Captain by 12 noon the day before baths are required.
    Baths are available for the Reserve battalion at LES BREBIS. Application should be made to the Town Major.

SECRET.

War Diary

Copy No. 4

34th Infantry Brigade Order No. 76.

11th. December.

1. 8th. Northumberland Fusiliers will relieve 9th. Lancashire Fusiliers in the Right Sector, and 5th. Dorset Regiment will relieve 11th. Manchester Regiment in the Left Sector of the Brigade Front on the night 13th/14th. December, 1917.

2. On relief 9th. Lancashire Fus. will go into Support and 11th. Manchester Regt. into Brigade Reserve at LES BREBIS.

3. All details for above reliefs will be arranged direct between Os.C. concerned.

4. All maps, defence schemes, log-books, working-party schedules etc. will be handed over on relief.

5. All dumps of R.E. material, S.A.A., Rockets, Grenades and trench stores will be handed over and signed receipts forwarded by relieved units to this office by noon, 14th. December.

6. The relief must not interfere with working parties, and work must be completed before relief begins, but relieving Bns. should keep off work on evening of 13th. December all men going on sentry duty first in the front line and their first reliefs, so that these men may be fresh for sentry duty.

7. Attention is called to this Office No. M.685 of 28th Nov. Battalions going to and coming from LES BREBIS must observe these distances.

8. Completion of relief will be reported by wire to Brigade H.Q. in B.A.B. Code.

9. ACKNOWLEDGE.

ISSUED AT 7 p.m.

F G Turner, Captain,
Brigade Major, 34th. Inf. Bde.

NORMAL DISTRIBUTION.

SECRET.

Copy No. 4

War Diary.

34th Infantry Brigade Order No. 77.

15th Dec '17

1. On the night 17th/18th December NUNS ALLEY SAP, NORMAN SAP, NESTOR SAP, and Sap at junction of NOGGIN & HELEN TRENCHES will be completely filled in, and barbed wire entanglements put across the spots where the heads of the saps now are.

    COMMOTION SAP and the BRICKSTACKS SAP are being retained for observation purposes.

2. 8th Northumberland Fus. will fill in NUNS ALLEY SAP and NORMAN SAP, and 5th Dorset Regiment will fill in NESTOR SAP and Sap at junction of NOGGIN and HELEN TRENCHES.

3. O's.C. B'ns. concerned will detail special parties for the task, and all the work must be completed before dawn on 18th inst.

4. New firebays in the main Front Line must be made before dusk on the 17th to provide new fire positions in place of those now in the Saps.

    Concertina barbed wire must be ready in the Front Line Trench to thicken the new wire as soon as it is put up.

5. The completion of the task will be wired to Brigade H.Q. by the Code Word "SATISFIED".

6. ACKNOWLEDGE.

F.J. Turner, Captain,

ISSUED AT 10.0 p.m.

Brigade Major, 34th Inf. Brigade.

DISTRIBUTION.

Copy No. 1. Office.	Copy No. 9. 5th. Dorset Regt.
2. -do-	10. 11th Manchester Regt.
3. Staff Captain.	11. 34th Machine Gun Coy.
4. War Diary.	12. 34th L. T. M. B.
5. -do-	13. 11th Division.
6. Bde. Signals.	14. 32nd Brigade.
7. 8th. North. Fus.	15. 33rd Brigade.
8. 9th. Lancs. Fus.	16. 86th Field Coy. R.E.

Copy No. 17. Centre Group Arty.

War Diary

SECRET.   Copy No. 4

34th. Infantry Brigade Order No.78.

Reference maps – Sheet 36.C. S.W.1. – 1/10,000.
                Sheet 36.C. N.W.3. – 1/10,000.
                HAZEBROUCK – 1/100,000.   19th. December, 1917.

1. 11th. Division will be relieved in the Line by 3rd. CANADAIN Division, who will carry out the relief with two Brigades. Each relieving Brigade will therefore take over the front of a flank Brigade, and one Battalion front of the Centre Brigade.

2. On relief the 11th. Division will be withdrawn to the BUSNES area.

3. Movements and reliefs will be carried out in accordance with the attached Table "A".
Details of relief, guides etc. will be arranged direct between Os. C. concerned.

4. Table "B" shows the sub-areas of the BUSNES area.

5. Transport of each unit moving by bus will move by road direct to new billets on the day preceeding the night on which its unit moves.

6. G.O.C. 34th. Brigade will command the Centre Sector till the relief is complete on night 22nd./23rd.

7. All Defence Schemes, Schemes for advancing in case of enemy retirement, aeroplane photographs, programmes of work, Secret letters and orders, which apply to the defence of the Sector, also Company and Platoon Commanders plans in accordance with para 11. of 11th. Division G.N. 173. (forwarded under this office N.831 of 13th. inst.) will be handed over to relieving units.
Instructions regarding maps to be handed over have already been issued.

8. A distance of 500 yards between Battalions, 100 yards between Coys. and 100 yards between units and their transport will be maintained on the march.

9. The completion of each relief will be wired to Brigade H.Q. by the Code "HAPPY XMAS".

10. Brigade H.Q. will close at ELVASTON CASTLE on completion of relief on night 22nd/23rd. and will open at NOEUX-LES-MINES as soon as circumstances admit.

11. ACKNOWLEDGE.

ISSUED AT .....7 h.m.......

                                                       Captain,
                                         Brigade Major 34th. Infy. Brigade.

DISTRIBUTION.

                                                                      P.T.O.

(2).

DISTRIBUTION.

Copy No. 1. Office.
2. -do-
3. Staff Captain.
4. War Diary.
5. -do-
6. Bde. Signals.
7. 8th. North. Fus.
8. 9th. Lan'. Fus.
9. 5th. Dorset Rgt.
10. 11th. Manch. Rgt.
11. 34th. M. G. Coy.

Copy No. 12. 34th M. T. M. B.
13. 11th. Division.
14. 32nd Brigade.
15. 33rd Brigade.
16. No.4 Coy. A.S.C.
17. 34th Field Ambulance.
18. 86th Field Coy. R.E.
19. Town Major, LES BREBIS.
20. 8th. Canadian Bde.
21. 9th. - do -
22. Centre Group Arty.

Copy No. 23. Liaison Officer.

SECRET.   Copy No. 1.

War Diary

ADMINISTRATIVE INSTRUCTION NO. 78.

== TO ACCOMPANY 34th. INFANTRY BRIGADE ORDER NO. 78. ==

1. Representatives of Units will report to Town Majors as under for the purpose of obtaining billets on the day previous to moving in:-

UNIT.	TOWN MAJOR AT.	BILLETS AT.	Date of moving in.
5th. Dorset R.	BURBURE.	BURBURE.	Decr. 21st.
11th. Manch R.	do.	do.	do.
86th. Fd. Coy R.E.	VAUDRICOURT.	VERQUIN.	do.
8th. Northd. F.	CHOCQUES.	LA PUGNOY.	Decr. 22nd.
9th. Lan. F.	do.	do.	do.
83 Fd. Coy R.E.	do.	CHOCQUES.	do.
34th. L.T.M.B.	NOEUX.	NOEUX.	do.
34th. Bde H.Q.	do.	do.	do.
34th. M.G. Coy.	ANNEZIN.	VENDIN.	Decr. 23rd.
34th. L.T.M.B.	BURBURE.	BURBURE.	do.
34th. Bde H.Q.	do.	do.	do.
34th. M.G. Coy.	do.	HURIONVILLE.	Decr. 24th.

11th. Manchester Regt. Billeting representative will arrange with Town Major for Billets and Transport Lines to be reserved at BURBURE for Brigade H.Q. and 34th. L.T.M.B. arriving 23rd.

2. Personnel of 34th. Brigade at Bomb Stores and on other duties in 11th. Division area will be relieved on 19th.-22nd. inst., and rejoin their Units. Units will forward to this Office by 12 noon 23rd. instant, nominal roll of all details employed in the present area who have not reported, showing employment. Personnel employed at 1 Corps School and 11th. Divl. Training Bn. will not be included.

3. Horse lines have been selected but not yet made at LA PUGNOY and BURBURE, and are not yet selected at HURIONVILLE. Steps will be taken to provide these at once with assistance of 86th. Field Coy R.E. and in conjunction with Town Majors concerned.
34th. M.G. Coy will wire to this Office site selected as soon as possible.

4. Trench Stores, Ammunition and Reserve Rations will be handed over and receipts sent to Brigade Headquarters by noon 24th. instant. Separate receipts should be obtained for rations.
Gum Boots on charge of Battns. at present are:-
        8th. Northd. F.   601.
        9th. Lan. F.   9.
        5th. Dorset R.   200.
Units will hand these over either to HARTS CRATER DUMP or to relieving Units, and receipts accounting for above numbers will be sent in.

5. Railhead for Leave Parties etc. will be LILLERS from 22nd. inst.

6. Refilling point will be notified later.

7. Lorries will be available on the scale of 2 per. Battalion, 1 for M.G. Coy and 2 per. Bde. H.Q. and L.T.M.B., they will be met by guides as under on day of march at 7 AM:-
Decr. 21st.	5th. Dorsets.	Church, LES BREBIS.
" "	11th. Manch. R.	Church, VENDIN.
" 22nd.	8th. North. F.) 9th. Lan. F.)	Church, LES BREBIS.

2.

7. Units.

    Decr. 23rd.   34th.M.G.Coy.)
                     34th.L.T.M.B.)   Church, LES BREBIS.
                     34th. Bde H.Q.)

    " 24th.   34th.M.G.Coy.   Church, ~~LES BREBIS~~. VENDIN

8. 34th. M.G. Coy will place two limbers at disposal of 34th. L.T.M.B. for the purpose of their move on night 23rd/24th. 22/23

9. Baggage wagons of Units will report to their Q.M.STORES at 7 A.M. on dates as under:—

    Decr. 20th.   11th. Manchester Regt.
    "   21st.   5th. Dorset Regt.
    "   22nd.   (6th. Northumberland Fus.
                    (9th. Lancashire Fus.
    "   23rd.   34th. Brigade H.Qrs.

10. O. C. Units will be responsible that a senior officer is in charge of embussing who will see that all busses are filled before moving off.

11. ACKNOWLEDGE.

                                          C L. Chute
                                                 Captain,
19/12/17.   Staff Captain, 34th. Infantry Brigade.

DISTRIBUTION.

Copies to all recipients of 34th. Brigade Order No. 78.

T. M. BURBURE.   T.M. CHOCQUES.
Brigade T.O.   Q.M. Northd. Fusiliers.
Q.M. Lancashire Fusrs.   Q.M. 5th. Dorset Regt.

TABLE "A" TO ACCOMPANY 11th. DIVISION ORDER No. 143.

DATE.	UNIT.	FROM.	TO.	REMARKS.
20th. Decr.	11th. Manch. Regt.	LES BREBIS.	VENDIN.	On relief by 8th. Can. Bde. hour to be notified later.
21/22nd "	5th. Dorset Rgt.	LINE (Left Front Line Bn.)	BURBURE.	Bus. Embus at M.2.d.5.8.
do,	11th. Manch. Regt.	VENDIN.	do,	
22/23rd "	8th. North. Fus.	LINE.	LAPUGNOY.	Bus. Embus at M.2.d.5.8.
do.	9th. Lan. Fus.	do.	do.	- do -
do.	34th. Bde. H.Q.	do.	NOEUX.	
do.	34th. L.T.M.B.	do.	do.	
23rd. Decr.	34th. M. G. Coy.	BULLY GRENAY.	VENDIN.	
do.	34th. Bde. H.Q.	NOEUX.	BURBURE.	
do.	34th. L.T.M.B.	do.	do.	
24th Decr.	34th. M. G. Coy.	VENDIN,	HURIONVILLE.	

(TABLE "B")

34th. Infantry Brigade Group Area.

Brigade Headquarters.	BURBURE.
5th. Dorset Rgt.	do.
11th. Manch. Rgt.	do.
	Sites for horse standings have not yet been selected.
8th. North. Fus.	LAPUGNOY.
9th. Lan. Fus.	-do-
	- do -
Field Coy. R.E.	CHOCQUES.
	Horse standings already exist.
M.G. Coy & L.T.M Btty.	HURIONVILLE.
	Site for horse standings not yet selected.
Field Ambulance.	BAS RIEUX.
	- do -

www.ingramcontent.com/pod-product-compliance
Lightning Source LLC
Chambersburg PA
CBHW081435300426
44108CB00016BA/2370